BILL

Marriott

BILL MARRIOTT'S
10 RULES OF SUCCESS*

1. Take care of the people closest to you, and they will take care of the people closest to them.

2. Publicly celebrate the success of those around you. Privately celebrate your own victories.

3. Figure out what you're good at and keep improving.

4. Do it now. Err on the side of action.

5. Talk less. Listen more.

6. See and be seen by the people you want to influence. Make your actions visible and yourself accessible.

7. Remember that success is always in the details.

8. Engage people who have the right qualities, even if they don't yet have the right experience.

9. Surround yourself with people who are smarter than you.

10. View every problem as an opportunity to grow; never give up!

* Revised by Mr. Marriott for more general application from his original Marriott-business-oriented "12 Rules of Success," as published in his *Marriott on the Move* blog, February 25, 2014.

BILL
Marriott

SUCCESS IS NEVER FINAL

HIS LIFE AND THE DECISIONS
THAT BUILT A HOTEL EMPIRE

DALE VAN ATTA

**SHADOW
MOUNTAIN**

Library of Congress Cataloging-in-Publication Data

Names: Van Atta, Dale, author.
Title: Bill Marriott : success is never final : his life and the decisions that built a hotel empire / Dale Van Atta.
Description: Salt Lake City, Utah : Shadow Mountain, [2019] | Includes bibliographical references and index.
Identifiers: LCCN 2019016801 | ISBN 9781629726007 (hardbound : alk. paper)
Subjects: LCSH: Marriott, J. Willard, Jr. (John Willard), 1932– | Marriott Corporation— Biography. | Hotelkeepers—Biography.
Classification: LCC TX910.5.M333 V36 2019 | DDC 647.94092 [B]—dc23
LC record available at https://lccn.loc.gov/2019016801

Printed in the United States of America
Lake Book Manufacturing, Inc., Melrose Park, IL

10 9 8 7 6 5 4 3 2 1

CONTENTS

CONTENTS

PROLOGUE

The air was still. *Dangerously* still.

But no one on the beautiful Lake Winnipesaukee could have suspected that peaceful Saturday morning in 1985 just how lethal the stillness might be for one of the area's most recognizable summer residents, Bill Marriott.

Bill had been coming to New Hampshire's largest lake for four decades. His father, founder of the large Hot Shoppes restaurant chain, had been bringing his family to the lake since the 1940s. The Marriott clan rightly considered the place a paradise on earth. Proof of its strong magic was that it was the only place fifty-three-year-old Bill could truly relax. His $3.5-billion company had 140,000 employees around the world. He had built or bought 144 hotels and resorts, turning Marriott into the largest company-owned hotel chain in the United States. Dozens more hotels were in blueprint or construction phases. Added to that were 90 kitchens serving 150 airlines around the globe, more than 1,400 restaurants, and catering services for 1,400 clients in university, hospital, and company cafeterias.

Bill's father, J. Willard, Sr., had lived to witness these successes, but he had died that summer, on August 13, passing peacefully at the age of eighty-four after enjoying a family barbecue at the lake. The

1

well-attended Washington, D.C., funeral had featured speakers such as former President Richard Nixon and evangelist Billy Graham. Now it was August 24, and most of the Marriott family had traveled from the D.C. area back to their summer vacation homes on the north side of the lake.

An important event was scheduled for Sunday. All the family were members of The Church of Jesus Christ of Latter-day Saints (known by some as Mormons). The Latter-day Saint community in Wolfeboro near the lake had been growing slowly over the years and had finally qualified for its own chapel, which had just been completed in June. A close friend of the family, Elder Boyd K. Packer, a member of the Church's Quorum of the Twelve Apostles, had promised J.W. before his death that he would personally dedicate the chapel. After speaking at J.W.'s funeral, he had joined the family at the lake on Friday, awaiting the Sunday dedication services.

Having an Apostle staying with Bill's newly widowed mother, Allie, was a spiritual comfort and a singular honor. When Elder Packer mentioned that he would like to go on a boat ride Saturday morning, it was a request Bill was happy to fulfill. There were few more joyful times for him than driving his baby blue Donzi Express Cruiser out on the sun-dappled waters of the lake, throttling up to speeds in excess of fifty miles an hour. Incessant daily winds had been whipping the lake into whitecaps, but that Saturday morning was perfect. Though not breezy, it was cool, prompting Bill to wear a wool sweater.

After breakfast he went down to his two-slip boathouse to prepare the Donzi. It was after 9:30 a.m., and normally Bill's three small grandchildren would have been swarming all over the boat, anxious to be with Grandpa. But their mother, Bill's daughter, Debbie, had slowed them down that morning, and they were just getting on the life jackets. Friend and guest Roger Maxwell, the longtime golf pro at a Marriott resort, walked out on the back lawn and saw Bill gassing up the portside tank. The hose connected to a line that ran up to

2

gas pump the Marriotts had installed mostly for filling up their cars. Refueling was routine for Bill, but that morning was so still, there was no breeze to disperse the gas fumes, and the vapors dropped down into the boat. Bill did not smell the accumulation, nor could he know that the boat's ignition switch was faulty. When he turned the power on to check the gas gauge, a spark ignited the gas.

The explosion rattled windows up and down the lakeshore, and the flames appeared to envelop Bill in a fraction of a second. There was no way he could survive. But then, within moments, Maxwell, the only eyewitness, saw his friend staggering through the lake shallows to the shore.

Newspaper reports would claim that Bill was blown out of the boat. But for Bill, who was literally on fire, a miracle had occurred. In the midst of the flare-up, he had heard a clear voice: "Get out of the boat!" Instead of being immobilized by shock, he had jumped into the lake.

Bill's wife, Donna, and son John heard the distinctive "whoosh" of a gas explosion, and they rushed out of the house to see the boat engulfed in flames. They were certain Bill must be dead. Grief turned to relief in seconds as Bill stumbled out of the lake, charred skin hanging from his hands, looking, as one witness put it, like "The Creature from the Black Lagoon."

Inside the house, John's girlfriend, Angie, was showering when she heard the explosion. Looking out a window facing the water, she saw Bill emerging from the lake. She swung into action, jumping out of the shower, ripping off the bedsheets, and bringing them back into the shower to soak them with water. Tossing on a T-shirt and shorts, she was out of the house in less than a minute, rushing down the yard to Bill, who had collapsed on the lawn with Donna and John ministering to him. Bill's polyester golf pants had melted onto his legs or been burned away, while the sweater, still hot from the fire, had prevented burns to his upper torso. The sweater came off, and Angie wrapped him in the wet sheets.

Someone called an ambulance, but the trip through the traffic-choked resort town of Wolfeboro would take too long. Maxwell loaded Bill, trembling with shock, into a car and sped the seven miles along country roads to Huggins Hospital. Doctors and nurses were alarmed at the third-degree burns over his body, as well as the possibility that fumes and flames had seared his lungs.

Bill's mother, Allie, soon arrived in the family station wagon with Donna, Debbie, and Elder Packer. Still fearing Bill might not survive, the family asked the Apostle to give Bill a priesthood blessing, which was done with consecrated oil and hands placed upon his head. Elder Packer felt inspired to promise not only that would Bill survive, but that he would not be scarred. He boldly pronounced that the accident would have some divine purpose, as yet unknown, beyond the miracle of his life being saved.

During the weeks of painful recovery, Bill had time to reflect on this life-altering event. He already had a strong conviction about God, the healing sacrifice of Jesus Christ, and the truth of the Church bearing the Savior's name. He knew without a doubt that he had been miraculously saved, that he was watched over from on high, that he had an important place in the world and a mission that included his family, his friends, his church, and his larger family of Marriott employees.

Among the condolences he had received after his father's death less than two weeks earlier, there was a particularly poignant note from family friend Coretta Scott King. The widow of the Reverend Martin Luther King, Jr., had written: "I pray that God will sustain you and help you to accept His will, knowing that all things work together for good, for them that love the Lord and are called according to His purposes."

Bill's life to that point had not been easy. Business for him had always been a kind of fiery battlefield with competitors, prices

4

fluctuations, the labor market, government regulation, and the seesaw of the economy. Overarching that was the most fiery flame of all—the hot temper of his Depression-era father, whose fear of debt led him to oppose many of the daring business decisions Bill had to make to build the Marriott empire.

Now the son was on his own. Though Bill couldn't know it, the challenging years ahead would include explosive growth in the 1980s; a crippling recession and Japanese stock market crash in the early 1990s that would nearly cost him the company; a potentially fatal personal health issue; the challenges of a world after 9/11, when his Marriott hotel between the Twin Towers was obliterated; and so much more.

He could not see that there would come a day when Marriott hotels would number more than 7,000, and he would be the world's undisputed number-one hotelier. But what he already knew that day in 1985 was more than enough. He knew that God loved him, that his family and friends loved him, and that his employees deeply appreciated his leadership.

Later he would say of that day, "I could hardly wait to get back to work." It was a lesson he had learned from his father, that a life of ease is an enemy to progress, both for the person and for the corporation— that, as Bill often put it: "Success is never final."

CHAPTER 1

PILGRIMS AND PIONEERS

Never before had twenty-one-year-old Elizabeth Stewart known such terror as she did during the predawn hours of November 15, 1850.

Elizabeth was traveling on the *James Pennell,* a fully rigged American passenger ship carrying her and 253 other passengers from England to America. After a difficult six-week journey, the tall ship rounded the Cape of Florida and sailed into the Gulf of Mexico toward New Orleans, less than a hundred miles ahead. Anxious to deliver his passengers on schedule, Captain James Fullerton had rigged the ship for full sail when it was hit by a hurricane shortly after four a.m.

In just ten minutes, the ship was disabled. The main mast was carried away so quickly that its brace smashed through the decking, nearly crushing a half dozen passengers lying in their bunks below. Rain poured through the broken deck, and Elizabeth and her fellow passengers below decks could hear the ship being torn apart above their heads. The worst was over quickly, but the seas rolled violently all night.

When the sun rose on a clear day, the crew and all the passengers had survived, but the ship was in serious trouble. It had been blown out into the Gulf of Mexico without any means of steering. Food and water stores were perilously low. They were so close to their destination, yet so far.[1]

For orphan Elizabeth Stewart, a great-grandmother of Bill Marriott, nothing ever came easily. Her childhood in Colmworth, Bedfordshire, England, had been one of poverty and toil. Her mother died when Elizabeth was only five, her father when she was seventeen. At eight she contracted smallpox and then later that year nearly drowned in a pond.

Sometime during this period, missionaries from The Church of Jesus Christ of Latter-day Saints knocked on her father's door. They told a compelling story about a fourteen-year-old boy named Joseph Smith who, while living in upstate New York in 1820, was reading the Bible and felt prompted to pray about which of the many Christian churches he should join. As he knelt in the woods near his home, the answer came in a vision. He said that God the Father and His Son Jesus Christ appeared to him and told him not to join any existing church. As word spread about his vision, the young boy was "ridiculed, hated, and persecuted," according to his own account.

In 1823, he received another vision, this time from an angel named Moroni, who had lived as a man in the Americas around AD 400. The angel told Joseph that near the farm was a set of metal plates on which was engraved a thousand-year history of an ancient civilization in the Americas. Joseph found the plates and translated them into what would become the Book of Mormon. At its core was an account of Jesus's visit to the Americas after His resurrection.

In 1830, Joseph Smith published the book and organized The Church of Jesus Christ of Latter-day Saints, which he maintained was the true Church of Christ restored to the earth. Within a decade, Smith was sending missionaries around the world, seeking converts to the new faith. The Latter-day Saint missionaries had significant success in Bedfordshire and elsewhere in England. Elizabeth, age twelve, and her brother William, seventeen, believed the revolutionary message. William was baptized, but Elizabeth waited until she was nineteen and living on her own.

By then, Smith had been murdered by a mob in 1844 near the Church's stronghold in Illinois. The Church was under the direction of his successor, Brigham Young, who moved the members to the Utah Territory to avoid more persecution because of their peculiar beliefs. Young sent out a call to all members of the Church, including those in England, to come to the valley of the Great Salt Lake—Zion— triggering an overland and sea exodus that lasted from 1846 to 1890.

By 1850, Elizabeth strongly felt the pull to gather with fellow believers to the Utah Territory. The square-rigger *James Pennell,* which had been chartered by the Church to take 254 Latter-day Saint converts on the first leg of their trip, set sail from Liverpool on October 2, 1850. Because Elizabeth had only a shilling left after she paid for her passage, she did not have money for food aboard ship. According to family tradition, she worked in the ship's galley to earn her meals.

By early November, the *Pennell* entered the Gulf of Mexico, but rough seas and unfavorable winds made it impossible for them to make landfall. Then came the hurricane. After drifting for several days, with provisions dangerously low, the *Pennell* was reached by a tugboat and towed to New Orleans. From there, the passengers took a steamer up the Mississippi River to St. Louis, where Elizabeth disembarked with still just a shilling to her name. "I was left to get along the best I could," she recalled.

Helping Elizabeth "get along" was her first love, a man whose name has been lost to the family. All that is known is that she kept his picture the rest of her life to remind her of his courage, gallantry, and sacrifice. One evening, while Elizabeth was carrying a kerosene lamp in one hand and a two-gallon container in the other hand, the lamp exploded, setting her on fire. "My sweetheart ran in and carried me out of the fire," she wrote. "He saved my life, and he died 18 days later from inhaling the fumes."[2]

She continued: "The fire burned me terribly, and the suffering was something great." In fact, her "burns were not well for three years." But just as would happen more than a century later in a fire that would engulf her own great-grandson Bill Marriott, Elizabeth's life was spared.

Elizabeth Stewart Marriott.

Her recovery, like his, was torturous; her face was also miraculously unscarred. Elizabeth's arms were marred with burned skin, but the most notable scar formed a V-shape beginning under her chin and extending about seven inches down her chest. One of her granddaughters recalled that her "neck was transparent, (as was her upper chest). You could see the organs when she breathed, and how she swallowed."[3]

Elizabeth stayed in St. Louis for two more years after the fire, working and relying on the kindness of strangers until she could afford wagon passage across the plains in the summer of 1853.

Her journey was typical of the Mormon pioneer saga—hunger, fatigue, heat, Indian encounters, the dead buried by the side of the trail. At night, wagons were drawn up in a circle for protection. After walking beside a loaded wagon all day, Elizabeth would gather buffalo chips for the cook fire and bake bread for the next day's journey. Around the campfire, the travelers would sing, recite poetry, and dance accompanied by a couple of violins. Early in the journey, she reported, "My shoes wore out and I had nothing but rags to wrap my feet in. It was a walk of 1,500 miles."

The wagon company arrived in Salt Lake City in a staggered fashion over several days in mid-September, and its members were cheerily welcomed by the city's residents. Elizabeth was destitute. "I had no home to go to, no money, and no way of earning any," she wrote. "All [in Salt Lake] were too poor to hire or pay for help. I offered to work for my board, if only I could get something to eat. But I still was not discouraged, because I knew that I had come to Zion and that the Gospel was true. The Lord had heard my prayers and helped me to come to this land I had so much desired."

Finding no employment in Salt Lake, she headed north to the small settlement of Kaysville and moved in with her brother William's family. It was while in that home, looking out the window one day, that she saw a man coming through the field toward the house. She wrote, "The Spirit whispered to me, 'That is the man who is to be your husband.'" It was William's brother-in-law, John Marriott. Elizabeth continued, "A few days later he came again and asked me to be his wife."

Elizabeth's descendants—including father and son J. Willard and Bill Marriott—were shaped by the stories of her journey to the New World, which were told and retold in the family. That frontier grit is in their DNA. Bill once said in a speech to a church group: "I often think about my pioneer ancestors who helped to pave the way for our family. Six of my eight great-grandparents walked across the plains pulling handcarts or walking behind covered wagons. They came in search of a place where they could be free from persecution. They had experienced great lawlessness. Their homes and farms had been burned, their leaders killed, their religion mocked and scorned. They had reason to doubt their future. They had reason to turn back. But they didn't. They went forward with faith and courage. They knew the work would be hard and that their faith would continue to be tested. But they believed in Jesus Christ. They picked up their personal burdens, marched forward, and came unto Him."[4]

It was Elizabeth's husband, John Marriott, who provided the mantra by which his descendants live: "There is no such thing as, 'It can't be done.'" John's respect for the job at hand was reflected in the fact that he always wore a white shirt, whether laboring on the farm, in the fields, or in his home.

Besides his unflinching will and dedication to work, John had the added advantage of being strong, which made him a legend of sorts in Ogden, Utah, where he lived. He could often be seen carrying 400 pounds of wheat in sacks at the same time. The story is told that once when two men began quarreling violently, John intervened by lifting both men up, one in each hand, banging their heads together, and dunking them in nearby water, thus bringing them to their senses. He was known to break many shovels because the handles couldn't hold the weight of the loads he lifted.

When John proposed to Elizabeth, he already had a wife, Susannah, but by that time the Latter-day Saints had re-instituted the Old Testament practice of polygamy. The majority of their men never practiced polygamy—perhaps primarily because they simply could not afford to support multiple households and dozens of children. Historical perspective suggests that one reason for the practice was that it provided a viable way for a community to care for higher numbers of single women like Elizabeth, who was poor, twenty-five years old, and without prospects.

After Elizabeth married, she was not whisked off to a new cabin— her thirty-seven-year-old husband could not afford to build one for his second wife. Instead, the home the new bride lived in for her first year of marriage was a wagon bed. Only a year into the marriage, John was assigned by Brigham Young to colonize a town near the convergence of the Weber and Ogden rivers, about three miles west of the new town of Ogden. He moved his first wife, Susannah, and their five children into a dugout in the new settlement. Pregnant with their first child, Elizabeth stayed in Kaysville until she could walk the eighteen miles carrying her six-week-old daughter.

John proved a natural leader in the new settlement, which the townspeople decided to name "Marriott." Elizabeth again lived in a wagon box in Marriott for six months, then moved to a windowless dugout where her baby slept on a shelf. Sometimes, after going to get water half a mile from the dugout, Elizabeth would return to find that snakes had crawled into her daughter's bed, seeking warmth. Later she lived in a small log room that was only about six feet high, with a sod roof. In the winter, the makeshift cabin was so poorly insulated that "our bread froze all the way through and had to be thawed out before we could eat it," Elizabeth recalled.

In December 1863, when the eastern American states were embroiled in the Civil War, Elizabeth gave birth to her second son, Hyrum Willard, nicknamed "Will." As he grew, he became opinionated and quick-tempered like his father. At about fourteen, Will moved out after an argument with John. He took up harness making and eventually married a distant Marriott cousin, Ellen Morris, and became a prominent farmer and sheepherder.

When it came to Will's courtship of Ellen, love was not mentioned in family histories. The same is true of his parents John and Elizabeth. There was a sense in both cases that the two Marriott men believed they were "rescuing" the women from an unmarried life of toil. While neither Elizabeth nor Ellen were noted for their beauty, both were diamonds in the rough who had proven in their early years to be more than a match for whatever life could throw at them. Both couples fell deeply in love during their long marriages.

John died soon after his son Will married Ellen. The young couple settled in the town of Marriott and had two children, first Doris ("Dodie") and then John Willard. As an adult, their son would be known as J.W. Marriott, the founder of a multimillion-dollar restaurant enterprise. But during his childhood years in Marriott, everyone called him Willard.

When he was three years old, Willard nearly died of typhus, which might have been caused by living next to a mosquito-infested canal. Dodie also got sick, as did the third baby, Ellen (also known as Helen).

Willard saw himself as the "man of the family" even at a very young age. When his mother was pregnant with Helen, she climbed a tree to pick apples, fell, and broke her leg. Little Willard became her nursemaid while she was bedridden, fetching whatever his mother needed.[5]

A big change occurred in 1905, when the family moved to the "grand estate." Owned by an Ogden racehorse breeder, it was the showplace of Marriott—100 acres of lush pasture with a two-story house, a twenty-stall barn, and a high white fence around the entire property. Even without indoor plumbing or electricity, the new house was considered a mansion by the townspeople. Will and Ellen's fourth child, Eva, was the first to be born there, followed by Paul and Kathryn ("Kay").

Ellen was pregnant with her seventh child when Helen and Eva, playing with matches, started a fire that burned down the mansion. Later, as a well-known restaurateur, Willard would remember that fire and attribute the spread of the flames to an unkempt house where chickens were allowed to wander and dirty linens lay in piles. As a result, he developed an obsession with cleanliness and order. But although Will may not have been tidy, he was industrious, and within six months he rebuilt the house larger than before. The last two children, Russell and Woodrow ("Woody"), were born there, for a total of eight.

Will was often away herding sheep so Ellen managed hearth and home. The family never went hungry, and Will always found enough money in the family accounts to be generous with his children. He loved to take the family on summer camping trips to the mountains. In the winter, there were horse-drawn sleigh rides with Will at the reins singing at the top of his lungs to the accompaniment of jingling bells. All the children of the town could count on Will to light torches around the frozen pond on his property so they could ice-skate after dark.

The Marriotts were the first family in town to own an automobile—a 1914 Buick touring car. When they drove the new car to church, the children from the Sunday School climbed all over it, and some even took the liberty of scratching their initials in the paint to commemorate the arrival of the town's first horseless carriage.[6]

In the winter, Willard's education was spotty, as he took on responsibilities at home while his father was frequently away in Salt Lake City serving in the Utah State Legislature. Willard was schooled through the sixth grade, often getting up at four a.m. to study. But high school was hit-and-miss.

As for his religious education, Willard credited the influence of his mother more than his father. In the winter evenings, the family would gather around the big stove, and Ellen would read the Bible to her children. On Saturday nights, Ellen would boil water for baths so the children would be suitably clean for church. There was no question that her children would follow the tenets of The Church of Jesus Christ of Latter-day Saints. She told them, "I'd rather have a stone tied around your necks and have you cast into the ocean than to have you forget your religion and not live it every day of your lives."

Willard had a natural entrepreneurial spirit that was evident at an early age. After helping grow the family's sugar-beet crop and tending to the cattle and sheep, Willard found time to engage in a variety of money-making ventures, such as raising rabbits and chickens, which he would sell in nearby Ogden. He demonstrated a Tom-Sawyer–like talent for managing his younger siblings. When the dreaded job of weeding and thinning the sugar beets came along, Willard would promise his siblings a cold soda pop for everyone who did their part. Leaving the others to start the work, Willard would go into town, buy the soda, and return to put the bottles in the cold stream that ran through their property. The children could see their reward as they worked.

Sheep were the family business, and Willard was a natural, just like his father. "My father always gave me the responsibility of a man," he said. "He would tell me what he wanted me to do, but he never told me much about how to do it and he never sent anyone along with me to show me how. It was up to me to find out for myself."[7] If Willard

14

displeased his father, he was whipped. Once he was locked in a closet for two hours and then sent to bed without supper. Willard inherited that temper from his father.

At the age of thirteen, Willard traveled to deliver summer supplies to a high mountain plateau pasture where Basque sheepherders were tending the Marriott flock. It was a thrilling time for Willard, outfitted with a big cowboy hat, a pair of woolly chaps, a six-gun strapped to his side, and a rifle and lariat secured to the saddle. One night, a rattlesnake slithered under his bedroll. When Willard discovered it in the morning, he took three shots at the fourteen-rattle snake and killed it, impressing the Basques, who had never seen such a large rattler. Another snake saved Willard from a smoking habit, he jokingly recalled. One day, he happened to be chewing a plug of tobacco the Basques had offered him when a rattler sounded off near his horse. In his surprise, the boy swallowed the repugnant wad, thus developing a distaste for tobacco.[8]

The next summer, when he was fourteen, Willard arrived at the high mountain range to find that bears had been picking off the sheep. Willard and a Basque sheepherder named Manuel followed fresh brown-bear tracks leading from one of their dead lambs up the mountain range. The terrain became so steep that they had to dismount and lead their horses. At one point, they heard crashing sounds coming toward them. While Manuel held the horses steady, the rifle-toting Willard saw a bear cub burst out, followed by a rampaging mama bear. She reared and then dropped on all fours, rushing forward as Willard took two shots, both of them hitting home. The cub dashed up a tree, and more crashing in the brush could be heard, which Manuel explained was the father coming for the cub. "You must shoot the cub," Manuel urged, and Willard did. The larger male bear turned back down the hill once that was done. The bearskins were hung to dry in an Ogden butcher shop, and a newspaper article told the story of the boy who had killed two bears in a single day.[9]

Willard was only fifteen when his father sent him alone on a train with thousands of sheep to sell in San Francisco. It was an adventure that opened his eyes to the world outside of rural Utah. He ran along the top of the moving train with a pole, jumping from car to car to sort out the piles of sheep that tumbled into each other every time the train put on the brakes. In San Francisco, Willard bought his first suit with long pants. He explored Chinatown, where he saw opium dens with men sucking on their pipes and staring dreamily. He ate exotic foods on the wharf, took the ferry to Sausalito, and watched in horror as a monoplane doing loops over the bay took a fatal nosedive into the water.

Then he wandered through the 1915 World's Fair, officially called the Panama-Pacific International Exposition, celebrating the completion of the Panama Canal. It "filled my head with dreams of travel and achievement and shining cities, world-makers, and world-shakers who never had to hoe a row of sugar beets in the blazing Utah sun or ride herd on a flock of sheep through a choking white cloud of dust," he wrote in his journal.[10]

The following year, at sixteen, he took the sheep by train to Omaha for sale. On the way, a conductor sized him up, determined he was too young to be traveling alone, and put Willard off the train in Cheyenne while the sheep went on to Omaha alone. Undeterred, Willard caught the next train, only to arrive in Omaha and find his herd had been mingled with others. He solved the problem by cutting the biggest sheep out of the mixed herd and claiming them for the Marriotts.

Back home, Willard was the only one of the children who was allowed to drive. Hence, he considered himself the unofficial owner of the family Buick. His dad had put him behind the wheel from the time that Willard's legs could barely touch the floor—a practice that peeved the town sheriff, a one-legged man called "Peggy" who himself had only a cart pulled by a Shetland pony. Peggy often would flag down young Willard to give him a lecture about safe driving.

But Willard's driving privileges would come to an abrupt end shortly after he turned nineteen, when Will and Ellen would sell their precious Buick to finance an important event in his life—a two-year proselyting mission.

CHAPTER 2

THE ROOT BEER STAND

For several days in late 1918, there was no scent of baking bread in the Marriott home, only the smell of sickness. No bed was empty; from four-year-old Woody to eighteen-year-old Willard and twenty-year-old Doris, all eight of the children were coughing, some were feverish, and some had nosebleeds. Will and his wife, Ellen, did not have enough strength to leave their own bed to help their children. In front of the house a makeshift rag flag flew, and on a placard nailed next to the door was a one-word warning in large letters: "INFLUENZA."

The whole Marriott family became victims of the deadly pandemic sometimes called the "Spanish flu." It was a virus so deadly that in less than a year it killed more people than the bubonic plague—the "Black Death"—had killed throughout the entire fourteenth century. Nothing else before or since—disease, famine, natural disaster, or war—has killed so many in so short a time. One-fifth of the earth's population became infected with the deadly flu, and more than fifty million died.

As near as can be determined, the pandemic first arrived in Utah in early October 1918. The infection spread so quickly that by mid-October, hospitals overflowed with patients. Most people were quarantined in their homes and required to fly the "flu flag." By the next month, the worst of the epidemic seemed to abate in Utah, but then

World War I ended on November 11, and public-health officials could not prevent celebratory gatherings in every town and city. Within a day or two, a second wave of infection occurred, worse than the first. In an act of desperation after Thanksgiving, Ogden's leaders closed the entire city to outsiders.[1]

The flu epidemic hit during Willard's senior year at Weber Academy high school. Between his absences for lambing in the spring and harvesting sugar beets in the fall, school was already "something of a hit-and-miss proposition," he wrote.[2] But when schools were closed by the epidemic for four months, there was no possibility that Willard would graduate in the spring of 1919. The epidemic finally abated that spring.

Willard would not be deterred from his plan to serve a two-year volunteer mission for The Church of Jesus Christ of Latter-day Saints after he turned nineteen in September 1919. His assignment was to the Eastern States Mission, headquartered in New York. His father worried that the Marriott family could not handle the double financial hit of a mission—the loss of Willard's help at home, coupled with the cost of supporting him while he was away. But Willard urged his father to have faith that it was the right thing to do. Will agreed and sold his beloved Buick, and Ellen sold her only precious possession, a gold watch and chain inherited from her mother. The money was used to outfit Willard with a new derby hat, crisp white shirts with celluloid collars, a suitcoat and pants, and shiny new black shoes. Then it paid for his train fare to New York City, with enough left over to cover his expenses for a few months.

The train pulled into New York's Hoboken station in early December. Willard took the subway under the Hudson River to Brooklyn to receive his assignment from his mission president, George McCune. He stayed at the Brooklyn mission home for a week for training. During that week, he looked up a cousin, Laura Bushnell, who lived with her husband, George, in a large upper West End

Avenue apartment. George was vice president and comptroller for the fast-growing J.C. Penney Company, which had moved its headquarters to New York from Salt Lake City only five years earlier. It was a very fortuitous family connection for the future businessman.

For his first assignment, Elder Marriott took the train to Burlington, Vermont, where he quickly acclimatized to the work—and learned humility. On his sixth day in Burlington, he wrote in his faithfully kept daily journal: "I am beginning to realize my divine calling, and responsibility I have fulfilling my duty. I can plainly see my transgressions, and what it would [have] meant if I had not stopped."[3] He soon demonstrated zeal in the work—sometimes too much zeal. On a New Year's Eve train ride to Hyde Park, New York, Elder Marriott condemned a man to hell for not listening to the gospel message.

One night in Burlington, he received a frightening phone call from the Mathers family, members of the Church. Their daughter Ruth had fallen off a forty-five-foot cliff by Lake Champlain. Doctors told her parents she was dying. Elder Marriott arrived at the family's home and asked to be alone with the unconscious Ruth, where he pled with God to know what he should do. Then he placed his hands on her head in the manner of Latter-day Saint priesthood blessings and promised her that she would live. In less than half an hour, Ruth was awake and asking for water. The experience greatly strengthened Willard's faith in his God and in himself.

Along with the high spots, missionary labor could be grueling. Rising from bed at an early hour, when it was 20 degrees below zero outside, Willard and his companion would preach door-to-door and on street corners. Elder Marriott's first experience with a street meeting was an unmitigated failure. "We spoke for 15 minutes to a telephone post & electric light. No one would stop," he wrote.[4] A few weeks later, another street meeting drew a hostile crowd that grew large enough to attract the attention of the local newspaper. The editor of the Rutland

Elder J.W. Marriott (left) with fellow missionary Hugh Colton, his future business partner.

Herald Reporter invited the missionaries into his office to talk religion and then wrote an upbeat article about their efforts.

More often than not, people's reactions ran from disinterest to anger at the missionaries. When Willard visited a local photo studio, the photographer told him he'd rather "be shot before being a Mormon." One angry woman "shut my fingers in the door," while another "acted awful hateful. She slammed the door and I hollered in saying she would feel sorry for slamming the door in my face. She came out with a mad rush and told us to get right out of there. Set the dog on us."[5]

In Colchester, near Burlington, Elder Marriott had the most harrowing experience of his mission. Protestants in the town were united in their antipathy toward the Latter-day Saints. Willard and his companion entered the town cautiously on June 16, 1920, and did some private preaching, but word of their presence spread quickly. One welcoming family invited them to stay for dinner and lodging, but soon the house was surrounded by an angry mob. Their hosts gamely defended the missionaries as the young men made a hasty departure, hiding out in a field.[6]

Throughout the moonless night, they heard swearing and cursing against "those filthy Mormons"; and, occasionally, they heard a rifle shot. At one lull in the hunt, the missionaries stood up to assess the danger and heard the sound of footsteps around them. Willard's companion kicked the nearest shadowy figure—a cow that bellowed in pain. Willard reported that at sunrise, after "ascending & descending hills, climbing over & crawling through fences & wading through dew-fallen grass,"[7] they managed to evade their pursuers. Persecution only seemed to redouble Willard's commitment. "The only time I am really happy is while I am preaching," he wrote.[8]

Toward the end of his mission, Elder Marriott had encounters with an impressive list of luminaries, including Babe Ruth, who hit his 140th home-run ball toward the surprised missionary.

Ruth was in the midst of what some historians argue was his best season ever, leading the New York Yankees to their first league championship. On July 30, the Yankees were on their home field playing against the Cleveland Indians. Anxious to see the Sultan of Swat play just once, Willard and his companion somehow got seats in the sold-out crowd of 38,000, and the great Bambino hit a home run.

"I was wishing Babe Ruth would knock a home run & he lifted one right to me," Willard wrote excitedly in his journal. "We were in the bleachers. I had my coat & a book in [my] hands so couldn't grab it & it hit a man in the head sitting [to] the side of me. Knocked him out for a few minutes. Feel like kicking myself for not throwing my coat down but it came so sudden."[9]

Willard never told anyone in his family about the moment, maybe because he had failed to drop his coat and reach for the ball. But, more than most moments in his early life, it allegorically foretold what would later become a consistent difference between J.W. and his son Bill. The father was cautious and disciplined, refusing to trade a bird in the hand for two in the bush. Bill became a risk taker who could pivot his company on a dime.

In the summer of 1921, J.W. received a letter from his mother warning that when the last $100 they had sent to Willard ran out, he would probably have to come home. Two weeks later, he got a letter from his father insisting he come home in September to start college. Then another letter came from his mother in August reminding him of sacrifices the family was making for him. Willard agonized over what to do. In the end, the mission president made the decision for him, sending him home ten weeks shy of his two-year mark.

The twenty-one months had changed him forever. "I developed beyond anything I could have imagined—in poise, vocabulary, knowledge, spiritually, and in working with people," he described decades later.[10] Not incidentally, he had made new friends who would prove pivotal in his early business ventures, including Franklin Richards, who would introduce him to the food-catering business, and fellow missionary Hugh Colton, who would be his first partner in founding the family restaurant venture. George Bushnell, the J.C. Penney executive and relative by marriage, would be an early investor who would introduce him to another key investor and adviser, Earl Sams, and to Lake Winnipesaukee in New Hampshire.

Finally, a stop in Washington, D.C., on his way home from the mission would prompt him to later choose the city as the best location for the start of a new restaurant business that his son Bill would later expand into an international hotel empire.

Willard turned twenty-one on that day he stepped off a Pennsylvania Railroad train at Union Station and got his first look at Washington, D.C. He never expected to live in the East, let alone begin a business there, so he thought this was his one chance to see the nation's capital.

The next morning, he hopped aboard a sightseeing bus, which took him on a tour of Arlington Cemetery, the White House, and the homes of the capital's most important leaders, including Reed Smoot, the highly respected senator from Utah who would one day become

Willard's father-in-law. In retrospect, the most memorable sight for Willard was a hardworking pushcart vendor who couldn't keep up with the tourists' demands for lemonade and ice cream in the sultry heat. That memory would later cause Willard to conclude that the District of Columbia was just the place for a root beer stand.

Back at home in Utah, Willard faced two obstacles to his college plans—he had no money and no high school diploma. A Weber College professor in Ogden saw potential in him and arranged campus jobs and classes that would give him high school and college credit. He buckled down to his studies, became student-body president, and graduated with a two-year degree in 1923.

That summer Willard and a friend took sales jobs with Baron Woolen Mills and were sent to the logging camps of northern California to sell long woolen underwear to loggers. On arrival at each camp, the partners would pick out two of the huskiest lumberjacks and dare them to try tearing the long johns apart. They never could, so orders for the $22 union suits piled up. The canny partners soon found they had to collect payment for the goods on Saturday, right after the loggers were paid and before they started drinking and gambling. Working eighteen-hour days, the pair each made $3,000 that summer.[11]

In the fall, Willard was admitted to the University of Utah in Salt Lake City, the oldest state university west of the Missouri River. His fraternity brothers at Phi Delta Theta included fellow missionaries Hugh Colton and Franklin Richards, who hired him to work at a catering company supplying university parties—his first foray into the food business. The next summer, Willard returned to the wool business and once again made $3,000.

Flush with cash and excited about his final year at the University of Utah, Willard went home at the end of summer, but there his ebullience was crushed. His father had borrowed money to buy a herd of 3,000 sheep in Elko, Nevada, and the sheep needed to be driven to

Tremonton, Utah. Will would trust no one but his son to do that, so Willard put his studies on hold. With the assistance of two Basque sheepherders, he drove sheep through the cold winter months, from October to May. He came close to freezing to death one night, and he lost 500 lambs to the elements, lions, coyotes, and poison water. He was eventually successful, but most of the sheep sales went to repay the bank loan. The unshakable legacy of that sheep drive was Willard's visceral distrust of debt, which would greatly impact the future Marriott company's business decisions.

After the sheep drive, he checked in with Baron Woolen Mills for a summer job, was made district supervisor of seven states, and quickly built up a sales force of about forty-five University of Utah students to work for him. Although there was no salary for the position, his percentage of the sales that year came to nearly $5,000. That nest egg allowed him to finish his senior year at the university. The highlight of that year was the day he rounded a corner and spotted a slender girl wearing a green dress that set off her beautiful brown eyes and abundance of brown hair.

"That's the kind of girl I'd like to marry," Willard told a friend, who responded that Allie Sheets was way out of a sheepherder's league.

• • •

Several decades before that chance encounter, a widow in Westvale, Yorkshire, England, was managing six young children and looking at a bleak future. Martha Hirst Taylor turned her life around by heeding the call of The Church of Jesus Christ of Latter-day Saints to immigrate to Utah. In 1888, she and her children made the long journey over sea and land to Salt Lake City. Eleven years later, Martha's daughter Alice married Edwin Sheets. Three years after giving birth to a son, Alice and Edwin had their second and last child, whom they named Alice, but who was always known as "Allie" to distinguish her from her mother.

When Allie was less than a year old, the family followed Edwin to law school at the University of Chicago. When they returned to Salt Lake City, Edwin settled into a law practice. He was also bishop of a Latter-day Saint congregation, and when the Spanish flu hit Utah, Edwin visited the sick and the dying without regard for the contagion. He died at the age of forty-four from pneumonia and influenza. A few months before his death, Edwin had a dream in which he was told that he was wanted "on the other side" to preach to the souls of soldiers who had died in World War I. He shared the dream with a friend, then swore him to secrecy until after he was dead.

The high regard in which Edwin Sheets was held is evidenced by the fact that amidst all the flu deaths occurring at the time, the *Deseret News* newspaper dedicated an editorial to Edwin's death: "His entire life was spent in true service to his fellow man, and although but a young man in years, his long experience and faithful devotion to duty has seldom been excelled by men gray with age."[12]

Edwin left his family financially secure, so his widow, Alice, had the luxury of throwing herself into religious and charitable work. She lobbied her church to build a children's hospital, which it did, and worked tirelessly as a volunteer at that hospital.

Although Allie Sheets had lost her father, she was not without privilege and opportunity. She excelled in school and studied piano under the organist for the Mormon Tabernacle Choir. She took Latin and geometry for fun and skipped eleventh grade. At the tender age of fifteen, she enrolled at the University of Utah. By the ripe old age of eighteen, her dance card was full and her goal was to marry a doctor.

She was definitely out of Willard's league, but he was undeterred and unembarrassed about his own pedigree. On their first date he showed her pictures of his sheep. Then he took her to the mountain range to view his family herd—which, unbeknownst to Allie, was really the bank's herd. The summer of Willard's graduation, he proposed and Allie accepted.

Much of their courtship was spent at a new establishment that was all the rage in Salt Lake. It was called the "A&W" (only coincidentally their initials), and it sold frosty mugs of root beer for five cents. Business was booming—5,000 sales a day—and Willard was reminded of the pushcart vendor he had seen that hot day in Washington, D.C. For Willard and Allie, the envisioned marriage of product (A&W) and place (D.C.) became the birth of a dream.

A&W was the creation of California businessman Roy Allen, who bought his root beer recipe from a retired chemist in Arizona. He tried it out at a roadside stand during a veterans' parade and was soon the purveyor of root beer at a half dozen stands in central California. Then, in 1923, Allen invented the modern drive-in. At the time, Allen had a partnership with one of his employees, Frank Wright, so they named their root beer "A&W." By the time Willard and Allie were sipping the root beer in Salt Lake City, Allen had pioneered the notion of root beer store franchises. Willard's cousin Sherman Marriott bought the franchise for Fort Wayne, Indiana. More important, Willard's mission friend Hugh Colton, who was attending George Washington University Law School in Washington, D.C., began pushing Willard to go in with him on an A&W franchise in the nation's capital.

That fall, Willard drove to Sacramento for a sit-down meeting with Roy Allen and came away impressed. In April 1927, he and Colton signed a deal with Allen and opened their nine-seat A&W franchise in a tiny storefront location on 14th Street in downtown D.C. Their grand opening was May 20—the same day that Charles A. Lindbergh took off from Long Island's Roosevelt Field in his single-engine *Spirit of St. Louis,* attempting the first solo flight across the Atlantic Ocean. Willard and Hugh opened their doors at ten a.m., and the customers soon began pouring in. Many were anxious to hear the news about "Lucky Lindy," so Willard rushed out and returned with a countertop radio so his customers could follow the minute-by-minute commentary on Lindbergh's flight. Many years later, when Willard and Allie shared a table with the Lindberghs at a White House dinner, Willard deadpanned to Lindy: "You know, we went into business on the same day, but you got all the publicity!"[13]

By the end of that first historic day, Willard and Hugh had served nearly 2,000 mugs of root beer. At only a nickel each, and with plenty of free coupons given away, the take that day was $73.10, but the newly minted entrepreneurs had nearly 2,000 converts to the A&W recipe.

Meanwhile, Allie Sheets was preparing to graduate from the University of Utah in June, and planning a wedding at the same time. Willard made it home in time to see her receive her diploma. Then he had a last piece of business before their wedding at eleven a.m. the next day. He needed a ring.

After spending a fitful night at his family home in Marriott, Willard got up early, took the tarp off his Model T, and headed north to Baron Woolen Mills, which still owed him about $3,000 in commissions from the prior summer. The manager was waiting for him, with a chill in the air. He was not going to pay because too many of the sales from Willard's crew had fallen through. A certain amount of "shorting" was expected, but never to such a degree. What he didn't know was that the mill had bought some expensive equipment, and Willard's commission was a budget casualty.[14]

The disconsolate bridegroom rushed off in his Model T to a bank in Ogden and asked to borrow $1,500, but the manager turned him down, citing Willard's father's poor credit history there. It was a humiliation Willard never forgot, and one that compounded his aversion to debt.

He was now broke and late for his wedding. When he called Allie, she was in tears, sure that he had stood her up at the altar. Finding it was "only" a money problem, she was overjoyed that the wedding would still occur, just two hours late. As they were about to enter the Salt Lake Temple, Allie's mother pressed four crisp $50 bills into Willard's hands. She had planned to use the money for a family wedding reception, but she knew they needed it for the long drive back to Washington, D.C.

In the late 1920s, there were few paved roads in America. The Model T was a sturdy vehicle, but it couldn't go much faster than thirty-five miles an hour. It frequently got bogged down in mud and all too often overheated on inclines—forcing the couple to stop and wait for the engine to cool down, then refill the radiator from the three-gallon can strapped to the running board. They spent their wedding night at a dilapidated hotel in the cowboy town of Evanston, Wyoming. The honeymoon trip took eleven challenging days, but J.W. (as he was sometimes called in adulthood) and Allie always remembered it with fondness. "We were very much in love and the 11 days went by all too soon," J.W. said.[15]

The Marriotts set up housekeeping in D.C. in an apartment building on New York Avenue, where the State Department is now located. One floor below were their new business partners, the Coltons. They quickly opened a second A&W franchise, and Allie was pressed into service as bookkeeper. Business was good, but not great. Marriott and Colton could not have survived the first year without reneging on key parts of their contract with A&W. This may have been a subconscious factor in J.W.'s future opposition to franchising Marriott restaurants or hotels. Deep down, he knew that he had started his business as a franchisee by not living up to the contract.

Marriott and Colton were often late in their payments to Roy Allen. And once they committed the cardinal sin of substituting another product for the A&W recipe when they ran short on the secret syrup. Allen caught them when he sent a quality-control spy to the store. The partners apologized, and Allen forgave them. They were his first franchisees east of the Mississippi, and Allen had a lot riding on their success.

Struggling to make money on root beer in the winter, J.W. took a train to California to ask Allen to let them sell food at the D.C. root beer stands, which was against their contract. Allen relented, and J.W.

J.W. in the doorway of the first Hot Shoppe, 1927.

headed back to D.C. to confer with Allie about menus. Hamburgers were not even considered because that particular meat was so low on the social scale that few restaurants offered it. They agreed that hot dogs and barbecue sandwiches would be good, and then, being Westerners, they thought maybe they could throw in some Tex-Mex offerings. Allie visited the nearby Mexican embassy and used her college Spanish to charm recipes out of the chef. Soon Allie was cooking up chili and tamales in their apartment. Because they were the first to feature those foods in a chain of stores on the East Coast, the National Restaurant Association later called J.W. "the father of Tex-Mex restaurants."

Word of the upcoming change to their root beer stores spread that fall of 1927, and a friend asked when they were going to open their next "hot shop." The Marriotts liked the name, especially using the old English spelling—"Hot Shoppe." Overnight they rebranded their locations from street-front root beer stands to warm, enclosed "Hot Shoppes," still offering the A&W product. A new restaurant chain was born.

By March 1928, Hugh Colton wanted to move back to Utah. Profits were anemic, and the business couldn't sustain two families. Colton offered to bow out. "We nearly tossed a coin to see who got the business," J.W. said in one interview. "Neither of us wanted it very bad." J.W. was still a cowboy at heart, and he also was tempted to return to Utah. The Marriotts finally agreed, reluctantly, to buy out the Coltons for $5,000, which J.W. had to borrow from a bank.[16]

The contract with Allen required the Marriotts to open something new in 1928—a drive-in restaurant unlike their walk-in establishments. It would be the first drive-in east of the Rocky Mountains. They found a spot on Georgia Avenue and wrangled with the D.C. government over the unique traffic and parking demands of a drive-in.

Among the innovations J.W. incorporated into his first drive-in was a food tray—invented by a friend for the Salt Lake City A&W stand—that attached to the car door. The young men who served the cars, called "curbers," wore A&W orange-and-black uniforms and hustled to receive their tips-only income. That image of the "Running Boy" soon became part of the Hot Shoppes logo. On an average weekday, more than sixty gallons of root beer were dispensed from the store's six spigots. Unlike the previous two stores, the drive-in with food was an instant success.

By the time the stock market crashed in October 1929, the Marriotts had eighty employees at three stores. Although the young couple wanted a baby more than anything else, that baby, Bill, would not be born until five years into the marriage. For the time being, Allie was content with their life. She penned a letter to her husband that March while visiting Utah. The most telling paragraph addressed her thoughts after visiting with a friend whose husband was a sheepherder: "He is out with the sheep & she is living home with her folks. He

J.W. and Allie Marriott in Washington, D.C.

comes in every 2 months for a week. She hasn't seen him for 7 weeks now & here I have only been gone 3 1/2. She says it's an awful life & never to let you do it. So if we sell hot dogs the rest of our lives, I don't care—as long as I can be with my sweetie 25 out of 24 hours."[17]

Only a few months later, when Hot Shoppes filed its first incorporation papers, Allie Marriott became the company's first president. J.W. was not even listed as a board member until the third board meeting. The game of administrative musical chairs continued the next day when J.W. was named president. The officer slate was set, probably more to fill in the blanks on incorporation forms than to represent actual company control.

Life in Washington without children was not all work for the Marriotts, however. They had a rich circle of friends, many of them Utah Latter-day Saints who had been invited into government service by Senator Reed Smoot. They met for church in a rented hall, and Sunday School was taught by a brilliant Latter-day Saint lawyer, J. Reuben Clark, who had become undersecretary of state during the Coolidge administration.

As 1929 closed, and the first waves of the Great Depression were felt across the country, the Marriotts looked for signs of trouble in their business and could find none. They were soon up to five restaurants, all in the D.C. city limits. They had founded their new business in the most Depression-proof city in the nation. The same could not be said for J.W.'s family back home. Will Marriott was effectively bankrupt. When his farm went on the auction block, the winning bidder, at $5,000, was none other than J.W. With some creative financing, he had saved his family's farm, but he didn't want his father to run it anymore, so J.W. spent another $6,000 to move his parents and sister Doris into Ogden.[18]

Hot Shoppe Number Five opened on July 2, 1930, the same day Allie's widowed mother married Senator Reed A. Smoot. The widow Alice Sheets, then fifty-four, had come to D.C. for a visit the previous spring. At church she met the senator, who, at sixty-eight, had been widowed for two years. He instantly set out to win her heart with a series of dates that were reported in the local press. After the wedding, their honeymoon was cut short by President Herbert Hoover, who needed Smoot in town on legislative business. The newlyweds spent their two-week honeymoon living at the White House. The first morning there, President and Mrs. Hoover gave a wedding breakfast in their honor, and the only other guests were J.W. and Allie. The new Mrs. Smoot wrote back home to Utah: "Can you imagine any little girl coming across the ocean and almost the width of the United States as a little emigrant, dreaming that she would ever become the wife of a Senator of the United States [and to find] herself, with her distinguished husband, the honored guest of the head of the United States government?"[19]

As it turned out, the extended Marriott clan would become accustomed to moving in such circles as their business empire grew, spurred on by the son who was born to J.W. and Allie on March 25, 1932.

CHAPTER 3

BILLY THE KID

B ill Marriott's race against time began the day he was born, when he first demonstrated a competitive nature and a need for speed.

His parents' best friends, Isaac and June Stewart, were expecting their second child at the same time as Allie and J.W. looked forward to their first. The two couples had the same obstetrician and the same due date, April 5, 1932. The obstetrician even booked adjoining rooms for the moms-to-be at Columbia Hospital for Women.

Allie began experiencing labor pains on the morning of March 25, and J.W. rushed her out of their apartment building and into his Nash automobile. As he raced down the street, the Stewarts, who lived only two blocks away, passed them in a speeding vehicle. Arriving at the hospital at about the same time, the two pregnant women were rushed into adjoining delivery rooms, and, as was the case in that era, the expectant fathers were relegated to the waiting room, where they wore out the floor with their pacing.

After three hours of labor, Allie gave birth to a seven-and-a-half-pound boy, whom his parents named John Willard Marriott, Jr. Two hours later, the Stewarts' second son arrived. Baby Billy had won his first race. It was Good Friday—a very good Friday for the Marriotts.[1]

Outside the happy Marriott home, the world was in the middle of the Great Depression, an economic event that sparked widespread up-heaval. In the United States, public discontent with President Herbert Hoover was at an all-time high, and he was being challenged for reelection by New York Governor Franklin Delano Roosevelt. For the first time in American history, more citizens left the country than immigrated into it, and the Dow Jones Industrial Average hit a record low of 44.22.

There were some bright spots besides Billy's birth that year. Norwegian ice-skater Sonja Henie dazzled the judges to win a gold medal at the February Winter Olympics at Lake Placid, New York, and the Los Angeles Summer Olympics netted so many medals for Americans that the second-place country, Italy, was almost 500 points behind. The New York Yankees swept the World Series again, with Babe Ruth and Lou Gehrig at their peak. A curly-topped tyke named Shirley Temple appeared in her first movie. A wrinkle-free fabric was invented, and Ford unveiled its V-8 engine, while Italian Guglielmo Marconi tested the first shortwave radio. For better or worse, a new era was beginning at the same time baby Billy was embarking on his life's journey.

When Allie's office in the apartment was converted into a nursery, J.W. rented a basement office in their building. Much of Allie's energy was taken up with the baby, so J.W. hired his first secretary and a book-keeper. His brother Paul mastered the restaurant business and became J.W.'s right-hand man. Paul had the brains and vision to facilitate J.W.'s plans for rapid expansion. Not long after Billy was born, it was Paul whom J.W. tapped to open the first Hot Shoppe outside the D.C. area, in Baltimore. J.W. also tasked Paul to negotiate the purchase of the A&W franchise in Philadelphia. But he would never need his younger brother more than in early 1933, when J.W. was given less than a year to live.

Franklin Delano Roosevelt was elected America's thirty-second president in a November 1932 landslide, which evidenced a major shift of many Republicans to the Democratic Party. It was because of FDR's popularity that Republican Senator Reed Smoot, who was running for a sixth term, lost his seat in a surprising defeat. When Smoot

Billy on a pony.

learned from radio and telephone reports on election night about the trend against him in early voting returns, he put his glasses into his vest pocket, took Alice by the hand, and said, "It's past our bedtime." J.W. and Allie had joined them for election night, and Smoot asked them, "When you're ready to go, would you turn out the lights?" The next morning, he told the Marriotts he would serve out the last months of his term, and then he and Alice would return to Utah so that he could fully take up his duties as a member of the Quorum of the Twelve Apostles of The Church of Jesus Christ of Latter-day Saints.[2]

The Marriotts attended FDR's inaugural ball, but to them the President's New Deal programs looked increasingly socialistic. Among the legislation were minimum-wage and union collective-bargaining laws that would challenge the bottom line for the Hot Shoppes and then the Marriott company for decades to come.

In March, several weeks after FDR's inauguration, Billy turned one, and his family moved into Senator Smoot's French provincial mansion at 4500 Garfield Street. It would be Billy's permanent home until he left for college. J.W. and Allie had felt that the seven-bedroom house was too elegant for their young family of three, but Reed and Alice Smoot couldn't find a buyer for the mansion, so they asked the Marriotts to house-sit. The Depression continued to discourage buyers, and eventually J.W. and Allie took over the mortgage for $35,000 and settled in permanently.

The Marriotts had barely moved into their new home when Allie urged J.W. to see a doctor about lumps that had developed under his arms and on the back of his neck. After a battery of tests, he was diagnosed with Hodgkin's disease, a cancer of the lymph glands. It was so advanced that five doctors told him it was incurable.

"How long do I have?" J.W. resolutely asked.

"Six months—a year at most," one of them replied, and the rest of the doctors concurred. They advised him that he might lengthen his life to a year if he took a long vacation and left his business concerns behind.

J.W. took their advice. He turned the business over to Paul and took Allie and Billy on a road trip. The threesome made their way up the Eastern seaboard, stopping at motels whenever J.W. was too tired to go on. At Moosehead Lake in Maine, they checked into a remote fishing and hunting camp called "The Birches." After a long stay, they headed south to explore J.W.'s old mission stomping grounds. Memories flooded back to him of more than one occasion when he had seen God's power heal someone. It occurred to J.W. that his illness was a test of his faith and it was time for him to seek out elders of the Church to give him a healing blessing.

Back home in Washington, he invited two Latter-day Saint men to his home, where they put their hands on his head and, after seeking inspiration, incredibly promised him that he would be healed: "We rebuke this disease. We believe, and we ask you to believe with us, in your mission of service to your fellow man and to your church, and we promise you that you will live to perform this mission."[3]

J.W.'s burden had been lifted. Within a few weeks, the lymphatic swellings decreased in size and then vanished altogether. His doctors were astonished. Within months, the same doctors could not find the faintest trace of Hodgkin's disease. By Christmas he was back at work. Not only was this a miracle for which he never ceased to be grateful, but he acknowledged that it obliged him to serve God in whatever capacity was asked of him for the rest of his life.

By 1934, J.W. had become the head of the extended Marriott family, even though his parents were still living. He had a strong sense of responsibility for his siblings, and the prosperity of Hot Shoppes enabled him to assist them financially. Doris, the oldest of the siblings and first to wed, had married a man who eventually abandoned her and her child, so she moved in with her parents in Utah. J.W.'s seventy-year-old father, Will, was a restless man, and, with Doris at home to keep her mother company, he went to Washington to work for his son in 1934, just as Billy was turning two.

Will Marriott became the Hot Shoppes' first unofficial personnel relations man. He made the rounds of the restaurants, getting to know all the employees. He also scoured the local markets looking for the best wholesale food deals for the restaurants. Judging meat was his specialty. A butcher once threw down a challenge: "I'll bet you a Stetson hat you can't tell me what grade of meat that is, or the weight within ten pounds." Will wore the Stetson proudly for the rest of his life.[4]

Billy saw a lot of Hot Shoppes during his early years. "When I was very small," he recalled, "I remember going with Mother to the Arcade Market on 14th Street with the sawdust on the floor and the fresh meat and chickens hanging up for display. Afterwards we would go by the old 14th Street Hot Shoppe. I particularly remember Number 5."[5]

Hot Shoppe Number 5 on Connecticut Avenue was the star of the chain, growing faster than the unemployment lines in the 1930s. "The cars used to line up on Connecticut Avenue as far as you could see to get in there," J.W.'s brother Woody recalled from his first job as a Number 5 carhop. "Everybody that worked as a carhop had to learn to run. You wouldn't dare go out of that door without running. That was my brother's idea of telling them [customers] that we were speeding up the service."[6] The man called the "Mayor of Connecticut Avenue" was Mack Woodward, the curb manager. He rode herd on the boys, teaching them how to carry their trays high and run with them. Woodward wasn't above making a little money on the side, charging the boys a small fee for the pencil stubs and windshield cards needed to take orders, requiring interest for any money he loaned them, and sometimes running a crap game in Number 5's basement.[7]

Billy found the hustle and bustle both fascinating and funny. The older boys told Billy tall tales, like the time one of them was carrying hot chocolate on a tray on a windy winter night, and the wind blew the whipped cream off the chocolate and sent it flying over his shoulder, where it froze in midair and then smacked into the head of the unsuspecting running boy behind him, knocking him out.

Sometimes there were inebriated patrons at the Hot Shoppes whose antics could be amusing. J.W. began to sell both light and dark beer after the Prohibition Act was repealed in February 1934. Because the dark beer looked like root beer, embarrassing mix-ups often occurred, with customers getting dark beer for the root beer they had ordered, and vice versa. So an unknown number of curbers elected to become unofficial taste testers. That made for some tipsy running boys before a more reliable identification system was established.

When Billy was three, in 1935, several key changes were made at Number 5 that increased patronage even more. News reports that year touted Number 5's modern broadcast system—seven transmitter poles for curbers to call in orders and a loudspeaker system to tell them when the order was up. The clever curbers and managers also adapted it as an early-warning system to thwart J.W.'s surprise inspections. When a curber spotted J.W. driving into the lot, he would quickly call in an order over the loudspeaker for "One Big Tamale!"—putting everyone on their best behavior.

J.W.'s surprise inspections were an early lesson in a management philosophy Bill would later adopt: "Management by Walking Around." J.W. once told a gathering of employees, "My biggest mistake is a nice office. I like it. My visitors like it. So I don't go visit the Hot Shoppes like I should. When I don't, I feel I miss something."[8]

Number 5 was known as the number-one restaurant hot spot in Washington in the 1930s. It "draws the fashionable night clientele of the city," noted one newspaper report.[9] When Dwight Eisenhower became president, he confided to J.W. that he and his wife, Mamie, had visited there at least once a week when Ike was an aide to General Douglas MacArthur. The Eisenhowers came for Allie's chili and hot tamales.

Perhaps the most colorful contemporary report on Number 5 was written by columnist Gil Miner of Maine's *Madison Bulletin,* who had been squired to the restaurant by a U.S. congressman he was visiting in June 1934. It was a hot summer night, and Miner wanted a cold drink. As if it were the Eighth Wonder of the World, the congressman bragged that he could take Gil to a place where he didn't have to get out of the car to order a cold drink, a hot dog, or a steak, and he could eat it from a tray attached to the car.

"This interested me," Miner wrote, "and in due time we arrived at the 'Hot Shoppes' on Connecticut Avenue. Believe me, it was 'Hot!' Parking spaces for over 1,000 cars, hundreds of young men bustling about taking orders and delivering them, dressed in snappy brown uniforms, with captains in outfits so white they'd make an admiral blush."

The columnist ventured indoors and introduced himself to J.W., who happened to be there that night. Miner invited Marriott to vacation in Maine. "I do already," J.W. smiled. "My family spends a month every summer at Moosehead. Do you ever go there?"

Miner was excited, in part because this was "the first time I had ever been able to talk things over with a living Horatio Alger," he wrote.[10]

After discovering the idyllic hunting and fishing camp on Moosehead Lake when J.W. was coping with his Hodgkin's disease diagnosis, the Marriotts spent seven summers there. It was one place where Billy could have his father's full attention. There were no telephones, so J.W. could not conduct business. The lake was too cold for swimming, but fish were plentiful, and the family spent many nights eating the catch of the day and then settling into Adirondack chairs facing the picturesque 800-foot Mount Kineo a half mile across the lake. When the talking faded in the evening, J.W. would wind up the portable Victrola and play favorite records such as "Drifting and Dreaming," "Stardust," "Moonlight Bay," or "Home on the Range."

During that pivotal period, J.W. gained an important new friend, mentor, and Hot Shoppes' most important outside investor, Earl Sams. He was president of the J.C. Penney Company and the boss of J.W.'s cousin-in-law George Bushnell. Sams was sixteen years older than J.W., and he had a personality, philosophy, and generosity that melded neatly with J.W.'s own character. The two developed a father-son relationship that began with the vital business advice Sams gave J.W. during their chats on the porch of the Samses' house at Lake Winnipesaukee in New Hampshire. Two important keys to Sams's success, which J.W. absorbed, were to never borrow money to expand and to hire only "good, clean-cut, decent workers." The employees needed to consider their work at Hot Shoppes as a service, not just a business.

Bushnell, who was well aware that J.W. had nearly worked himself to death a few years earlier, also counseled him: "I do not think it necessary for a man to work 18 hours every day. In fact, I know he cannot keep it up." Bushnell also believed in respecting the community. "Some storekeepers look upon a town as a mine out of which they are going to take all the treasure they can without putting anything in except the pick and shovel and their hands. The Creator never intended us to do that. We live with one another to serve, to build, to inspire. This is our duty toward our communities."[11]

Sams and Bushnell were preaching to the choir with J.W., but it was encouraging for him to have his own operating philosophy confirmed by men who had already made their fortunes. In the future, the trio's foundational business rules would have a powerful impact on the boy who overheard their adult talk. Billy would one day teach the same principles to hundreds of thousands of employees of the Marriott hotel empire.

As the Hot Shoppes business grew, in part with the addition of A&W franchises, Billy found his place in the company. His earliest recollections of the business were from trailing behind his father visiting the restaurants. There were proud moments when J.W. asked his opinion, using Billy as a one-boy focus group. At five, Billy couldn't yet read, but his father showed him the 1937 mock-up for the first-ever Hot Shoppes children's 35-cent menu. It became an instant success and was put in all the Shoppes.

Billy was growing up fast. After attending nursery school on Macomb Street, he started kindergarten at the Horace Mann School in 1937. J.W. and Allie took Billy on a trip to the Pacific Coast that year, stopping in Utah to visit the Marriott grandparents. Grandpa Will had returned to Ogden from working in D.C. earlier in the year, and he was happy to take his visiting son and grandson on a pheasant-hunting trip, which produced a memorable photo of the three standing next to a car with their trophies.

In August 1937, J.W. opened Hot Shoppe Number 8 at the south end of the 14th Street Bridge on the Potomac River. Much of the surrounding land was vacant; the area's subsequent dominant building, the Pentagon, was not constructed until years later, during World War II. The only real business nearby was the small Hoover Airport across the street from Number 8. It was the first out-of-city location for the Hot Shoppes chain. There were no houses in the area.

Within a couple of days of the grand opening of Number 8, J.W. noticed a customer who was waiting for a flight out of Hoover Field. The man asked the waitress to find a container so he could take two quarts of hot coffee on the plane with him. She obliged and got a good tip. A few days later, J.W. visited Number 8 again and watched as another airport customer bagged a sandwich to take with him on his flight. An idea lit up J.W.'s mind, and he paid a visit to Captain Eddie Rickenbacker, the famous World War I flying ace who owned Eastern Airlines. J.W.'s proposal was simple: "Why don't you buy my food for your passengers and charge a little more for their ticket?" Rickenbacker liked the idea and signed up with Hot Shoppes, making J.W. the pioneer of independent in-flight catering. The basement of Number 8 was converted into the company's first airline kitchen. Bill rememberd the bustle of that kitchen from when he was a young boy. It was a humble beginning for what would eventually—under Bill's leadership—become the largest airline catering service in the world.

In the summer of 1938, affable Uncle Woody worked in the basement of Number 8, slicing thirty-five turkeys a day for airline meals. Woody became an asset to J.W., who made him vice president of store operations that year. Born and raised in Ogden, Utah, Woody had known few black people. When he went to work for J.W., he quickly noticed the number of minorities on the payroll. "Well, Willard, you've got quite a few blacks working for you, don't you," he commented.

J.W. eyed his younger brother carefully and then responded, "Woody, I don't discriminate against anybody. But I want to tell you something—those blacks are more religious and more dependable than some of the white trash I've hired and fired from the South. That's why I hire so many of these men and women. They're hardworking, loyal, honest, and more Christian than a lot of whites I've met!"[12]

• • •

As 1938 drew to a close, Billy had good reason to be excited about an upcoming family event. His mother was expecting a baby. After almost seven years as an only child, he was finally going to get a younger brother or sister.

On January 9, 1939, in the middle of a heavy snowstorm, nine-months-pregnant Allie was invited to the home of Louise Bennion, her closest friend, for a sewing bee. That afternoon, the sewing and conversation hummed along until Allie began having labor pains. At least a foot of snow had accumulated on the ground, and Allie arrived at Columbia Hospital only an hour before baby Richard ("Dick") Edwin Marriott was born at six p.m.

The boys' only living grandfather, Will, was anxious to see his new grandson, and he traveled from Utah by train in the spring just in time to see D.C.'s famous cherry blossoms. The seventy-five-year-old Will seemed hale and hearty, except for a chronic stomach ailment.

At the time, Washington was abuzz with the anticipated visit of Great Britain's King George VI and his wife. The royals had accepted President Roosevelt's invitation to visit the former colonies, the first time a reigning British monarch would set foot on U.S. soil. Billy rose early on June 7, 1939, to get a good viewing spot for the welcoming parade on Massachusetts Avenue with his parents.

Grandfather Will wasn't all that interested in seeing the British monarch. His father, John Marriott, had happily left that country decades earlier for greater opportunity in America, and Will wasn't about to look back. So Woody took him on an outing to the Virginia countryside. They drove in Woody's Buick convertible to the ranch where Woody boarded his horses. Will was thrilled to spend a couple of hours horseback riding—which, fittingly, turned out to be the last activity in which the retired Western rancher would ever engage.

Woody drove his dad back to the Garfield Street home about four p.m., several hours after the Marriotts had returned from the parade. Will lost his balance as he got out of the car, striking the open car door with his side, his Stetson hat flying off down the driveway.

"You all right, Dad?" Woody asked anxiously.

"Oh, boy!" he responded. "That was a hard knock."

Still holding his side, Will went through the house to the sun porch to report to J.W. and the rest of the assembled family that he was going upstairs to rest. "I hit myself on the car door getting out of

Woody's car," he explained. "It hurts." J.W. called a doctor, who said there was nothing to worry about and gave Will some morphine so he could sleep through the night.[13]

The next day, Will was in terrible pain. J.W. called for an ambulance, which took Will to George Washington University Hospital. There he slipped into a coma. He lingered for a few days and then died. The Marriotts asked for an autopsy, which revealed that the fall against the car door had ruptured his aortic artery; he had eventually bled to death.[14] Allie's stepfather, Elder Reed Smoot, was the principal speaker at the funeral. After the service, a steady stream of callers at the Jackson Avenue home pressed envelopes of money into widow Ellen Marriott's hands, explaining that they were returning money Will had given them without question when they had asked him for a loan. Many of those who repaid the money were strangers to the family.

At the end of that eventful summer of 1939, seven-year-old Billy went on his first airplane trip. The family flew from Washington to Boston. At a stopover in New Jersey, little Dickie was temporarily set on top of the airline counter when comedian Red Skelton happened to pass by. He took one look at the eight-month-old and pronounced Dickie "the cutest baby I have ever seen," Bill recalled. That trip to Boston turned out to be their seventh and last summer at Moosehead Lake. It was the summer J.W. made a momentous decision regarding his son's education. Though Billy had done fairly well in first grade at the public school, his father decided he could do better in another setting. J.W. made arrangements for Billy to attend second grade in the fall at the private Quaker school known as Sidwell Friends.

Sidwell's reputation for academic excellence was such that it was the school several U.S. presidents chose for their children. Billy was sociable and made friends easily there, but the relationships did not go deep. "I had friends at Sidwell, but not any real close friends," Bill recalled. Perhaps he might have had more friends at Sidwell if there had been other boys who shared the familiarity of his religious traditions. In later years, he could joke that there were twice as many Buddhists at Sidwell as there were Latter-day Saints; he was right. The official Sidwell 125-year history detailed the religious affiliation of Sidwell students when Billy was enrolled as "386 students . . . including 69 Episcopalians, 54 Presbyterians, 24 Methodists, 23 Catholics, 17 Jews, 15 Quakers, 14 Christian Scientists, two Buddhists and one Mormon."[15]

With Billy growing older, J.W. increased his son's chores. "My younger years were somewhat lonely," Bill explained, even after his brother came along. Billy's relationship with his father became complicated at an early age. There were plenty of rules and high expectations, but not much time for affection. "My parents consistently used the carrot-and-stick approach. My dad was very concerned that I would turn out to be a playboy like other rich men's sons. So there were always goals to be met—high grades in school, chores to do around the house, etc. My father's aggressiveness and desire for perfection in his son were mediated by a kind, thoughtful, understanding mother who would always listen and try to help. Without her continued love and support, I don't know what the outcome would have been."[16]

Most of his chores were outdoors—raking leaves, washing cars, mowing the lawn. He regularly shined J.W.'s shoes, which he often had to do twice in a row to satisfy his father. J.W. was a perfectionist, and Billy got the brunt of that—a pattern of father-son conflict that continued into Bill's adult life in business. J.W. was always looking for better ways that his sons could do something. Once he told Billy to rake leaves and then watched as his son carried the leaves in bunches to a basket. "Why don't you move the basket where you work instead of walking back and forth?" J.W. said. Bill called it "my first lesson in productivity and one I'll never forget."[17]

If the car was dirty on a Sunday morning, J.W. refused to leave for church until it was washed. "We rarely got to church on time," Bill said. *Quit* was not a word in the Marriott lexicon. "My dad was never satisfied. Every day provided an opportunity for me to do better, and

Dad was never reluctant to let me know it. On the other hand, my mother was quiet and rarely criticized. She didn't have to, since I got enough from my dad."[18]

Billy unconsciously drank in more lessons of perfectionism as he followed his father on Hot Shoppes inspections. J.W. required that floors be mopped from two buckets—one for clean water and one for dirty. Then he invented a bucket with two compartments. "He insisted that the parking lots be hosed down every night. He fussed about the dust on the venetian blinds. He wanted the hot food so hot it would burn your tongue; the cold food ice cold." Billy once saw an argument between J.W. and a Hot Shoppes manager about the amount of salt on a hamburger. The manager threw away ten burgers before J.W. was satisfied. "He worried about the appearance of the waitresses—not too much makeup, no fingernail polish, proper hair nets, and, back then, stocking seams straight." Male waiters were not allowed to have mustaches that dipped below the corners of their mouths.[19]

J.W. was demanding with his employees, but he compensated with unexpected compassion. When Allie took young Billy to the family doctor for an earache, Billy was surprised that his mother was on a first-name basis with several African-American men in the waiting room. He found out that his father had put the doctor on the payroll to take care of the workers—his own version of employee health insurance. Later J.W. added a surgeon to the payroll, too.

Outside of work and chores, Billy saw little of his father, though J.W. tried to be home for most dinners. Once when he left on a train trip out of Washington, he wrote the family a note that summed up the two sides of J.W. Marriott: "My dear Allie & Boys . . . I have never felt so badly in my life about leaving you. I almost got off the train at [Silver Spring, MD]. But as you say, when I get anything in my head I can't get it out. Wish I were different but guess you will have to put up with what you got tied to for 'better or for worse.' It is hard to understand human beings & especially JWM."[20]

The Marriott family in 1939: Allie, Billy, J.W., and Dick.

Though J.W. was spry, Allie was becoming increasingly debilitated by arthritis, so much so that she was unable to attend the February 1941 funeral of her stepfather, Reed Smoot, in Salt Lake City. It was the equivalent of a state funeral for the former senator and respected Apostle. Among the eulogies and stories told about Smoot, his step-grandson, Bill, had a favorite. It came from the grueling three-year Senate hearings in the early 1900s when fellow senators refused to seat Smoot because he belonged to The Church of Jesus Christ of Latter-day Saints, which had once endorsed polygamy. Smoot himself was strictly monogamous, and Senator Boise Penrose of Pennsylvania rose to his defense. Glaring at one or more of his Senate colleagues who had a reputation for philandering, he famously declared: "As for me, I would rather have seated beside me in this chamber a polygamist who doesn't polyg than a monogamist who doesn't monog!"

Those family memories and other experiences taught Billy at a young age that his religion was controversial and often misunderstood. But the Marriotts remained firm in their faith, and Billy grew up in the comforting environs of the growing Latter-day Saint community in Washington, D.C.

CHAPTER 4

THE WAR

Nine-year-old Billy Marriott woke up on the morning of Sunday, December 7, 1941, not particularly excited about going to church. The meeting dragged on, and his attention wandered. As Billy sat, half listening and half daydreaming, nearly 5,000 miles away, family friend Captain Mervyn Bennion, the husband of Allie's best friend, Louise, woke up in his quarters aboard the battleship *U.S.S. West Virginia* in Pearl Harbor. He was going ashore to attend Latter-day Saint services in Honolulu. While Captain Bennion completed his Sunday morning routine, Billy arrived home, finished eating his lunch, and headed to the basement to play with his train set. About the time that Billy was turning on the operating switches, Captain Bennion was shaving. It was 7:50 a.m. Hawaii time, and the captain liked a close shave, especially when he was going to church.

Though it seemed to be a relaxed day in paradise, Captain Bennion was not entirely at ease. When the fleet was at sea, there had been a few alarming encounters with Japanese submarines. Captain Bennion believed that the battleships should spend more time sailing than berthed in Pearl Harbor, where the shallow waters and close confinement made them vulnerable to attack. High command heard his objections, along with those of several other officers, but would not change the orders.

At 1:25 p.m. in D.C., Billy's trains were running fast. It was 7:55 a.m. Hawaii time, and the first wave of Japanese fighters and bombers coming from the east struck Battleship Row. The *West Virginia* was hit by two aerial bombs and seven torpedoes, which tore two gaping holes on its port side. Captain Bennion rushed out of his quarters and was headed for the flag bridge when shrapnel sliced through his stomach. He fell to the deck, and a pharmacist's mate rushed to bandage him quickly before the captain ordered the sailor to tend to others. For the next ninety minutes, Bennion listened to reports and dispatched orders. He refused to be taken below for medical treatment, even when the second wave of Japanese planes began their bombing and strafing runs.[1]

One hour into the ordeal, Bennion's family and friends were alerted to the Pearl Harbor attack. At 2:30 p.m. EST, every radio station broke into its regular programming and announced the news. J.W. shouted down to Billy in the basement to turn off his train set and hurry upstairs. "We listened all afternoon as the first reports of the Japanese attack on Pearl Harbor took place," he recalled. "We were all very worried about our good family friend Capt. Mervyn Bennion on the battleship *West Virginia*."[2]

A half hour after the radio alerts began in D.C., a fire broke out on the *West Virginia* and several sailors tied Captain Bennion to a ladder and hauled him up to the navigation bridge. Smoke and flames soon threatened that location, and Bennion ordered them to save themselves. A few minutes later, the pharmacist's mate who had stayed with the captain heard him say, "I'm gone." He took his last breath. The *West Virginia* sank at 2:30 p.m.—8 p.m. at the Marriott home—with the captain's body still on board.

When the Marriotts heard Secretary of the Navy Frank Knox over the radio speaking about one valiant, unnamed navy commander, they had no idea he was talking about their friend. "The dying captain of a battleship displayed the outstanding individual heroism of the day,"

Secretary Knox said. Louise Bennion was informed of her husband's death several days later. An overflow crowd including Billy, his parents, and senior military officers gathered for a memorial service in the Washington chapel of The Church of Jesus Christ of Latter-day Saints. The captain was posthumously awarded one of the first Congressional Medals of Honor of the war, and two years later, Louise christened a destroyer named in her husband's honor.

Bill never forgot listening to the president's famous address to Congress. With a radio in each classroom at his Sidwell Friends School, every student heard Roosevelt's chilling opening words: "Yesterday, December 7, 1941, a date which will live in infamy, the United States of America was suddenly and deliberately attacked by naval and air forces of the Empire of Japan." Throughout the seven-minute address, the students sat in silence; then they stood for the national anthem.

As with most others on the home front, the Marriotts' everyday lives were changed by the war. They equipped their basement as a bomb shelter, and Allie volunteered many hours for the Red Cross, as well as providing meals for visiting servicemen she met at church. At the Hot Shoppes, J.W. coped with the reality of a diminishing male workforce. He put his brother Woody in charge of the personnel department. Woody's solution was to drive to North Carolina to recruit young women eager to leave their mountain homes for work in the city. He signed up 150 women, after helping two-thirds of them fill out papers, since they could neither read nor write.

As he prepared to bus them back to Washington, Woody got a call from J.W. ordering him to cancel the recruitment because D.C. had just ruled that, with gas shortages, private cars could not be used "to go from home to places of amusement, including restaurants." Business would suffer, and the Hot Shoppes would not need any new employees. But Woody didn't think the edict would stick, so he ignored his brother's order and arrived back in D.C. with a busload of eager workers. As he expected, D.C. had already rescinded the brief restaurant restriction. It took some time for the mountain girls to acclimatize to city living and restaurant work. Most of them used snuff or chewed tobacco, and they used large empty tomato cans for spittoons, which they hid whenever J.W. came around.[3]

Gas rationing prompted Billy's first contribution to Hot Shoppes. "Since I rode the bus and the streetcar to school, I was the only member of the family who knew the routes." J.W. mined Billy for ideas about how to encourage bus ridership to bring customers to the Hot Shoppes. "This was the first time I was asked to contribute to the business, and I was very excited and honored to be asked. I really felt I had grown up with the company."[4]

Allie was too ill to go on a family vacation in the summer of 1942, so Billy picked out a two-month-long summer camp on Cow Island in Lake Winnipesaukee, reasoning that his parents might enjoy visiting with the Samses and Bushnells when they dropped him off or picked him up. But Camp Idlewild was not as fun-filled as he thought it would be. "I was only ten and had never been away from home before," Bill recalled. "I became very homesick but endured the two months. My parents came to see me once, and when they left, I thought I'd die."[5] Billy was so skinny his parents had hoped he would pick up ten pounds at camp. Instead, he came home ten pounds lighter, with hemorrhages in both eyes and a bad case of the flu. But he had also learned how to swim and won all the top awards at the camp.

Billy was so afraid to begin fifth grade at Sidwell in the fall of 1942 that he staged a sickout. He had "heard so many bad things about one teacher that I was really scared. My folks let me stay home for the first three days of school because I was so terrified." Then his mother calmly reasoned with him. "Billy, you can't stay home forever. You've got to go." So, on the fourth day, he arose and went. "The teacher ended up being okay," he recalled.

During the next year, J.W. shut down curb service at Hot Shoppes to curtail gas consumption. Then he deftly changed things by moving

Hot Shoppes into an industrial "mass feeding" market, contracting to run workplace cafeterias at industrial sites and government buildings.

The summer of 1943 began a decades-long Marriott family tradition of vacationing at Lake Winnipesaukee, New Hampshire, in a home that they first leased, then purchased. The following summer, Billy sustained his "first big injury" while he was playing "King of the Hill" on a raft. Another boy pushed him off, but Billy refused to let go and slammed into the edge of the raft, earning a scar that stayed with him for life.

Sixth grade at Sidwell was memorable for Billy because it was that term when he found his first non–Latter-day Saint friend for life, Gilbert "Gibby" Grosvenor. As an adult, Gibby would succeed his father as president of the National Geographic Society. He told a reporter that in those early Sidwell days, neither he nor Billy felt pressured to follow in their fathers' footsteps. "My father and Bill's father used to joke that they refrained from pushing us to join the family business because it would have backfired." Despite that deliberate lack of parental direction, Billy never dreamed of being a scientist, an explorer, or a baseball star, Gibby recalled. He wanted to be a successful businessman like his dad.[6] (As adults, both Bill and Gibby served for many years on each other's corporate boards.)

The Marriotts had one neighbor who fascinated young Billy. Anita Patton was the only sibling of General George S. Patton, upon whom she doted. She wanted to be close to her brother when he returned home on leave from the war, so she moved in across the street from the Marriotts. In her basement, Ms. Patton had a collection of white mice in cages equipped with treadmills and other interesting equipment. "I used to go over there and play with the little white mice," Bill recalled. "She gave me two to bring home, so I put them in a glass cage. Somehow they got out, copulated with some house mice, and we had grey mice running all over the house."

Ever-changing war rationing restrictions continued to challenge

J.W.'s ability to keep his Hot Shoppes open and making a profit. The sale of beer had always been a nettlesome issue for teetotaler J.W., so when his beer allotment was cut by one-fifth due to rationing, he happily took it off the menu. Sugar, butter, and meat were strictly rationed so as much as possible could be sent to the front. Hot Shoppes creatively substituted many meatless dishes on the menu, such as soufflés, macaroni, and vegetable platters. It was a notable achievement that J.W. kept every Hot Shoppe open during the war. By comparison, the popular Howard Johnson chain had 200 franchise restaurants at the beginning of the war, but only 12 remained in business at the end of the war. J.W. not only managed to increase his business through the new line of industrial cafeterias, but he also managed to improve his restaurants' popularity.

Billy Marriott particularly looked forward to turning twelve years old. That was the age at which he would become a deacon in the lay priesthood of his Church. In addition, he could join the Church-sponsored Boy Scout troop. A week before Billy's momentous birthday, J.W. and Allie took their son to New York City. The Marriotts went to a few Broadway shows, but there was only one thing on Billy's mind—the big Boy Scout store and headquarters at 2 Park Avenue. He had his Scout registration card firmly in hand—his ticket to the acquisition of his first Scout uniform and other desired Scouting supplies.

"My eyes popped out of my head as I saw all that wonderful camping equipment. I used up all my allowance money and begged for whatever funds my parents would let me have to acquire the most complete set of Scout equipment I could get," he recalled.

As soon as he got home, Billy tried packing his new knapsack for a campout. "I neatly packed all the equipment into my knapsack together with enough canned food to last for a week and was prepared for my first overnight camping experience. When I went to hoist the bulging knapsack off the floor and onto my back, I couldn't lift it. It was so heavy I could only put it on my back by getting my dad to help me place it on the kitchen table so I could back up to the table to put it on. When I finally did get it on, it almost pulled me over backwards. There was no way I could go on a long hike with all this—I couldn't even walk across the room! I decided I had a lot to learn about Scouting."

Because he had joined the Scouts during World War II, Billy participated in some war-related community service, including distributing pledge cards for war bonds and savings stamps, promoting victory gardens, standing ready to serve in medical emergencies, and collecting aluminum, wastepaper, and salvage. "When we had collected the required amount of paper, we were given an Army type medal with a red and white ribbon, and from it was hanging a gold medal with General Eisenhower's face on it. I wore this medal on my Scout uniform proudly."

Becoming an Eagle Scout required earning at least twenty-one merit badges. There were two in particular that were the most difficult: Bird Study and Camping. For the Bird Study badge, the Scout was required to personally observe and describe forty species of wild birds. Billy aced the badge because his winter vacation in Florida put him in one of the most bird-rich states in the country. His potential Waterloo was the Camping merit badge. It required at least fifty nights of sleeping outdoors, at least ten of those on backpacking hikes. He almost gave up. "How was a city boy ever going to sleep out-of-doors for fifty days and nights to pass this particular requirement when there was no Scout camp available nearby?" He accomplished the ten overnights during hikes with his Scout troop, and then determinedly pitched a tent in his backyard for the remaining nights.

The final hurdle was to make a fire by rubbing sticks together. "I twisted the stick but it only got warm. So I twisted it harder and harder and faster and faster. It began to smoke, but there was no spark. It smoked some more. I began to breathe hard and fast as I worked. I inhaled the smoke and my eyes began to water. I began to cough and tears were streaming down my face. I was just about ready to quit

Billy, fifteen, as an Eagle Scout in 1947.

when, through the smoke, I spotted a small spark which began to show a bright red. It was truly the most beautiful thing I had ever seen!"[7]

Less than 10 percent of Boy Scouts ever achieve Eagle Scout rank, and the average age of those who do succeed is seventeen. Always a hard charger, Billy was awarded the honor only a few months after his fifteenth birthday.

• • •

As Billy attended eighth grade in the fall of 1945, America still had postwar food shortages. Because many items were still rationed, Hot Shoppes' initial growth immediately following the war was slow. However, in December, J.W. and his brother Paul secured the exclusive Miami-based Eastern Airlines in-flight catering contract from its president, Eddie Rickenbacker.

By Christmas 1945, J.W. had developed an interest in ancient civilizations in Mexico. He planned a two-week trip with Billy and Allie to see major Mayan and Aztec ruins in Mexico and Guatemala. Ever since his Church mission had ended twenty-five years before, J.W. had not kept a journal. But, seeing a bright future ahead in the postwar years, and excited about the trip, he started keeping a daily diary again in 1946, about the time of the trip. The family toured ruins and went to a jai alai game and a bullfight. On the way home, they stopped in Miami for their usual February vacation there. By then, Billy had already missed three weeks of school, so he flew home while his parents drove.

The long drive back gave them time to talk about J.W.'s possible retirement. The trouble was that neither of his brothers—Paul or Woody—could take over the business, so J.W. abandoned the retirement dream. When they arrived home, he faced new responsibilities when the Church hierarchy appointed him as one of the leaders of the Washington D.C. Stake, a collection of all of the congregations in the capital area. J.W. was daunted, but he agreed to serve in the volunteer position.

During this eighth-grade year for Billy, he went with Gibby Grosvenor to a testing center to determine his strengths for future career choices. As he recalled years later, "My friend was good with his hands and was told he'd make a great surgeon. They studied my test scores for a long time and said I could name most of the animals in the zoo. Maybe I should go into business, since I had no specific talents that they could find." At the same time, a Church Apostle and family friend in Salt Lake City proudly typed up an index card recording: "Billy Marriott [is the] only boy or girl in his class who doesn't or hasn't smoked. He has the best marks of any student in the class."[8]

At this point, J.W. began considering switching Billy to an even harder private school, the Episcopalian-run St. Albans School for boys. "My parents decided to turn me over to the Episcopalians after the Quakers had done their best," he later joked.[9] For a brief time, J.W. threw himself into being a more present father with his son. He took

Billy to a shooting range and signed him up for horseback-riding lessons. One wonderful activity was going with his dad in April to the opening game of the Washington Senators 1946 baseball season, when President Truman himself was on hand to throw out the first pitch.

The father-son bonding continued on May 20 when J.W. invited Billy to help him pick up a new family car—a grey '46 Ford Super Deluxe Station Wagon. It was the premier "Woodie" of the postwar era, so nicknamed because the sides, rear, interior, and roof were paneled with wood. Not long after, Billy was sitting in the driver's seat trying to manipulate the stick shift when his dad came out of the house to go to work. J.W. took a long look at his son, then tossed him the car keys and said, "Drive me to work." Billy had never driven before.

"I barely got out of the driveway. He told me how to use the clutch, put on the gas, put on the brake. The car was jumping all over the place," Bill remembered. "His office was on Upshur Street, so I had to go all the way across town with him." J.W. did offer some instruction, and he was patient. "He didn't really get excited or nervous. I think he thought it was pretty funny." Billy didn't think so, especially when J.W. made him stop on a steep hill. "He wanted to see how far I'd roll back, or whether I would stall the car trying to move back up the hill. I was a complete nervous wreck by the time we got to his office."

That summer, J.W. decided fourteen-year-old Billy was ready for his first job at Hot Shoppes. "For one month, I sorted out the pink, yellow, and green invoices and stapled them together. That's all I knew how to do. But I was getting $2 or $3 an hour, and I think I got $40 in cash when I was done."

By the next fall, as Billy attended his first year at St. Albans, the postwar pace of the Hot Shoppes' business began to pick up again, and J.W. cut back on family time. Billy looked to other men to fill that gap, and there was no one like Bill Werber, a former major league baseball player who later went into the insurance business and snagged J.W. as one of his best customers. In his post-baseball life, Werber became an avid bird hunter, and he took J.W. and Billy hunting with him several weekends in the fall of 1946. A few favorite tales from those outings made it into Werber's 1981 book, *Hunting Is for the Birds.* On one occasion hunting quail, J.W. felled a bird, but Billy's gun jammed. J.W. and Werber kept shooting. "All the while, young Billy was trying to get that bad shell out of his gun and cursing like a defeated pirate on a sinking galleon. I thought his dad would burst a blood vessel laughing, yet he only made one comment: 'I didn't know he knew all those cuss words.' Then Billy, in great disgust, heaved his automatic into the honeysuckle where he later retrieved it, and carefully wiped it clean."

Werber subsequently took the time with Billy to counsel him about the need for self-control. But Werber loved Billy's spunk. He chuckled while they were hunting quail at Front Royal, Virginia, on a hot day and Billy asked for a taste of "Mr. Werber's beer." J.W. responded testily, "You know you can't drink beer," and that was that.

Billy was one of the most determined hunters Werber ever flushed quail with, and that was abundantly evident in another story Werber liked to tell. He and the Marriotts were hunting in a steady rainfall. They parked and waited for an hour, hoping the rain would stop. Finally Billy insisted they get out and hunt in the rain. "Come on, Mr. Werber, let's go," Billy begged. "Let the dogs out. This is the last day I have to hunt."

Werber acquiesced, though he figured the dogs would not be able to pick up a scent. Incredibly, the dogs immediately went on point in a field, and the three hunters shot several quail. When the dogs followed the retreating quail into the nearby woods, Billy begged to be able to follow into the dripping trees. "No way, Billy," Werber replied. "It's a waste of our time. It's so thick you couldn't get off a shot in there." The dogs headed for the pines anyway. The hunting trio stopped just short of the tree line when the dogs locked on two coveys of birds. They made perfect shots. "We might as well try a couple of other fields," Werber then suggested to J.W. "We're wet now. We can dry out later."

Werber reported that J.W. "could have killed me. He had no stomach for this self-flagellation—and, truth to tell, had I been with anyone other than the ebullient younger Marriott, I wouldn't have been slopping around in all that stuff."[10]

• • •

The Episcopalian influence was strong at St. Albans High School, but that didn't faze Billy since Christ is also at the center of the Latter-day Saint faith. Though Billy gave his father no serious cause for concern regarding his morality, J.W. decided at the beginning of 1947 that it was time for an important father-son talk. The two boarded a train for a six-day trip to Lake Winnipesaukee and Montreal.

They checked into the Colonial Arms Hotel near the lake, then drove to the lake, where the caretaker had made a welcoming fire. Billy went ice-skating for the first time. "Did well but ankles weak," his father observed. On Saturday evening, J.W. mustered enough courage to have the talk about "the birds and the bees" with his son, which had been the main purpose of the trip. From school chums, Billy already knew the basics of sex. Neither was comfortable during the talk, but J.W. was forceful about expecting his son to remain chaste until he was married. "I'd rather see you come home in a pine box than see you come home at all after getting a young lady pregnant," the father admonished.

Billy was at St. Albans in his freshman year. While moderately popular, he avoided the boys he called BTOs—Big Time Operators—and he certainly didn't want to be one. J.W. was generally pleased with Billy's progress and demeanor, but it was not always so. For example, about this time, J.W. reported in his journal coming home from a Church meeting and "strapp(ing) the boys for not going to bed." Bill remembered the razor strap for many years after, but said his dad only used the strap "a couple of times."

J.W. continued to take time to go hunting with Billy and Bill

Billy with his first car at St. Albans.

Werber, even buying two of Werber's well-bred English setter hunting dogs, which J.W. and Billy named "Marriott's Judy" and "Marriott's Tip." Sometimes Billy took his gun out to do some hunting with pal Tyler Abell. It became increasingly difficult for him to find the time, though, as the Hot Shoppes continued to evolve and J.W. fretted over one of his senior employees—his brother Paul. Once a charismatic, charming leader full of ideas, Paul had become erratic, exhibiting Jekyll-and-Hyde behavior that might have been an undiagnosed bipolar disorder exacerbated by increasingly heavy drinking. J.W. was optimistic when Paul married and had a child, but the effect of fatherhood was short-lived. None of these family details concerned young Billy, but he would eventually have to deal with the repercussions in future years.

Billy found plenty to occupy himself. Visiting the University Club in downtown Washington, D.C., he began weight lifting, with disastrous results. "I lifted a weight above my head and it kept on going," he recalled. "Instead of letting go of the weight I held onto it, and it jerked my right shoulder out of joint. It tore it right out. The moral is that I should let go when I know that danger is approaching, but I never did." Afterward, his right shoulder would easily dislocate with any strenuous physical activity.

On his sixteenth birthday, in March 1948, Billy earned his driver's license. At the same time, the *St. Albans News* reported that he was academically third in his class for the midterm marking period. At the end of his sophomore year, he was reelected class treasurer for the next year. That summer Billy worked on his dad's motorboat and drove it in Lake Winnipesaukee races. That boyhood need for speed—which he never outgrew—made his mother nervous. "That's how I started getting my gray hairs," she recalled, especially when he "raced against older men who would try to get him in a wave and swamp his boat."[11]

But for Billy, the racing provided rare moments of relaxation. He later related in a speech at a Florida marine event: "I've grown up near the water and have been driving power boats since I was twelve years old. A short thirty-minute boat ride can be one of the quickest refreshers that I know. To me there is nothing more relaxing than standing behind the wheel of a powerful boat."[12]

CHAPTER 5

ANCHORS AWEIGH

On Billy's seventeenth birthday, J.W. proudly took his son to shop for the young man's first car. J.W. could afford to spoil his sons, but he generally chose not to. He required obedience to his rules and ungrudging acceptance of chores at home. He expected the boys' best efforts at school and adherence to the Church's strict moral and health codes, which included no sex before marriage and no alcohol or tobacco. Billy had done most everything his father had asked, and his father rewarded him with a 1949 Ford, with all the independence that came with that for a young man.

At the end of Billy's sophomore year, J.W. bought an impressive inboard speedboat—a seventeen-foot Higgins. J.W. enjoyed going for a fast ride with his son and would sometimes invite friends along, including the George Romney family, who visited in the summer. The Detroit-based Romney had been the chief spokesman for the auto industry during the war, and was then a top executive with the Nash-Kelvinator company (soon to be American Motors). J.W. and Romney had membership in The Church of Jesus Christ of Latter-day Saints in common and were close friends. Romney named one son Willard after J.W., though the boy would become better known by his middle name, Mitt.

At school, in addition to co-managing the basketball team, Billy joined *The Albanian* yearbook staff as an ad salesman in his senior year. The yearbook reported that many of the advertisements appearing in the volume "are due to his tenaciousness and efficiency."[1]

His parents were pleased with his activities, his academic performance, and his behavior. After one Sunday church meeting, J.W. wrote in his journal: "We had quite a discussion with Billy as to whether he should go to a party after the meeting." It was an issue because Latter-day Saints encourage a quiet Sabbath observance with little extracurricular activity. "We left it up to him, so he went, and came home at 12 o'clock, the time he said he would come home. Billy is a fine young man. He is 100% honest. He tells us what he does when he goes out, and we never have to worry about his coming home with liquor on his breath. He has good moral habits, and we are mighty proud of him."[2]

Billy's St. Albans days were formative in his religious development, even though he had few friends who shared his particular faith. As an adult, he told a Church audience about his high-school years: "I was often called upon to defend my religion to those classmates who make fun of it. I thought about Elizabeth Stewart [his pioneer ancestor] and her sacrifice for her beliefs. As I defended my church, I too came to believe it was true. To strengthen my convictions, I studied and tried to learn more about our teachings and doctrines. The more I learned and prayed about them, the more convinced I was that the church to which I had been born was indeed the Church of Jesus Christ."[3]

After graduation, Billy was the only St. Albans senior headed for a Western university—the University of Utah—but his independent streak steered him away from his father's Phi Delta Theta fraternity; he planned to pledge Sigma Chi instead. No matter where Billy went, J.W.'s hope was that his son would find a Latter-day Saint wife, and the odds of that were higher in Utah.

Thus it was that when Billy headed to Lake Winnipesaukee with his family for their summer 1950 vacation, the family was in great spirits. Billy had made up his own mind about college, and that decision made his father and mother happy. Unfortunately, only two weeks into the vacation, just twenty-two days after Billy's high school graduation, the world turned upside down.

North Korea invaded South Korea on June 25. America was again at war, only five years after the previous war ended. Unlike his father during World War II, Billy was of prime draft age. His well-laid plans were plunged into the great unknown.

In the fall of 1950, Billy drove his Ford across the country to Salt Lake City to begin college. To everyone he met, he was now "Bill," having shed the "Billy" of his youth, except when he was with family and old friends. The rush chairman for Sigma Chi that fall was Sterling Colton, son of J.W.'s first business partner and longtime friend Hugh Colton. He and Bill would become close friends for life.

In its centennial year, the university was still in the midst of postwar turmoil and transition—at the tail end of a postwar boom that peaked with more than 12,000 students, who had to make do with inadequate housing and cramped classrooms. Instead of living at the fraternity house, Bill chose dorm life in a converted army hospital on the grounds of Fort Douglas adjacent to the campus. Intending to join his father's company, Bill opted to major in banking and finance.

From his first day of class, Bill realized that the "U" was going to be a walk in the park compared to St. Albans. "I thought it was amateur night in the beginning," he said, which meant he had more time for socializing. "I didn't do great my freshman year because I became interested in girls." (For Bill, that academic slip meant a few B's among mostly A's.)

In those days, the "U" had a community college feel; the vast majority of students went home to their families at night. Fraternities flourished because they provided a center for social activity, which was one reason Bill joined Sigma Chi. He found a lifelong friend in fraternity brother Bruce Haight from Palo Alto, California. The most difficult issue Bruce and Bill wrestled with during their first freshman months was their desire to serve missions for their church when the federal government wanted them as soldiers for the Korean War.

Bill went ahead with his mission plans, hoping to leave the summer after his freshman year. He also scheduled an appointment in Washington at Christmastime for a patriarchal blessing: a special priesthood blessing pronounced by an ordained patriarch that provides direction for the future and understanding of God's will for the individual. The patriarch placed his hands on Bill's bowed head and pronounced, among other things, that he would someday serve a mission. But the Church was soon warned by General Lewis B. Hershey, director of the Selective Service System, that no religious deferments would be given to young men to serve missions, and those already out on missions might be drafted into the army at any time.[4]

After the Korean War, in 1955, Congress passed a resolution giving Latter-day Saint missionaries ordained-minister status, allowing them ministerial deferments—but for Bill it was too late. He never served a full-time mission for the Church as a young single man, though he did later serve as an adult in a succession of missionary-related Church positions. Although he keenly felt the loss of the opportunity to serve a traditional mission, he was never one to harbor regret or take too many backward glances. He said in later life, "I do the best I can and trust in the Lord that that is good enough."[5]

Unlike the previous World War, the Korean "police action" was unpopular with most Americans. To the young men of draft age, the conflict was not a clear defense of the homeland, and its purpose was not compelling enough for many to volunteer for the military. Bill Marriott was no exception. He looked for a fallback plan that would prevent his being drafted to the front lines. Student deferment for those who took a minimum of twelve credit hours at the university was good for a limited time, but he knew it was better to join the Reserve Officer Training Corps (ROTC), which guaranteed enlistment as an officer. His preference was for the navy, but its ROTC roster was nearly full.

After impressing the right commanders, though, he was admitted to the navy ROTC. While he couldn't be drafted, this gave him a good opportunity to serve his country.

During Bill's freshman year, another pivotal event occurred: he found that he loved working in his father's restaurant business. Even before Bill's plans to go to college in Utah, J.W. had thought about opening a Hot Shoppe in Salt Lake City. One of J.W.'s friends, also a former sheepherder, Stephen M. Covey, had opened a hotel-restaurant-filling station in the mid-1930s near Granger, Wyoming. He called it "Little America." The way station in the middle of nowhere was such a success that Covey built a Little America motel and coffee shop in Salt Lake. In 1950, weary of the coffee shop part of the business, Covey sold it to J.W., who remodeled it as a Hot Shoppe, opening it during Bill's freshman year. It was the company's twenty-third restaurant and the only one in the West.

J.W. was on hand to greet more than 500 guests who jammed the shop for the grand opening. Bill was working hard in the kitchen. From his first day on the job, Bill said, "I liked the pace—the ability to interact with employees and customers, and just the speed of the business. When you get busy in a restaurant, things become very chaotic, and I kind of liked that."[6]

When Bill returned home after his freshman year, his father had a new acquisition to show him: a sprawling farm in Hume, Virginia. J.W. longed for a taste of his Western cowboy upbringing, which the farm would give him, so Allie finally capitulated to the purchase.

Besides, there was a health-related reason for the property. J.W.'s face had turned sallow; after a battery of tests, doctors diagnosed his ailment as hepatitis. He was hospitalized for six weeks and given intravenous glucose and penicillin to repair the damage to his liver. The doctors advised that the best thing for recuperation was total rest. Allie agreed that it was time to find a farm, which would serve him intermittently as a recuperative oasis.

Fairfield Farm was originally owned by King Charles of England in

Fairfield Farm.

the 1600s and eventually became the estate of James Marshall, brother to noted Chief Justice John C. Marshall of the Supreme Court. During the Civil War, it was used by the Confederate army as a temporary head-quarters. A Belgian baroness whose husband was taken captive by the Nazis used it as a refuge for her part-Jewish family during World War II.[7]

After J.W. bought the 2,200-acre Fairfield Farm in 1951, the Marriotts made a half dozen overnight visits there that first spring and summer, staying in a little cottage on the estate because the manor house was dilapidated. Bill was busy that summer after his freshman year working in the "kitchen engineering" department of the company, but he went at least once to see the new farm, enjoying its beauty but not the outdoor ranch life. That was not a passion he shared with his father.

When Bill returned to the University of Utah as a sophomore, he went back to work at the Salt Lake Hot Shoppe. The previous spring, he had reported often to the breakfast chef at four a.m. and helped prepare the meals for the day. It was then that the infamous Deep Fat Fryer Incident had occurred. After one lunch hour, his shift manager asked Bill to clean out the fryer used for cooking French fries. "I cooled it down and drained out most of the grease. I got soap, and a hose, and hot water and shoved it into the fryer and all of sudden the whole thing started to foment, foment, foment, foment and it just bubbled up all over the fryer, all over the kitchen, all over the floor, all over me. It was the biggest mess you ever saw in your life."

In the fall of his sophomore year, Bill was now put in charge of the grill and steam table five afternoons a week. Bill learned to do every job during his college years except waiting tables. By his junior year, he was a shift manager, and in his senior year, when he was busier at school, he became a supervisory inspector.

The store manager, Jerry Clark, was a navy reservist who tried to interest Bill in naval aviation. Bill's interest faded the day Clark took him for a flight in a trainer and demonstrated a high-flying loop. "He did it two or three times, and then he said, 'Now you try it.' I almost crashed the airplane. And I had thrown up all over the place." After they landed, the mechanic "took one look inside the plane and said, 'Get some rags and clean it up. It's your mess.' So I did. I decided right then and there that I wasn't going into naval aviation."

While he was home one Christmas, Bill met Russell and Dantzel Nelson, new Latter-day Saint friends of his parents who would become important in Bill's life. Lieutenant Nelson was an army doctor at the Walter Reed Medical Center. In the future, he would become a world-renowned heart surgeon and then, at the age of ninety-three, the President of The Church of Jesus Christ of Latter-day Saints. He was the second close family friend in Washington who would become the Church's President in later years. The first was Ezra Taft Benson, who served as Secretary of Agriculture during the Eisenhower administration.

At the end of his sophomore year, at his father's request, Bill drove to Los Angeles to scout drive-in restaurants. "At least once a year, someone from our company did a drive-in tour of California, which was the drive-in capital of the world," Bill recalled. Both the good weather and the high level of auto ownership spurred the fast-growing industry, whose giants got their start in California. From Sacramento in 1919, Roy Allen had launched what would become the large A&W franchise chain. From Glendale in 1937, Robert Wian had begun another successful chain, called "Bob's Big Boy." And in 1948, the McDonald brothers switched from barbecue to hamburgers in their San Bernardino restaurant and had expanded to a half dozen franchisees by the time Bill went to Los Angeles in June 1952.

What interested Bill the most on the scouting trip was a new revolving-wheel-based check-order system he observed at one drive-in. Bill raved about it to his dad when he returned to Washington, so J.W. directed him to test it at the Philadelphia Hot Shoppe on Market Street. The system was simple: a curber took the order and clipped it to the wheel at the kitchen's edge. The cook filled the order and turned the wheel to return the ticket, which the curber presented as a bill to the customer. "Dad put me in charge of the new wheel, getting the food out and calling the curbers in," Bill said. "I was making so much noise that the neighbors complained I was too loud on the loud-speakers, so I had to stop screaming."

At the time, J.W. was in the middle of one of the biggest business decisions of his life—whether to convert Hot Shoppes from a family company to a publicly traded firm. J.W. decided to take Bill into his confidence. Back in Washington, only a few days before Bill returned to school for his junior year, J.W. invited Bill into his study for a review of the pros and cons of going public. They debated until eleven p.m., with Bill firmly on the side of not selling any stock, keeping it "in the family." He was so adamant that J.W. recorded in his journal: "Billy doesn't want us to sell *any* stock."[8]

Meanwhile, J.W. was dealing with the most nettlesome issue of his life—his brother Paul, who was still managing the In-Flite airline catering. Earlier in the year, J.W. thought the only way his own health would improve was if he could remove the stress caused by having Paul at headquarters. Paul believed he should be an equal partner, and he was jealous of anyone else who won J.W.'s ear. Paul's drinking and un-happiness spilled all over the River Road headquarters and cost the In-Flite division an important contract at Newark Airport.

J.W. had warned Paul he would have to move the In-Flite offices to a separate location, hoping to remove the friction Paul caused. Paul said he would move only if the larger family corporation divested itself of any ownership in the catering operations, giving it all to him, but J.W. re-fused. Privately, he began working on a plan to buy Paul out completely, partly driven by J.W.'s continuing interest in taking the company public.

Only a couple of days before Bill returned to college in January, J.W. told him that he had made up his mind to take the company pub-lic. Unfortunately, Paul was still a factor, increasing his demands and complicating the stock sale. Still, J.W. couldn't bring himself to fire his brother. Instead, he signed a ten-year management agreement keeping Paul on the catering payroll. By the end of that decade, Bill would be the new president of the company, and it would fall to him to fire his uncle Paul because his dad, even then, could not do it.

March 17, 1953, was set as the date for Hot Shoppes, Inc., to go public. The company was to be sold over the counter, which was a step down from a stock exchange. J.W.'s reputation was a key factor in the sale. One Virginia broker confided to J.W., "I wouldn't touch your stock if you were not the head of the company." The price was set at $10.25 a share. On offering day, the success could not have been more stunning. After the investment houses opened for business that morning, the phones never stopped ringing. Every share was sold in only two hours, and the calls for orders were still coming in. Every goal J.W. had for the sale was achieved. The company's working capital had been increased by more than $1 million, while the Marriotts were still in full control since they still owned two-thirds of the outstanding stock. J.W.'s three brothers—Paul, Woody, and Russell—all did very well with the IPO, and would eventually become multimillionaires. J.W. made the most, more than $1 million on this first sale.

On the last day of the year, J.W. and Allie met with their bishop to pay their tithing, defined by The Church of Jesus Christ of Latter-day Saints as 10 percent of one's annual increase. When the personal checks and donated stock shares were added up, J.W.'s and Allie's total contribution to the Church that year was $132,743.50. "Sure glad to be able to pay it," he wrote in his journal. "The Lord has been exceedingly good to us."[9]

In the days immediately after the stock sale, J.W. was in a mood to celebrate, and he planned a trip with Bill. He flew to Salt Lake City and the pair took off for Las Vegas, where J.W. wanted to check out the drive-ins, restaurants, hotels, and the gaming business. Once they arrived, J.W. was appalled at the "awful gambling," which he concluded was a waste of time and money. Both father and son loved Nevada's no-speed-limit highways, though. "A nice day. Drove 120 miles per hour. Good visit with Bill," J.W. recorded.[10]

Bill finished his junior year with A's and a rare B in Labor Relations, where he learned of the challenges that unionizing posed to corporations. Once back home, Bill frequently joined J.W. for restaurant inspections and lengthy business discussions. The father-son relationship began to subtly change. After seven years of journals in which Bill was referred to either as a "good boy" or "fine boy," J.W. penned his first criticism. "Billy very selfish & can't see much good in anybody," his father wrote one evening.[11] Bill later acknowledged that it was a fair complaint from his father at the time.

In June, father and son shared a moment of harmony when they picked up a beautiful, classic wooden speedboat named the *Dolphin*. When they first took it out on the water, the 160-horsepower engine smoothly skimmed the boat across Lake Winnipesaukee at forty miles per hour. The *Dolphin* soon became the sentimental favorite among family members and was kept in pristine running condition in Bill's family for decades. A few weeks after the *Dolphin* purchase, it was time for Bill to ship out on a much bigger boat, the *USS Columbus*, a World War II heavy cruiser.

As part of navy ROTC requirements, all midshipmen were dispatched on a summer training cruise, and it was a happy coincidence that Bill and Bruce Haight were assigned to the same cruise. Berthed in Norfolk, Virginia, the *Columbus*, whose nickname was "The Tall Lady," was an impressive sight for the two college men—674 feet long, bristling with armament. In all, there were 358 ROTC midshipmen assigned to the cruise from forty-nine universities. They rotated around, learning all duties on the ship. The first port of call was the Coco Solo Naval Base on the Atlantic side of the Panama Canal Zone, and then on to Port of Spain, Trinidad, and then Guantanamo Bay, Cuba. The only previous foreign countries Bill had visited were Mexico and Canada, and now he added three more to that list in as many weeks. When the ship returned to Norfolk, Bill and Bruce drove to Washington and then on to Lake Winnipesaukee for two weeks before returning to college.

Bill later lauded the "U" for being the place that "inspired me to continue to study and learn."[12] None of his professors came close to matching the impact of speech professor Dr. Royal L. Garff. He rarely sat down to lecture, preferring to be always on the move among the students. He believed that the only way students could learn the value of public speaking and gain confidence in it was by doing it before an audience. "Royal made you do it," Bill said. "He taught you to stand up, to speak up and to shut up."[13]

Occasionally, Professor Garff would tell his students stories about his family, speaking with great pride about his oldest daughter, Donna, who was then enrolled as a freshman at the "U." That didn't catch Bill's attention until one day when he saw a pretty blonde girl waiting at the bus stop. Excitedly, he asked a friend who was riding with him if he knew the girl. The friend was a handyman at the Chi Omega sorority house, where she had pledged. "That's Donna Rae Garff," he replied. He subsequently introduced the two, and Bill's world changed in that moment.

CHAPTER 6

HEAVENLY FLOWER

In 1857, at the age of fourteen, Peter Nielsen Garff pushed and pulled a handcart 1,500 miles across the American frontier with one of the most ill-fitted, poorly led immigrant companies ever to make the journey. Speaking no English, Peter traveled with his parents and four siblings and a large group of Danish converts to The Church of Jesus Christ of Latter-day Saints. They had crossed the ocean and embarked on their long trek from Iowa City, Iowa, in mid-June of an unusually hot summer.

Peter's younger brother Lauritz explained in his short account: "The untold suffering and hardships that we . . . suffered during this long journey from Denmark, would require more time and space [to recount] than will ever be taken in this life, at least." When they arrived at Fort Laramie, Wyoming, the only Garff still able to walk was Peter. The rest of the ailing family was consigned to a wagon and ox team, while Peter, sometimes alone, pulled the handcart the rest of the way.

By the time the lead handcart with a wilted Danish flag attached to it reached Salt Lake at the end of the eighty-five-day trek, the company had lost fifteen of their number, including Peter's father and sister. It was left to the fourteen-year-old boy to seek lodging and to care for the family.[1]

As Peter's grandson Royal Garff wrote, Peter matured on a farm that "he carved from the primitive and rugged earth and rescued from the gullies, sagebrush and rattlesnakes" in Draper, at the southeast end of the Salt Lake Valley. Peter was twenty-six when he married sixteen-year-old Antomina Sorensen, another Danish convert, who had crossed the plains four years after him.[2]

Over the next twenty years, Antomina bore twelve children, the sixth of whom was named Royal Brigham in honor of Brigham Young. Royal B. was raised on the Garff farm and at a young age developed an attachment to Rachel Ann Day, who lived on a nearby farm. The childhood sweethearts married in 1902 and named their first son Royal Lovell.

Young Royal worked at his grandparents' farm and his parents' grocery store in Salt Lake City. He served a Church mission to New Zealand and attended the University of Utah and Northwestern University in Chicago. Royal's younger brother Ken had bought a gas station in downtown Salt Lake, which was the beginning of what would be a highly successful auto dealership. During Royal's Northwestern years, he earned extra money ferrying cars bought at Chicago discount prices to Salt Lake, where Ken sold them.

While visiting back home in Salt Lake in the summer of 1931, Royal met a girl from Alamo, Nevada—Marba Stewart, one of twelve children of prominent Las Vegas cattle ranchers William T. and Artemesia Stewart. Royal and Marba had a whirlwind courtship and married that fall in Evanston, Illinois. They lived in Evanston for a decade, while Royal earned his master's and PhD degrees from Northwestern. Then he worked for several years as director of retail training for Chicago's Montgomery Ward company.

The couple was overjoyed at the arrival of their first child, daughter Donna Rae, on June 10, 1935. Their second daughter, Joanne, came nearly three years later. While Marba was pregnant with their third

Donna (at right) with her parents, Marba and Royal Garff, and sister Joanne.

child, Dennis, the Garffs moved to Salt Lake City, where Royal joined the University of Utah as a professor of speech and marketing.

Royal and Marba used their savings for a down payment on a home within walking distance of the university. The fourth and last Garff child, Linda, was born in 1943, and the following summer Royal went to New York City, where the legendary motivational trainer Dale Carnegie took note of him and offered him a job. Royal was attending the Carnegie Institute to become a certified course instructor, and the famous and wealthy Carnegie himself sat in on a couple of his speeches. "Royal, you've got what it takes!" he inscribed in a gift book to Royal. His instructors added that they had "never been around anyone who had such a good speech background or who had such infectious enthusiasm," he wrote to Marba. Carnegie was pressing him with a job offer, which meant moving to New York, but that didn't attract Royal. He concluded that "most of these people in these big cities do nothing but run around even more than I do. . . . I'm really happy to be living out West. I want to see if I can do well with this public speaking business, then try to get out of debt and really enjoy our families, children and life in general."[3]

Everything was on an upward trajectory until one day the following spring when Professor Garff uncharacteristically failed to show up for class. Marba had just received the tragic news that she had breast cancer, which in those days was tantamount to a death sentence. Donna was in the fifth grade when her mother had a double mastectomy. At just ten years old, Donna began to cook for the family and to take on other household chores. That summer of 1946, the cancer abated. Marba allowed Donna and Joanne to vacation at her parents' Las Vegas home, sending them off with a bit of advice: "Have a good time and remember, when you do your part and help the most, that is when you are the happiest. Be careful and don't do foolish things."

The financial strain of surgery, hospitalization, and treatments for Marba was heavy on Royal, but his brother Ken Garff, the prosperous car dealer, came to the rescue. "In trying to meet the crisis alone, I could have lost most of our resources," Royal said. He took a two-year leave from the university, and Ken hired him for an office job at the dealership at nearly three times his university salary.

In early 1947, when Donna was in sixth grade, Marba's cancer returned. Grasping at alternative treatments, she traveled to Brooklyn, New York, while Royal stayed home with the children. Their good-bye at the Salt Lake City train station was the last time the children ever saw her. Royal eventually joined her in Brooklyn, leaving the children in the care of a friend.

In Royal's first letter home to Donna from New York, shortly after her twelfth birthday, it was clear that he was putting heavy responsibility on her young shoulders. Hospital expenses were $120 a week, he informed her, and he was trying to live on $1 a day—40 cents for his room and 60 cents for his meals. Some days he subsisted on leftovers from Marba's hospital meals when she could not eat. It was up to Donna to keep expenses down and to act as his secretary by forwarding his most important correspondence and bills. Donna was also primarily in charge of her siblings.

On July 17, Royal wrote "dearest Donna Rae" to thank her for being so "dependable, our partner in building a good home." He hoped she was taking her tonic and iron pills every day, but she was not to use his typewriter, or her siblings would be jealous. And she was to use only "a little" lipstick. "We want you to be thought of and respected like your Mother and not to be a loud, showy person. So take it slow and you'll be a lot happier in the long run." A week later he wrote, "Your Mother is having a very difficult time—suffering a great deal. It's certainly hard on your Daddy to sit here and watch it and not be able to do much about it." Several days after that: "Mother's stomach is still terribly swollen causing terrible pain."[4]

Finally, in a letter dated August 7, Royal wrote Donna, "We are with you and the other [children], sweetheart—no matter where we are or you are. And even if your Mother cannot get better, you must always feel she is near us, as she always will be." Four days later, Marba died at the age of forty.

Back at home, Royal hired a series of caregivers for the children and went back to work. The next year Royal married a widow, Maxine Rice. She had been determined not to remarry, but after she met Royal's children, they began to pester him: "Daddy, get married!" And so they did. Maxine encouraged the children never to forget Marba. "I loved Marba, even though I never met her. She bore these darling children." Within months the children were all calling Maxine "Mother."

Donna was by nature stoic, rarely showing emotion. She internalized her anxiety, which then created a form of eating disorder and need for excessive sleep. Maxine suggested that Royal take Donna for regular morning walks "in hopes of alleviating her anxiety and building her appetite." It worked, and Royal cherished the one-on-one time with his daughter. Donna became accomplished at both piano and dance. Her strong suit was the hula, embodying Hawaii's "Sweet Leilani, Heavenly Flower" when she danced.

Donna registered to attend the University of Utah in the fall of 1953. She was determined to graduate before entertaining any thoughts of marriage. So the last thing she wanted was a date with a senior named Bill Marriott, who she rightly suspected had come to Utah to find a Latter-day Saint wife. The first few times he asked her to school functions, she turned him down. Then Bill had a crackerjack idea.

In the first week of December, Sigma Chi put on its annual ball and banquet, at which one woman was elected the "Sweetheart of Sigma Chi." Bill cleverly nominated Donna and then called her to tell her she was on the list, without telling her he had nominated her. "I'm supposed to take you to this banquet, so I'll come pick you up," he said. She didn't win, but Bill was the perfect gentleman. That didn't make securing the second date any easier. Weeks went by, and Donna finally said yes to an invitation to one of Bill's ROTC dances. Ten-year-old Linda was very impressed with her older sister's date. "You could hear him coming a block away. I will forever remember that wonderful white navy uniform he had on," she remembered. But Donna's head was not easily turned by wealth or good looks.

A buoyant Bill returned home for Christmas, where his dad spent hours counseling him, trying to smooth some rough edges. J.W. wrote in his journal: "Billy is critical of anyone who gets in his way or who seems to be superior, but will outgrow that." On Christmas night before a crackling fire, his parents and Grandmother Alice Smoot gave Bill advice about love and marriage until 1:30 a.m. "Discussed the type of girl for Bill," J.W. wrote. "Good family requirement."[5] When Bill flew back to college, he was more determined than ever to court Donna, who fit the requirements.

The turning point for Bill and Donna's future occurred in April when they went to dinner with J.W. and Allie in the elegant Empire

Bill in his navy dress whites.

Room of the Hotel Utah in Salt Lake City. To Bill's parents, Donna was bright, beautiful, enjoyable to be with, and well rooted in the Church. Until that evening, Donna had had no idea who the Marriotts were. After the dinner, her sorority sisters educated her. "The Marriotts are really *it* back there in the East," one friend said. "Don't you know anything about the Marriotts?"

"No," Donna answered, "but I DO really like his parents a lot."

Soon, they were dating once a week, and near the time of Bill's graduation, they were seeing each other every day. On graduation day, June 7, 1954, Donna could not help but be impressed with her beau as he was commissioned as an ensign in the navy, wearing his dress whites. Bill and Donna had tickets for a graduation dance that evening, but they never made it. "Bill started talking to me about the business and what he wanted to do in the company," Donna recalled. "He told me about his uncles—how two of them were letting down his father. He told me how hard his father was on him, and if it wasn't for his mother he didn't know where he would end up. We sat and talked for hours and hours. He told me everything. We never went to the dance."

79

In July, Bill had to report to the navy. Before that, he accompanied J.W. on a business trip and to the opening ceremonies of the New York Thruway. J.W. had won the lease to operate nine restaurants along the 148-mile stretch between New York City and Albany. Approximately seventeen miles apart, the Hot Shoppes thruway restaurants comprised a monopoly that became a significant new revenue stream for the company.[6]

Bill paid little attention to the ceremonial speech that day given by Governor Thomas E. Dewey, the one-time presidential candidate who was then at the end of a decade as the state's notable governor. Instead, Bill's eyes were riveted on a bright red Ferrari, one of the first Ferraris ever seen in America. After the ribbon cutting, an auto cavalcade of vehicles commenced down the superhighway, with Bill and J.W. traveling in J.W.'s Cadillac convertible. But Bill was absorbed with that $16,000 foreign sports car ahead. At the first opportunity, Bill boldly asked the driver if he could ride with him. The driver agreed, advising: "Don't touch the back of the seat because it's very thin and you'll dent the metal." Bill clambered into the front passenger seat and sped along more than forty miles of the new superhighway in the exotic sports car. "That was a big deal," he remembered.

Bill and Donna wrote each other frequently that summer. Late one July evening, only a week or so after his arrival at the navy supply corps school in Georgia, Bill filled up his pockets with quarters, walked to the nearest public telephone booth, and dialed Bryce Canyon Lodge in southern Utah, where Donna was waiting tables and performing in a variety show. The lodge manager who answered the phone said Donna was busy changing into her hula costume for the evening show, but Bill insisted that she be summoned. When she picked up the phone, he got straight to the point. He loved her and wanted to marry her, so would she marry him? Donna was speechless. When she recovered sufficiently, she asked him to wait for her answer until she had talked with her parents.

The next morning, he ordered a dozen red roses to be delivered to her. The card was typical Bill—no excess verbiage: "Love you, Bill."

Royal Garff was not happy when Donna phoned him. He liked Bill well enough, but he wanted his daughter to finish college. But after some thought and consultation with his own mother, he gave his blessing. Now that the most important part of his future was assured, Bill, along with best friend Ensign Bruce Haight, hunkered down to his studies at the school for the navy supply corps, a fitting training for Bill's plan to work for Hot Shoppes when his navy service was complete.

Without Bill's knowledge, J.W. had been pulling strings to secure a naval post in Washington for him. Bill was summoned to an interview in Washington to discuss possible assignments.

"Tell me, Ensign Marriott, are you disabled?" the navy captain asked.

"No, sir," Bill replied.

"Is your father disabled in some way?"

"No, sir," Bill said, wondering where this was going.

"Do your parents need you here in Washington?" the captain continued.

"No, sir," Bill answered. The captain shuffled his papers for a moment and then informed Bill that pressure had come from "above" for Bill to receive a Pentagon job because of an unspecified family need for him to be close to home. Bill left, embarrassed that J.W. had been lobbying the navy to keep him in Washington.

Back home that Friday evening, J.W. was disconcerted that Bill had undone his careful campaign. The two talked late into the evening. Bill explained that he neither wanted nor deserved special treatment, but he allowed that he was worried about getting married if he was going to be away for months at sea. Again without Bill's knowledge, J.W. worked the phones all weekend trying to ensure a D.C. job. The effort failed.

Bill was assigned to the Norfolk-based *U.S.S. Randolph* aircraft carrier. It was not the Pentagon, but it was docked in the closest naval base to Washington and was scheduled to be in port for much of his navy service, which meant he and Donna could live in Norfolk when they married. Bill was still in supply school when the *Randolph* left for a six-month Mediterranean cruise. He was assigned to fly to Europe and join the ship after Christmas. Donna flew to Washington to spend Christmas with him.

Even though both Bill and Donna had grown up in four-bedroom houses, the Marriotts' home seemed huge to her. "Big living room, big dining room—we didn't grow up in a big house at all. I was pretty awestruck." That feeling was compounded by an invitation to have dinner with President Eisenhower and First Lady Mamie at the Marriotts' Fairfield Farm. The Marriotts' close friend Ezra Taft Benson, who was both Secretary of Agriculture and an Apostle in their Church, had been pressing the president to visit the farm and enjoy some hunting, guided by Bill Werber.

An anxious J.W. called Werber a couple of weeks before the event. "I've got myself into a big problem and you have to help me. I've told the president we have a lot of birds down there, and maybe I oversold him." Fairfield did have a good number of birds, but they were at the edges of the heavily pastured farm. Eisenhower was used to hunting in Georgia, where his hosts "seeded" a small secured area with birds. Werber advised J.W. to do the same, so he brought in 100 adult quail from Pennsylvania and released them near the farm.

By the time the big day arrived, J.W. had a cold and a high fever, but he rallied to join his guests. Donna was swept away when Bill walked her into the manor house's front room to meet them. Huge logs crackled in the fireplace, lighting the sparkling ornaments on the Christmas tree with flickering flames. Four hostesses from Hot Shoppes attended to the guests' every need. The day was unusually frigid, with a wind-chill factor below zero.

"What do you want to do, Mr. President?" J.W. asked him. "Do you want to go hunting? We've got fine opportunities for you to kill some birds, if you'd like, but it's awfully cold outside."

The president paused a bit, then turned to Ensign Marriott and asked, "What do you think we should do?"

Bill was surprised. "This was the commander in chief, and I was just the lowest form of animal life in the navy—and he was asking me what I wanted to do," he remembered.

Bill quickly replied: "I think we should stay inside by the fire."

The famous Ike grin spread over the president's face, and he responded, "I think your suggestion is great. Let's do that."

The short episode made "a tremendous impression" on Bill. "I could see almost immediately how a man of his stature could deal with egos like Montgomery, Patton, Churchill, de Gaulle, and Stalin during World War II. He gave them the respect of asking and considering what they thought."

After that, the dinner was almost an anticlimax for Bill, but not for Donna. She soaked up every moment, including the family program that the Bensons' four daughters had prepared for the president and first lady—a typical "family home evening" like those observed weekly in devout Latter-day Saint homes.

After Christmas, Allie took Bill and Donna to New York City for several days. The visit was filled with sightseeing and dazzling Broadway shows. On January 6, Bill flew out to join the *U.S.S. Randolph* anchored in Valencia, Spain. He and Donna would not see each other until three days before their wedding, almost five months later.

Bill's last name would one day loom large on dozens of European hotels, but he took his first trip to Europe aboard a slow-moving U.S. Navy Constellation cargo plane. He arrived on January 10, 1955, and the *Randolph* weighed anchor, leaving Valencia five days later.[7]

Two weeks after Bill joined the crew, his superior, Lieutenant Mickey Finn, wrote privately to a navy captain who was a friend of J.W.'s that Bill had been given "the job of Sales Officer which entails three Ship's Stores, one Soda Fountain, one Foreign Goods Store, the Clothing and Small Store retail and bulk, the Ship's Laundry, Cobbler Shop, Tailor Shop, about eight storerooms including one holding 700 cases of beer!; two Barber Shops, and deal with vendors at various ports visited. So you can see where Ensign Marriott will be a very busy young man, picking up an immense knowledge of business."[8]

Meanwhile, J.W. was busy pulling strings for another unwanted surprise for Ensign Marriott. He hatched a plan with the wife of the *Randolph's* commanding officer to fly himself, Allie, and Donna to one of the ship's ports of call in Italy for a shipboard wedding, complete with an arch of crossed sabers. J.W. called the father of the bride to tell him the good news. "Shouldn't you ask Donna what she thinks?" her father gamely responded.

J.W. did, excitedly springing his surprise on Donna: "How would you like to go to Europe with us and see Bill and we'll have the captain of the ship marry you while we're there?"

"It was just like a bolt of lightning. I mean, it was exciting to think about, but I hadn't heard anything about this from Bill—and I found out they hadn't even asked him," Donna recalled. She diplomatically reminded J.W. that she and Bill wanted to marry in a Latter-day Saint temple. But J.W. had already thought about that. "You can be married a year later in the temple," he insisted. (The Church of Jesus Christ of Latter-day Saints in that era required couples who married in "till death do us part" civil ceremonies to wait a year before their marriage was ratified in a temple ceremony "for time and all eternity.")

Donna said she would get back to him after she talked with Bill. Knowing the "surprise" was about to be revealed, J.W. made a shore-to-ship call to Ensign Marriott and dropped the plan on him. Bill didn't like it, but as he had learned to do with his father, he held his tongue and called Donna.

"We can't do it," he told her. "What are you going to do? Follow me from port to port and just see me when I can get off the ship for a few minutes? That's ridiculous!" Donna agreed and continued waiting in Utah. Bill sent a terse January telegram to his parents: "Prefer to wait until June for wedding."

Not to be deprived of a visit with their son, J.W. and Allie met up with him in Cannes, France. J.W. had brought a news clipping from the *Washington Evening Star*, which illustrated just how ubiquitous Hot Shoppes had become. In a Protestant Sunday School class in Chevy Chase, Maryland, one youngster was showing off his Bible picture cards to a pal while his mother happened to be listening in the next room. "This one is Jesus in the manger," the boy explained. "This is Jesus at school. This is Jesus as a young man." Finally he came to the picture of the Last Supper. "This one"—he hesitated for a moment—"This one is Jesus at the Hot Shoppe."[9]

After Cannes, it was back to the *Randolph*. Bill had his job well in hand, though there were occasional hiccups, like the Wormy Cigarettes Incident. The ship had a large case of cigarettes infested with worms. The accounting regulations didn't allow Bill to just throw away merchandise, so he sent them over to a supply ship. Shortly after, the *Randolph* captain called him up to the bridge.

"Why did you send over those cigarettes?" he asked Ensign Marriott.

"Because they're no damned good!"

If the captain was amused, he didn't show it. "Well, [the other captain] is going to send them back, and we're going to accept them."

That was that. "I had this big space in our storage inventory that was now useless because of those dead cigarettes. I tried to get rid of them, and I couldn't," Bill said. "That's the difference between the navy and a commercial business."

During his months aboard the *Randolph*, Bill and a lieutenant who shared his faith met each Sunday for Church services. They were the only two practicing Latter-day Saints among the *Randolph*'s 3,500-man complement. Both were appreciative that every night, after the sound

Donna and Bill on their wedding day in 1955.

of taps, one of the ship's chaplains prayed for the crew over the PA system.

In Salt Lake, Donna was feted at no fewer than eight luncheons at four different country clubs, as well as a country club dinner and another dinner party at a private home, four bridal showers, and one tea, all of which threatened the thin bride's waistline.

The *Randolph* arrived in Norfolk on June 18, and Bill hurried to Utah. On June 29, in the Salt Lake Temple, Bill and Donna faced each other, kneeling across an altar with mirrors behind each of them that stretched their images into eternity. In a simple ceremony, surrounded by family and friends, they were sealed "for time and all eternity."

Afterward, Apostle and family friend J. Reuben Clark, who performed the ceremony, offered some advice: "Don't ever go to bed angry. You won't be able to kneel down and say your prayers together if you're angry with each other." The two took the advice to heart. "I only remember about five times in our six decades of married life that we've had a problem," Donna said. "And that was only when one of us was overly tired—at the end of the day when the kids weren't good, or Bill had a hard trip or something."

Nearly a thousand friends and family members attended the reception that followed. It took indefatigable Donna more than six months to send out handwritten thank-you notes for the 436 gifts.

The next day, Bill and Donna flew to Calgary for a week in the Canadian Rockies in a room at the Banff Springs Hotel, a magnificent structure built in a combination of Scottish baronial and French chateau styles.

Their first home was an apartment in Portsmouth, Virginia, less than ten miles from the Norfolk naval base. From there they had easy access for trips to Washington once or twice a month. Bill was one of the first that summer to taste a new double-decker hamburger that Hot Shoppes was trying out. J.W. had modeled it after Robert Wian's signature sandwich in California, called the "Big Boy," which also became the name of his restaurant chain. But Hot Shoppes had a different "secret sauce," with a recipe that included chili, A-1, Tabasco, and Worcestershire sauces. The burger was called "Mighty Mo," after the massive *U.S.S. Missouri* battleship.

At Christmas, J.W. and Allie hosted a party for the newlyweds and 250 Washington guests. Back in Norfolk, Bill was promoted from ensign to lieutenant junior grade, and shipped out on the *Randolph* for two months. Donna waved good-bye, closed up their first home, and flew to Salt Lake City to spend the spring with her family.

The *Randolph's* first port of call during the Caribbean cruise was Mayport, Florida, where the ship anchored for almost two weeks. While there, Bill was alarmed to learn that his father had become seriously ill, with an acute pain in one of his arms. Surgeons cut a large muscle in his shoulder to clean out an excessive calcium deposit in one bone. J.W. was well enough to fly with Allie and Donna to Cuba when the *Randolph* docked at Guantanamo Bay. Bill met his wife and parents in Havana, but his folks found the city dirty and congested, so after a few days they moved the vacation to Miami. At the end of his leave, Bill hitched a ride on a navy transport back to Cuba.

Because of his assignment on the Caribbean cruise as wardroom mess officer, Bill was relieved of his responsibility for the Geedunk (the ship store), the barber shop, the cobbler shop, and the laundry. But the new job wasn't any easier. "The wardroom provided three meals a day for several hundred officers, all of whom had high expectations about what they should be eating and how it should be presented," he explained.

His greatest challenge was dealing with the stubborn World War II veteran "stewards" or cooks, who were mostly African-American or Filipino. Hence the Battle of the Meat Loaf. "I got into it with them about how they were making the meat loaf, so I gave them our Hot Shoppes recipe for it. They ignored me. They wanted to cook the way they wanted to cook, and their meat loaf was, well, terrible. They were tough as nails, and they didn't give a crap about me, or anything else. When I tried to pull rank on them, the meat loaf only got worse. This went on for weeks until I finally folded my cards and crept away, dropping the family recipe back into my sea bag. And they continued making crappy meat loaf."[10]

When the *Randolph* returned to its home base on May 1, that was the last of Bill's sailing days in the navy. He owed the military just two more months of service, so he and Donna rented a small apartment in Portsmouth for that short period. "I loved being at sea," Bill reflected, and he gained useful knowledge as one of the managers of a large floating hotel with a massive guest list. "Brief as it was, my navy experience has carried over in many large and small ways. I still shine my shoes every day."[11]

MOTOR HOTEL DIVISION CHIEF

While on a visit to Washington before he left his navy service, Bill drove to Hot Shoppes headquarters at 5161 River Road for some career planning with his father. Having outgrown the Upshur Street offices, J.W. had built a new three-story air-conditioned Hot Shoppes headquarters—the fifth since the company was founded in 1927—on a ten-acre tract in Montgomery County, Maryland. J.W. and his executives had moved in a year before, in May 1955.

Bill's plan had always been to join his father's company once he completed his navy service, which, with the end of the Korean War, had been shortened to two years. Bill would soon join the company, which had more than 5,000 employees and was experiencing rapid growth. Its annual sales from restaurants and catering were $29 million.

As Bill drove past the beautifully landscaped grounds, he admired the front of the building, shining with blue-green solar glass and porcelain panels. After parking, he walked the circular driveway to the entrance, with its ultramodern marquee. In the reception area, he relished the feeling that this was the place he would begin his chosen career. On the first floor were some of the executive offices, including those of three of his uncles.

Bill's destination was the third floor—the home of the boardroom

and his father's executive suite. He bypassed the office of Milton Barlow, the Harvard-educated finance expert who was a capable executive but a prickly man. A year before, Barlow had badgered J.W. into creating a number-two position at the company, executive vice president, with himself as its first occupant. At the time, J.W. wrote in his journal that he would have to "take a chance on his questionable public and personnel relations." After Barlow's promotion was announced there was "no shouting and cheering" among the normally upbeat Hot Shoppes executive ranks, but, J.W. wrote, "I believe they will accept him."[1]

Bill entered his dad's office at the west corner of the third floor. Above the mantel of a fireplace was a polished set of Texas longhorns. On the walls were several Western paintings, as well as a couple of original oils by Dwight Eisenhower, gifts from the president. J.W. invited Bill to sit down for a pro forma "job interview." His first job after the navy would be in restaurant operations at headquarters.

June 1956 was a busy month for Bill as he mustered out of the navy in Norfolk. He and Donna bought a house at 5214 Parkway Drive in the Kenwood neighborhood of Chevy Chase, Maryland. "It was the smallest house in Kenwood," Bill recalled. He sold some Hot Shoppes stock from his trust to buy the house outright at its $52,500 price. Donna was pregnant that summer and frequently sick.

When Bill first began work at the family restaurant business, the world was very different. As he humorously related in a speech decades later: "It was 1956, and Eisenhower was president. Bunnies were small rabbits, and rabbits were not Volkswagens. We thought deep cleavage was something the butcher did and outer space was the balcony at the movies. We never heard of FM radio, computer chips, CDs, artificial hearts, word processors, yogurt, and guys wearing earrings. We had bvds but no DVDs. Grass was mowed, Coke was a cold drink, and pot was something you cooked in!"[2]

Bill's first boss couldn't have been a better one—Iva de Freese

Bill in the kitchen at his first job with Hot Shoppes.

Savage, Hot Shoppes' top chef. Hired away from Schrafft's renowned restaurant chain, it was she who developed, wrote, and tested more than 4,000 standard recipes that J.W. accepted as the culinary bible for the company. He promoted her to head the company's research department, which made her the first female in the Hot Shoppes management hierarchy.

One of Iva's first assignments for the eager young man was "to tackle the sandwich wrap issue—the best way to keep a hot sandwich hot and fresh. Foil wraps were coming out then, but they sweated the sandwich too much. There wasn't anything like the plastic boxes today that allow a hamburger to breathe. We finally ended up copying what Big Boy was doing out in California—a very light, thin paper wrap almost like wax paper which held the heat and didn't make them too soggy."

Not all of Bill's ideas worked. Another Iva assignment was "to find out why we couldn't serve our customers faster. I collected some

menus, and then I looked at the guest checks, which showed what customers were really buying. I found out that there were over 200 printed items on our menus, but there were another 200 items made for special orders, from peanut butter and jelly sandwiches to french fries with brown gravy. When we reduced the number of items, we speeded up the service, reduced our food cost, and reduced our kitchen labor. But the big mistake I made was not asking our customers what they wanted. So I cut items I shouldn't have cut and left selections on the menu I should have taken off. I made unilateral decisions with no customer input—and I made some bad mistakes."[3]

One of his more memorable tasks was to compare restaurant sales between Hot Shoppes and the much larger Howard Johnson's national chain, which through franchising had grown rapidly from a dozen restaurants at the end of the war to more than 400 units. "I was amazed that the comparable Hot Shoppes had sales that were double, and even triple, Hojo's. I tried to define why this was. I studied the management style of my dad and Howard Johnson, whose restaurants were poorly run. My dad thought it was because most of Hojo's restaurants were franchised and we weren't, but that wasn't really it. Howard Johnson and Dad were both charismatic leaders. Both were superb salesmen. But Howard Johnson concentrated on making money and living a lavish lifestyle. My dad concentrated on people: his associates and customers. These were two very different cultures. While Howard Johnson spent his time on his yacht in Florida in winter, and Nantucket in summer, Dad spent his time in the kitchens worrying about quality, and he spent time listening to his people. That was the difference in the quality and greater success of Hot Shoppes versus Howard Johnson."[4]

After Bill had spent six months with Restaurant Operations, J.W. gave him a new assignment in public relations, working for the company's veteran PR chief. The course of Bill's future was set when he was assigned to take on the PR and ad work for the company's newest venture: a Marriott motor hotel along the Potomac River.

Years before, J.W. had bought five acres of prime land on the Virginia end of the 14th Street Bridge, intending to use it for a new headquarters building and commissary, particularly with the convenient railroad siding next door for shipping supplies. Corporate legend perpetuated the idea that J.W. decided to build a hotel after he received a purchase bid from a hotel company for the property. Such a bid was received, but only *after* J.W. had decided that Hot Shoppes would build its own motel or hotel there.

In that era, hotels were large downtown facilities with few parking spaces. Motels were mom-and-pop operations along highways with plenty of parking but fewer rooms. In the early 1950s, the pioneers in motel chains were Holiday Inn and Howard Johnson. Though J.W. never intended to go into the hotel business, when he did, he decided he wanted a much grander facility than was then available. It would be a "motor hotel," since it would be neither a typical hotel nor a motel. J.W. had to fight against his own stodgy board of directors to push the Twin Bridges motor hotel plan, featuring a tower up to five stories and a total of 375 rooms in eleven sprawling buildings, which J.W. declared to be the "largest motor hotel in the world" when it opened in January 1957. With its daring architectural features, elegant restaurant, Western frescoes, and hourglass swimming pool, it was unlike any "motel" the motoring traveler had ever seen.

At the grand opening, J.W. experienced something he had never known with any of his restaurants: the name *Marriott* in lights. Shortly after the ribbon was cut, Bill was summoned to the phone to take a call from Texas oilman Jack Wrather, who owned two popular TV shows, *The Lone Ranger* and *Lassie*. Wrather had built a hotel for Walt Disney near his new Disneyland park, and business was slow. He was in desperate need of good hotel management.

"They say you're opening a brand-new motor hotel there in Washington," Wrather began. "Is that true?"

"Yes," Bill replied.

"Well, I own the Disneyland Hotel. It has about 100 rooms and it's not doing well. How would you like to come out to California and manage the Disneyland Hotel?"

Bill put his hand over the phone, motioned his dad over, and explained the situation. "Should we go out and take a look at this hotel?"

"No," J.W. groused. And then he betrayed his wariness of the hotel business he had just stepped into. "We probably can't run the one we've got!"

Bill got back on the line and declined, thus turning away the first offer for a line of business that would one day become Marriott's bread and butter.

However, the call gave Bill an idea that germinated for the next two months before his father asked him, "What do you want to do around here?"

"I'd love to run the new hotel," Bill answered firmly.

"Well, you don't know anything about the hotel business," his father responded.

"Neither does anyone else around here," Bill countered.

"Okay," his father said, "go ahead." And that was that. Bill Marriott was now the proprietor of his first hotel.

In its earliest year, prospective guests could drive up to the lobby window of the Twin Bridges Marriott, examine 3-D Kodachrome prints of the various room designs, and select the one they wanted to stay in. They were given a key and then followed a bicycle-riding bellboy to their room. "We charged $9 and $1 for every extra person in the room," Bill said. "When we were really busy during the tourist season, we would look inside the cars to see how many people were in there. If it was only one person or two, we would send them on their way. But if they had two kids, a mother and father, we would jump at it. That way we would get $12 out of those rooms."

Bill started room service from scratch. "Talk about a hands-on, making-it-up-as-you-go-along experience. I had just officially moved over from the food-service side of the company. At the end of my first month on the new job, I found myself putting together room service trays and filling guest orders myself. Not that I was any kind of expert on the subject! I quickly trained two or three other people, and they took it from there."

His very first "executive decision" involved, of all things, ice buckets. "I was looking over our expenses for Twin Bridges and noticed a pretty hefty sum under the category 'Other.' A little investigation revealed that guests found our plastic-covered, cardboard ice buckets so sturdy and convenient that they were filling them up with ice and drinks to take on the road. At a dollar apiece, the loss of hundreds of buckets in a year would have quickly eaten up our meager profits, so I ordered permanent ice buckets to be placed in each room, and we were back in business."[5]

The same month that the Twin Bridges Marriott opened, newly reelected President Eisenhower asked J.W. to chair the food committee for the inaugural ball, which included a perk of prime seats for himself, Allie, Bill, and seven-months-pregnant Donna at the inaugural parade. The parade was impressive, but J.W. described the food planning in his diary as "a real strain. My last inauguration work I hope."[6] Little could he or Bill have guessed that a decade later, J.W., at an older age, would chair the entire event for two successive presidential inaugurations.

In mid-March, Bill and Donna finally invited his parents over for dinner. It had been six months since they had moved into the Kenwood house. Donna was soon to deliver their first child, and she steeled herself for J.W's possible inspection of her housekeeping, remembering how he had repeatedly checked for dust when he visited the newlyweds' Norfolk apartment. Instead, probably because of Donna's condition, J.W. was on his best behavior.

On March 30, shortly before eight a.m., Donna's contractions increased enough that she told Bill it was time to go. He rushed her to nearby Garfield Hospital, and, about five hours later, baby Deborah

Donna and Bill with their first baby, Deborah.

arrived. She appeared to be healthy, but the doctor had a concern about her heart. One month later, the Marriott family doctor added his concern when he thought he heard a heart murmur; it was possible she would grow out of it, he said.

In addition to new fatherhood, Bill was learning the ropes of hotel management. Because of the prime location and resortlike facilities, high occupancy by summer travelers was fairly assured at Twin Bridges from April to October, but J.W. had made almost no provision for nontourist business. Bill quickly made the rounds of defense contractors around the country to lure their business when they visited the Pentagon. That was a short-term solution for the off-season. Bill determined that the long-term solution would be conventions.

Twenty-first-century hotel guests would have trouble envisioning the "amenities" of Twin Bridges, the pioneer of the motor hotel. Rooms were only $9 a night, but there were no marketing programs, no reservation system, no computers, and no meeting rooms. But there was also no competition. It was the first real motor hotel of any size in the suburbs.

"As competition increased, we added all the services," Bill said, "a reservation system, an ice-skating rink, ballrooms and meeting rooms, sales staff, a specialty restaurant to supplement our coffee shop, and an accounting organization. It was tough convincing meeting planners to meet anywhere but downtown, but we did."

The ice-skating rink was an immediate hit, generally having more skaters than the rink could reasonably accommodate. Special guests one Christmas Eve included the family of Ezra Taft Benson. Bill was never a good ice-skater, so he stood on the sidelines to cheer the others on. Secretary Benson, who had not been on skates in many years, should have done the same. An hour after taking to the ice, Benson took a bad fall, dislocating his shoulder.

As the hotel became more profitable under Bill's management, he began to see a new direction for the company that would take it away from restaurants. "I was leery about the long-term viability of the Hot Shoppes restaurant business. It was a very complicated business and was labor-intensive. It took an awful lot of effort to earn any money. Plus, we had run out of locations in the Washington area so we had started to expand into other cities on a haphazard basis. I saw hotels as a new opportunity, a new way for the company to grow." That meant Bill needed to pressure J.W. into approving additional hotels. He didn't think it would be an easy sell; his father was, at heart, a restaurateur, and he also loathed borrowing money for construction.

In late 1957, J.W. and Allie went to the Soviet Union for three weeks with a delegation of restaurant operators and caterers as part of a business exchange program. While they were gone, Bill and Executive Vice President Milt Barlow cooked up the idea for a second hotel on land just outside D.C. next to the Rosslyn, Virginia, Hot Shoppe Number 12. Like the Twin Bridges Hotel, this site was at the end of another bridge over the Potomac—this time, the Key Bridge. When J.W. returned, he surprised Bill by liking the idea. It fit his notion that bridges were excellent traffic choke points to build a business.

Bill was so excited about the hotel that he upstaged his father with an unscripted public announcement. The occasion was a banquet where J.W. was receiving an award from The Advertising Club of Washington. J.W. made a twenty-minute acceptance speech, which was well received. But a correspondent from the *Salt Lake Tribune* reported, "[I]t was his son who made the news by disclosing that a second multi-million-dollar Marriott Motel is going to be built here." The headline read, "Ex-Utahn Gets Spotlighted—But Son Steals the Show."[7]

· · ·

In March 1958, Bill flew to Dallas to inspect the Hot Shoppes In-Flite kitchen there. At the last minute, he set up a meeting with land developer "Big John" Stemmons, who owned reclaimed river bottom land called the Trinity Industrial District in Dallas and wanted to build a hotel there. The Marriotts looked like they might make good partners. With one hotel in operation and a second under construction, Bill was no neophyte. But forty-nine-year-old Stemmons, who had substantial business experience and wealth, was bigger than life to the small-time hotelier who was just a few days short of his twenty-sixth birthday. Big John was a kind man, full of humor, and he treated Bill as an equal.

During one of their conversations, Stemmons taught Bill a powerful business lesson regarding "enlightened self-interest"—the idea that if you had concern for the well-being of your community, your community would support your business. Stemmons loved his "village," as he called Dallas. At the end of their memorable meeting, Stemmons recommended that Bill see his Trinity Industrial District partner Trammell Crow, who wanted to pay for the construction of a hotel in the district. Bill returned home, excited to brief his father about the idea.

J.W. was pleased, but he made it clear that he didn't have full confidence in Bill's bargaining skills. "You don't know what you're doing," he said. "I'm going to send Milt with you, and you'll learn how to negotiate from him." Chafing a bit, Bill took Barlow back to Dallas with him, as ordered. Because they were all straight talkers, Bill had developed a solid relationship with John Stemmons and his brother Storey. But at the meeting, when Barlow took over, a chill came into the air. The brothers didn't like him. "He wouldn't listen to them," Bill recalled.

So, the sharp Dallas dealers decided to clean Barlow's clock. The Stemmons brothers controlled the negotiations and tipped the deal to their benefit. Barlow didn't appear to realize what had happened, but Bill did. "Those Texas boys cleaned him out, and we ended up with a deal that was better for them than us," Bill said. "I said to myself at the time, 'That's the importance of listening and not thinking you know it all. Always try to find out what's on the other person's mind, and work with them, and you both might get what you want.'"

Barlow also spurned Bill's recommendation of Trammell Crow as their Dallas hotel's partner and financier. Barlow preferred to deal with Wall Street, so he took Bill with him to New York City and secured a loan from Equitable Life for the Dallas hotel's construction. Plans were begun for a Dallas Marriott, which would open two years later.

But Bill's gut instinct about Crow had been dead-on. Crow became one of the greatest developers America has ever seen. He went on to build the famously successful Dallas Market Center, the Peachtree Center in Atlanta, and the Embarcadero Center in San Francisco. He founded the Wyndham Hotel chain and become a serious competitor to Bill Marriott's hotel chain.

• • •

In the early 1950s, the Civil Rights movement had begun to pick up steam, which impacted Hot Shoppes. Among the Jim Crow laws still on the books in Virginia was one mandating that "every person [operating] any public hall, theater . . . place of public entertainment or public assemblage [including restaurants] shall separate the white race and the colored race . . ." Even into the late 1950s, J.W. did not dare violate that law, which the state was willing to enforce. For a while, J.W. did what many other restaurant owners were doing; Hot Shoppes in Virginia were for "whites only." Finally, in June 1960, he invited the first African-American diners into Virginia Hot Shoppes. The unilateral move, which flew in the face of the state's tradition, was seen as a pioneering civil rights act and heralded by the National Association for the Advancement of Colored People.

As for the Hot Shoppes working staff, minorities made up 70 percent of the restaurants' workers. Still, J.W. was wary of having out-of-the-kitchen black female waitstaff, fearing customers would balk. Bill finally told him, "Well, people will get used to it. You've got to do it!" J.W. tested the waters by first designating several black women to serve as "aides" to white waitresses. As they became a more familiar sight in the dining room, several black women were each assigned to be the sole waitress for a section. The change was not entirely trouble free. A busload of Southern tourists stopped at the Bethesda, Maryland, Hot Shoppe, and the white travelers were clearly shocked when a black waitress asked to take their orders. They asked for the manager, Bill's uncle Russell, and complained to him about the woman. Russell cordially invited them to leave. They conferred together, and hunger won out. The travelers stayed and ate quietly.

The decision to serve alcohol created more anxiety for J.W. than integration of his customer base and waitstaff. The Church of Jesus Christ of Latter-day Saints strongly discouraged drinking, and J.W. was also experiencing an alcohol-fueled family tragedy with his younger brother. Paul's marriage had failed, in large part due to his drinking. J.W.'s journals are full of profound disappointment regarding his brother. Sometimes Paul would promise J.W. that he would stop drinking, but then he would fall off the wagon. In 1959, J.W. notified Paul he was going to be relieved of his duties running the company's Industrial Feeding Division (factories and hospitals) because of his erratic behavior. Paul went on a bender, adding heavy doses of sleeping pills to the mix. J.W. frequently went to Paul's apartment to check on him and make sure he was still alive.

Hot Shoppes already sold alcohol at its Albany restaurant along the New York Thruway, but that hadn't been J.W.'s choice. It was a requirement of the contract with the state. His son Bill's proposal to sell alcohol at their Philadelphia hotel restaurant was understandably more difficult for J.W. It was his own hotel, and no outsiders were twisting his arm. Bill had two hotels operating at that time, another under construction, and several more contemplated. If they were going to be in the hotel business, he felt they could not avoid selling alcohol. J.W. consulted with some friends in the Church leadership, but they told him it was his decision.

Bill pointed out to his father that Virginia allowed members-only private clubs to which members brought their own liquor, so J.W. reluctantly allowed him to open a club at Twin Bridges. The Windjammer became a favorite Capitol Hill watering hole for members of Congress, and another of its attractions was the fine view of National Airport plane traffic.

J.W.'s vision of his small company based on family sit-down restaurants was slowly being eroded. From Bill's scouting trips to California and elsewhere, he reported that "fast-food" restaurants were here to stay and were gaining ground on family restaurants. The California-born McDonald's franchise chain was expanding rapidly across the country. Bill reported that the profits for the fast-food joints, which offered takeout, were higher than those of Hot Shoppes.

In addition, Hot Shoppes was already primed for the arrival of the commercial jet age. From the small beginnings bagging sack lunches at Hot Shoppe Number 8 near an airfield, the company snagged the Pan American World Airways contract in 1958 to cater the first Boeing 707s off the assembly line. Since 707s were seven feet taller than any other commercial airplane, Hot Shoppes invented a servicing truck that could jackknife up to the door.

Proud of Bill's progress, J.W. proposed to the board in late 1958 that his son be given a new position as vice president of the motor hotel division. The board vote was unanimous. That was Bill's first Hot Shoppes board meeting, and it was a memorable one. "We only had two hotels in our hotel division, but I was a vice president, so it was a big deal for me," he said. He had found his niche in the company.

Despite that vote of confidence, J.W.'s chronic harsh criticism of Bill became a difficult private struggle. On paper, J.W. facilitated and supported each promotion for his son, but in reality, he also derided Bill's efforts on a regular basis. "If it hadn't been for Allie, Bill would have been just beaten into the ground by his father," Donna observed. "She was such a supporter of his, such a saint, even when he was little. When his father didn't like the way Bill polished his shoes and would make him do it again, Allie would sit on the floor with him, take off all of the old polish, and help him put on the new polish. Time and again, she would have to step in between Bill and his dad to help him get through the tasks that weren't done quite right in his father's mind."

Bill said that if it hadn't been for his mother, things would not have turned out as well for the Marriott family. "I certainly was not always right, nor was I ever as wrong as my father believed I was. My mother was a great referee, mediating and softening the blows. And my wife was always beside me to pick me up, dust me off, and send me back into the ring again. I could never have been successful without the love and support of these two great women."

The more responsibility that Bill received in the company, the more J.W. berated him. That conflict was evident when J.W. went to inspect Bill's nearly complete Key Bridge Hotel in late March 1959. "I had stayed up 24/7 for months to get that hotel opened," Bill recalled. "I never worked so hard in all my life. And my dad walked into a room and stared at the drapes, which were very full and heavy. And then he let me have it."

"Who was the stupid person who put those drapes in here?"

"I did," Bill responded.

"Why would you do this?"

Even after years of his father's parsimonious praise and nit-picking complaints, Bill was still shocked. J.W. had not offered a single positive word about the way the rest of the hotel and its furnishings looked. "I had worked for almost three years to get this hotel designed, built, staffed, opened, and my dad says nothing going through the hotel— but then he sees the drapes and goes ballistic. So I went ballistic. I wasn't about to take it."

Bill gave his father a piece of his mind. "You're impossible to work for!" he barked, and then he walked out of the room and went home.

Allie witnessed the fireworks and lit into J.W. when they got home, demanding that he apologize. In his journal that night, he wrote: "Bill and I had one of the worst arguments I have ever had with him. Doubt if he and I will ever get along. I don't think he likes me much. Surely doesn't like the way I do things and I can now see where his mother stands too."

But J.W. did not apologize. Instead, as was the pattern, it was Bill who made the first move for rapprochement, calling his father the next morning to iron things out. "Bill called and (he was) very sad. Allie sad also. She says I am terrible and I agree," J.W. wrote.[8]

Bill was stung by his father's seemingly random rebuke, but over time he came to see method in J.W.'s madness. In a speech to Marriott managers four decades after the drapes episode, Bill recalled: "It took me a long time to figure out that he was just continuing to raise the bar and to seek perfection in all that he did and in everything that had his name on it, including me. He was never satisfied—never. It was frustrating working in such an environment. It created a lot of stress. But I knew he wouldn't fire me and he knew I wouldn't quit. So we had a Russian standoff. As the years went by, I came to realize that our company had become a great company because of his never-ending quest for perfection. Although he was very tough, he was successful in continuously challenging me and our executive team to always do better. Today, our belief that success is never final is what separates our company from our competitors."[9]

• • •

On April 15, 1959, Bill's first son made his appearance. They named him Stephen Garff Marriott. Two months later, the Key Bridge Motor Hotel opened to great fanfare. The Marriotts almost didn't make it to Dallas for the opening of their third hotel in September 1960 because of a hurricane—Hurricane Donna, ironically. At the time, Donna Marriott did not like socializing at hotel opening parties. She was pregnant with their third child and skipped more than one meal at the Dallas hotel because of nausea. The mayor of Dallas cut the ribbon before a crowd of about five hundred who "all raved about our beautiful place," reported J.W. "Nothing like it in Texas or the U.S. Outdid Las Vegas in a clean way."[10]

Despite its beauty and prime downtown location, the Dallas hotel struggled at first. "Dallas was a dog for a year. It took us that long to develop the business, and then it took off," Bill said. Three years after it opened, Bill added more rooms to the hotel, thus taking the "world's largest motor hotel" title from his own Twin Bridges.

The next hotel Bill built—in Philadelphia—was Marriott's first purely suburban hostelry. "It was not downtown," he said. "It was not next to an airport, and it was not on a major highway. It was just a big suburban hotel." J.W. had bought the land for $30,000 in the 1940s. It was just outside the city's limits in the upscale Bala Cynwyd neighborhood, a block from the heavily traveled Schuylkill Expressway and less than five miles west of the center of Philadelphia, which then had a population of four million and was the fourth-largest city in the country. When a contingent of Philadelphia businessmen had offered J.W. $1 million for the property, his response was, "Why?"

"We want to build a hotel there; it's a better location than any you've got in Washington." J.W. turned them down and years later gave Bill the go-ahead for the Philadelphia City Line hotel.

The board's approval presented J.W. with a new wrinkle on an old problem—serving alcohol. The first three hotels had been built in Virginia and Texas, which were "dry" states. Pennsylvania, on the other hand, was a "wet" state that allowed the sale of alcohol in hotels except on Sundays. Bill commissioned a report from hotel consultants Horwath & Horwath, which concluded that the hotel would be successful in the early years primarily because of expected "extensive local use of the restaurant and bar facilities." Bill knew they had to sell alcohol, and he advised his father accordingly.

J.W. still agonized over this decision in discussions with Bill, who had no similar misgivings. Bill advised J.W. to once again consult the Church leadership, this time the Church's eighty-seven-year-old President, David O. McKay.

"As you know, Brother Marriott," President McKay told him, "the Word of Wisdom also enjoins abstinence from the use of tobacco, except as an herb for bruises and for sick cattle. Moreover, it enjoins abstinence from the consumption of hot drinks, such as tea or coffee."

"Yes, President, I am aware of that."

"Well, then, I will ask you as one brother to another, suppose a sheepman, like you were, goes into a grocery store owned by a Mormon to buy supplies, and he wants cigarettes for his men. If the storekeeper says—'Sorry, we don't carry tobacco in any form because it's against our religion'—why, the customer won't come back the next time. If he wants coffee for his men and the storekeeper says—'We disapprove of it, and we don't want your men to drink it either'—he won't come back again. He'll go to the store down the street not only for his tobacco and coffee, but for everything else he needs. In the long run, this could put the storekeeper out of business, don't you agree?"

"Yes, President, it could—very easily," J.W. responded.

"As I see it, Brother Marriott, if you don't satisfy your customers' wants and needs, you could be running the same risk. If liquor today is an essential part of the service that the hotel and restaurant industry offers to its patrons, it seems to me that you're obliged to sell it to them. To sell it to them doesn't mean that we approve of drinking, any more than to sell a gun means approval of using that gun to commit a crime. The patron who believes as we do is not compelled to buy liquor, nor, indeed, is anyone. But it is the patron's life, his money, his right to decide for himself, not ours."

President McKay cautioned J.W. against liquor sales in any family-oriented Hot Shoppes, and concluded, "It is hard sometimes to find the right path in these confusing times. But I know you will find it, and I know you will follow it."[11]

When J.W. returned to Washington, Bill saw a changed man, at least in regard to this troublesome question. It was clear that his father felt unburdened by his talk with President McKay. Liquor was made available for patrons of the sophisticated specialty hotel restaurants and lounges, but never in the Hot Shoppes or in other company eateries where youngsters went.

Bill, himself, was deeply grateful for President McKay's pragmatic counsel. Even though he had made the same points, his father accepted the advice more fully when it came from his Church leader. Because of J.W.'s frequent recounting of that meeting, it provided pivotal guidance for Bill in his own business dealings long after his father was gone.

Bill's increasing role in corporate decisions did not overshadow the big strides that J.W. continued to make himself. One of those was company profit sharing. He began thinking about it as early as 1945, when his brother Woody raised the idea in discussions about creating a company pension fund. Hot Shoppes had a young workforce for whom retirement plans held little allure, but profit sharing was a different matter.

In 1960, following the example of the pioneer in profit sharing, Sears Roebuck, the Hot Shoppes board voted to enact a profit-sharing plan with contributions into the fund from payroll deductions and matching corporate contributions. It replaced the company pension plan. Initially it was calculated that the fund would have $500,000 in it by 1963. The actual figure was nearly $2 million. After twelve years, it was $42 million. The kitty grew as it was invested in company stock. Minimum-wage workers in a lowly Marriott kitchen job realized they could look forward to hundreds of thousands of dollars upon retirement if they stayed for thirty years.

In addition to loyalty and longevity, the effect on employees was increased emphasis on efficiency and the bottom line, because every dollar in profit for the company meant money in the fund for employees. J.W.'s penchant for frugality became a company-wide habit. Employees at all levels with an eye to profit were less interested in costly company perks, such as gifts on the occasion of a promotion, because those extravagances cut into profits. The program also had the effect of negating any benefits that unionization might bring employees.

CHAPTER 8

THE SON RISES

Though Bill had hobnobbed with politicians, he generally stayed away from politics and was very wary about his father becoming too involved with a single candidate during the heated 1960 presidential election between Vice President Richard Nixon and Senator John F. Kennedy. Republican friend Cliff Folger asked J.W. to be one of an elite group of twenty "VIPs" who would contribute up to $30,000 for Nixon's campaign. "Cliff promised to make me an Ambassador or something, but I am not interested," J.W. wrote. Instead, he supported Nixon because he found him to be "a brilliant man, full of sound ideas."[1]

As the campaign heated up in the fall, he agreed to chair "Restaurant Voters for Nixon." He viewed the Democratic candidate, Senator Kennedy, as "a smart fellow but immature and dishonest." J.W. felt that even though he was taking "a calculated risk" siding with Nixon, "there is no alternative." Bill urged his father, for the good of the company, not to become too enmeshed in the Nixon campaign.

With a Kennedy win, it was the second political mistake that year that Bill had advised his father against. The first was J.W.'s attempt to personally lobby outgoing President Eisenhower for a federal contract—an effort that blew up in his face.

In April 1960, J.W. went to the White House to talk to Eisenhower about plans to build Dulles Airport outside D.C. J.W. was anxious to get a federal contract for food service at the airport. Used to mixing friendship with business, and accustomed to an easy relationship with the president, J.W. likely had no idea he was crossing a line. Ike was "very friendly" when J.W. asked for help during the face-to-face visit, but the next day a White House secretary called with a curt message. "The President had talked with Gen. Pete Quesada and he would see me. The rest is up to me." As the head of the new Federal Aviation Administration, Quesada had sole control over who got Dulles contracts.

J.W. met with Quesada five days after the Oval Office visit, but it was "a waste of time." Hot Shoppes would not get the contract. Quesada didn't say so, but Eisenhower could not risk the appearance of favoritism for a friend. "My father did a lot of amazing things, but this was one of the dumbest—and I thought it would be," Bill recalled. He understood what J.W. didn't, that the president couldn't help him, and Ike would likely have to sell all his Hot Shoppes stock as a result of the request. Thus, in one short, ill-advised visit, J.W. cost the company a key contract and its most prominent stockholder.

During the 1960 presidential campaign, Milt Barlow had launched an unrelenting campaign of his own to become the president of Hot Shoppes. In mid-October, J.W. received a letter from Barlow almost demanding that he be allowed to replace J.W. as president, become a member of the board, and get 50,000 shares of stock and a strong deferred compensation package. "Most colossal nerve I have ever experienced," J.W. wrote.[2]

J.W. arranged the board position for Barlow, but when J.W. and Allie went on a round-the-world trip in early 1961, he left written instructions that if anything happened to him, Bill would take over as president. After J.W. returned safely, he asked Bill what he would do if Barlow were his problem.

Bill had little use for Barlow and his crusty personality and focus on petty issues. Barlow once called him on the carpet for violating company policy by authorizing a car radio for one of his top executives who traveled frequently on company business. "It's only an $8 radio!" Bill protested.

"That makes no difference," Barlow fumed. "You violated company policy. Get that radio out of that car."

Bill came away convinced, "This guy can't run this company if that's the way he's going to act and treat people." So when J.W. asked Bill what he should do about Barlow, the answer was blunt: "Get rid of him." J.W. took his son's counsel with a grain of salt. On the plus side, J.W. viewed Bill as "a fine, accomplished young man," "fairly religious," possessed of "an analytical mind," and a "hard worker," according to his journal. But he also saw in Bill "lots of fire—impetuous, sincere, inferiority complex. Not too tolerant but improving."[3] In retrospect, Bill said his father's assessment of him then was fair.

J.W. was not someone who could bring himself to fire anyone, so he hired a consultant to assess Barlow's future with the company. The consultant said Barlow should never be president, and if he threatened to resign, J.W. should let him. J.W. agonized for weeks while Barlow pressed his case and continued to stumble. Without consulting J.W., Barlow raised the price of Hot Shoppes soft drinks from 10 to 15 cents. J.W. found out only when he visited one of the restaurants. Complaints poured in to headquarters, and J.W. ordered an immediate rollback.

J.W. assigned Barlow to negotiate a partnership with American Motors, and J.W.'s friend AMC President George Romney, to build a hotel on Times Square in New York City. It was Bill, however, who briefed the AMC board and won over most of its members with his detailed report. Barlow subsequently angered enough of the board members that the deal languished and eventually fell apart.

Concurrently, Bill laid the groundwork to buy prime hotel property at the entrance of the Los Angeles Airport. Barlow was dispatched to close the deal, but he didn't like the price, which Bill knew was a steal. Barlow told the owner he wouldn't pay that price. "Fine—don't buy the land," the seller replied, and sold it to a competitor. Bill continued to fume over Barlow, and J.W. continued to fret. It would be more than a decade before Bill could build a hotel in Los Angeles—and that one was farther away from the airport entrance.

Marriott's fourth hotel, next to Newark Municipal Airport in New Jersey, was the first that the company bought instead of built. The owner was headed to prison on charges unrelated to the hotel, so Marriott picked it up for the fire-sale price of $690,000 and operated it for seven years until it was sold for a large profit to the federal government to make way for a freeway interchange.

Next up was the Philadelphia City Line hotel, which featured Bill's first serious tangle with labor unions. The AFL-CIO picketed the construction site just before the grand opening because they had been unable to organize Marriott employees. Former President Eisenhower had promised to cut the ribbon himself at the opening in July 1961, but he canceled rather than cross the picket lines. The unionized construction workers also refused, leaving Bill to scramble family and corporate employees to put on the finishing touches. Barlow put a stove in the kitchen. Dick Marriott assembled tables. Donna's younger sister Linda, who was visiting that summer, made beds and vacuumed. Bill put down baseboards.

The day before the hotel opening, Allie got a call from the Hotel Utah in Salt Lake City, where her elderly mother, Alice, was a full-time resident. The widow of Apostle and Senator Reed Smoot had been found dead in her room. J.W., Allie, and Dick flew to Salt Lake City while Bill had to stay behind to oversee the grand opening rather than attend his beloved grandmother's funeral.

That summer of 1961 brought family joys and sorrows. Donna and Bill's third child and second son, John Willard Marriott III, was born May 4, 1961. Paul Marriott continued his descent into alcoholism, and on May 21 he took an overdose of sleeping pills and went into a coma. When he recovered, he pledged to J.W. that he was a changed man—but by July he was drinking again. J.W. worried that the airline catering customers Paul worked with would lose confidence in Hot Shoppes. Still, though Paul was dragging the In-Flite business down with him, J.W. would not fire him. By August, J.W. was losing sleep over his brother. "He is very depressed and very mad at me. Drove by his house at 7:30 a.m. but couldn't rouse him. I'm afraid he will take an overdose of sleeping pills."[4]

Meanwhile, Bill and Donna had a scare with five-year-old Debbie. She loved riding the ponies at Fairfield Farm, and on May 30, against Allie's protests, J.W. put Debbie on a horse named Tony. Debbie's heart murmur worried Donna, but J.W. tut-tutted. "It's a tame horse, and I'll be right with her." Then, as Bill watched in horror, Tony galloped away with Debbie and tossed her off. She hit the ground so hard she was knocked unconscious. Bill ran through the field, scooped her up, and carried her inside to a couch. As they waited anxiously for Debbie to regain consciousness, Allie and Bill lit into Grandpa Marriott.

Debbie's heart ailment, diagnosed as *tetralogy of Fallot*, had begun to be more pronounced when she was about two years old and the blue tinge of her fingernails that signified a lack of oxygenated blood appeared intermittently. The Mayo Clinic's preeminent surgeon, Dr. John Kirklin, recommended surgery. The heart-lung machine necessary for the operation had been used but not perfected, but in 1962, Debbie could wait no longer. One pioneering cardiac surgeon of that era, Dr. Russell M. Nelson (the family friend who would later become President of The Church of Jesus Christ of Latter-day Saints), described the risk for Debbie. "We didn't take anybody on for surgery who we thought could live for another year with what they had. We didn't know what the mortality rates were because we were just starting, so our conscience would allow us only to do patients who were on their way out. If they made it through the surgery, they won. If they

Johnny, Stephen, and Debbie.

didn't, they were right where they would have been anyway. Every case was a skirmish into the unknown."[5]

The night before Debbie and her parents left for Rochester, Minnesota, and the Mayo Clinic, three-year-old Stephen and eighteen-month-old John got into a fight. Baby John's ultimate defense was to cry and hold his breath, which he did until he passed out. He fell against the kitchen door, which knocked out one of his teeth. A family friend who was a dentist popped it back in that night, but it came out again and John swallowed it.

Bill, Donna, and Debbie flew to Minnesota on Monday, November 5, where Debbie was then checked into the pediatric ward of the Mayo Clinic's Saint Mary's Hospital.

The operation was scheduled for 7:45 a.m. on Thursday. Bill and Donna arrived early that morning to visit with Debbie before she was moved from her "big iron crib." Bill called it "one of the most difficult moments of our life—seeing her go down that hall to that operation without us." The one bright spot was that the anesthesiologist, instead of using the cold gurney, picked her up and carried her in his arms all the way into the operating room. The operation lasted nearly four hours. For sixty-four minutes, Debbie was connected to the heart-lung bypass machine through her femoral artery. When Dr. Kirklin opened up her heart, he found that she had only two defects instead of the predicted four. He worked efficiently to repair them.

Many open-heart patients in the 1960s who survived surgery died in the days immediately following the operation. On the second night, Bill and Donna received a terrible phone call in their hotel room. Debbie was not doing well, and might not make it. "We were on our knees all night praying that she might be spared," Bill recalled.

The medical resident who had been assigned to stay was fortunately there when her heart went into fibrillation. He used CPR and drugs to revive her. He shakily confided to Bill the next day that Debbie appeared to have died for two or three minutes. Neither of her parents knew for more than a decade that Debbie had had an out-of-body experience. It was profound and real to her, but she did not feel comfortable sharing it until Dr. Raymond Moody's 1975 best-selling book, *Life After Life*, revealed that others had had similar experiences.

"I remember leaving my body—the room couldn't hold me," she said. "I felt a lot older, like an adult, and I knew what was happening— what the doctor was doing to revive me. I had the most wonderful, peaceful feeling. I thought, 'This is great. I am free from this pain. . . . And I've never felt this great love ever before.' I felt like I had this tractor beam of love pulling me out of that room. I knew instinctively it was the Savior, and that this amazing love was pulling me toward the Savior. I thought, 'Why do I want to go back there when I can go here?' I didn't get as far as 'seeing the light' that others talk about, but I was given a choice—not in words, but spirit-to-spirit."

During that experience, she had a view into her parents' hotel room, where she saw them praying. "My dad had his head in his hands and he was crying. When I saw that, I said to myself—or out loud, I don't know—'I can't do this to my dad.' The second I made that decision, I was back in that sick little body, being that sick little girl again. I love my mom dearly; we get along great. But there is something really special about my relationship with my dad. I've always felt that part of the reason my life was saved was to help my dad out the best I can while he lives—to be his confidante and his friend."

Debbie's brush with death was a turning point in Bill's life. Developing, building, and managing hotels was all well and good, and those efforts would continue to demand a great deal of his time and energy. But Debbie's miracle prompted Bill to pledge renewed dedication to his family and a greater consecration of time and talents to God, in and out of the workplace. However, the demands of the corporation were about to test that resolve.

In 1963, J.W. was weary and looking for a way out of the daily grind of directing the family company. In January, he wrote: "Very frustrated with business. Don't know how long I can take it." A month later: "Not much peace in this life. Wish I could get rid of all my business." J.W. thought one of his sons would succeed him, and he had great hopes set on Bill, who was seven years older and more experienced in the company than Dick. But in J.W.'s view, Bill was not yet ready for a promotion, particularly since he hadn't found a successor to run the hotel division if he rose in the ranks.[6]

As he had many times before, J.W. turned to a favorite consultant for advice. His name was Harry Vincent, and he would become a critical adviser and close friend to Bill for more than half a century. In 1960, Vincent had reviewed the executive ranks of the company and told J.W. that Milton Barlow was not the successor J.W. was looking for. In 1963 he had not changed his mind. J.W. continued to ruminate for two months until he came to a tentative decision, which he revealed to the board in November 1963: "For much too long, the top management of this company has been lacking in drive and purpose," he told them. "I've been standing to one side hoping that some kind of strong, unified management team would emerge, but it hasn't. So I'm going to run the company the way it used to be run until we can solve our problem. I'm in charge. I'm the president and chief executive officer. Until further notice, I intend to exercise full control."

Convinced now that he would never be president, Barlow told J.W. he would like to leave the company "in a year or so." J.W. was relieved, but he still needed to decide on a new president. In the midst of those company discussions, America was undergoing its own painful presidential transition.

On Friday, November 22, at 12:30 p.m., President John F. Kennedy was assassinated in Dallas. By early evening, Bill was finally able to connect with Bill Tiefel at the Dallas hotel to get a report. Tiefel had been deployed for six months to oversee the expansion of the hotel. He reported that Dallas hotel personnel were additionally saddened by the murder of the well-liked Dallas policeman J.D. Tippit, who worked as an off-duty security guard at the hotel. Lee Harvey Oswald had shot and killed Tippit forty-five minutes after he shot Kennedy. Also shot was Texas Governor John Connally, whose family was welcomed to stay as long as necessary at the Dallas Marriott Hotel while the governor was treated at a nearby hospital.

One unexpected result of the assassination was its effect on a Las Vegas Del Webb company executive named Jim Durbin. It prompted him to make a career decision that cleared the way for Bill Marriott's promotion less than two months later.

Durbin had been born in a hotel that his parents owned in Indiana. He grew up learning the business from his parents. The Marriotts got to know him during the eight years he worked at the Hotel Utah in Salt Lake City, where he rose to be assistant manager. He was particularly attentive to Allie's mother, who lived in the hotel during those years. Bill had tried without success to recruit Durbin. Kennedy's death and other personal losses left him rethinking his own life. "My wife and I decided not to play it safe anymore. It was time for a change."

Durbin accepted a job as executive vice president of the hotel division under Bill. When he interviewed in Washington, almost as an afterthought, J.W. asked him to meet with Milt Barlow. That brief meeting killed the deal. "Mr. Barlow didn't have the warmth or the spark in his eye that Bill and his dad did." After the interview, Durbin called to tell J.W., "Quite frankly, Mr. Marriott, I can't work with Mr. Barlow." Pregnant seconds of silence followed on the phone before Durbin heard an intake of breath and these words: "Don't worry about that. When you come in February, Mr. Barlow will not be here, and my son will be in his place."

There was a critical difference in the management styles of Bill and his father. Bill could fire nonperformers with little hesitation. But J.W. was not constitutionally able to fire anyone, no matter how much they deserved it. So, when New Year's Day 1964 came and went, J.W. had not yet met with Milt Barlow to let him know that he would be replaced by Bill as executive vice president before February. Instead, he hired Harry Vincent to do one more management study. Vincent accepted the assignment even though he had already given J.W. his opinion of Barlow.

On January 6, Vincent met with J.W. to deliver his findings. "It was the unanimous opinion of everyone I interviewed that it would be highly desirable for Bill to be EVP," Vincent reported. "While I cannot sort out how many were for Bill as much as they were against Milt, I can tell you that all your top people said it would be a great idea and a great change." J.W. called Board Director Don Mitchell for advice. "You've got to let Milt go now," Mitchell urged.

"I can't do it," J.W. responded.

"I'll do it, then," Mitchell countered. And he did.

The announcement of Barlow's resignation and Bill's promotion was set for Tuesday, January 21, after a board meeting. At four a.m. that day J.W. got out of bed and wrote a list of guidelines for Bill to follow:

> Keep physically fit, mentally and spiritually strong;
> Guard your habits—bad ones will destroy you;

Pray about every difficult problem;

People are No. 1;

Decisions . . . have all the facts and counsel necessary—
then decide and stick to it;

See the good in people and try to develop those qualities;

Manage your time;

Details—Let your staff take care of them;

Think objectively and keep a sense of humor. Make the
business fun for you and others.

Since the list was reproduced in a 1977 biography of J.W., some of Bill's hotel general managers over the years framed the advice and hung it in their offices as a daily reminder. Bill was particularly moved by his father's letter, and he thought the advice was sound. "I tried to follow it, but it wasn't my Bible. I didn't wake up every morning at six a.m. and read it like he told me I should do. I did the best I could."

Bill hit the ground running as executive vice president. He had to. For two months, J.W. was absent from the office—laid low with both a gastric ulcer and an ear infection that nearly cost him his hearing. During those two months when Bill was effectively head of the company, not once did J.W. fret in his journal about Bill's performance. Instead, he was uncharacteristically effusive in his praise for his son. For himself, Bill was not filled with confidence. He was just thirty-one, and he had a lot to learn about the non-hotel portions of the business.

By April, J.W. was on the mend enough to put in an inspiring performance at Brigham Young University. The men's student association had tapped him to receive its Exemplary Manhood Award. J.W. worked for more than a month on his speech. A dozen students, including young Jeffrey R. Holland and his new wife, Patricia, prepared a skit reviewing J.W.'s business career. (Holland later became president of BYU.)

Holland related the fiasco that followed: "The hour came and

J. Willard came. But not a single student appeared." The sponsors had forgotten to publicize the event, and the cavernous basketball arena was empty. "Now here is the part that matters, and which I will never forget as long as I live," Holland continued. "Mr. Marriott said to the very red-faced and totally distraught young sponsor of this event, 'Let's begin.'" The student stammered and said, "No one is here." To which J.W. replied, "You are here and I'm here and these kids in this skit are here, let's begin." Holland finished the story:

> So to an absolutely empty fieldhouse—as dark and void as the world before creation—J. Willard watched the skit, laughed, and applauded on cue, and accepted the honestly and lovingly awarded plaque.
>
> Then he spoke. He spoke to the 12 or 15 of us in the skit, plus the 3 or 4 student sponsors, and a few others who had come in, friends of friends. As we all hurried out to sit on the front row, before an absolutely barren podium, save for the dignified and beautiful image—the standing figure of J. Willard Marriott.
>
> [He] gave that night one of the most stirring and heartfelt talks that that little handful of students had ever heard. His topic was: "Think, Work, Pray." I remember the message to this day.
>
> But what I especially remember was the dignity and the grandeur, and the absolute unequivocal Christian compassion that a very important man demonstrated to some very chagrined students. He could have been angry. He could have sulked. He could have exploded. He could have stormed out of the building. He could have reminded everyone of how demanding his schedule was and how far he had traveled, and how monumentally offensive such an experience was. All of that was absolutely true. . . .

But he did not speak one word of any of it. Regardless of how much he may have felt like doing it, he did not do any of it. He spoke as if the whole world were present. And he acted as if this was the greatest compliment and the highest award he could ever be given. It was simply one of the most profound demonstrations of compassion and humility I have ever seen in my life.[7]

Another family member was also gathering accolades that summer. Allie was rising in the ranks of the national Republican Party, becoming the first woman to serve as treasurer for the party's national convention. During the convention in July in San Francisco, the press lauded her as "cool and competent" amidst the pomp and chaos. She had to sign every check—from $3.50 for staples to $35,000 for the use of the Cow Palace convention hall. Arthritis pain in her right hand became significant as she worked through all the banking. Outside the family, no one knew of her struggle.

The convention itself, which saw the nomination of conservative Senator Barry Goldwater, was otherwise an unpleasant experience for the Marriotts. Goldwater fractured the party, leading to the landslide victory of Lyndon Johnson in November.

With each passing week that summer and fall of 1964, J.W. stepped further back from control of the company. Bill was riding a wave of success, and he used it to persuade J.W. that it was time the company became part of the New York Stock Exchange. And if it did, then the company's name would need to change, since it was becoming more identified with the Marriott hotels than Hot Shoppes restaurants. A name change would cause confusion, J.W. argued, so Bill proposed and J.W. approved an intermediate moniker, "Marriott-Hot Shoppes, Inc."

Though he had made a few missteps, Bill's swift growth in the EVP job and widely acknowledged leadership success prompted board member Don Mitchell to persistently pose a question to J.W. throughout

J.W. Marriott, chairman, and Bill Marriott, president.

October: "Is there any good reason to wait any longer to make Bill the president?" J.W. could not come up with one.

As chairman of the board and CEO, J.W. would still have ultimate control of the company, but he warmed to the idea of letting go of the day-to-day responsibilities. He made the decision; he would step away as president during the November 10 annual shareholders' meeting and nominate his thirty-two-year-old son to take his place. Asked by a reporter later what it was like to turn his life's work over to his son, J.W. replied: "Great—it was the greatest thrill I've ever had. Besides, I didn't want to work so hard anymore."[8]

The shareholders' meeting was held at the Twin Bridges Marriott. First, the shareholders approved the change in the company name to Marriott-Hot Shoppes, Inc. Then, a beaming and emotional J.W. stood up to read a short, prepared statement that would change the company forever:

For nearly four decades, I have headed our company's operations, and—with the help of many dedicated, talented people—I have been privileged to see the business grow from a small root beer stand to a major national chain with annual sales which are now approaching the $90 million level.

I feel it is my responsibility to shareholders to turn over the active management of the company to a younger man.

Our Board of Directors feels that the outstanding job done by J. W. Marriott, Jr., both as executive vice president of Marriott-Hot Shoppes and as president of our Marriott Motor Hotels Division has qualified him to assume the responsibilities of president of the corporation.

However, I expect to be around for a long time as Chairman of the Board to assist in every way I can to be helpful to the continued growth and development of our company.

From the podium, J.W. looked down into the hundreds of upturned faces. Attendants stood by in the aisles with portable microphones for stockholders wishing to ask questions or offer opinions.

"Any discussion?" J.W. asked. The attendants scanned the audience; no one moved.

"All in favor raise your right hands."

Every right hand in the audience went up. Some raised both hands. On the platform where the corporate officers sat, everyone stood up. The stockholders broke into cheers. Arms outstretched, J.W. and Allie surrounded their son.[9]

CHAPTER 9

NO TIME FOR SERGEANTS

In his first year as president, Bill Marriott opened a hotel that put the company on the map and would eventually lead him to become the world's foremost hotelier. It was located in downtown Atlanta, and in the early 1960s it was a $12-million gamble for Bill, who had built his first four motor hotels in suburban locations.

He first got the idea during a stopover in Atlanta, where he had a conversation with a motel owner who bragged that his motel was running at 100 percent occupancy year-round. Bill realized that the city needed a first-class convention hotel, and he determined to build it. The site he chose was the beginning of the gamble—a piece of land in Buttermilk Bottom, a home to drunks and homeless people. Jim Durbin said, "After we opened the hotel, we still had to go out every morning and clean up the whiskey bottles that were on the street in front of the hotel."

Most of the hotels Bill proposed prompted intense battles with his father, who hated debt. But Atlanta was an exception. J.W. was persuaded that Atlanta was a thriving city on the way up, with little competition in the hotel market, although he was taken aback by the scope of the project—$12 million and 500 rooms. Bill needed a marketing team to fill those rooms, so he raided the Hilton Hotels chain. "I took all the Hilton people I could get my hands on."

Bill already had on his staff Winthrop W. "Bud" Grice, an indefatigable, P.T. Barnum type who, along with Bus Ryan and Bill Tiefel, became the nucleus of Bill's hotel marketing team.

In anticipation of the Atlanta opening, they did millions of dollars in presales to guarantee that the hotel would be booked for months to come. The guests at the grand opening in 1965 did not know that the hotel was not quite finished. Ryan said, "The whole back end wasn't finished—it was raw concrete. So we draped things off and put flowers everywhere so nobody could tell." Except Grice made a mistake while leading one tour of VIPs when he pulled back a drape to show them a ballroom, and it was still under construction. "He recovered so quickly that he persuaded them our presales had been so successful that we were already building our expansion," Ryan recalled.

Years later, *Business Atlanta* praised Bill's "bold bet" when he chose the city for his small company's disproportionately large investment.[1] Ryan summarized the nature of the gamble: "When Bill opened Atlanta, it was a big hotel for our little company. At that particular time, for us, it was like a canary giving birth to an elephant."

On the food side of the business, J.W. was slow to recognize the serious competition McDonald's fast-food franchises created for Hot Shoppes. But Bill understood and answered the challenge with the company's first fast-food restaurants, which opened just three months after Bill became president. A 1974 profile on J.W. in the *Washington Post* said his failure to see the fast-food trend coming was "proof that he had lost his touch, that he passed the torch to his son none too soon."[2]

By the time Bill became executive vice president in January 1964, McDonald's had made significant inroads into Hot Shoppes' customer base. The local McDonald's franchisees were spending a whopping $500,000 in advertising alone. "They advertised price and they advertised convenience, and we couldn't offer either one. We had to do something," Bill said. The first thing he did was fast-track a concept that had been kicked around for a takeout-only "Junior Hot Shoppes." Younger brother Dick, who was attending Harvard Business School, backed Bill with a detailed paper on the subject. J.W. bowed to both his sons and gave Bill the green light.

Bill settled on Stouffer's food service executive Peter Plamondon to run the Junior Hot Shoppes experiment. Plamondon had already met J.W. and Allie. He and the Ryans had visited Lake Winnipesaukee, where, Ryan recalled, "We sat in the living room after dinner. Mrs. Marriott was darning socks, and Mr. Marriott was in his slippers. It was an incredible experience. The Marriotts took you in as family." Ryan, who had worked for Hilton, thought at the time, "I never sat around with Conard Hilton in his slippers at his place." Plamondon thought, "I've got to join this company!"

Bill has often said, "We just copied the McDonald's menu," but Marriott was actually much more innovative than he remembered. At the time, McDonald's was still offering only one meat, the 15-cent hamburger. But Bill and Plamondon came up with a three-meat menu for the Junior Hot Shoppes. For beef, they had the Royalburger, a double-decker cheeseburger which was really the Mighty Mo without the lettuce. (Not until four years later did McDonald's roll out the Big Mac.) They also had fried fish on a bun. A similar sandwich was being offered on Fridays by the McDonald's Cincinnati franchisee in an effort to capture its large Catholic population. But McDonald's founder Ray Kroc wrote that he "did not want any damned fish stinking up our restaurants." He refused to adopt the Filet-O-Fish nationally—until after Junior Hot Shoppes proved they were popular on every day of the week. Finally, Hot Shoppes added "Pappy Parker's Smoky Mountain Fried Chicken" to the menu. This was nearly two decades before McDonald's added Chicken McNuggets in 1982.[3]

Several hundred well-wishers showed up in a heavy snowstorm on January 30, 1965, for the opening of the first Junior Hot Shoppe

A Junior Hot Shoppe in 1965.

in the southeast D.C. suburb of Marlow Heights. A planeload of top McDonald's executives flew in and observed the business for hours.

J.W. was not happy that the new restaurant was only a walk-up. "This is ridiculous. Put a dining room in," he said. That resulted in an argument with Bill, who said, "I can't afford to put in dining rooms. We're trying to compete with McDonald's, and they don't have dining rooms."

"They will," J.W. replied. On this, Bill wisely bowed to his father's wishes, and for every subsequent Junior Hot Shoppe, he added indoor seating. It was their biggest innovation yet—becoming the first national fast-food chain to add indoor seating—and J.W. deserved the credit. Within a year, McDonald's mimicked the Juniors. In fact, Ray Kroc hired the same contractor who had built the Junior Hot Shoppes to convert more than 100 of his McDonald's for indoor seating.

Bill added one more innovation, an invention well ahead of his competitors. It was a cash register with preset keys—such as one labeled "Hamburger"—that automatically entered the price. When National Cash Register began selling the Marriott-spawned registers to the company's competitors, Bill filed a patent lawsuit. Though it was established that the register had been a Marriott brainchild, the court ruled in favor of NCR, which had engineered the actual equipment.

Dozens more Junior Hot Shoppes were constructed in D.C., Maryland, Virginia, Pennsylvania, and Texas. J.W. showed up for the opening of the fiftieth because it was right across the street from the River Road headquarters. He would frequently eat there, particularly if he had grandchildren in tow.

Overall, the Juniors were a great success, but the chain was launched with a fatal flaw. "We got off the ground well," Plamondon said. "We caught the curve at the right time. We had great real estate, a fine concept, and better products than McDonald's. We became more successful, in fact, than full-service Hot Shoppe restaurants. What we missed was the franchising component." J.W. refused to turn the restaurants over to franchisees, fearing they would not maintain his high standards. The only other option was a massive Marriott capital infusion to build a nationwide chain of company-owned Juniors. But then, the company would never have had the capital to keep building hotels. "There just wasn't enough money to do both," Bill said, "nor was there enough executive talent to carry both out. So we had to choose which road to go. I felt we could make more money in the hotel business than we could make in the restaurant business, so that's the way we went."

A company is known by the people it keeps. Bill searched for and cultivated talent not only in the executive ranks of competing hotel chains but in the trenches, too. John Randolph had been just sixteen when he joined Hot Shoppes in 1930 (two years before Bill's birth) making tamales in the basement of the Connecticut Avenue Hot Shoppe. When he was promoted "upstairs" to the dining room as a busboy, he earned extra money on the side babysitting young Bill.

In the 1940s, J.W. moved to stave off possible unionizing efforts by appointing Randolph to a management position as the company's personnel representative, a rare position for an African-American in those days. "His job was to listen to the hourly employees' troubles and grievances and resolve them, or give them to my dad to resolve," said Bill. "The general managers were scared to death of him because they knew he had direct access to my dad."

Randolph was beloved by the workers because they knew they could count on him in any emergency. If the problem was financial, he would tip off J.W., who frequently and secretly paid for health-care costs not covered by the employee medical plan. Randolph found apartments and houses for employees and visited hospital rooms to offer solace. He planned employee funerals—and even the funerals of some of their spouses and other relatives. J.W. bought Randolph a conservative black Chevrolet sedan so he would be appropriately outfitted for funerals.

Another longtime employee was Bill's first boss, seventy-four-year-old Iva de Freese Savage, director of the test kitchen and quality control. Savage first learned to cook at the age of twelve in Piedmont, Alabama, when her mother went blind. She graduated from the Alabama College for Women with a home economics degree and took her skills north, eventually landing a bakery job with Hot Shoppes.

Most famously at the company, it was Iva Savage who came up with the Mighty Mo and the signature strawberry pie, but she also created winning recipes for onion rings, shrimp Creole, breaded veal cutlets, chicken noodle soup, and many other dishes. She was highly attuned to the economics of her recipes. If a dish called for five shrimp and six were served, that could be the difference between profit and loss on that meal. Every recipe was broken down to its smallest detail per portion, even for parsley garnish. Her recipes were distributed to every Marriott chef and manager, all of whom had to attend her "food school." Under no circumstances was a chef to deviate by so much as a pinch of salt from the original recipe. After she was crippled by an auto accident at the age of seventy-nine, Iva told Bill it was time for her to retire. He reluctantly accepted her resignation, but before she died at ninety-six, she joined Bill to launch a "Back to Basics" program that stressed many of her recipes and quality standards.

Hanging on to faithful lifetime employees was a pleasure; firing nonperformers was the bane of J.W.'s existence, and thus he was relieved to hand off that chore to his son. "Dad would not fire people," said Bill. "He would yell and scream at them and then he'd give them a raise. That's just the way he was." The problem was that "many had started with the business when it was only $200,000 a year and now we were an $80 million business," Bill added. "Some of them were in way over their heads. They had really made a great contribution, but the company had outgrown their abilities."

Although the terminations were necessary, it was an agonizing period for Bill because among the approximately thirty-five managers Bill discharged were friends and relatives. One executive recalled Bill being "physically sick" during the pink-slip period. Another executive observed: "He was young, and a lot of the people he was letting go had changed his diapers." The worst aspect of Bill's layoffs included the forced retirement of his own uncles. They had become multimillionaires, which made it an easier pill to swallow, but it did not relieve the strain on Bill.

First to get notice was Paul Marriott. His heavy drinking had led to serious slippage in his executive capabilities. Paul knew it was coming, and he took it well when Bill asked him to retire in 1965. The termination of Woody Marriott was a much more difficult proposition. Fourteen years younger than J.W., Woody believed for many years that he would be his older brother's successor. That made for strained relations with Bill as Woody tried to protect his turf as vice president of restaurant operations. He had been in command of almost every division of the company except hotels, but the company was outgrowing his skills.

By the end of Bill's first year as president, he let Woody know that he was being "retired" from his position over restaurants. But then J.W. promoted him to "senior vice president" and gave him a raise. Woody had no specific duties other than to offer advice and represent the company at various ceremonial events. Then, in 1967, J.W. put Woody on the board of directors. His previous bitterness toward Bill seemed to have dissipated, and not once did he vote against Bill at a board meeting.

The retirement of Uncle Russell Marriott, eleven years younger than J.W., was the most drama-free and consensual departure. Russell was an upstanding man, but he did not have the drive of any of his three brothers. When Bill sat down with fifty-four-year-old Russell in 1965, he pointed out all the good qualities he admired in his uncle, but indicated that Russell had risen as high as he could in the company and appeared to lack enthusiasm for the job. Russell agreed, and he was not upset when Bill asked him to informally step down. He was allowed to stay on the company roster, but would not be required to go to work.

In his early years as president, Bill realized that the looming presence of J.W. was a force to be reckoned with and possibly a drag on Bill's ambitious plans to acquire more hotels. The reality was, J.W. couldn't stop his son. "I knew he wouldn't fire me and he knew I wouldn't quit. He would not have allowed anybody else to put the company at risk to build multiple hotels. It wasn't in his makeup." J.W. wrote privately of his doubts at the end of Bill's first year as president: "Management has stars in their eyes. They are dreamers."[4]

Jim Durbin, who observed the father-son relationship up close, said J.W. was a "devil's advocate" who delighted in "the role of Monday morning quarterback critiques. But as the chairman, he had line-item veto rights, and he used them. Bill would debate and debate and get a quasi-yes and he'd get a little further and then the Chairman would rethink it again and come back with more debate. 'Don't bankrupt me!' he would tell Bill."

When J.W. prevailed, the results could be long-term, as with the time J.W. stood in the way of Bill buying a second hotel in Atlanta. The John Portman–designed hotel with the industry's first signature atrium went to Hyatt. Perhaps no other hotel in American history had more of an impact on the entire industry as did the iconic Atlanta Hyatt Regency. "At the time, Hyatt was a second-class motel outfit. But when the Regency opened, a steady stream of people passed through the hotel simply to stand in the 'Awesome!' spot in the lobby," said Bill. "In no time, almost every major city wanted a similar showplace hotel—and cities were lining up to pay for them. Hyatt Regencies soon sprouted up in key markets around the country."

For many years, Bill confessed in speeches that passing on the Atlanta project was one of the worst decisions he and the company had ever made because it allowed Hyatt to become a tough competitor.

When J.W. first saw the 5.2-acre site in New Jersey where Bill wanted to erect the sixth Marriott Motor Hotel, he had a hard time believing his son was serious. It looked like the middle of nowhere. Across the street were a barn, a couple of chicken coops, and a cow. He could not get over that cow. Whenever Bill's hotel people mentioned the Saddle Brook hotel project within J.W.'s earshot, he would interject, "Isn't that the place with the cow?"

Where J.W. saw a cow, Bill saw enormous potential—close to New York City with plenty of regional office buildings in the area. J.W. obligingly attended the hotel opening, but he wasn't in a good mood since nearby I-80 was still unfinished and the cow was still living across the street. J.W. continued to consider it a risky proposition, but he was wrong. "Pound for pound, it was the most profitable hotel we had in the first twenty years because it was small," Bill said. "We had more than 90 percent occupancy from the day it opened. It just went like gangbusters."

Less than a year after Saddle Brook opened, J.W. was fully occupied trying to help his friend George Romney get elected president of the United States. Since Bill was handling the Marriott business, J.W. had both the time and energy to throw himself into the organization of Romney's presidential campaign. Romney was governor of Michigan, and his staff and presidential campaign advisers clashed throughout 1966—a period when J.W. was one of the few voices of reason. Bill was too busy to join in the Romney effort, but he was concerned about the stress on his father, which became most evident in late November as the Romneys and Marriotts vacationed together in Puerto Rico for Thanksgiving.

On a previous Puerto Rican vacation with the Romneys, Bill had been swept into Romney's frenetic lifestyle when J.W. and Bill had played a round of golf with him. Romney's friends called it "compact golf." Instead of playing one ball for eighteen holes in leisurely fashion, Romney played two or three balls at the same time, proceeding on the run from one to another, for at least six holes. Both J.W. and Bill kept up for a while but then let Romney move ahead on his own.

During the Thanksgiving 1966 vacation, Bill could see what a strain Romney's demands were putting on J.W., so he cautioned his father to take a backseat on the campaign. But J.W. was too committed to disengage from what he saw as a righteous cause, and an exciting one. It was a heady thing for the sheepherder from Utah to find himself not only a witness but a participant in historic events.

On January 17, 1967, J.W. was at home when he had a near-fatal heart attack. He was hospitalized for a week. Not until a decade later, when J.W.'s 1977 biography was published, did Romney realize the role of the campaign in J.W.'s crisis. He wrote J.W. then, "Until I read your biography, I did not know the magnitude of your giving and friendship. Not until then did I know your support and involvement in my Presidential campaign could have cost you your life."

Romney's wife, Lenore, wrote, "How does one say 'Thank you' when another has risked his very all? George is quite shaken—and I am also—and we both want you to know how deep is our appreciation—and our remorse."

J.W. responded with grace: "I appreciate all the nice things you said in your letter . . . but your campaign was a very exciting thing while it lasted. Unfortunately, I did get very sick, but that probably would have happened anyway."[5]

• • •

Robert C. Wian was only twenty-two years old in 1936 when he opened his first restaurant and what would eventually become the "Bob's Big Boy" chain. Though he was an innovative entrepreneur, Wian was not a first-rate businessman, which frustrated his board of directors. So, when Bill went to Los Angeles in late 1966 looking for a deal with Big Boy, Wian was receptive. "I had never been involved in a big acquisition of anything before," Bill recalled. "I was on my own. I was thirty-four years old and I was dealing in the big leagues."

Bill negotiated a complex stock purchase that resulted in paying the equivalent of $7 million for twenty-three Bob's Big Boys in Southern California and a franchise program of 580 more restaurants in thirty-eight states. The deal closed in May 1967 and included a seat for Wian on the Marriott board of directors.

J.W., who had supported the deal, was upset when he learned that Bill had kept Wian as president of Big Boy at his old salary, which was higher than J.W.'s. Forced to mollify his father, Bill went back to Wian and asked if he would agree to a salary cut to "even things out" in the merger; he reluctantly agreed. J.W. was also miffed that the fifty-three-year-old Wian set his own hours, which amounted to part-time. Wian was at the stage where he was not interested in keeping up with the Marriotts, but he didn't fully realize it until May 1968, after a four-hour tour with Bill of possible restaurant sites. After the two men had looked at twenty possible sites in one day, Bill said, "We've got all the money you need. Let's build them all!" Within a few days, Wian resigned as a board member and Big Boy president.

The purchase of Big Boy connected Bill to a network of experienced franchisees who were full of ideas regarding the fast-food business. A couple of them had started a small Fort Wayne, Indiana, roast-beef restaurant chain called RoBee's, and they wondered if Bill would be interested in buying them out for $1.25 million. He did, though J.W. was skeptical. "Big speculation in my book," he groused in his journal.[6] Bill saw only one significant roast-beef competitor—Arby's—which had already launched a trademark lawsuit against RoBee's for the "phonetic similarity" of their name. Bill decided a new name and a celebrity endorsement were needed. Thus began his business relationship with Roy Rogers, the singing cowboy of the silver screen.

Rogers—who at one time had his name on more than 400 products, second only to Walt Disney—signed an agreement with Marriott in 1968; it was one of the best bargains Bill ever made. Rogers was paid a $100,000 signing fee, plus $300 per year for each restaurant in operation for the first ten years of the agreement. For $2,500 a day plus expenses, he would make whatever promotional appearances Marriott requested and would also do TV and radio commercials. More than 100 Roy Rogers restaurants were operating by the end of that first year.

In 1967, Marriott bought Arizona's legendary Camelback Inn in Scottsdale, Arizona. It was a desert playground for the rich and famous, including the Marriotts, who began vacationing there when Bill was sixteen. When he got a tip it was for sale, he quickly cut a deal for $2.7 million, and then called his mother.

"How would you like to own Camelback Inn?" Bill asked her.

"Oh, I can't believe it!" Allie excitedly responded.

"It's true," Bill confirmed. "We're going to have it."

Although Allie was thrilled, J.W. was not. He loved staying at the Camelback Inn, but he didn't think it was a good idea to buy a resort that was open only eight months of the year, from September to May. J.W. stewed about the deal and then "gave Bill a fit," Donna recalled.

During the negotiations, J.W. called Bill and ordered him not to buy the resort. It was too expensive. The next morning, Bill was at a breakfast meeting near the resort when a waiter summoned him to the phone. It was J.W. "What are you going to do about Camelback?" he demanded.

"Well, you told me not to do it."

The Camelback Inn and grounds.

"I've decided you can do what you damn please!" said J.W., and then he hung up.

Later, when Bill turned the final negotiations over to Jim Durbin, J.W. tried to enlist Durbin's aid to stop the deal. But Durbin pulled a fast one. "I told the chairman [J.W.], 'If we don't buy it, Del Webb's going to buy it tomorrow,'" Durbin recalled. It was not true, but it worked. "That old competitive instinct came out in the chairman. He had his wife call me back because he was ill. 'My husband says go ahead and buy it, Jim.'"

From the first, Bill knew he might have an uphill battle keeping the resort's most loyal guests. The Marriotts were not well-known in the West at the time, nor among the jet-setting, upper-crust clientele. It didn't help that a local newspaper headlined the acquisition, "Hamburger chain buys famous resort." But in a few short months, Marriott won over the frequent guests by preserving the atmosphere of the resort while spending millions for badly needed upgrades.

In the spring of 1968, Bill took his family to Camelback for a ten-day vacation and celebration of his birthday—a tradition that would continue for the next half century. J.W. and Allie were already there when Bill, Donna, and the children arrived. That 1968 vacation for J.W. and Allie lasted two months, and they returned for one to four months every subsequent year. In spite of J.W.'s initial opposition, Bill said, "Dad loved owning that hotel, and he loved living there. I think it added ten years to his life."

After his January 1967 heart attack, J.W. did not return to the office for four months, and then he worked part-time. He reengaged with the Romney for President campaign, but in a more behind-the-scenes role. By June, he complained in his journal that only he and investment banker Cliff Folger were funding Romney's campaign, and that had to change. He made plans for a high-powered campaign kickoff event.

The biggest hoopla the Marriotts experienced at their Lake Winnipesaukee summer complex occurred during the official four-day Romney campaign kickoff, which started on the evening of July 4, 1967. More than 200 supporters greeted Romney's plane at Laconia Airport on the lakeshore. Bill came by car and J.W. by boat to deliver the dignitaries to the Marriott lake house. The following morning, Romney held a press conference on J.W.'s porch. Allie complained, "Newsmen everywhere—trampling over my flower beds!" Having spent days preparing for the extravaganza, an exhausted J.W. snuck over to Bill's house that afternoon and slept for several hours. In the evening, the Marriotts held a reception for 250 people.

The next day, a high-powered lunch with a dozen top Republicans was held in the den, with Allie serving lasagna. Another reception followed, this time involving nearly 100 New England newspaper editors and owners, along with their spouses. J.W. snuck away for a nap again. Two more days of receptions and press conferences followed.

For several months, Romney was the clear Republican front-runner—until the media began incessantly replaying his claim that he had been "brainwashed" by U.S. diplomats and generals during a visit to the Vietnam war zone. In frustration, J.W. wrote Romney privately with advice: "Don't have a news conference unless you have something newsworthy. All they do is rehash Vietnam and brainwash, and you must know by now they want you on the cross. You are too good for most of them."[7] The Vietnam remark proved too difficult for the candidate to overcome. "George's Waterloo," J.W. called it, but he hung in there with his friend.

On December 20, J.W. was meeting with Romney's campaign manager when a sharp pain hit him in the head and neck. It had not been a heart attack, but several days of testing could not determine the cause. The day after Christmas, a frustrated Bill called in a neurosurgeon, who determined that a blood vessel had burst in J.W.'s brain. On December 28, Ellen Marriott, J.W.'s mother and Bill's grandmother, died in Utah at the age of ninety-nine. Because he was still hospitalized, J.W. couldn't attend the funeral.

Two months later, Romney's presidential campaign ended. The man who had lost the 1960 presidential election—Richard M. Nixon—staged a comeback and surged past Romney in the Republican primary. In November 1968, he defeated Vice President Hubert Humphrey, the Democratic candidate, and won the presidency.

• • •

Bill was determined to be a different kind of father than his dad had been. "My dad was very hard on me and Dick. And consequently, I was not as tough on my kids. I wanted to create a relationship. Of course I would tell them the things they should not do, and give them rules, but by and large, I let them alone. I let them do their own thing. I decided to love them."

Being a father and running a major corporation in his thirties was a serious challenge, and it required sacrifice and scheduling. If he was in town, Bill was always home for breakfast and dinner. Saturdays were the children's days. He took them to see the ships and the U.S. Naval Academy at Annapolis or to watch boat races on the Potomac River.

Typical of that era, when the children misbehaved, Mom threatened: "Just wait until your father gets home." Bill was the disciplinarian. Once, when John was six, Bill put the disobedient boy over his knee for a spanking. Bill had barely commenced the discipline when John bit him in the thigh. Bill was so shocked that he tossed the boy off. After a second or two of stunned silence, "we all started laughing so hard, including Dad," Debbie recalled. "We all had a good laugh and that was the end of it."

"Dad didn't get mad very often, and when he did, it was usually because of Grandpa. But one night, he got mad at me," Debbie said. "I was a night owl and I would always sneak back downstairs. He'd chase me back upstairs, but one night it made him mad, and he told me so. Before I fell asleep, he came back upstairs and sat on my bed and apologized. From him, I learned, it's okay to tell your kids you're sorry, and you're human."

Throughout the children's growing-up years, the Marriotts kept their modest Kenwood home. Bill wanted his friends and fellow Church members to feel comfortable, not awed, when they came to his house. Both he and Donna believed their children could be raised more normally if they were not living in a mansion. Though the Marriotts could afford it, neither a nanny nor a cook was hired during the family's early years.

Stephen recalled, "We all had to have our toys picked up and everything ready for my dad to come home for dinner because my dad and grandfather often fought. If we were ready, that wouldn't spill over into being upset with us when he came home from work." Donna confirmed her son's memory. "The friction between their grandpa and dad made things a little tougher at home than they might have been otherwise. There were times he'd come home very distraught, and he wasn't as patient then as he might have been otherwise."

After dinner, Bill would retire to his den to work, but he had an open-door policy for the kids. It was in that den that they received some of their most treasured encouragement and counsel. "He made us feel like we were the most important people in his life," Debbie said.

She remembered only one fight her parents had. "It was over a piece of banana cake. I was eight. Ten hours a day he'd work, and then bring four or five hours of paperwork home. He was so busy that night he wouldn't come back to the table for dessert. Mom was upset. She got her bags out; she was going home to her mother. Dad started to laugh. I thought it was the end of the world. He put his arms around her and told her he loved her. It was so stupid, like happens in every marriage. Otherwise, they never fought. They were always affectionate, held hands and all that stuff, which was great for us to see. It also lent a lot of security to our home, especially when he wasn't there as much."

Two years younger than Debbie, Stephen was a temperamental child. In retrospect, it's likely that Stephen's temper and fits of anger were the early symptoms of health issues that would eventually rob him of his hearing, his sight, his ability to walk, and, ultimately, his life. The bouts of anger began when he was a baby. As he grew, Stephen became a holy terror, to his sister in particular. One night while young Debbie was setting the table, he hit her over the head with her favorite Jack and Jill radio, which sent her to the hospital for stitches. Twice when they were with a babysitter, Stephen became furious that Debbie wouldn't let him play with her friends. The first time it happened, he went out to the garage and hammered the fenders of her bike. The second time, he threw a knife at Debbie, which missed by inches and stuck into the wall.

Bill and Donna were beside themselves in handling this unpredictable son, even consulting a child psychiatrist at one point. "All the shrink said was, 'He is carrying a lot of anger,'" Bill recalled. "As we reflect on it, we believe he didn't know how to express himself otherwise when he was not feeling well." Yet Stephen grew up to be perhaps the most spiritually inclined of the Marriott children. Once, while visiting the Garff grandparents in Salt Lake City, eight-year-old Stephen and six-year-old John were playing together outside and drank water from a garden hose. Their uncle Dennis, a practical joker, rushed out with pretended alarm and told them the exterminator had just been there, which meant the hose water had not been flushed and was still poisoned.

"You only have five minutes to live," he told them. John ran into the bathroom and stuck his finger down his throat. Stephen fell to his knees and begged God to let him live, promising to serve Him all the days of his life, if his life was spared.

Grandpa J.W. Marriott had a soft spot for his namesake grandson, little Johnny. In many ways, John was more like his grandfather than like his father, Bill. "I always had a hard time communicating with my dad over the years," John said. "I was more like my grandfather. I liked the outdoors. I liked to have an honest debate and dialogue about important things and be challenged and to challenge others. My dad didn't like to argue with me. He got frustrated and felt challenged. He took it personally, as a criticism, which was not the way I meant it."

New Hampshire was the only place where Bill would relax. That was never more true than after the summer of 1970, when Bill bought a sleek, baby-blue, thirty-four-foot Donzi Express Cruiser speedboat. Even J.W. was impressed with it, particularly after he raced his son and lost. "Bill's goes 55 m.p.h., mine 50," he lamented.[8]

The Lake Winnipesaukee summers proved to have such a gravitational pull that every one of Bill's children established homes there, and *their* children are hoping to build houses for their own young families.

CHAPTER 10

RISKY BUSINESS

Midway Airport had been Chicago's primary airport for more than a decade when J.W. built an in-flight catering kitchen there in 1956. Six years later, when all commercial traffic was shifted to O'Hare Airport, Marriott followed, building a kitchen just for its American Airlines contract. When Bill inspected the new kitchen, he resolved to build a hotel next to what was then the world's busiest airport.

It may be hard for readers in the twenty-first century to realize that there was a time when the Marriott name was not known in most of America, much less the world. After the ground breaking for a Marriott in Chicago in 1966, advertising man Aaron Cushman heard about the planned hotel and asked around, "What's a Marriott?" No one seemed to know, Cushman wrote in his memoir. "The best answer I could get was that they were a tiny company headquartered somewhere in the East."

Bill hired Cushman, who visited the company's Maryland headquarters and began to work closely with Marriott's team in Chicago. The jaded Chicago ad man became a Marriott convert. "They had some very unusual characteristics. These people really cared. They were motivated like no one I had ever met before—they were a different breed of cat. They loved what they were doing and absolutely ignored the hours they poured into the job."

Cushman and his firm worked hard to successfully secure daily mentions or photos of the Marriott hotel project, but Bill balked at his plans for grand opening stunts. "After investing millions of dollars, I don't understand why I can't just open the door and walk in—or routinely cut a ribbon," Bill complained to Cushman during a Chicago taxi ride.

"You *could* do that," Cushman allowed, "but you won't get more than a couple of columns on the real estate page. We need to excite the newsmen to leave their downtown desks and get us a photograph on the front or back page of every daily paper and 30 seconds of TV footage on the evening news."[1]

Bill approved the plans, and it worked. For the December 1967 opening of Marriott's eighth hotel, voluptuous beauties dressed as mermaids surrounded the ribbon cutters next to a then-novel year-round indoor-outdoor pool. A giant six-foot replica of a hotel key was inserted into a twelve-foot mock-up of the real main entrance, then hoisted aloft by helicopter and symbolically dropped into Lake Michigan, signifying Marriott's permanent open-door policy.

Prior to the grand opening, when the hotel advertised for job seekers, more than 2,000 people showed up, forming a line around the hotel more than a block long. Among the hopeful applicants was a blind man, John McDonald, a father of four. He had already applied to and been rejected by more than fifty companies. Marriott hired him to be a silverware sorter in the hotel kitchen. He surprised everyone with his rapid and efficient sorting.

In a 1982 speech, Bill fondly related: "Whenever I can, I like to visit our hotel at O'Hare Airport in Chicago. Each time I do, I enjoy chatting with John. [He] has a perfect attendance record—no easy task because he has to get up at 4:30 a.m. to catch a bus each working day. That dish room is one of the best in our company. John always has a big smile, and constantly inspires others with his diligence, enthusiasm, and hard work. He's been a great motivator for me personally. Sometimes when I'm on the run and I ask myself if all the hassle is worth it, I think of John in Chicago, cheerfully sorting silver that he will never see. So I go ahead with the task at hand."[2]

At the same time that Bill was building new hotels, he was also adding rooms to his older hotels. When it came to a projected twelve-story tower at Key Bridge, he found himself in the middle of a heated environmental controversy—even as Lady Bird Johnson was praising his support of her beautification initiative.

The First Lady was a fan of Hot Shoppes because her two daughters were. One of Luci Johnson's close friends was a waitress at the Twin Bridges restaurant, so she frequently stopped in for a Mighty Mo hamburger and chocolate milkshake. When sister Lynda wanted to have a private talk with her mom, she persuaded Lady Bird to go to a Hot Shoppe drive-in for lunch in a nondescript car. Newspaper columnist Betty Beale wrote of such outings: "This is the most private way that the mother and daughter can eat together without being disturbed by telephone calls or any of the other frequent White House interruptions."[3]

Lady Bird also appreciated the landscaping Marriott had donated for the traffic circle in front of the Key Bridge hotel, and she wrote to tell Bill so: "How generous you have been to give so much beauty to the Rosslyn circle area of this city!" she said in a June 1966 letter.

Only a few months later, an Arlington, Virginia, citizens group protested what they considered to be Marriott's unsightly plans to add the twelve-story tower at Key Bridge, raising the existing two large neon Marriott signs to the top. The Arlington County Planning Commission had approved the plans and refused to back down, even after Senator Bobby Kennedy and Interior Secretary Stewart Udall entered the fray. Udall derided Marriott's plans for a "garish commercial intrusion" to the Potomac riverfront. Intent on being a good neighbor,

Bill wrote Secretary Udall that he would reconsider the matter. The company would "endeavor to do whatever it can to cooperate with you."

A few weeks later, the First Lady invited Bill and Donna for a bus tour and White House luncheon that would focus on her beautification efforts in the capital city. Bill and Donna were featured in an accompanying photograph as they examined a model of a proposed public school amphitheater. "Bill Marriott says he feels peculiar going to the White House for lunch when he still hasn't changed his mind about putting a 14 by 47 foot neon sign atop the addition to the Key Bridge Marriott," one article noted.[4]

By the time Bill opened the addition in 1970, he had muted the controversy by shrinking the size of the sign and dimming the neon. In time, even that twelve-story building would be dwarfed by other high-rise buildings, including the prominent *USA Today*-Gannett twin towers.

One of Bill's prime goals as company president was to qualify the company for a prestigious listing on the New York Stock Exchange (NYSE). The path to the listing began in April 1965, when the board of directors approved a 2-for-1 stock split, increasing the total number of shares from roughly two to four million and doubling the number of shares Marriott family members held.

To qualify for the NYSE listing, lawyers and brokers advised Bill and J.W. that the family would have to shed the family-owned real estate companies that leased properties to Marriott-Hot Shoppes (MHS) for hotel and restaurant operations. Neither Bill nor J.W. wanted to spend any MHS capital to buy the real estate companies from the family. Instead, they traded the companies for 249,669 more shares of MHS stock, which substantially increased their holdings a second time. After that, Bill and J.W. thought the family was holding too many shares. So the family put up 500,000 shares in a "secondary stock offering." That still left J.W. and Allie owning nearly 11 percent of the company, and Bill, 7.49 percent. The sale netted J.W. and Allie $3.8

Celebrating the listing of Marriott-Hot Shoppes on the New York Stock Exchange.

million each. The checks for Bill's three uncles ranged from $1 million to nearly $3 million. Having sold the least amount of stock, Bill received a check for $1,009,375. At the age of thirty-four, he had officially become a cash millionaire, though on paper his net worth had already exceeded that amount.

Just before the NYSE listing, Bill split the Marriott stock 2-for-1 for the third time in less than eight years. On August 26, 1968, Bill, Donna, J.W., and Allie flew to New York City and proudly stood on the VIP balcony when the opening bell rang and their stock—under the tickertape symbol "MHS"—began to sell at 32¾ a share. Bill and J.W. each purchased 100 Marriott shares to kick off the trading.

Because Bill was running the company so well, J.W. had plenty of time in the second half of the 1960s to focus on several projects for The Church of Jesus Christ of Latter-day Saints, the most important of which was the need for a temple in the Washington, D.C., area. Bill concurred wholeheartedly and assisted where he could.

The last time there had been a Latter-day Saint temple east of the Mississippi, it was in Nauvoo, Illinois, and that had been destroyed by arsonists more than a century earlier. On frequent occasions, when J.W. hosted visiting Church leaders, he would take them to several locations that he and other local Church members thought would be good sites for a temple. The tour always ended at the most favored site, in the suburb of Kensington, Maryland—a wooded hill overlooking the Capital Beltway. In 1962, President McKay finally approved the purchase.

One concern for the conservative Church leadership was the explosive Civil Rights movement, in which the nation's capital was the target of protests and riots. The fervent hopes of the Marriotts and other area Church members seemed to be dashed when Washington, D.C., erupted in six days of rioting following the April 1968 assassination of the Reverend Martin Luther King Jr.

Bill's younger brother, Dick, vividly recalled those dark days because he was managing the Langley Park Hot Shoppe. "I remember walking out of the front door on Friday, wondering why we did not have many customers, and then seeing a row of tanks coming down the street. There were big clouds of black smoke in the distance. . . . We were wondering what was going to happen, because we were on the outskirts of a predominantly black neighborhood. We were not sure if we were going to get burned. But we had a lot of wonderful people working at the Hot Shoppes—both black and white."

Local Church leaders responded with compassion. When D.C. Mayor Walter Washington asked for emergency assistance for tens of thousands of victims, the Latter-day Saints responded with what the mayor called the best-organized relief program in the city. Bill himself dispatched dozens of Hot Shoppes trucks with relief donations, including an estimated 185,000 meals. Just weeks after the riots, Apostle Harold B. Lee traveled to Washington on other business and, alarmed

by the devastation and unrest, advised the Marriotts that a temple in Washington would have to wait.

J.W. couldn't wait. Two months after Washington burned, Church leaders asked J.W. if he would consider moving to Salt Lake City to accept a "big job in the Church," meaning a full-time leadership calling. "I [said] I couldn't handle [the] job with responsibility because of my heart trouble—but would give $500,000 for a temple in Washington."[5] It was classic J. Willard Marriott; he changed the subject and offered the Church a huge incentive to proceed with the family's most desired project. The persistent campaign worked. Incredibly, only seven months after the city was in flames, President McKay made the announcement that the Church, which had been founded by New England men and women, would symbolically return to the East with a temple in Washington, D.C. The ground-breaking ceremony that the Marriott family attended that December was a very happy day.

On matters spiritual and personal, the Marriotts were united and loyal. But that harmony often ended at the office door. Disputes between father and son reverberated around the extended family.

The strong-willed and protective Donna Marriott was never going to be her father-in-law's favorite, and she was fine with that. She became a gatekeeper at times for Bill. Sometimes, when the father and son had a conflict at the office, J.W. would try to continue the argument over the phone, interrupting Bill's dinner or family time. Donna would refuse to put Bill on the phone. His father had hounded her husband enough for the day, she said, and she wasn't going to put him through. On a few occasions, when it got particularly acrimonious, Donna would call and ask Allie to intervene, occasionally dangling the possibility that Bill could easily quit the company, start his own business, and leave the aging J.W. in the lurch.

J.W.'s feelings toward his son and corporate heir were deeply complex. He was proud, and yet deep down he had to know that Bill had set the company on a profitable trajectory that J.W. himself had neither

the will nor the vision to do. Often, after Bill received attention or praise in the media, J.W. would pick a fight.

Bill became sensitized to that reality, and, when it was possible, he put his father front and center at events such as hotel grand openings. J.W. enjoyed the limelight and Bill did not, so that worked for both. When J.W. opposed one of Bill's ideas, if Bill waited long enough, J.W. would generally come around and even praise him.

As happens with many aging company founders, J.W. also wrestled with feelings of increasing irrelevance. His expertise was food service, but that industry had a narrow profit margin, while hotel development, with its more substantial growth possibilities, was clearly the wave of the company's future. In that field, Bill had superior knowledge and skill. "My father didn't understand the hotel business, but he thought he did," Bill said. If it appeared that Bill wasn't listening to his advice about the hotels, a frustrated J.W. became louder and more acrimonious. "Talked business with Bill 20 minutes & bad feelings," he wrote in his journal. "I better stay away from business. I shouldn't criticize but I never could tell Bill anything. Guess I'm not diplomatic."[6]

It didn't help that as the company moved forward in the latter part of the twentieth century, J.W.'s mindset was still stuck in the Depression, when hotels failed and when debt began to haunt J.W. like a specter. Friends and family—including Bill—often blamed the sometimes-prickly relationship between father and son on their disagreement over corporate debt. But, as with anything else involving human personalities and a shared family past, there was more to it. Bill's son John, who loved both of them, offered frank insight:

"My dad doesn't vacillate. He decides. My grandfather liked to talk through every decision, worrying about whether it was right or not. Actually, he liked to argue about everything, and my dad didn't. My dad's very sensitive, and he doesn't like to be criticized. Nobody likes to be criticized, but he *really* doesn't like to be criticized. Sometimes he takes suggestions or ideas as personal criticism, when they aren't meant that

way. Now add in his own father, who often intended to criticize my dad. So my grandfather would push his buttons, and dad would go nuts."

This relationship dynamic came to a head on J.W.'s sixty-eighth birthday. After a sleepless night worrying over Bill's hotel expansion plans, J.W. went to the office that day and let Bill have it. It was worse than any previous tirade Bill had endured, so he left the office early, very upset. "He was shaking so much, I thought he was going to have a heart attack," Donna said. A birthday party was planned that night at J.W.'s, but Bill refused to go. J.W. called to apologize. "I wouldn't let him talk to Bill," Donna recalled. "I said, 'You're killing him! You've got to leave him alone.'"

Later that night, J.W. penned a self-aware journal entry:

> Thought of my shortcomings.
>
> The rate at which Bill is going with the business— he signed deals today on large convention hotels, New Orleans, 42 stories, $28 million, and Los Angeles Airport, $25 million. And we are still looking for locations—adding to six present hotels & six more we haven't finished building.
>
> I remember when all big hotels went bankrupt in the '30s. I'm a coward I guess. Don't like debt. No peace with the creditors breathing down your neck.
>
> Still, we are going great now. Bill doing a marvelous job with his team of tigers. I only discourage him. I really should step out & let him go his way—only a weight around his neck.
>
> I lost my temper today with Bill & it made me sick. Gave me a bad headache—which I can't afford. Bill was so depressed & sick he didn't come to my birthday dinner, which made me feel worse.
>
> But I am 68 today & I suppose too old to change—

> to go at Bill's speed. I am a [propeller-driven] DC-3
> vintage. He is a 707 jet.[7]

Two months later, J.W. was offered a diversion. Richard Nixon had been elected president and wanted J.W. to chair his 1969 inaugural festivities. J.W. accepted the post at once, having known Nixon since the 1940s. Bill was elated. The job was a big boost for his dad, whose doldrums evaporated with the prospect of being part of national history. "I was happy to see him divert his energies away from the company, because he was at that time more of a hindrance than a help," Bill said.

Bill and Donna felt duty-bound to attend several inaugural events, in addition to hosting parties for airline executives and others on behalf of the company. Bill's heart swelled with particular pride, though, when he saw his parents sitting behind the Nixons during the swearing-in, and then leading the parade to the White House in the first car, a top-down convertible, with the Mormon Tabernacle Choir not far behind. At a cost of $2.85 million, it was the most expensive inauguration yet—but the bill was entirely covered by private donations and the sale of tickets and souvenirs. Proving J.W. was a captain of private enterprise, the inaugural committee ended up with a surplus of $1,016,000. Throughout the next year, in consultation with First Lady Pat Nixon, J.W. parceled the profits out to worthy civic projects.

While J.W. was diverted by the inauguration, Bill was busy establishing a Marriott presence in New York City, buying and remodeling the venerable old Essex Hotel in the heart of midtown Manhattan along the south border of Central Park. The renamed Marriott Essex House opened in April 1969. In the same way that Conrad Hilton elevated his profile when he bought the Waldorf Astoria, so too did the purchase of the Essex House raise the stature of Marriott's hotel operations.

As part of the deal, Marriott inherited a unionized workforce. Marriott executives estimated that the hotel had about a third more staff than they actually needed—a featherbedding situation that was a

source of ongoing frustration for Bill. He explained to *Forbes* magazine: "At the Essex House, a dishwasher can only wash dishes and a glass-washer [must wash] glasses. The broiler cook cannot cook with the deep-fat fryer. We don't have this in other places. A salad girl can work the salad block for an hour, then turn around to the sandwich block. And if she wants to be a cashier, we'll give her a crack at it, or at being a hostess."[8] Instead of serving their members well, the unions prevented the Essex staff from having the easy upward mobility that occurred in the rest of the Marriott company.

Less than a month after taking over the Essex, Bill took over management of his eleventh hotel, his first outside the United States. It was Acapulco's newest and tallest hotel, the beachfront Acapulco Marriott Paraiso del Pacifico, built by a Mexican millionaire and managed by Marriott. In the 1950s and early 1960s, Acapulco had been a playground for the wealthy, but by the late 1960s, the Paraiso was able to capitalize on a new accessibility to middle-class Mexicans and Americans.

None of Bill's previous hotels proved as difficult or frustrating as his twelfth, which was eight years in the making. In 1961, when Bill had first wanted to build in Boston, he had rejected an expensive downtown location in favor of the Newton suburb. It was a beautiful spot, formerly a park, and Bill wasn't the only one who thought so. But a small group of dedicated Newtonian preservationists rose in protest. Bill had not anticipated any zoning problems and was surprised by the zeal of the local opponents, who delayed the project more than four years, fighting a legal battle all the way to the Superior Court of Massachusetts. Marriott won the case and broke ground in 1967.

For the next two years, J.W. fretted about the $10-million construction price tag and worried over many details. Harry Vincent recalled, "To build the Marriott in Boston at the cost being considered meant you had to have a $100 room rate, which was unheard of when the project began. No hotel could ever command a $100 per room rate, and it was very hard for Bill's father to break out of that mindset, so he resisted that project." The hotel opened with a $125-a-night rate and boasted better than 80 percent occupancy, becoming one of the most reliable stars of the Marriott chain.

Vincent concluded: "J.W. was a wonderful, attentive, conscientious, dedicated person—but not a risk taker. It is absolutely clear to me that the performance of the Marriott corporation in growth, profits, and return to the shareholders has been many-fold more effective under Bill, Jr., than it was or would have been under his father."

A common misperception—even within the Marriott corporation—is that Bill spent most of his time on hotel development after becoming president in 1964. Yet at the time the company was primarily a food-service business. The Hot Shoppe restaurants, Big Boy coffee shops, Roy Rogers fast food outlets, industrial cafeterias, and in-flight catering made up more than two-thirds of the corporate profits. Out of necessity, Bill threw himself into the struggling airline catering business, which provided a third of the company's income.

Because of Uncle Paul Marriott's spotty management, when Bill took over airline catering it was losing $100,000 a year. He discerned early that the best way to beat his competitors was to infuse large amounts of capital for kitchens and to take risks. The contracts with airlines were notoriously breakable. For example, in Bill's first summer as president, Northwest Airlines canceled an agreement with Marriott. "We have just built a $500,000 kitchen and before we get in it, they cancel!" J.W. lamented in his journal.[9] No caterer could win an exclusive agreement to service an entire airline because no caterer had a kitchen to provide fresh food at every one of the airline's airport stops.

Bill felt the greatest potential for airline catering growth was not in the U.S., but overseas. Less than a year after becoming president, he bought Cervesio Catering, which had a monopoly at the Caracas, Venezuela, airport. It was Bill's first experience with foreign employees, and a rocky one at that. He had been impressed with Cervesio's 40

percent profit margin, but then learned that some of that profit came from questionable practices. "They were taking trays off the incoming flights and reusing the food that wasn't eaten. If there was a dessert or a salad that hadn't been touched, they'd stick them on the outgoing flight. We had to put a stop to that." Bill's next overseas acquisition was a Puerto Rican airline caterer. Then he expanded to Italy, Greece, Portugal, and Spain.

The fact that Bill correctly foresaw and prepared for the coming age of jumbo jets gave the company a big head start in servicing them. With the ability to carry more than 360 passengers, the Boeing 747 was going to change the way Marriott In-Flite did things. In short, they would have to meet the challenge of putting together the biggest carry-out operation in the world every time they serviced a 747 flight. He needed more storage and bigger kitchens full of labor-saving devices, and he needed them now. So his team fast-tracked a ninety-day build model that could be reproduced at any airport.

The last big hurdle was devising a truck that could deliver the food modules by hydraulic lifts to the galley doors of the towering 747s. Trucks on the market that might do the job cost $25,000 each, which was too expensive, and they weren't specifically made to off-load food crates. Marriott needed to design and produce its own fleet of special trucks. One day, Bill Martin, director of In-Flite's construction and maintenance, was driving down an expressway behind an American Linen truck. He saw dirty laundry stored on the roof, away from the clean linen in the trailer. Eureka! At only $15,500 each, Marriott soon had a truck with a back elevator and a wider deck that permitted efficient loading across the roof of the deck.

Pan American Airways launched the first 747 service route in the United States on February 4, 1969, from the San Juan airport. That day, Marriott became the first independent airline caterer to supply a 747. Marriott quickly established a reputation as the fastest and most efficient jumbo jet supplier, and the contracts multiplied rapidly.

Marriott's In-Flite division also became the first caterer for the Auto-Train food service between Florida and Virginia.

After a decade of hard work and close attention to the In-Flite Division, Bill had produced significant results. He had secured one-quarter of the domestic market. By the end of 1974, he had made significant inroads into Europe, adding London and Frankfurt kitchens. In Africa and Asia, he had opened facilities in Johannesburg and Guam. Bill had clearly launched In-Flite on a path that would soon make it the largest and most dominant airline caterer in the world.

Bill's business expansion required him to hobnob with government agencies and politicians, but, unlike his father, he kept a professional distance. Nixon made Bill a member of the president's Advisory Council for Minority Enterprise based on Marriott's own much-praised program for advancing minority employees up the corporate ladder. Bill took the advisory council position seriously and used it to lobby the president for breaks for minority business owners.

The president only "lobbied" the Marriotts once. In a private meeting in the Oval Office, Nixon asked the Marriotts to hire and keep an eye on his younger brother, Donald. He was an inveterate wheeler-dealer with a penchant for embarrassing his brother. Though the Marriott name does not appear on the president's official schedule for that day in December 1969, Bill later confided details of the meeting to friend and syndicated columnist Jack Anderson. Anderson summarized it thus: "Delicately, the President asked the Marriotts to keep his brother out of trouble. 'I want to be sure that Don has no dealings with the federal government,' said the President. 'I want to be sure that Don is never asked to do anything that would embarrass this office.' Then the President added as an afterthought: 'Don is the best salesman in the Nixon family.' The Marriotts agreed to watch over Donald."[10]

Bill was actually amenable to the hire. Several years before, one national airline had inexplicably dropped a Dulles Airport in-flight catering account with Marriott, and Bill asked why. Was it dissatisfaction

with Marriott service or pricing? Bill asked one of the airline's executives. "No," the airline executive confided. "It was Donald Nixon. He came to see us on behalf of his client (a Marriott competitor). We suspect that someday his brother is going to be President of the United States, and we decided to go with him because we needed that relationship." So Bill thought that hiring Don might be able to bring the Marriott company new business. And, in fact, Don soon brought that national airline account at Dulles back to Marriott.

In early 1970, Nixon asked J.W. to form an "Honor America Committee" for Independence Day. The stated purpose was patriotism, but Nixon was really looking for a way the "Silent Majority" could mount a rally to counter anti–Vietnam War demonstrations that were plaguing his administration. For five weeks, Bill didn't see his father at the office while J.W. planned the patriotic event, which included the Reverend Billy Graham and comedian Bob Hope, both of whom became close friends of the Marriott family. A crowd of 450,000 showed up on the Fourth, but Bill and his family were not among them. He was in the hospital recovering from an emergency hernia operation.

The media frequently referred to the Nixons and senior Marriotts as "good friends." During Nixon's presidency, he invited J.W. to White House meetings or dinners on twenty-one occasions, and to another fourteen presidential events outside the White House. Contrary to appearances, however, they were not real friends. J.W. admired Nixon and backed his political initiatives, and Nixon appreciated J.W.'s loyalty and support. But it was a professional acquaintance, not a friendship.

The main Nixon administration official whom J.W. and Allie actively cultivated as a friend was Attorney General John Mitchell, along with his garrulous wife, Martha. The Marriotts invited them to a warm winter vacation at Camelback in February 1971. The following Thanksgiving, the Mitchells were invited to dinner at the Marriott farm in Virginia. A snowstorm kept Bill and Donna away that day but also allowed Bill to keep the Nixon cabal at arm's length. It was not that

he was prescient enough to anticipate trouble. He was simply too busy to hobnob, and he remembered that the one time his father had asked President Eisenhower for a business favor, it had gone badly.

Though Allie did not need or pursue Republican political assignments, she was in the thick of it with J.W. She was tapped to be treasurer of three successive Republican national conventions—1964, 1968, and 1972—and she was also a longtime Republican National Committee (RNC) representative from the District of Columbia and rose to be an RNC vice chairman during the Nixon administration. In terms of generational impact, however, Allie's longest-lasting public contribution was to help guide the John F. Kennedy Center for the Performing Arts from its founding to its full flowering as its advisory committee chair, appointed by Nixon.

While J.W. and Allie enjoyed the regard of the president, Bill was dealing with the negative fallout of employing Nixon's younger brother. On Sunday, January 30, 1972, after church, fellow Latter-day Saint congregant and friend Jack Anderson, the highly prominent journalist, took J.W. aside and told him he (Anderson) was on the verge of publishing a series of hard-hitting stories on Don. J.W. conferred with Bill, and both thought it might be a good idea to have Don fly to Washington from his California home and meet with Anderson to answer questions.

The next day, J.W. called Nixon aide John Ehrlichman to warn him, which set off a presidential panic. Nixon hated Anderson because of his scoops on Nixon shenanigans, which had won Anderson a Pulitzer Prize and put him at the top of Nixon's infamous "Enemies List."

As heard on the White House tapes, Nixon spent hours obsessively discussing Anderson, Don, and the Marriotts. "The older Marriott claims to have some kind of influence with Anderson," Ehrlichman reported. He advised that Nixon not get personally involved with his brother's troubles. "He just has so many flies on him right now that you shouldn't get into it." Ehrlichman called J.W. and asked for help

with Anderson to soften the upcoming Don Nixon stories as much as possible. A week later, Anderson published his columns on Don. Even Nixon was astonished that Anderson, with a bow to his friends, absolved the Marriott corporation and President Nixon of Don's questionable-but-not-criminal wheeling and dealing.

What neither the president nor J.W. knew was that Anderson had uncovered a much bigger story involving Don and a potentially criminal business deal in the Pacific area. Because Anderson thought that J.W. would tell the White House, he provided the details only to Bill. "I've got the goods on him, but he works for you and it will probably hurt your company even though you aren't involved." After Jack laid out the specifics, Bill asked him not to publish the more damaging story. "Please, as a favor to me and my dad, don't run it," he recalled asking.

Jack Anderson rarely passed up a scoop of that political magnitude. He went through several hours of soul-searching, considering not only his friendship with the Marriotts but also his respect for Bill's integrity. Finally, with resignation, he called Bill and promised not to run the blockbuster. "It was a big deal," Bill recalled. "I knew it was a really big deal for Jack to do this. We never forgot that kindness."

While Bill steered clear of the Nixon administration, he had a hint of the chaos through the eyes of his close friend Jon Huntsman, whom he knew from Church association as well as from Huntsman's marriage to Karen Haight, sister of Bill's best man, Bruce. As the Watergate scandal unfolded, Huntsman was trying to tactfully ease his way out of the White House, where he was serving as Nixon's special assistant and staff secretary, taking a detour from building his own corporate empire.

Bill once described Huntsman as a true friend, "one you can count on in any situation. When you're up or down, happy or sad, he is the one who listens and understands and who asks nothing in return but your friendship."[11]

They were two friends who were also not above pranking each

other. In the summer of 1972, Huntsman, newly freed from the White House job, took a vacation with the Marriotts at Lake Winnipesaukee. They had taken their families in two station wagons to an outdoor pageant in Palmyra, New York. Bill had combined the trip with a stop to inspect the new Rochester Marriott, and both families had left with fruit baskets from their overnight stay. The caravan of station wagons was at a stoplight in Bennington, Vermont, when Huntsman leaned out of his window and lobbed an overripe peach into Bill's windshield. Bill returned fire. "We held up traffic through two light changes with one of the best fruit fights you've ever seen. The cars were a mess, and so was the town," Bill recalled. "It's a wonder we both didn't land in jail!"

A year later, as the Watergate scandal exploded, both Huntsman and the Marriotts came to realize just how close they had innocently come to getting dragged into the morass. As the indictments of Nixon's top aides rolled forward, J.W., Bill, and Jon met on May 19, 1973, to discuss the unfolding events. The attitude for all was, "there but for the grace of God go we."

Huntsman confidentially related to the Marriotts how he had almost been pulled unwittingly into the middle of Watergate. Shortly before he resigned, Chief of Staff H. R. Haldeman instructed Jon to solicit a $100,000 cash campaign contribution from Jon's former employer, Dudley Swim. Swim and his wife were both from Twin Falls, Idaho, and she was a Latter-day Saint convert. The Marriotts were also longtime friends of the Swims, partly because Bill had frequent business with Dudley, who was chairman of the board for National Airlines, an In-Flite customer.

Haldeman pledged that Swim would be made ambassador to Australia if he ponied up the money. Making ambassadors of major campaign contributors is a routine presidential practice, but the *cash* donation was out of the ordinary. Swim agreed to the contribution, but he wanted to write a check. Haldeman said no, and Swim

reluctantly agreed. Jon explained to the Marriotts that it was not until the Watergate revelations that he realized the Swim donation would have been part of the secret slush fund used to pay for illegal campaign operations.

Huntsman actually made the airline reservations to pick up the money from Swim at his California home. The day before the flight, Dudley Swim unexpectedly died of a heart attack. "His passing saved me from becoming an unwitting bagman in an illegal contribution scheme," Huntsman confided to the Marriotts. J.W., feeling a bit queasy, wiped his own forehead. All J.W.'s campaign contributions were by check, but if a Nixon aide had ever asked him for cash, he realized he might have given it, assuming it was a legal request. If he had done that, how quickly all those years of Marriott reputation building would have been undone! [12]

CHAPTER 11

THE PERFECT STORM

A fanfare of fifes, a roll of drums, and a cloud of 2,000 balloons accompanied the grand opening of the Crystal City, Virginia, Marriott hotel in January 1970. It was Marriott's thirteenth. Three months later, three generations of Marriotts were on hand for the ribbon-cutting ceremony for number fourteen, the Dulles Airport Marriott outside Washington, D.C. Bill's marketing people favored spectacular grand-opening ceremonies, which sometimes went awry.

For the Dulles opening, an expert archer was hired to shoot a balloon that was tethered above the hotel's lake. Inside the balloon was a mock-up of the key to the hotel's front door. The balloon was supposed to burst, dropping the key into the lake, signifying that the hotel didn't need a key because it would never close. It was a stunt repeated with various themes at other Marriott openings, but this time the winds were gusting at 20 miles per hour. The archer missed four times before a hotel employee waded into the water to pop the balloon. Next came three flag-bearing skydivers jumping out of an airplane at 8,500 feet. They were aiming for the small island in the middle of the lake, but the wind carried two of them out of sight, and the third landed in mud at the edge of the lake.

The high winds were a symbolic harbinger of external factors that would seriously threaten the company's upward trajectory in the 1970s. In just a few years, national and international crises—including war, an oil embargo, a stock-market crash, high inflation, and the downfall of a president—would send the country into the worst recession since the Depression. Without any warning of those coming rough seas, Bill Marriott entered the new decade with an optimistic business plan of expansion and diversification.

"It was the age of conglomerates," Bill recalled. "It was a time when Wall Street expected companies to grow in different ways. I was always asked, 'What new businesses are you getting into?' 'What's the next big thing you are doing?'"

One thing Bill planned in 1970 was a proliferation of franchised "Marriott Inns," which would soon dot the country. Although J.W. obstinately opposed franchising, the rationale behind Marriott Inns was sound. Holiday Inn was doing well with a franchised national chain, and even Hilton was building "Hilton Inns" at locations that couldn't sustain a full-fledged hotel. This would be Marriott's chance to get into smaller cities as well.

Gray McCullah was hired to drum up franchisees. Bus Ryan on the marketing team recalled the day McCullah arrived back at headquarters with a briefcase full of $15,000 checks from people who wanted to buy into a Marriott: "These were doctors, lawyers—anybody who had $15,000 and thought this was going to be the key to their life's new fortune, which was the way Gray had sold it to them." In just a few months, McCullah had collected more than five hundred checks from prospective franchisees, totaling more than $7 million.

Instead of being elated, Bill was alarmed. Who were these people? Did they have a good location for the Marriott Inn in mind? Could they manage the Inn? Not one check was to be cashed until the applicants were vetted. Only about ten passed muster in that first round. One year into the program, more than fifty qualified franchisees had been signed up, and the company was planning to open Marriott Inns at the starting rate of twenty per year.

The next "new thing" was a venture into the "specialty dinner house" market, not in hotels. The first restaurant was Port O' Georgetown in a historic 1820 warehouse in Washington, D.C. Next was the Joshua Tree steak-and-lobster restaurant in McLean, Virginia. A few days before that opening, Bill joined other Marriott executives for a dinner to test the staff and kitchen. Future billionaire Jon Huntsman, J.W., and Dick joined Bill at his table. Between them, they sampled all the fare on the menu. Midway through dinner, a nervous waitress spilled a container of melted butter all over Bill's new suit and tie. Huntsman never forgot Bill's reaction. "He was not upset. He reassured the waitress that everything was just fine. He couldn't have been more gracious or gentlemanly. Then, after Bill wiped at the spots with a wet napkin, we went right on with the meal and forgot about it."

The third restaurant was the biggest of all—the size of a football field. For two decades, the D.C. government's Redevelopment Land Agency had tried to revitalize the southwest waterfront along the Potomac River's Washington Channel. But not until Marriott came along did the $25-million project get off to a running start. Marriott envisioned a 900-seat seafood restaurant giving patrons a sweeping view of the monuments upriver. The company bought the rights to the name and menu of a popular seafood restaurant nearby, Hogate's, and tore it down. Bill's new Hogate's was instantly more popular than the old one had been. Several weeks after the opening, J.W. recorded that there were "200 people waiting in line." Not only was Hogate's one of the largest seafood restaurants in the country, but it grew into what trade publications determined was the number-one restaurant in the United States in sales volume, grossing more than $6 million annually.[1]

Marriott's next venture was a charter vacation business called Marriott World Travel. It was a low-investment business from which Bill expected quick profits and a window into travel business operators abroad. At the end of its first year of operation, Marriott World Travel had moved more than ten thousand people to and from Greek and Caribbean islands.

Bill had barely begun the new enterprise when he decided to buy a cruise ship line. Others would later conjecture that Bill just wanted his own fleet of ships, but that was not the case. The new business was a natural, if adventurous, outgrowth of the direction in which the company was headed. Still, "the idea of cruise ship operation back then was pretty exciting for Bill," recalled Harry Vincent. Donna, too, noticed an extra spring in Bill's step as he proceeded with a fleet purchase. "The cruise ship business was doing very well at that time and Bill—loving ships—was happy to get into it."

The best buy at the time looked like the highly reputable Sun Line, with two ships cruising the islands off of Greece: the *Stella Maris* (Star of the Sea) and the *Stella Oceanis* (Star of the Ocean). A third, much larger ship under construction was the *Stella Solaris* (Star of the Sun), scheduled for its maiden voyage in 1973. Holland America Line owned a big share of Sun Line and was interested in selling. That began many months of intense international negotiations with both Holland America and Sun Line owner Alex Keusseoglou.

J.W. and Allie flew to Athens to meet Keusseoglou and to inspect the ships. J.W. didn't like the idea of having a partner, but Bill argued that Marriott needed a knowledgeable partner because he knew nothing about the business. J.W. and Allie found Keusseoglou to be a charming Greek captain on the order of Aristotle Onassis, but Allie didn't trust him from the first. "He talked too fast," she later said. Keusseoglou treated them to an overnight cruise to Crete. Once back in Athens, J.W. agreed when Allie pronounced: "It's time to go home. Greece is for the Greeks." J.W. reported to Bill that he did not feel good about going ahead with the purchase, though he conceded that Keusseoglou ran a first-class operation.

No one was more instrumental to the purchase than General

Counsel Sterling Colton, who was the only one capable of dealing with the mercurial Keusseoglou. Sterling's father, Hugh, had been an original cofounder of Hot Shoppes. Sterling had become a fast friend of Bill's when they both attended the University of Utah, and the two had kept in touch as Sterling became a star at a Salt Lake City law firm.

Two years after becoming president of Hot Shoppes, Bill asked Sterling to uproot the Colton family from Salt Lake and come work for Bill. Sterling didn't hesitate. After Sterling had spent two years as an assistant general counsel, Bill promoted him to the company's top legal position in 1970, and he helmed the company's growing legal staff with much-lauded excellence for the next twenty-five years. Bill never had a better, more level-headed and consistent adviser and friend at Marriott than Sterling Colton.

The Sun Line deal, which occurred only a few months after Sterling had been promoted to general counsel, proved to be a real baptism by fire. It was "one of the most complex legal, financial, tax and accounting problems in which Marriott has been involved," Colton noted contemporaneously in the company's newsletter. The first two ships had formerly been owned by a Liberian company and two Greek companies. These, in turn, were owned by the Holland America Line, a Dutch company, and Keusseoglou, a citizen of Greece.

If that weren't confusing enough, Marriott was subject to the laws of the United States, which meant the acquisition had to be made through a new Bermuda subsidiary, so that the contracts were subject to arbitration under the laws of England. Since the investment was made overseas, it was restricted by the regulations on foreign investments imposed by the Office of Foreign Direct Investment. This also happened at a time when the international monetary markets were in a state of great confusion. In fact, the final contracts were executed two days after an additional devaluation of the dollar was announced.

Just prior to the closing, certificates of incorporation, bylaws, contracts, insurance policies, and many other documents were assembled.

The closing itself took place at the offices of the Handelsfinanz Bank in Zurich, Switzerland. "That the transaction finally took place smoothly is a tribute to the skills of all involved, particularly Sterling Colton," the Marriott newsletter article concluded.[2]

What was missing from that public account was an unprecedented event that occurred behind closed doors at the final board meeting regarding the deal. J.W. had finally reconciled himself to the venture, but, when it came to a vote, Allie said, "No." J.W. looked at her with disbelief and said, "Allie, you have never voted against me before. Why are you voting no?" She said, "I do not like boats." Harry Vincent was there and had his own theory: "There was more to it than not liking boats. Being the kind of lady that she was, that was all she would say. What she meant was, 'I do not trust this man Keusseoglou.'"

Bill assumed his mother was acting on intuition more than business analysis, and once Sun Line was under Marriott ownership, her misgivings seemed to have been misguided. For the first eighteen months, Sun Line profits rolled in and it looked like smooth sailing ahead for Bill's fleet.

In February 1971, *Forbes* magazine did a cover story on Bill, describing the trajectory of the company from root beer stand to conglomerate, with most of the growth under the direction of the second generation. In only "six years since Bill took over, Marriott has almost quadrupled in size and had a sales volume of $315 million in its latest fiscal year." At the same time, with the company's unique profit-sharing program, Bill's piloting of the corporate ship had lifted his participating employees with that rising sea. At the end of a thirty-year career, a $3-an-hour dishwasher retired with $577,000. An executive after the same thirty years retired with about $2 million. "We have at least a dozen millionaires who have retired from this company," Bill told *Forbes*—and that didn't count his three uncles, who had retired with substantial fortunes.[3]

J.W., though not yet ready to retire completely himself, turned seventy-one in September and was "depressed over his age," according to Allie. An incident aboard the *U.S.S. John F. Kennedy* two weeks later accentuated that. As a representative of his Church, J.W. was invited by the chief of navy chaplains to join a chaplains group meeting on the aircraft carrier. "I climbed about ten flights of stairs to the bridge to watch the maneuvers of the carrier [when] I got sick. The medical officer thought I was having another heart attack, so they put me on a helicopter and took me to Portsmouth Naval Hospital where I had at least ten doctors work on me," he wrote in his report to Church leaders.[4] The navy doctors found nothing more serious than overexertion.

Whereas 1971 had been a relatively balmy year between Bill and his father, 1972 was often cloudy with recurring storms. On New Year's Day, Allie recorded that the two "had a session—1 hour—both worn out after." Two weeks later, she arrived for a board meeting only to discover that the run-up executive committee meeting had been a knock-down, drag-out experience for her husband and son. "Stormy session," she recorded. "Went one hour over time—[J.W.] and Billy at odds—they both looked awful when the Board Meeting began— Billy shaking all over—[J.W.] flushed. Too bad they get each other so upset."[5]

J.W. knew he was driving his son crazy, but he just couldn't help it. In a speech to Marriott managers on January 17, he said, "I wish I had been born under another star instead of Virgo, which makes one orderly and particular. My wife says I make myself and everybody else miserable. I guess misery loves company. In my youth, my father was everything but orderly. He let the chickens run through the house; I had to chase them off with a broom. Dirty clothes were piled up on the staircase, which is one of the reasons our house burned down and for six months we slept in tents, sheds and with the neighbors. I was brought up in an environment which was anything but orderly, and yearned for such a life."[6]

It wasn't just his obsession with cleanliness and perfection, but J.W.'s desire to keep the business neat and tidy, that was splitting him and his son. Bill's dizzying expansion and diversification were unsettling to J.W. He began to feel like an anachronism. The *Los Angeles Times* profiled Bill's impressive reign as the company's president, while minimizing his father's foundational role. Although J.W. penned a complimentary note to Bill about the article, it had a rueful twist. "Congratulations—keep it up, [but] it makes the 'old man' look like a third-rater."[7]

In March, Bill opened the St. Louis Marriott, followed by the New Orleans Marriott. He had earned a respite at Lake Winnipesaukee that summer, where the Marriotts were joined by twenty-five-year-old Mitt Romney, his wife, Ann, and their two small boys. Mitt was on his way to Boston to attend Harvard graduate school. The Marriotts were impressed with Mitt and his family, and the Romneys fell in love with the lake. Years later, they would build a home there, and, like his dad, Mitt would announce a run for the presidency from the lake.

In August, the Marriotts were in Miami for the Republican National Convention, where Allie was serving as the convention treasurer for the third and last time. The convention nominated President Nixon as the party's candidate. It also included a frightening moment for Allie that put her on the front page of the *Washington Post*. When she and others arrived at the Fontainebleau Hotel for a fund-raising dinner, they were confronted by several hundred screaming demonstrators at the hotel entrance. "They kept shouting at me, 'Keep the rich out! Keep the rich out!' I thought they were going to grab my handbag," she recalled. Not one to be deterred, however, she ran to the corner of the hotel where television news trucks were stationed behind a six-foot fence. One of the newsmen gallantly handed her a box. She stood on it, hiked up her evening dress, and artfully climbed the fence to safety. Visibly trembling as she related this to the *Post* reporter at the gala, she added, "I was never so scared in my life."[8]

In November, the greatest moment thus far in Bill's career was tainted by a row with his father. J.W. was nursing an injury from an accident on a trail motorcycle at the lake. Adding to his physical un-ease was the emotional fragility he felt as board members pushed for a corporate charter change so Bill could be appointed to the new po-sition of CEO. It didn't help when *Newsweek* published a story mini-mizing J.W.'s contribution, writing: "Bill Marriott, Jr., has steered the Washington-based company on a decidedly different course from the one his father envisioned. [He] has transformed [a] moderately success-ful 45-year-old chain of 45 restaurants and four hotels into an inter-national giant in the highly competitive food and lodging business."[9]

On November 20, the day before the annual shareholders meeting where Bill was to be promoted to CEO, a small argument with his dad quickly escalated into the worst they ever had. According to J.W.'s journal, "I criticized some of Bill's men. He tore into a rage . . . and cancelled his staff meeting and went home. I should never criticize his operation again. A terrible situation between us."[10]

Bill was so furious that, for the first and only time, he left his car in the parking lot of the River Road headquarters and walked to his Kenwood home, hoping to cool off. He didn't. Donna was shocked at her husband's appearance. "There were some awful times—there really were—and this was at the top. His father had been so miserable to him that I thought he'd even been crying on that walk home. He was very, very upset and said he had had it. He was going to leave the company."

Donna phoned Harry Vincent, who called Bill. "I can't stand it any longer," a resolute Bill told Vincent. He had considered his options and thought the prospects were excellent for a better job with much less aggravation. For the sake of his own health and his father's, it seemed that it was time to cut the cord. Vincent realized this was not minor petulance but a reality that could well lead to Bill's resignation the next day, so he mounted a full-court press. Marriott Corporation could not succeed without Bill at its helm.

Vincent asked Bill to meet him at the Metropolitan Club for a face-to-face discussion. He rallied other board members, who persuaded Bill to go through with the promotion the next day. If J.W. didn't change, then Bill could resign later. Then two board members called J.W. and told him to stand down. "Bill is going to take over whether you want that or not. So please calm down and back off," one of them said. J.W. was nobody's fool, and, reading between the lines, he knew that the board might well vote him out altogether if he didn't make things right with his son.

"The next day Bill's dad was just like syrup," Vincent recalled. Twelve hundred Marriott shareholders gathered for the annual meeting, and J.W. could not have been more complimentary of his son. Bill responded that he was "proud to be the son of Mr. Marriott" and led the shareholders in a tribute to J.W. and Allie. The shareholders approved Bill's promotion.

Now, Bill just had to keep it up—which was not a foregone conclusion. In a matter of only weeks, the stock market would crash and plunge America into a deep recession accentuated by cataclysmic political tumult.

The decade of the 1960s was a period of remarkable American prosperity by almost every measure, including an escalating gross national product, a lower unemployment rate, and a booming stock market. The early 1970s saw occasional hiccups in the stock market, but the market kept climbing until the Dow Jones Industrial Average soared above 1,000 for the first time the week after Nixon's reelection. On January 11, 1973, the market came tumbling down. Since the initial drop was nowhere near the single-day crash that had sparked the Great Depression, there was little alarm. Unaware of the perfect storm on the horizon, Bill went about his business as usual.

J.W. had reluctantly agreed to chair the second Nixon inauguration. The $4-million inauguration was a success and once again ended with a surplus in the budget. Most memorable for J.W. was the White House church service before the inauguration, for which thirty members of the Mormon Tabernacle Choir were flown in to provide the

The Marriott Center at Brigham Young University.

music. Nixon and the others in attendance rose to their feet when the choir sang its signature hymn, "The Battle Hymn of the Republic." "I don't think there was a dry eye in the audience," J.W. recalled.

Two weeks later, that proud memory was very much on J.W.'s mind when Allie, Bill, and Donna joined him for the dedication of the massive new Brigham Young University basketball and events arena, the "Marriott Activities Center." Former Hot Shoppes executive and now BYU executive vice president Ben Lewis had approached J.W. in 1969 for a contribution to build a new sports arena. J.W.'s alma mater, the University of Utah, had just named its new library after him, in part because he had donated $1 million toward its construction. Lewis goaded his old friend: "Shouldn't you be giving to the Church's university?" he needled.

"Well, how would you feel if I sent you a check for $100,000?"

Lewis replied, "I'd feel much better if it was ten times that amount."

J.W. laughed, and soon a check for $1 million was in the mail.

In his speech at the dedication, J.W. said, "I am sure all of you know how important a good image is. Businessmen spend millions of dollars to build a good image; institutions make their greatest effort to do the same, and we as individuals make it a life's work." Then, becoming emotional, he reflected on a future when his descendants would likely attend the university. "I want to ask them to remember that it is the responsibility of all our family to see that their name is worthy to be more than an identification sign on this building."[11]

The value of a good name was also on Bill's mind as investigations by the media and Congressional committees tried to drag Marriott into the scandalous maelstrom spawned by a burglary the previous June at the headquarters of the Democratic National Committee in the Watergate office complex.

Although the Marriotts never did anything untoward or illegal, some shareholders were concerned about any Marriott association with the Nixon administration. During the annual shareholders meeting in November 1972, Bill was peppered with questions about possible Marriott links to the Watergate scandal, including questions about Don Nixon. Bill deflected them, but afterward he made an appointment to see Don at his California home, where Bill planned to fire him.

Even before Bill got on the plane, Don called his brother. Nixon's secretary Rose Mary Woods then called J.W., asking him to save Don's job. "Rose Mary said the President would appreciate it if we would hold up on Don until he got better [healthwise]," J.W. recorded.[12] Father and son conferred and reluctantly agreed to give Don one more year. A month later, J.W. put together a handwritten account of what Don had done and not done for the company. He realized that in the middle of a recession, they couldn't afford someone who wasn't pulling his weight, so he agreed several weeks later to let Bill notify Don of an "early retirement" package. This time there was no call from the White House.

In general, the Marriott connection to the Nixon administration was of far less concern to Bill than the failing economy, which the

White House had also mismanaged. On November 19, 1973, the stock market hit its lowest point in nineteen years. Marriott stock dropped to $21.50 from $41 earlier in the year. The next day, at the company's annual meeting, Bill worked hard to reassure the nervous stockholders, particularly about energy shortages. He appointed someone in each of the company's divisions to implement a 20 percent energy cut. Many of the company's restaurants were located in neighborhoods where the majority of customers came from a radius of only two or three miles away, so "I don't expect any dropoff in sales," Bill told the shareholders meeting. As for hotels and airline catering, Bill predicted: "When gas [supply] is reduced, people drive less, fly more, and stay at our hotels." His optimism was soon tested.

Ten days later, Marriott stock dropped to $16 a share. "We may have an energy-induced depression," J.W. wrote with alarm in his journal. Gas stations voluntarily closed on Sundays, which decimated Marriott's toll-road restaurants. Many states imposed gas rationing. A federal law was passed making 55 miles per hour the maximum speed limit across the country. State governments asked citizens not to put up Christmas lights.

The energy crisis and Nixon's Watergate crisis dragged on into 1974. Bill implemented a ninety-day moratorium on new construction and adopted austerity measures. More than 500 jobs—including Donald Nixon's—were eliminated in a two-month period, most by attrition. Both the toll-road restaurants and Sun Line cruise ships went deeply in the red. Then, in July, Turkey invaded Cyprus and began a shooting war with Greece. All Greek cruise ships were ordered to return to port so they could be used for troop transports. "Our Greek partner radioed our ships to stay at sea for another two or three days and go around in circles until the war was over," Bill recalled. "He thought the war was not going to last very long, and it did last only a week—but that was long enough to lose all of our business." There were 1,000 cancellations for Sun Line cruises on the invasion's first weekend, beginning a Sun Line loss in the millions of dollars.

With the resignation of President Nixon in August 1974, the number-one American concern became inflation. New President Gerald Ford warned that if oil prices continued to escalate, there would be another worldwide depression. By Labor Day, Bill began to feel that the company might not be able to stay above water if the recession continued for another year.

After two years of decline, the stock market finally hit bottom on December 6, having lost half its value. Marriott stock, however, did not drop to its lowest point until two days before Christmas, when it hit $6.25 a share. The company had always posted fiscal year earnings increases in the double digits, but the cumulative effect of 1973 and 1974 forced Bill to report in fiscal year 1975 that the company had a double-digit (12 percent) earnings loss for the first time in Marriott's half-century history. Bill had good reason for feeling grateful even as he reported the historic loss. The recession had caused many companies to fail, and even blue-chip firms had posted greater losses than Marriott. On the plus side, Bill had learned lessons that proved invaluable as he steered his company through future economic storms.

CHAPTER 12

BICENTENNIAL BISHOP

When Marriott announced that it was going to build America's largest airport hotel in Los Angeles, it barely made a stir on the West Coast, where the Marriott name still was not familiar. The company had been operating restaurants in Southern California for several years, but those were under the Big Boy name. The first time the *Los Angeles Times* wrote a story on the hotel development, they misspelled the company's name in the headline and throughout the article as "Marriot," with only one "t."[1] It was not uncommon for Californians then to pronounce the name Ma-ra-ti, "like we were an Italian food company," one executive recalled. "The name Marriott is not quickly recognizable here," the Torrance, California, *Daily Breeze* reported in spring 1973. "It will be, however, when the new Marriott Hotel opens in September."[2]

Construction of Marriott's $24-million Los Angeles hotel was finished ahead of schedule. Boasting 1,020 rooms, the eighteen-story hotel was the largest Bill had ever built. Few buildings in Southern California could equal its facilities, which included 150 meeting and banquet rooms to seat from ten to two thousand people. That was 44,000 square feet of meeting space, which Marriott executives sometimes referred to as "the convention hall with the hotel on top."

A glance at the 150-page checklist that General Manager Jerry Best

Debbie and Bill greet Glenn Ford at the grand opening of the Los Angeles Marriott.

carried with him in the preopening days shows how mind-boggling a task it was to open such a hotel. On the supply side, for example, Best needed 11,716 pieces of clothing for staff, 1,000 bags of sand for ashtrays, 60,000 Marriott cocktail stir sticks, 400 panels of teakwood for the dance floor, 1,075 copies each of the Gideon Bible and the Book of Mormon (which Bill always included in every Marriott guest room), 20,000 shoeshine mitts, 93 dozen fly swatters, and 25 ice-carving chisels.[3]

The afternoon of the grand opening, Bill had an unforgettable daddy-daughter time with sixteen-year-old Debbie, who was his "plus-one" in Los Angeles. Bill took her to the junior ballroom, where he and Debbie were two of the few allowed to watch one of the most famous men in the world go to work. The hotel had set up a boxing ring for Muhammad Ali prior to his rematch with Ken Norton four days later at Inglewood Forum, two miles from the hotel. The man Bill and Debbie saw in the specially designed Los Angeles Marriott hotel ring was prepared to win, which he subsequently did. "I will never forget being with my dad and watching Muhammad Ali spar in that hotel ballroom as he prepared for one of his big fights," said Debbie. "It was just so amazing!"[4]

The star-studded "President's Dinner-Dance" for the grand opening included emcee Bob Hope, Glenn Ford, Pat Boone, Roy Rogers, Nancy Reagan, Zsa Zsa Gabor, astronaut Buzz Aldrin, and, memorably, John Wayne. Bill recalled: "He was a very large man and a man of few words, but he let me know exactly what he wanted—a drink—when he said, 'I understand liquor flows like glue at Mormon parties.'"

Debbie was there cohosting with her father because Donna was home, eight months pregnant. No one was more surprised than Bill and Donna when she became pregnant twelve years after John's birth. David Sheets Marriott arrived on October 1, 1973. His birth capped a frenetic year for Marriott, including one day in May when Bill broke ground for three hotels in three states. The trio of events was ceremoniously called "The Great Groundbreaking in the Sky" because it was done from the air. The day began in Kansas City, Missouri, where a chartered jet picked up civic officials and the media for a flyby of the hotel site. Aboard the plane Bill pushed a button, and smoke bombs went off below on the hotel site, signifying the ground had been broken. The drill was repeated for hotels in Denver and Newport Beach, California.

Four hotels—Los Angeles, Kansas City, Denver, and Newport Beach—had all been planned and financed before the recession began. Once Bill recognized the impending economic challenges, he shifted corporate strategy. He alerted the board's executive committee that the new Marriott strategy was to own only 25 percent of the hotels with the Marriott name on them. The other 75 percent would be built and owned by someone else, but branded and managed by Marriott. It was a sea change that could mean less profit on the hotel side, but more capital freed up.

To J.W.'s dismay, another part of Bill's corporate belt tightening was selling off nonperforming Hot Shoppes. By 1973, the number of restaurants had dropped from its peak of forty to twenty-five. J.W. had opposed every sale. "To him, it was like selling his children," Bill said. So it was a very, very sad day in 1974 for J.W. when the board voted with Bill to sell his "favorite child," the Connecticut Avenue Hot Shoppe.

Number Five had been a cash cow for the company since it opened in 1930. In the basement had been the company's first commissary, and it had become a city landmark where celebrities and political heavyweights hung out. Even more sentimental, it was the premier Swing Era place where thousands of young men courted the girls who became their wives. But by 1974, the location had become crime-ridden, causing profits to plummet. The land was more valuable than the restaurant's decreasing annual profits, so Bill sold it to National Bank of Washington for their new headquarters.[5]

As the papers were about to be signed, the bank's lawyers said it appeared a sewage easement had not been paid thirty-five years before, and the deal could not proceed. When the Marriott representative called Allie, she affirmed that it had been paid because she had written the check. In less than an hour, she located the canceled check in an attic box, and the sale closed. "I looked for the check for Connecticut Avenue everywhere," Allie wrote that day. Along the way she "tripped over the pad under (J.W.'s) desk and sprained my ankle," but she found the necessary proof, leaving her both exultant and sad. "We have had it since 1930. Goodbye, #5 . . ."[6]

Marriott was also selling or converting other unprofitable ventures. The company tried to sell its interest in the cruise ships after the Cyprus war, but there were no takers. The popularity of the fast-food Jr. Hot Shoppes had waned, so the company sold several of the locations and converted others into Roy Rogers restaurants. The most innovative measure was the conversion of Camelback Inn casas to timeshare condominiums, with sale prices ranging from $42,000 to $300,000 a unit. Then Marriott did the same at Essex House in New York City.

Under the new hotel-management strategy, Bill made a concerted effort to find prime locations abroad. The Middle East offered the most immediate opportunities. In Cairo, Bill cut a deal with the government of Egypt to manage a Marriott-designed, Egyptian-financed hotel adjacent to a former palace. In Tehran, he signed a contract to design and manage a hotel to be built by the Shah of Iran's Pahlavi Foundation. In Jordan, Bill found tourism officials excited about the prospect of a Marriott hotel in Amman, partly because U.S.-Jordanian relations had warmed during the Ford administration. King Hussein was honored at the first State Dinner that President Ford scheduled, with J.W. and Allie among the invited guests at the dinner, held just a week after Ford assumed the presidency.

One country in which Bill decided he was not going to manage a hotel for the foreseeable future was the Soviet Union, which he was able to scout firsthand as a delegate for a 1974 trade group tour to the USSR. During Bill and Donna's first night in Moscow, they shivered in the 55-degree temperature of their Intourist Hotel room until Bill decided to take advantage of the probability that the KGB was bugging their room. "We figured they were listening to us, so we complained loudly, 'Why don't they turn up the heat? What's the matter with these Russians! Don't they know we can't get any sleep in a bedroom that's only 55 degrees?' Within a few minutes the heat was turned on. You could hear it come on as we complained."

At every lunch and formal dinner for ten days, the Soviets started with vodka, and they were at first offended that Bill did not imbibe. "I told them I was a Mormon, and they didn't understand what a Mormon was. I had to tell them, it's like being a Muslim. As soon as I said Muslim, they associated it with a religious belief and they respected it. It was no problem from then on. So, I was a Mormon Muslim in Moscow."

The more Bill expanded Marriott holdings, the more J.W. fretted, and the worse his health became. After a cardiologist diagnosed a weakened heart, J.W. always carried nitroglycerin pills to counteract chest pains often brought on by stress. Whether or not either of them realized it, Bill's hotel expansion plans were held hostage by J.W.'s health.

Theme parks seemed to be a natural extension of the company's product line, and they had the side benefit of distracting J.W. from his fears about hotel proliferation. A survey of the amusement park business

Bill signs the contract licensing the use of Warner Brothers characters at Great America theme parks.

in the early 1970s proved it was a rapidly growing industry. Bill had demonstrated his go-big-or-go-home philosophy with other Marriott lines of business. So once he set his mind on theme parks, the only question was whether Marriott would buy existing parks or build new ones. Buying was easier at the outset, but it proved to be an elusive quest.

Disney dominated the industry, followed by the Six Flags operation based in Texas. Bill had begun negotiations with Six Flags for a merger or buyout, but their parks were simply too profitable for them to want to sell. Theme park consultants Economics Research Associates, which also advised Disney, suggested that Bill look at locations in Washington, Chicago, and San Francisco. With the bicentennial celebration of America's founding on the horizon, Bill opted for a patriotic concept and chose the name Great America.

On January 26, 1972, Bill booked the National Press Club for the announcement of his most ambitious endeavor yet. The $65 million-plus Great America theme park was the "largest and most significant" venture undertaken in the company's forty-five-year history, Bill told the press. Plans called for four different entertainment areas. The largest would be a 100-acre park themed as an adventure through America with plenty of thrill rides. He was also planning a marine life park, a ride-through animal preserve, and a New Orleans replica. Each of the four centers would have continuous live entertainment. It would be the most diverse family entertainment complex in the country.

But his plan to build the first park in Howard County, Maryland, north of Washington, was stymied by neighborhood opposition. After nearly a year of battling the locals and the county government, the project was denied the necessary zoning. He had better luck at the other two sites. For San Francisco, the company found a willing partner in one Marriott stockholder, actor Fess Parker, aka Davy Crockett and Daniel Boone. Parker owned land near the southern tip of San Francisco Bay in Santa Clara, where he had hoped to build a Davy Crockett–themed amusement park. Marriott bought the land, and the Santa Clara City Council obligingly rezoned it for a Great America park. At the same time, a half continent away, the company found land between Chicago and Milwaukee on I-94 in the small village of Gurnee, Illinois, and bought it for a second Great America park. Marriott continued to search around Washington but decided to leave the field after being shut out in Virginia as he had been in Maryland.

• • •

As he contemplated providing memorable experiences for children at his theme parks, Bill was actively involved in rearing his own children. Being one of the wealthier families in America created the risk of those children being spoiled, so Bill and Donna wanted to do all they could to prevent that. "My parents had the philosophy that we only spend money on education and travel," Debbie said. "We didn't grow up with fancy cars or a big house." The only exception was that each of the children got a car when he or she turned sixteen. Bill explained, "That was about the only thing we indulged in, but it was probably because we didn't have to drive the kids around then."

If the Marriott children wanted money, they could work for it. Debbie's first summer job for the company was at the front desk of the Key Bridge hotel. "I really tried hard to distance myself from this perception people had that 'you're a Marriott so you must be rich,'" she said. But one day she simply had to use the Marriott name, which led to an all-time favorite Marriott family "gotcha" story.

A woman and her elderly mother arrived to check in at the hotel. When Debbie asked for her credit card, the woman refused to provide one. Debbie explained that hotel policy required either a credit card or cash payment.

"I'm best friends with Bill Marriott!" the woman huffed. "He trusts me, so it's not a problem. My mother needs to go to the bathroom, so you need to check me in right now!"

"I'm sorry, I can't do that," Debbie calmly responded. "It's against our policy."

The woman was furious. Looking at Debbie's name tag, which had only a first name, the lady sputtered: "I can't believe anybody would hire you, Miss Debbie. I'm going to call Mr. Marriott right now and tell him what terrible people he has working on his front desk."

With a smile, Debbie replied, "Well, if you would like to talk to Mr. Marriott, I will dial the phone number. But I can tell you right now that my dad is not in his office. He's out of town."

The lady turned white as a sheet. Then, Debbie recalled, "She took her wallet out and started throwing credit cards across the desk—hard!" It was a rare moment when the Marriott children would own up to their famous name. Once when Donna was away with Bill on a business trip, J.W. sent his chauffeured limousine to take the grandchildren to school. Debbie and her brothers refused to get in.

Humility was one of the greatest lessons Bill and Donna felt they could convey to their children. By their behavior over the decades, no one could accuse them of showboating at public functions or acting as if they deserved the spotlight. Bill felt strongly that the family wealth threatened to make his children prideful if he and Donna did not pass on their own natural self-effacement. "We used to say, 'There are no big shots in this family.' And that's the way we've operated," Bill said.

The lesson worked, even during the teenage years, when adolescence tends to induce a sense of entitlement. In 1970, *Washington Post* magazine writer John Carmody joined Bill and his family for several weeks of close observation. He concluded in his comprehensive profile: "Bill Marriott has a family that looks as if it had just marched out of a life insurance commercial. . . . Their church is an integral part of their lives: they truly do pray together and play together. When they are out in public the boys shake hands solemnly with the grownups and they all, mom and dad and the kids, fall into a laughing, easy comradeship that makes the people at the next table, or wherever, look and smile back without quite knowing why. It is, in sum, one of those families a great many people in the United States still hope to have."[7]

Like every father, Bill was less than happy with the boys who were dating his daughter, especially if they kept her out past curfew. "Dad would wait up. Then, when my date and I arrived, he would come charging out the door to yell at me to get inside. He had a sparkle in his eyes because he got a real kick out of thinking all my boyfriends were scared of him," Debbie said.

One night, Bill himself had a fright when he got home and was confronted by a knife-wielding man. Longtime employee Martin Buxbaum lived nearby, and his daughter was babysitting the Marriott children that night. She called her father frantically to report, "There's someone trying to get in the back door."

Buxbaum grabbed his hunting knife and sprinted to the Marriott house. His daughter let him in the front door, and he rushed through to the back door to confront the intruder, who was still tinkering with the lock. The "intruder" turned out to be Bill, who was more than a little surprised to be met by one of his employees brandishing a knife.

Buxbaum blurted out defensively: "Why don't you come in the front door like a normal person?"

"Because it's my house!" Bill said.[8]

Bill built a house at Lake Winnipesaukee for his own family, near J.W.'s home there. The nearest Latter-day Saint chapel was in Laconia, forty miles away. The family would drive the distance in Grandpa J.W.'s red convertible with the top down. At the lake, the pace picked up when Bill bought his swift 1970 Donzi Express Cruiser. The children loved speeding along the placid lake at more than 50 miles per hour with their dad at the helm, where he seemed happiest. A catamaran sailboat also joined the family "fleet."

None of the children was expected to go into the family business. "Dad never really brought business discussions home. Business was not thought of as a dinner-table discussion topic," Stephen said. "He didn't pressure us to go into the business, but I know he hoped we'd go into it. He always had summer internships available for us, so we could learn at early ages if that's what we really wanted to do." Stephen's first summer job was flipping hamburgers at a Roy Rogers restaurant.

In spite of his career demands, Bill put his Christian faith first, which included serving in a succession of ecclesiastical positions in The Church of Jesus Christ of Latter-day Saints. At the local level, the Church has an unpaid lay ministry. The members are "called" to assignments, and they can decline, but few do. In terms of the organization, a ward is a single congregation, and a stake is a leadership umbrella over several wards. Stakes are governed by a three-member presidency and twelve men on a "high council." Bill became a high councilor in the Washington D.C. Stake in 1974.

The most rewarding high council assignment for Bill was his role in the opening of the Washington D.C. Temple in 1974, a building for which his father had lobbied over the years. The massive, six-spired edifice covered with white Alabama marble was showcased for the public during an open house in September and October. A total of 758,322 visitors toured the temple. Bill was tasked with hosting a day for business VIPs. They began their tour with breakfast at the Key Bridge Marriott, where Bill had salted the crowd with Latter-day Saint executives from the company among the tables to answer questions about the Church. In conjunction with the open house, Allie, a Kennedy Center board member, arranged for a September concert by the Mormon Tabernacle Choir at the Center, which was attended by newly inaugurated President Gerald Ford and the First Lady.

More often than not, Church work for Latter-day Saints, even famous ones, is anonymous or behind the scenes. Few in the Church in high or low positions escape the thankless task of setting up or taking down chairs for church meetings or cleaning the buildings. Bill was not above that duty. On the Saturday before the D.C. temple dedication services, Allie reported that Bill was exhausted from carrying chairs up six flights of stairs in the temple for two hours. "It made him sick, since he was still weak from the stomach flu he just got over."[9]

Life-altering personal events in the summer of 1975 competed for Bill's attention. Debbie graduated from high school and went off to Brigham Young University, and the family became fully aware of Stephen's multiple health issues. When Stephen was about twelve years old, he began to lose his hearing, but it was a couple of years before either he or his family realized it. His parents had gotten used to Stephen's "What'd you say?" during conversations. A few days after Debbie's graduation, Donna felt prompted to ask Stephen, "Are you not hearing me or just not listening?" Stephen thought about it for a moment, and then he said that maybe he couldn't hear as well as other people. He was soon diagnosed with a severe and potentially degenerative hearing loss. "My dad put his arms around me, and he sometimes cried with me. He also spent all day waiting with me at hospitals."

In the same month as Debbie graduated and Stephen was diagnosed, Bill received a significant change in his Church assignment, to become bishop of his ward—the equivalent of a pastor. He reluctantly agreed to what essentially amounted to a full-time volunteer job. The day before the news was announced to the Chevy Chase Ward, J.W. did something almost unheard of in the Church. He called the President of the Church to ask that Bill's assignment be rescinded. He knew President Spencer W. Kimball would give him a respectful hearing because they were friends. Kimball took J.W.'s phone call and listened as J.W. said Bill was simply too busy at Marriott to be a bishop on the side. "This calling was approved by our First Presidency, and we're not going to reverse it," Kimball replied.

A key reason for Bill's unhesitating acceptance of this new call was his admiration and respect for the man who had issued it, President Kimball. In four short years, the Church had successively lost three prophets to death. The first two were ninety-six and ninety-five years old, but the third, Harold B. Lee, was a close Marriott family friend and was just seventy-four when he died. "A terrible shock," J.W. lamented in his journal. "A great friend of ours for 40 years. The Lord wanted him or he would have stayed."[10]

Unlike his three immediate predecessors, Kimball had dealt with serious health issues throughout his life; the year before he became President, he had undergone open-heart surgery at the age of seventy-seven. The Marriott family knew Kimball to have a spirit far stronger than his body. He had stayed at the Marriott home in 1957 on his way to New York for an operation for his throat cancer, and he had greatly impressed Bill and J.W. with his insistence on performing extensive duties in spite of his illness.

"If someone were to ask me who was the most powerful and influential man in the world today, it would be President Kimball," Bill unabashedly pronounced during the Latter-day Saint prophet's life. "He is the most dynamic leader of the Church in this century. But to me, his greatness is in compassion and humility. He has said his life is like his shoes: to be worn out in service. He has been an example of complete submissiveness to the will of the Lord, of meekness and love."[11]

For President Kimball's part, Bill's acceptance of the call to serve as bishop increased the prophet's fondness for his friend's son. In letters to J.W., President Kimball often inquired after Bishop Marriott, calling him "delightful," "excellent," and "a credit to the Marriott name."[12] In one of the sweetest moments in Donna's memory, after a standing-room-only regional meeting at the new Washington D.C. Stake Center, President Kimball took the time to stop and give two-year-old David a kiss on the cheek.

Another life-changing event occurred in the summer Bill was called to be a bishop. On August 26, 1975, J.W. suffered a massive heart attack while vacationing with the family in New Hampshire. That afternoon, fourteen-year-old John was on the tennis court playing with his uncle Dick when they heard Allie scream from the window, "Come quick! He's having a heart attack!" Allie called for an ambulance, and J.W. was taken to Huggins Hospital. Ironically, the previous year J.W. had contributed funds for an intensive care unit there, but it had never been used because the hospital couldn't afford the extra nurses that were needed to staff it. Bill flew up from Washington, and the family hovered at the hospital for an anxious week of prayer and fasting. On September 8, J.W. was transported by ambulance to Massachusetts General Hospital in Boston, where the diagnosis was grim: J.W. probably needed multiple bypasses, but he might not survive the surgery. After three weeks he was sent home to regain enough stamina to have heart surgery.

Three days after returning home, J.W. suffered another heart attack and was rushed by ambulance to Georgetown University Hospital, where he spent two more weeks. No one in the family believed that J.W. was out of the woods when he returned home from the hospital on October 15. On November 6, he went into shock from a reaction to medication and was again rushed to the Georgetown hospital.

During J.W.'s fourth hospitalization, Bill suggested his father go to the Mayo Clinic for more tests when he was well enough to travel. Doctors there determined that surgery would not help. Rest and medication were the best and safest treatment. The family huddled and decided it was best if J.W. and Allie rested at Camelback. Arizona's weather and the resort's spalike atmosphere were palliative to J.W. for the next five months. He beat the odds and survived another ten years.

Bill was deeply grateful for the prayers of many friends, family members, and Marriott associates, but it was Allie whose ministrations were paramount. At his father's funeral a decade later, Bill said, "The doctors gave my father little chance for recovery, but they didn't know my mother. Nor did they recognize the healing power of our Father in Heaven. It was Mother's complete dedication to Dad's every need that helped to add ten precious years to his life."

Bill also played a role in prolonging his father's life. He innately knew that beyond a certain point, J.W.'s stress about the hotel expansion program might prove fatal. So he curtailed his hotel development vision throughout the 1970s. Instead, he directed the company's extra capital to other ventures. Those were less stressful for his father, but they also delayed Bill's drive to become the world's largest hotelier.

Donna and other family members believed that Bill's service as a bishop was also instrumental in J.W.'s survival. Deeply imbedded in every Latter-day Saint's core beliefs is the idea that God often blesses those who give selfless personal sacrifice. "We were doing everything we could medically to help Bill's father," Donna concluded. "But I knew that the fact Bill was willing to serve as bishop, no matter how hard that was, blessed his father's health."

Bill's ready acceptance of the call to service might have been the greatest act of faith he had ever shown. He felt ill prepared and thought the timing couldn't be worse. As the CEO of a $732-million company in the middle of a recession, his plate was already full. He coped by delegating and organizing and by using his business skills at church to make sure the trains ran on time.

He found himself in charge of a large contingent of Hispanic Latter-day Saints who were absorbed into the heavily Anglo Chevy

Chase Ward when their own congregation was disbanded. The Hispanic members felt they had lost their footing, so Bill created a "translation booth," from which English-to-Spanish translations of sermons were transmitted via headphones to the Spanish speakers seated in nearby pews. When one of them spoke from the pulpit, a simultaneous translation into English was piped into the chapel.

The work of a Latter-day Saint bishop is partly administrative but also heavily weighted with one-on-one care for congregants and pitching in alongside everyone else. True to the family motto, Bill's "no-big-shots" behavior impressed everyone. He was often one of the last to leave after a ward social event, and, with his family, he could be found in the church kitchen doing dishes and mopping the floors.

An important work for a bishop is bringing disaffected Latter-day Saints back to the fold. The Church keeps members' names on the ward records, even if the person drops out of Church activity. One woman in Bill's ward hadn't attended any Church meetings in forty-nine years. Every time Bishop Marriott called her, she hung up on him. He stopped at her home several Saturdays in a row, and she never answered the door. "I finally said, 'This is one person—maybe I better spend my time on the ones whom I can help.'"

It took more than a year to locate one inactive woman, but finally Bishop Marriott learned that she was working in a local hospital. When he visited her there, she was aloof until she revealed an interest in music. Bill asked her to join the choir, and she began coming to church, gradually providing fellowship and service to others.

One man hadn't been to church in sixteen years when Bill finally located him. He was a heavy smoker and an addicted coffee drinker, and he also enjoyed wine—all violations of the Church's health code. He felt out of place attending ward meetings. "Despite the many demands on Bishop Marriott, he found the time to meet with me five different times in a three-month period, always encouraging me to give up these habits. He was very personable and easy to talk to. But then, on the fifth time, he said, 'If you have a cup of coffee or a cigarette, come to church anyway. We want you back.' It was a refreshing approach," the man recalled. "It took a lot of pressure off me, and it worked."

Bill said, "Some of the happiest moments I ever had as a bishop were when a member came to me and said, 'I want to come back. I've been outside the Church for many years and I have not found happiness. I know that the other way is not good. I want to return to the gospel.' What a great thrill and blessing it was to bring back just one member to that joy."

As a bishop, Bill presided over Sunday worship services, performed marriages, conducted funerals, attended ward socials, and went on ward campouts. It was, perhaps, the latter that was the greatest challenge. He hated camping and would outfit a full bed in the back of his station wagon to avoid sleeping in a tent. David Fell, who was the ward executive secretary for Bishop Marriott, recalled that Bill would also don a sleeping mask that made him look like the Lone Ranger. "That's how he survived the campouts. But he came, and that spoke volumes."

As a bishop, Bill could perform marriages in Maryland. At least one of those ceremonies was unforgettable. The couple arrived forty minutes late. Bishop Marriott looked over their marriage license and panicked; it was a Virginia license, not good in Maryland. "So Bill bundled this couple in his car, dashed over to Virginia, and got them married in a civil ceremony," Fell related. "When he brought them back, the bishop did not tell anyone what had happened. He did everything except pronounce that he was doing it by the authority of Maryland, and no one was the wiser. He had a very slick way of doing it so that it sounded like it was a done deal, rather than having been done in between."

Regarding funerals that took place while he was bishop, Bill was able to handle the sad occasions with compassion and equanimity. The tragic death of Burr Johnson aboard a U.S. Navy destroyer was the cause of a particularly notable funeral. Johnson, his wife, and their children were Latter-day Saints, but he came from an Episcopalian family. (His mother was secretary to Bill's former St. Albans headmaster, Canon Charles Martin.)

Before the funeral, Canon Martin wrote J.W. about how impressed he was with Bill's sensitivity: "Immediately after Bill got the news, he went over to see the family. Yesterday, he was over again arranging all of the details of the service, from the music to the pallbearers. . . . It did me good to see a man with Bill's responsibilities giving the time, the interest, and the concern he was giving." The Episcopalian minister was also amazed at the support other members of the Church gave to the family. "I am going to call together our clergy at School [St. Albans] and say, 'Look, my friends, this is an example of the way we must support one another and this is an example of what lay people in the church can do.'"[13]

Bill had reason to be pleased with the way his ward pulled together at such trying times, but he was not happy when someone fell short of doing his or her part. His second counselor, Steve West, who also happened to work at Marriott, provided a unique perspective about Bill's growth as a leader in a nonbusiness situation.

"I remember a grave situation where we had somebody who was not doing what Bill wanted done. At work, you can say, 'Do it,' and the person does it. If they don't, they're fired. As bishop, Bill could say, 'do it and do it and do it'—and in this case, it didn't get done. Finally he said, 'We'll just have to remember that we're all volunteers. They don't get paid for doing this. They're doing it because they want to, and at the point they decide they don't want to, you lose all control. We have to keep them wanting to.' This refined Bill's capabilities as CEO because keeping people wanting to do things was good for business. You can be aggressive, you can be gruff, you can be a prima donna. But if you lead a group who follows because of desire, you are an exceptional CEO."

Perhaps only in The Church of Jesus Christ of Latter-day Saints could a Fortune 500 CEO counsel with a Church member about a deeply personal issue one day and then report to work the next morning and make multimillion-dollar decisions. "As bishop, I was dealing with every kind of thing imaginable—marital problems, kids on drugs, people in abject poverty who couldn't get jobs," Bill recalled. At first, he wore himself out in the effort. "It took about six months before he realized there was no way he could solve all those problems. He wasn't a trained psychologist. He was just one man. He decided he could do no more than to do the best he could and pray that would suffice," Donna said.

David Fell recalled once being tasked by Bishop Marriott to accompany a young ward member with serious psychiatric problems back to his home in Salt Lake City for treatment. "I was very nervous he would have a psychotic episode along the way, and then we reached O'Hare airport and it was bedlam. Suddenly, a man from Bill's In-Flite services at the airport tapped me on the shoulder and whisked us along to the connecting flight, right through his friends at security and the airlines." Bill paid for the flights himself.

One of the hardest parts of Bill's job as bishop was when he took the time to personally counsel ward members only to have the problem get worse because the supplicant didn't follow his advice. Once, Bill received a long-distance phone call from the mother of a young woman he had counseled about her marriage. The daughter had disregarded his advice, and things had not improved. "I thought [the mother] was going to tell me I told [the daughter] all the wrong things," Bill said. Instead, she reported that she told her daughter, "If you go to counsel with the bishop, you should do what he tells you to do. If you don't—and you haven't—you shouldn't counsel with him, or complain."

Sometimes the calling could be very frustrating, even depressing. "He worked very hard at keeping husbands and wives together," recalled David Fell. "Once, he mentioned to me that he had just finished eight hours of counseling with a couple, trying to keep them together. But they had already planned a divorce, and he finally realized that they had gone through all those hours to try to get him to decide who would get custody of the dog. That really irritated him, as it should have." Fell added that instead of being a bishop who held a lot of Church inquiries over moral transgressions, "he held a lot of hands. He preferred to counsel them back to righteousness, rather than excommunicate them."

Among the things that affected Bill most deeply as bishop was the impoverished Hispanic members who were determined to pay tithing. "They were not making much. They were going without needed clothing in order to pay their tithing. I had these little South American ladies come in and give me their tithes of $5 or $10, knowing that was maybe a full 10 percent of all they'd made in the week. It brought me to a much better understanding of, above all, their faithfulness."

Looking back on Bill's time as bishop, Donna considered it nothing short of miraculous that her husband could fit it all in. "When he became bishop, I didn't know where he would find the extra time he needed to do it," she said, "but the Lord blessed him to carry out his calling. We had a wonderful spirit in our home. He was able to do what needed to be done as bishop, still keep up with his job, and always be at home when he was needed." Blessings aside, though, the time-consuming calling could not help but sap some of his energy. "He had very, very long Sundays," Donna recalled. "First there were the church meetings, and then he'd stay after church to counsel with people in his church office. After that, he'd make hospital visits or go to the members' homes to talk with them. Then he'd go to work Monday morning just wrung out. People couldn't understand why he was so tired on Monday. They'd all been out playing golf."

During this time, Bill struggled with the downturn of a new chain restaurant venture—Farrell's Ice Cream Parlour Restaurants. The mid-1972 acquisition for $10 million had seemed like a good idea at the time. Founder Bob Farrell had successfully married entertainment with well-priced ice cream specialties to produce a winning concept. The restaurants had a "Gay Nineties" theme—1890s, that is—with bright red-and-white decor and employees energetically serving customers in straw boaters and period dress. Every parlour had a player piano, and the tabloid-sized menu featured sandwiches as well as ice cream treats delivered with noisy fanfare. When a group ordered "The Zoo Sundae," the huge dairy treat was carried enthusiastically by employees around the restaurant on a stretcher to the accompaniment of wailing ambulance sirens. Free sundaes for birthday customers were a big draw, and the parlours were doing high-volume business at shopping malls in the West.

Restaurant Group President Mike Hostage was hot about the prospect, so Bill decided to pick it up and let Hostage run with it. Bill liked the idea of owning a group of ice cream shops and "not reinventing the wheel. To try and duplicate what Bob Farrell had done would have taken a lot of time and may or may not have been successful. He had the charisma, expertise and ability to run these places. They were fun and different. Great ice cream and great family entertainment. It made sense for us to acquire it."[14]

When Marriott bought Farrell's, the company had twenty-one ice cream restaurants with sales in eight states of $7.7 million the previous year. An additional thirty-seven franchised units in six states and British Columbia, Canada, brought in $13 million more. The fact that sixteen of the twenty-one company-owned units had been built in the previous three years promised an appealing growth trajectory. In fact, in two years, Hostage tripled the number of company-owned Farrell's to sixty profitable restaurants across the United States and in Canada.

In retrospect, Bill observed: "Farrell's was handled all wrong. With weak management, we expanded too fast over a wide geographic area. They had big-time business on birthdays, but there weren't enough birthdays. They made money for two or three years, and then failed miserably." Farrell's was partly a victim of the recession, when overall business in retail malls declined, and Bill eventually sold it for roughly a break-even price.

Meanwhile, Bill was intent on opening a hotel in Europe. Over nearly a decade, Bill went on a half dozen hotel-scouting trips abroad, one of them in the company of legendary movie star Douglas Fairbanks, Jr., who had solid business contacts with hoteliers in Great Britain and

Germany. Bill learned while on a Fairbanks-arranged 1965 trip to Munich that "Europe was controlled by a bunch of cartels that kept out all the competition. The Munich city council locked us out of the city, but took us to a place we could build way out in the country. We walked away. I told them, 'We aren't going to do anything in Germany until you get your act together and allow free enterprise to be free.'"

What Bill wanted most was a suitable site for someone else to build the hotel and Marriott to manage it. He finally found a site in Amsterdam and a partner, the massive Watney Mann brewery company, who agreed to finance the $15-million real-estate purchase and construction through a Dutch subsidiary. J.W. was happy with a deal that required not one cent of corporate investment, while the company stood to make money even if the hotel owners did not.

The grand opening of the Amsterdam Marriott in March 1975 was a major media event. For his part, J.W. may have been more excited about the new Marriott Tulip a Dutch grower had developed for him and Allie. After the grand opening, they took home 100 bulbs to plant in Washington and at Lake Winnipesaukee.

Two weeks after the Amsterdam grand opening, Marriott opened its first destination resort built from scratch—the Lincolnshire Resort complex north of Chicago. At its center was the 400-room hotel with an eighteen-hole championship golf course, ski runs, bicycle trails, health club, ice-skating rink, indoor and outdoor swimming pools, and a live theater venue.

Many things can go wrong at a ribbon cutting, and the Marriott preference for quirky grand-opening stunts added to the unknowns. This time it was a lion named Zamba who had to break through the ribbon and eat a slab of raw meat shaped like a hotel key (the usual symbol that the resort didn't need a key because it would never close). On cue, Zamba devoured the "key," and then a power fluctuation caused the lights to flicker. The 450-pound Zamba panicked and broke from his leash.

With the trainer in hot pursuit, the lion ran up the aisle and dashed across several rows of terrified guests. He made it out an exit door to the lobby and into a hall before the trainer wrangled him back onto the leash. Amid the pandemonium, the wife of one of Marriott's franchisees was so frozen to her seat that the huge lion bounded right over the top of her. News reporters rushed to her with microphones. "Are you all right?" they asked. With impressive aplomb, the Jewish woman replied: "Well, with all these Christians here, I knew I was safe from the lion."[15]

• • •

In May 1977, after two years in his Church calling, Bill was released as bishop to take an assignment as the first counselor in a new Washington D.C. Stake presidency. After the reception honoring Bill as the outgoing bishop, Allie recorded with exultation: "All said Billy was the best Bishop they had ever had."[16] It had been a time when Bill said "the need to rely on the Lord became very important to me."

Longtime friend Jon Huntsman observed a few years after his friend's release as bishop that "the happiest I've ever seen Bill was when he was bishop—when he was literally working around the clock with families who didn't have anything. He seemed to thrive in that atmosphere. He radiated a sense of inner peace and contentment."[17]

Two decades after his release as bishop, Bill reflected that the service "really brought me to a much better understanding of our associates in our company—what kind of problems they have in making ends meet, in trying to raise their families, trying to get their kids to do right, trying to provide healthcare and pay the light bill, the heat bill, the rent. When you're the CEO of a company, it's hard to really understand what's going on in people's lives that are working down in the trenches. The Church job gave me more empathy. I became a better listener because of it. Those two years became an anchor in troubled times. No question about it."[18]

CHAPTER 13

HIGH ANXIETY
AND MIRACLES

The bicentennial spring and summer of 1976 brought a whirlwind of exciting activities. First was the March 20 opening of the Great America at Santa Clara, California. The *Washington Post* called the theme parks the company's "biggest investment gamble in its history," and Bill felt every bit of that risk, in spite of the huge crowd of 20,000 on the first day. "There are a few butterflies in my stomach—maybe a whole herd of them, for that matter," he said at the time. "We think we are moving into the right business, in the right way, at the right time."[1]

At the end of May, Bill and Donna flew to Gurnee, Illinois, for the opening of their second Great America. Only 7,000 people braved a torrential downpour that day. Bill obligingly sat in the front seat of the Gurnee double corkscrew roller coaster for the first ride—in the rain. When he got off a little shakily, a reporter asked how he felt. Bill smiled: "You know, there aren't many of us CEOs who can say we just got off our latest roller coaster. Of course, some of us feel like we're on them every day."[2]

Two weeks later, he was at the Washington Monument, opening the first of the free "Music '76!" summer shows that Marriott sponsored for the United States bicentennial. Four days later, he was back at Santa Clara, opening a new 300-room Marriott hotel. Three days after that, he and Donna boarded a Concorde jet for the first time, to enjoy a one-week trip to Amsterdam, Russia, and Finland. A few days after they returned, they joined in the bicentennial Fourth of July weekend celebrations in the nation's capital.

At the request of President Gerald Ford, the Mormon Tabernacle Choir gave a series of performances at those celebrations. On Saturday morning, July 3, local Latter-day Saints including Bill and Donna gathered for the dedication of the new visitors' center at the Washington D.C. Temple. That evening, the Marriotts joined Church President Spencer W. Kimball and U.S. President Ford in the President's Box at the Kennedy Center for the Honor America Day (HAD) musical production. As head of HAD, J.W. had overseen all the planning, except for one surprise.

The program was scheduled to end with the Tabernacle Choir and audience singing "The Battle Hymn of the Republic." But first, HAD's vice chairman stepped to the microphone on stage, and Stephen and John Marriott entered from the wings wearing their Eagle Scout uniforms. Attendants carried a small table to the center of the stage, on which was displayed a porcelain statue of a pair of wild mustangs in full gallop. It was a gift from the grateful HAD committee to a patriot who had worked hard to honor his country. "Now, Steve and Johnny, go find your grandpa," the HAD official instructed. The boys carried the statue from the stage as the spotlight played over the audience and then landed on J.W. in the President's Box. His grandsons emerged from the back of the box to present him with the gift.

Bill was proud and moved by the honor for his father. At the center of this vivid mental snapshot for him was the sight of his Eagle Scout sons standing with the President of their Church, honored grandparents, and the President of the United States. Church, family, and country—all lined up in a joyful tableau.

● ● ●

By the early 1970s, the Marriott headquarters on River Road could not contain the rapidly expanding staff. Six of Marriott's divisions had to be transferred to other office complexes nearby. Responding to the urgent need for a new headquarters, Marriott found a site in Bethesda, Maryland, at the intersection of Interstate 270 and Democracy Boulevard. The company soon had a design for an impressive seven-story building. Every other floor was set back fifteen feet and planted with ivy on the three terraced levels, giving it a lush pyramid facade. The 537,000-square-foot building would hold all 1,400 headquarters personnel from every major Marriott division, with room to spare.

The ground breaking was set for May 21, 1977, the fiftieth anniversary of the company's founding. Reminiscent of their first trip across the country, J.W. and Allie gamely rode to the event in a top-down 1927 Model T Ford. Bill unveiled the cornerstone, which identified the new structure as "The J. Willard and Alice S. Marriott Building." In September, the company hit a perfect milestone for its golden year, $1.03 billion in annual sales at the end of its fiscal year. A round of laudatory stories about the company spread across the country, touting the nickel-a-mug root beer enterprise that had just surpassed $1 billion for the first time. In one interview, Bill confidently predicted that they would cross the $2 billion mark in five years or less. He did it in four.[3]

Marriott family fortunes rose with the company's success. As much as wealth brings a comfortable living to those who have it, it may also create an envy from others that can turn potentially dangerous. Once when Debbie argued with her father over a curfew violation, he sat her down and confided his reasons for being protective: "I haven't wanted to talk about this, but . . . part of needing to know where you are, and wanting you to be home, is because we've had some threats against our family." As Debbie reflected on her childhood, she realized that on at least three occasions a police car had been stationed outside their house for several days and nights. "I found out later that Dad had received death threats from a few lower-level employees he had to fire."

The most serious and dangerous plot against the family was planned by a law-enforcement officer during the summer of the company's golden year.

The previous year had been full of occasions when Marriott ceremonial functions had required a police escort, such as the one for a bus carrying VIPs to the bicentennial Fourth of July fireworks. Riding the lead motorcycle that day was U.S. Park Policeman Paul Shepherd. He had been at the Marriott home on two other occasions, but that day was the first time Bill met and spoke with him, and Shepherd seemed friendly enough. Bill had no inkling that the officer was "a cold, calculating desperate individual who would chuck a whole career for big money," as a federal prosecutor later described him.[4]

Shepherd was a fourteen-year U.S. Park Police veteran who, in mid-1977, planned a series of kidnappings because he "was tired of being a poor cop." In July, he contacted a thrice-convicted felon to help plot three kidnappings—one of the senior Marriotts, Redskins Coach George Allen or his wife, and former U.S. Transportation Secretary John A. Volpe, who owned a large construction company.

The felon expressed interest, but then, wanting to curry favor with law enforcement, he notified the FBI. They asked the felon to arrange an introduction between Shepherd and FBI undercover agent Edward Robb, who posed as "Eddie Rossi" and hinted of Mafia connections. Shepherd explained the plan to "Rossi": they would go to J.W.'s home and abduct him or Allie for a $500,000 ransom. "If I get in that house and something goes wrong," he said, "I'll cut that old lady's head off and leave her bleeding all over the floor." Later he added, "I'm just so damn tired of being poor. I don't really care [about killing anyone]. I just want the money."[5]

Shepherd also planned to involve his older brother, Billy, who would be their lookout. Whichever senior Marriott was kidnapped, he or she would be held at Shepherd's girlfriend's place.

The next day, unaware of the unfolding conspiracy, the Marriotts were vacationing in New Hampshire. (Shepherd hadn't taken into account that his victims were not even at home.) On Friday morning, July 29, the FBI called Bill at Lake Winnipesaukee and gave him a role in the sting. The following Tuesday morning, after he had returned from the lake, Bill drove his father's car into the driveway at J.W.'s house and went inside, making it appear from a distance that he was J.W.

Shepherd had to work that day, so he told Rossi to kidnap J.W. Rossi assumed Shepherd would have a lookout near the house—probably his brother—to make sure the deed was done. A "stolen" Hot Shoppes truck soon wheeled into the driveway, and two FBI undercover agents dressed in company coveralls entered the house. Shortly after, they came out with a body bag supposedly containing J.W., but actually stuffed with blankets and pillows.

Just before nine a.m., "Rossi" called Shepherd. "Everything's real good! The meat's in the van," he said in code. Shepherd waited a few minutes, then went to an outside pay phone and called Bill. This was a crucial moment for the kidnapping case. Bill had to act shocked, wait for the ransom demand, and agree to pay it. Only then would the FBI have an airtight case. Bill played his part well. After Shepherd hung up, FBI agents swooped in for the arrest. Minutes later, FBI Director Clarence M. Kelley issued a press release about the kidnapping plot and the arrests of Shepherd and his brother.

Bill was less rattled about the day's events than he was when he testified against Shepherd at a trial the following October. The defense attorney zeroed in on Bill, asking about his net worth and other questions designed to elicit sympathy for the poor kidnapper. Bill recounted: "He was trying to make the family look bad. 'Oh, so you get a motorcycle escort to drive you around Washington in a bus? You're a big shot, aren't you?' That really upset me—he was trying to deflect from his client's guilt, and make the victims look bad. 'You deserve to be kidnapped—showing off all your money!' he said, or something like it. It was awful; it was bizarre." The strategy didn't work. After twenty hours of jury deliberation, Shepherd was found guilty and sentenced to fifteen years in prison.[6]

If notoriety and wealth brought risks, they also gave Bill a platform for political and social change. He came to life as a political activist in the late 1970s. It was a time of great political awakening for America's captains of free enterprise. Many of them realized that unless they entered the political arena, American capitalism in general would erode, and the future of their companies would fall victim to an expanding government, with attendant increases in regulations, taxation, and inflation.

Due to President Lyndon Johnson's Great Society initiatives, the importance of American business had diminished in favor of government programs. A liberal philosophy gained a strong foothold in the nation's politics. Though ostensibly conservative, the Nixon administration— through economic programs, regulatory actions, and an increase in government size—accelerated an antibusiness climate.

First to raise the warning cry was lawyer Lewis Powell, who in 1971 wrote a memo to the U.S. Chamber of Commerce leadership while he was chairing one of their committees. (This was only a few months before Powell was named as a U.S. Supreme Court Justice.) In the memo, he opined that pro-business conservative thought had lost much ground to the New Left, which was the growing fashion on college campuses among America's future leaders. The Chamber must rise up and engage in this war of ideology since, in Powell's view, it was well equipped to lead the charge on behalf of free enterprise.

The Chamber initially failed to accept the challenge, but Powell's writings on the subject motivated others to do so. Colorado brewer Joseph Coors funded a think tank, the Heritage Foundation, to engage in conservative lobbying on Capitol Hill. After three-quarters of a century, the National Association of Manufacturers (NAM) moved its offices from New York to Washington, D.C., in 1972.

Bill watched the evolution with interest. For years, he had left the political schmoozing to his father, while he concentrated on Marriott's

bottom line. But in the wake of the 1976 presidential victory of pop-
ulist Jimmy Carter, Bill realized he could no longer stand on the
sidelines. He accepted a nomination to the Chamber Board in April
1977. The group's announcement of Bill's election was glowing: "The
national Chamber is gaining a giant in one of the country's fastest-
growing industries . . ."[7]

At first, still wishing to avoid the messiness of politics, Bill focused
on the Chamber's education efforts. In a much-quoted passage from
one of his speeches, Bill said, "I cannot understand why courses in
free enterprise are not absolutely required of our young people in high
school and college. . . . We have to educate our educators and educate
our young people about the world around them. We are a free enterprise nation, and we must insure that the next generation knows the
basics of our capitalist system."

The array of Carter-spawned legislation that directly threatened
Marriott and the American economy as a whole had propelled Bill into
the political arena. For example, Carter proposed legislation to end the
so-called "three-martini lunch" by severely curtailing business tax deductions for meals and entertainment. "The three-martini lunch is so
rare that it is basically a myth," Bill declared to the press. "The average
businessman's lunch is a hamburger and Coke costing $3 or less. The
Hotel and Restaurant Association is violently opposed to the legislation,
as am I. If it's enacted, within the first year we'll have to cut about 2,700
permanent jobs at Marriott. This would be an absolute imperative response to what we estimate as the loss of our expense account volume.
And this will happen across the board for the entire lodging/food service
industry—which incidentally is the third largest employer in our country." The facts were so indisputable that unions, realizing the potential
massive job loss, joined in opposition, and the legislation was killed. That
legislation, however, was only a small symptom of the greater problem.

"I think inflation is our biggest enemy, and second is the increasing role of government in our lives. Almost everything being done in

Washington is inflationary," Bill told one reporter. In a related speech he lamented that the government "was actually legislating increased inflation instead of taking bold steps to reduce it."[8]

Exhibit A was the federal minimum-wage legislation introduced in February 1977, proposing automatic raises in the minimum wage every year for the next four years. Bill was a firm supporter of the need for a federal minimum wage standard to protect workers, but he also believed that once a baseline was established, the market should determine increases. Profit margins were slim in the food business. In D.C., the local government had thought it was helping low-income workers by passing wage increases significantly higher than the federal standard. The impact on Marriott alone between 1975 and 1979 was the closure of fourteen restaurants and loss of 1,300 jobs, many of them filled by minority youths.

As Carter's minimum-wage legislation was working its way through Congress, Bill said he "went to the White House and begged a member of the president's staff not to increase the minimum wage." He was politely ignored. He got the same response from members of Congress who told him they couldn't buck the labor-union support of the bill.

The legislation passed in November 1977, mandating a nearly 46 percent increase in the minimum wage through annual step-ups over four years. Bill hunkered down with his people to put together an immediate response that would preserve the company's bottom line for its stockholders—which meant hundreds more layoffs in the next few years. As he went through this planning process, his anger escalated.

In early 1978, Bill resolved that he had to do more. The perfect opportunity to launch his vigorous campaign for free enterprise was at a speech to the American Marketing Association (AMA) on February 24. The fire-breathing address became a classic:

> For the first time in my own business career, I'm compelled to speak out in protest. We face an inability or unwillingness among public leaders to consider the

true consequences of their actions. We see these leaders cave in consistently to the vocal few. There's been a serious loss of vision, and the problem spans the entire nation, whether they are federal officials, state, or local, whether they are elected, appointed, or civil servants.

I've finally realized I can't just keep tending to my own business and hope things will work out. It's getting late—I've got to step forward. I am proud of our great country, of our free enterprise system, of what business and industry has done. Of course, we're not perfect. We make mistakes, too. But our system works. We're capitalists—and we should be proud of it.

Business provides eight out of every ten jobs. It provides capital investment and products and services and taxes and dividends that make this country go. And, there's so much more we could do if government will just get its knee off our chest. . . .

And so, I suggest a revolt. A taxpayers' and business leaders' revolt against far more government than we need, or deserve, or want, or will stand for, or will pay for. . . .

Business is not guilty until proven innocent—as so many people seem to think today. Our business system is good. It's not business *and* society. It's business *for* society. . . .

We are all in business. . . . We are in a position of influence. I respectfully suggest that we have a great responsibility to help turn this thing around.[9]

Once Bill was in, he was all in. Over the next three years, in speech after speech, he fervently focused on the cause of free enterprise. He created the Marriott Political Action Committee and the Marriott Local and State Political Action Committee. Those corporate PACs used targeted political contributions to back candidates who understood the vital role of business in America.

For his main platform, however, he favored the Citizens Choice initiative of the U.S. Chamber of Commerce, ramping up his involvement with that lobbying group to the point that he was elected its chairman in May 1979. Under his leadership, it soon quadrupled its membership and carried significant weight on Capitol Hill. Concurrently, Bill helped the Chamber itself become a lobbying juggernaut.

In retrospect, it's clear that Bill's high-profile political activism was timely. There is little doubt that presidential candidate Ronald Reagan's promise to "get the government off the backs of the people" was key to his dramatic victory over Carter in 1980.

With a government more in sync with what Bill had outlined, America's economy boomed during Reagan's two terms. There was not one federally ordered increase of the minimum wage during those eight years—yet many more low-income workers were employed and were paid higher wages than they had been during the Carter era. As Bill had foreseen, the market was able to improve their lives and employment prospects within the rising economy better than any government mandate ever could.

• • •

The Marriott family expanded in 1978 when Debbie married Ron Harrison, who turned out to be an asset to the family and the company. Ron had served a Latter-day Saint mission in Taiwan and was fluent in Mandarin. After the engagement, Ron's father sat Debbie down for a lecture; he didn't want Marriott wealth ruining his son or destroying his confidence. Though he had substantial offers from several top engineering companies and Apple, Ron wound up building a career at Marriott, working his way up through the ranks and making his mark at every level.

Seven weeks before Debbie's wedding, Bill's oldest son, Stephen, embarked on a Church mission. The previous October, Bill and Donna had taken him to a hearing specialist in Los Angeles. Stephen had hoped to be told that his hearing would get better, and he had prayed fervently that at least it would not get worse. So when the doctor told him his hearing had not deteriorated, he was grateful. But there were other health issues. No matter what he did, he could not add any muscle or weight to his thin frame. In early 1978, Stephen was diagnosed with hormone deficiencies that precluded muscle improvement, weight gain, or normal production of testosterone. It was the last prognosis that most alarmed Stephen. He wanted children, so he agreed to hormone-replacement therapy, which included a multiyear series of painful shots.

Any one of those three issues—hearing loss, general frailty, and the need for medication that was not available in many places of the world—was serious enough to disqualify him from serving a mission. The combination was practically a guarantee that the Church would not take the risk of sending him. Stephen continued to pray, feeling that he had his parents and God in his corner. The fact that Stephen's health ultimately didn't disqualify him was probably due to the fact that the Church leadership knew the Marriott family and their record of service to the Church. Stephen was assigned to go to Vancouver, British Columbia, to work in the mission office there.

Bill recalled the day he and Donna dropped Stephen off in Salt Lake City to begin his training. "He had two big suitcases with everything he owned, and everything we thought he'd ever need on his mission," Bill recalled. "He was losing his hearing, and weighed maybe a hundred pounds. He couldn't carry the suitcases up the stairs, so they had to send someone to help him." As the parents left, they could not help but feel anxiety for their son and the challenges he would experience during the next two years.

Although Latter-day Saint missionaries are not normally allowed to see their families, because of his special circumstances, Stephen was permitted a rare visit from his parents and his brother, John, in the spring of 1979. They were on their way home from an eleven-day tour of the People's Republic of China.

Over several years, J.W. had developed friendships with the top Communist officials of the PRC's liaison office in Washington, D.C. When one was promoted to a high government post in Beijing, he invited J.W. to China on a government-hosted tour. The group that went in the spring of 1979 was made up of five couples—J.W. and Allie; Bill and Donna; Debbie and Ron Harrison; Jon and Karen Huntsman; the Marriotts' friends Mark and Lola Austad—and two teenagers, John Marriott and Peter Huntsman.

They would be among the few Westerners allowed behind the Red Curtain. Three years before, the murderous and repressive Cultural Revolution had finally ended with the death of Mao Tse-tung and the unseating of the Gang of Four that had ruled in his dotage.

"It was that very unique window of time—right after the Cultural Revolution, and before an explosion of Western influence," Ron Harrison recalled. "All the people we saw were still wearing the same blue or black Mao suits. All the women had the same haircuts. Everybody walked or rode bicycles; there were almost no cars. It was all still so uniform. Think of it—a billion people, uniform, the same."

After spending a few days in Hong Kong, the Marriott group took a train to Canton and checked into the twenty-six-story White Cloud Hotel. The experience echoed Bill's trip to the Soviet Union. Although the Canton hotel was only three years old, it was filthy. The sheets were old tablecloths with food stains on them. The towels were rags that also were used to mop the floors. Everybody kept their socks on and slept on top of the sheets, not between them. Surprisingly, the ultrafastidious J.W. was the least put off. "He was raised in a dirty old house in Utah, so it was like going home for him, I guess," Bill laughed.

Ron chose not to let the Canton guides know he spoke Chinese. As he listened to them conversing in Mandarin about the Marriott group, he realized they were aware of private conversations that had taken place in the hotel rooms, which were obviously bugged. In Shanghai, the next stop, Ron dropped the ruse. Debbie recalled, "We were in a park and there were about 300 or 400 people surrounding us, just staring at the Westerners, gawking like we were Martians. . . . So Ron stood up on a bench in the park and started speaking to all of them. They were all stunned that a Westerner could speak Chinese. He started joking with them, and they were all laughing."

Neither Bill nor J.W. were fans of exotic food, especially food that came with heads still attached, so Ron vetted their menus. J.W. had filled a suitcase with Rice Krispies, peanut butter, dried soup, and other snacks. Bill had not packed any survival food. "Ron spoke the language, and that saved us," he said. "It seemed like he spent most of his time in the kitchens trying to negotiate something we could eat."

While in Beijing, Bill scouted hotel locations, which pleased the PRC's minister of tourism immensely. But the discussion between the two, though courteous, did not go well. Acting as translator, Ron summarized the minister's terms: "We have our own [Communist] party hotels. We'll let you build your own hotel on your dime. We'll let you bring your own people in. But we'll tell you what groups and individuals can stay at your hotel, and only after we have filled our party hotels first. And then, after five years of your attempts to make a profit, we'll probably nationalize your hotel and make it ours."

Bill remarked drily, "I guess they're not ready for us yet."

After a stopover in Tokyo, Bill, Donna, and John flew home via Vancouver. Stephen, who had looked like a thirteen-year-old when he arrived on his mission, was bigger and stronger. They took him shopping for larger clothes and to a restaurant where he wolfed down the meal. He was thriving, and his parents bade him farewell with confidence that he would be okay.

The trip to China had started the day after Debbie graduated from BYU with highest honors as a Phi Kappa Phi. When she and Ron returned from China, they moved to Dallas, where he had a summer engineering internship with Texas Instruments Co. and Debbie worked at the front desk of the Dallas Marriott North hotel. Debbie was soon pregnant with twins, and they moved back to Utah for Ron's final year at BYU. On October 22, Debbie went into labor, only twenty-two weeks into her pregnancy. At the hospital, the nurses seemed non-plussed and refused to notify Debbie's doctor.

"I got really scared and tried to track down my parents," Debbie recalled. Donna had gone with Bill to Munich, Germany. When his secretary finally reached him, it was three a.m. in Munich. Bill and Donna got on their knees and prayed. Then Bill called Debbie to assess the situation and learned that her doctor had finally arrived to find her in grave condition. He learned firsthand from his terrified daughter just how dire the circumstances were. As Debbie recalled, "My dad flipped out and called my doctor, yelling and swearing at him. He told the doctor I was in labor, and he'd better leave immediately, whatever he was doing!" The doctor did, and was shocked to find she was dilated to five centimeters. "He went into panic mode, and complained that 'the nurses didn't tell me it was *this* serious.'" (One of them was subsequently fired over the dangerous misdiagnosis.) Bill and Donna caught the first flight home.

At a time when there were none of the labor-slowing drugs that exist now, the best the doctor could do was put Debbie on an alcohol IV. A relatively new drug to slow labor, Vasodilan, had potentially hazardous heart-related side effects, and Debbie's heart was already compromised. The growing team of doctors took Ron aside and presented a terrible choice. "We have medicine that will save Debbie, but the twins will be aborted. Or, we can save the babies, but Debbie's health will be so compromised that she will probably die. What do you want to do?"

Setting the no-win decision aside, Ron gave Debbie a priesthood blessing, praying to slow down the labor. Then he consulted a cardiologist, who advised that Debbie's heart was probably strong enough to handle a small dose of Vasodilan. Bill had also martialed spiritual forces, alerting Apostle and family friend David B. Haight in Salt Lake City of the crisis by telephone. Elder Haight drove to the hospital in Provo and gave Debbie a second blessing. His words seemed to promise a positive outcome.

By the time Bill and Donna arrived in Utah, it was still up in the air who might live and who might not. After three days, the Vasodilan had worked well enough that Debbie was out of the woods, but the babies were not. Doctors advised that she must not deliver the twins until thirty-two to thirty-four weeks if there was to be any hope of their survival. Her hospital bed was tilted on blocks with her feet higher than her head, and there she stayed for two months.

Bill had to return to work in Washington, but, without fail, he called every day. At one point, when he could tell that his daughter was particularly depressed, he flew to Utah to stay with her for four days. "He just sat by my bed all day long, holding my hand, chatting with me," she said.

Ron came up with a way to help Debbie reach the thirty-four-week mark. Doctors had said that every two days in the womb, the babies were gaining three ounces. So, every other day, Ron brought her a three-ounce box of Jell-O and slowly built towers of boxes on the window ledge in the hospital room. One week out of every three, Donna came out to stay with Debbie at the hospital, doing needlepoint and holding her daughter's hand. In the early hours of December 11, the twins were born. Scott came out weighing four pounds, eight ounces, and Mark, four pounds, five ounces.

Six months later, Debbie and Ron took a vacation to Hawaii, leaving the babies in the care of Bill and Donna in Maryland. One moment with Grandpa was preserved on film in the corporate archives. "My dad was so proud, and he figured this was a way to drive home the point he'd been making with his senior executives about efficient time management," said Debbie. With some flourish, Bill arrived at

Bill with Debbie's twins, Mark and Scott.

a meeting, carrying in each hand a grandson in an infant carrier. He placed them in the center of the boardroom table and said: "These are my grandchildren, Scott and Mark. I want you to know that my daughter listens to me. Two kids at one time—now, that's productivity and management!"

When the twins were born, Stephen was in the last six months of his mission. He had begun to lose his sight, but he didn't tell anyone, including his parents. He wanted to live the "no-big-shots" family credo on his mission, so he couldn't abide special treatment. Once, Elder Haight wrote him to inquire about his mission. All letters were forwarded through the mission office, where another missionary had written over the front of the envelope, with an arrow pointing to Haight's name: "What kind of joke is this? You probably know Pres. Carter too, right?"

Stephen was even nervous about his father's phone calls, which were an exception to mission rules. Once, he wrote in his journal, "Dad called me again tonight. It was great talking to him and mom

211

but I wish he wouldn't call so often simply because of mission rules."[10] Stephen lived by the rules. The fact that he couldn't control his crippling health issues probably explained why he thrived in a rule-driven missionary system. It was a triumphal return home for him in June of 1980. Less than two months later, John departed for his mission, which turned out to be a vastly different experience from his older brother's.

To his parents' chagrin, John ran with a faster crowd in high school. Like so many teens, he was determined to find his own way in the world and not do what his parents expected him to do, which strained their relationship. Though they were upset with some of his choices, they also did not try to control him. They saved their fire for two ultimatums—he must attend BYU, and he must go on a mission.

Provo, Utah, and BYU were a culture shock for John. He begged his parents to allow him to transfer to the University of Utah, and they agreed. But they refused to capitulate on the mission. Bill hinted that it might be a condition of John making his career in the family business. "I was told that if I didn't go I would probably be pumping gas for the rest of my life. Maybe they figured I'd flunk out of school, that I'd be a derelict or something. So I felt I had no choice." It was not in John's nature to be bitter, so he resigned himself to the prospect and accepted a mission assignment to Tokyo.

"Living in Japan was a great experience," John recalled in interviews. "I was at a very impressionable age, and I got a lot out of it. The Japanese are real perfectionists. I learned people aren't necessarily right or wrong—they're just different. I baptized over a hundred people, learned the language and the culture, and have returned regularly since then on business trips."[11]

While John was on his mission, Stephen married Juliana ("Julie") Baughman. His health challenges continued to worsen. Around Christmas of 1981, Bill recorded in his journal, "Debbie and Stephen got into a big fight about Stephen's driving ability. Just like they were back in grade school!"[12] But it was much more serious than that.

One night, Stephen was driving in Washington, D.C., with Julie and Debbie as passengers. Debbie remembered: "Stephen kept running red lights . . . and we almost got killed. I started screaming at him, 'What's the matter with you? Didn't you see that light?' Apparently, he didn't." Not only did Stephen refuse to admit his failing eyesight, but he wouldn't let Debbie get behind the wheel. She told him she would never ride with him again.

In January 1983, Julie and Stephen had Bill and Donna's third grandchild, Jennifer Rae. "I tell you, the day of miracles has not ceased!" wrote Stephen, who had once been told by doctors that he could never have children.[13]

Meanwhile, Debbie was pregnant with her third child, and that pregnancy was not going well. Her husband had finished an MBA program and was being recruited by top engineering firms. Bill added Marriott to the list of those recruiting Ron, but he was reluctant to pressure him to join the family business. Although Ron was an engineer, he was beginning to think about more people-oriented work, which Marriott would offer. But, he said, "I wanted to be my own guy. I didn't want to be viewed as someone who would take the easy way. I wanted to be successful on my own, and I knew I could be."

In the end, he chose family, and Bill made him sales manager of Marriott's Rancho Las Palmas resort in Palm Springs, where he had trained in the hotel business. Debbie went into premature labor at twenty-seven weeks. There was no facility to handle premature newborns in Palm Springs, so she moved in with Ron's sister in Palo Alto, California, to be near Stanford University hospital. Christopher was born on February 16, 1983, only one month early, weighing five pounds, ten ounces, which was not as small as the twins. But it quickly became clear that all was not well.

Chris was diagnosed with hyaline membrane disease, which is now known as infant respiratory distress syndrome (IRDS), a lung deficiency. He was put on a respirator in the Neonatal Intensive Care Unit

(NICU), and doctors told Debbie he was dying. "They were going to take Chris off the respirator so I could hold him for the first time—and so he could die in my arms. I was in absolute hysterics and told them to wait until Ron got to the hospital. By the time he arrived, and we walked to the NICU, the pediatrician said Chris had begun to respond a little, so they would wait and see what happened."

Meanwhile, Bill arrived in time for a powerful spiritual experience. As the doctors stood back, Bill, Ron, and Ron's father put their hands on the baby's head as Ron offered a blessing. Not only did he promise life, but he blessed it to be a healthy life. The NICU doctors had been present during many kinds of anxious prayer circles and healing ceremonies, but this was something else altogether. Chris's survival seemed too much to hope for, no matter the faith of the family. Yet, against all odds, Chris began to heal. Not only that, but the other three babies in the NICU made the same progress, when doctors had expected all four to die. The doctors were scratching their heads because they had never experienced such a wholesale turnaround in the NICU. Debbie told them about Latter-day Saint priesthood blessings. "You can't be in a NICU and not believe that there's a God," one of them replied. "We're not very religious, but we know God is here, and was during that blessing."

Bill was profoundly moved by the miracle. He discussed it with the man who had become his spiritual mentor, Elder Marvin J. Ashton. The two had become good friends when Bill served on a Church board that Ashton chaired. "Can a blessing for one person affect others in the room?" Bill asked Ashton. The Apostle smiled. "Of course it can, Bill. You had faith in that room. Ron had faith. Debbie had faith. Others had faith. The room was filled with it. Those other little babies needed that blessing, so the Lord spread the spirit and the words to them as well. He 'suffered the little children to come unto Him' and live, and they did."

CHAPTER 14

HOTEL HOPPING

For the grand opening of the Portland Marriott in April 1980, Bill had crafted a nostalgic return to the Northwest for his father, who had spent his college summers as a salesman in the logging camps. "Fifty-three years ago, I came to the Northwest to sell woolen goods to the loggers in Bend," J.W. told the crowd. "They bought my woolen underwear at $22 a suit, which was a lot of money then, but it lasted five years. There were no chainsaws back then; everything was done by hand."

With that said, Bill picked up a two-man crosscut saw to begin sawing a log, which would also cut the ribbon. On the other end of the saw was Portland's mayor. It was a simple stunt that seemed impossible to flub. The small log had even been precut to within a couple of inches of its diameter. The problem was that Madame Mayor had had a couple of drinks and couldn't pull her end. "I started laughing, she started laughing, and everybody got to laughing," Bill said. Another guest jumped in to replace the mayor, and the opening was completed.

The Portland Marriott had been problematic from its groundbreaking. The location, a block fronting the Willamette River, was superb. The builder financed the construction, and Marriott agreed to buy it when it was completed. A series of misfortunes beset the project, including a severe winter, a concrete shortage, and two lawsuits—one from an environmental group and one from a competing hotel chain—seeking to halt the construction. The project took two and a half years, "twice as long as we had anticipated," Bill noted. But they succeeded in the end.

Next on Bill's agenda was the grand opening of the Marriott Hotel at the Seattle-Tacoma International Airport in January 1981, built in partnership with Alaska Airlines. This time, Governor John Spellman had been asked to join Bill in an authentic Native American dugout canoe in the hotel pool, where they would paddle a short distance and cut the ribbon. But the day before, during a practice run, the unsteady canoe dumped the hotel's marketing manager into the water. So, a "scheduling conflict" arose, and the governor sent his attorney general instead.

Bill arrived at the last minute from the grand opening of the Des Moines Marriott the day before. When the time came for the canoe event, Bill and the attorney general donned elaborate Native American headdresses and were solemnly marched to the pool by drumming Tillicum Village Indians. The two men stepped carefully into the carved cedar dugout. A local reporter recounted, "Three lifeguards waded chest-deep and like pallbearers guided the tipsy canoe across the treacherous waters. [The two men], in Indian headdresses and three-piece business suits, quickly did their duty and then even more quickly clambered out of the canoe." As with prior grand-opening stunts, the event paid off. The news photos of two distinguished men in a canoe in a pool were picked up by newspapers across the country. Some called it Bill Marriott's "Northwest Passage."[1]

The opening duties for the Des Moines and Sea-Tac hotels prevented Bill from being present during a historic event for the new president of the United States, Ronald Reagan. His election victory had been a personal victory for the Republican Marriotts. J.W. funded the transportation and lodging for the Mormon Tabernacle Choir so they could appear in the inaugural parade. The Marriotts had invitations to all the inaugural events. Bill and Donna attended the inaugural gala and had grandstand seats for the parade.

But three days later, Bill was surprised to receive a call from the State Department. A ranking official transmitted the president's request to book the entire Crystal City Marriott in Virginia the following Tuesday. At the precise moment Reagan had taken the oath of office, fifty-two American hostages who had been held by radical militants in Tehran for 444 days were turned over to U.S. officials. Reagan wanted to meet them and their families at the White House, but they needed a private place to stay. The only conflict for Bill was that he had to attend back-to-back hotel openings. He called his parents, who agreed to greet the guests when they arrived on January 27.

The hotel was entirely emptied of other guests. J.W. and Allie drove to Crystal City at three p.m. and waited in a suite, watching the White House ceremonies on TV until the former hostages departed for the hotel. At five-thirty p.m., Allie and J.W. joined about 500 people in front of the hotel, including the staff. The Marriotts shook hands with each of the ex-hostages and their families and hosted them all for four days at no charge.

When Bill considered the political upheaval that had precipitated the Iranian hostage crisis, he could not help but be grateful that the Tehran Marriott had never been built. Having courted the Iranian government of Shah Mohammed Reza Pahlavi for four years, Bill finally nailed down a deal during a trip to Tehran in July 1974. The Shah's Pahlavi Foundation offered all the financing. Marriott would be responsible for the design and management of the hotel in return for a significant percentage of gross sales. Construction had not yet begun four years later when fanatical Muslim clerics unseated the Shah, prompting him to flee and live in exile. If the hotel had been built, extremist Muslims would have taken it over in 1979.

"The Mideast is where the action and the money is," Bill had declared in the mid-1970s, ramping up a major expansion in that area when he still had only one hotel in Europe.[2] He hedged his bets carefully by making sure that all of the Mideast properties would be management contracts only. Bill's first completed hotel in the region was built adjacent to Riyadh Airport in Saudi Arabia; it opened in 1978. The Dhahran Marriott opened not long afterward in Saudi's Eastern Province. A second hotel opened in Riyadh in 1980, and another in Jeddah, Saudi Arabia, in 1984.

Amman, Jordan, was a special case. J.W. personally had raised the idea of an Amman Marriott with King Hussein at a 1974 state dinner hosted by Vice President Gerald Ford. Hussein's American wife, Queen Noor (Lisa Halaby), created the Jordan Society to improve Jordan's image in the United States. From his airline catering connections, Bill knew the queen's father, Najeeb Halaby, who was CEO of Pan American Airways. Halaby asked Bill to sit on the board of the queen's Jordan Society. The last thing Bill needed was to serve on another board, but he agreed for the sake of his company's Middle East projects.

The Amman Marriott opened in January 1982. By that time, the Amman hotel market was already overbuilt, and Bill was concerned. "Jordan should not have any more five-star hotels until they fill the ones they have," he explained during a press conference. "We are well aware that we are entering a highly competitive situation, just as we did in Saudi Arabia, where our hotels are now among the country's most successful. Marriott's great strength lies in guest service, superlative facilities and powerful marketing."[3]

The jewel in Marriott's Mideast crown, however, was always going to be Cairo. Marriott began negotiating in 1972 with the safest partner in town, the Egyptian Government Organization for Tourism and Hotels (EGOTH).

The following year, EGOTH made a verbal agreement with Marriott for an extraordinary site on Gezira Island in the middle of

Laying the cornerstone for the Cairo Marriott.

the Nile River. At the center of the hotel complex would be the royal palace that Emperor Napoleon III of France had built in 1869 for his consort, Empress Eugenie. The government had tried to run the palace as a hotel, but it had deteriorated over time, so EGOTH turned to Marriott to be managing partner.

A few months later, Marriott's hotel president, Jim Durbin, was shocked to see a photograph of the Egyptian minister of tourism shaking hands with two Sheraton executives after signing a deal for the same site. To add insult to injury, one of the Sheraton executives was Durbin's younger brother, Robert, which prompted a headline: "Two Indiana Brothers Have Their Own Mideast War." Marriott fought back and forced EGOTH to honor their original deal.[4]

No other Marriott hotel took as long to build as Cairo—seven years. Many of the best Egyptian construction workers were away in Saudi Arabia, where they could earn twenty times or more what they were paid in Egypt. Marriott's Architecture and Construction (A&C) chief, Jack Graves, oversaw the construction, which was an exercise in frustration. "We are used to backhoes to excavate a basement, but Cairo didn't have them. Instead, we had women with cloth sacks on their heads hauling debris out of a basement," Graves said. The workers worked at their own pace, which is to say slow. "We had to pat them on the back and thank them for just about everything they did in order to keep it going. To motivate the concrete crews, we got a goat every morning and staked it in the middle of the project. Whoever poured the most concrete by the end of the day got the goat. Before that job was through, we had bought every goat in Cairo and some chickens, too."

When it was finished, the Cairo Marriott was the largest hotel in the Middle East, with 1,260 rooms. Marriott's restoration of the palace, in consultation with Egyptian antiquities experts, was nothing short of spectacular. For the grand opening in 1983, Marriott pulled out all the stops. Never before had the company spent so much on a launch. "We had over 100 important customers there. . . . We had airline presidents, bank presidents, insurance company officials, travel agents, and travel media writers," Bill reported at a company marketing meeting a few days after the event. "We marched them around in the desert for four days and when they couldn't stand that any longer we put them on our fresh clean Sun Line cruise ships and let them look at the beautiful blue waters of the Aegean Sea."[5]

At the next board meeting, J.W. complained about the expense of it all, reportedly about $500,000. Bill defended the cost, noting that "the resulting public relations benefits exceed anything we have done before."[6] Bill knew that J.W.'s irritability about the Cairo event also stemmed from disapproval of the hotel's government-operated casino—a first for Marriott.

The temptation for hotel chains to add lucrative gambling operations began to increase in the late 1960s. Hilton jumped in with both feet in 1971, becoming the first company registered with the New York Stock Exchange to operate gambling facilities. By 1985, half of the company's operating income was derived from gambling—largely from two Las Vegas hotels.[7] Even Holiday Inn wanted a piece of the pie and acquired the casino and gaming giant Harrah's. By 1983, one-third of Holiday Inn's revenues were from gambling. Five years later, revenue from the chain's casinos was equal to its hotel lodging revenue.[8]

Marriott had grappled with the issue first in 1972 when offered an opportunity to manage a casino hotel in Las Vegas. The Church of Jesus Christ of Latter-day Saints not only discouraged gambling of any kind by its members but was also outspoken about the evils of gambling. But as the CEO of a publicly held company, Bill was required to thoroughly investigate gaming as a new revenue stream for the company. He sent a team to Las Vegas for a week to do a market analysis. The team returned with a positive report. However, the project ultimately died for lack of a suitable site and financing.

Over the next two years, as Bill examined the gaming industry more closely, three primary arguments against Marriott involvement formed: Marriott had no experience managing casinos, bankers were wary to loan money for construction, and the moral and ethical implications continued to trouble Bill. Barron Hilton warned him that there were some unseemly aspects to the business. For example, large casino hotels lured high rollers with expensive perks such as free suites and even prostitutes and drugs. Bill couldn't imagine buying into that culture.

He was equally wary about the risk to his customers. Gambling could destroy people's lives with a single roll of the dice. "When you see old men and old women taking their Social Security checks and going to Las Vegas and spending the day and blowing it all and having no money, this is serious business. It's not good to make your money that way," he told one interviewer. In the early days of Atlantic City's development as a gaming destination, Bill went to see it. He wrote in his journal: "Atlantic City is a very unhappy place. Everyone is trying to strike it rich. Most of the people were of moderate means and couldn't afford to be there in the first place. It was sad."⁹

Casinos became a significant issue for Marriott in 1976 with the possibility of acquiring the Del E. Webb Company. When Bill began negotiations with their CEO, Bob Johnson, he was hoping to acquire only lodging properties, which included Mountain Shadows, the resort hotel near Camelback Inn. He did not want Webb's four Nevada hotel casinos.

Nevertheless, Johnson issued a public announcement on August 2 that Marriott was offering to purchase all of Webb's properties in Arizona, California, and Nevada—which prompted a call to Bill from the President of his church, Spencer W. Kimball. He recounted to Bill his own sad experiences with friends from his hometown in Arizona who had lost all their money to the lure of Las Vegas gambling.

No Church President would ever in practice require a member of the Church to walk away from a legal business. "I can't tell you how to run your business," Kimball told Bill, "but I would like to strongly suggest that you do not get into gambling, that you do not go into Las Vegas. It would be a terrible thing for you to get into."

Bill's respect and love for his ecclesiastical leader was great, and Kimball's words had such a sobering effect on him that he shared them with others. As a result, when the Del Webb deal fell through, a rumor spread among Marriott executives that it was because President Kimball had ordered Bill to drop it. But at the time there was no deal for the casinos, and Bill's preferred position was still to acquire only the Del Webb lodging facilities.

When Bill updated the Marriott board, to his surprise, the two longest-serving "outside" board directors, Don Mitchell and Harry Vincent—neither of them Latter-day Saints—argued strongly that the company should stay out of Las Vegas for the sake of the company's image. "I'm a reasonably active Protestant, and I am absolutely opposed to the gambling milieu in our country. I think it's very, very destructive," Vincent explained. In the end, Del Webb itself pulled out of the negotiations, deciding not to sell any assets at that time.

It is ironic, then, that Bill brought up the gaming issue again a few days after the deal evaporated. The board was firmly committed to staying out of the casino business in Las Vegas, but Lake Tahoe was a different story. Investor Brooks Parks had a partially completed hotel and casino there on the Nevada-California border. He hoped to partner with Marriott. At a board meeting, J.W. objected strongly. The issue of the Cairo Marriott came up, where a casino was required by the government partner. But the Marriotts viewed government-run "amenity casinos," like the slot machines and blackjack games on most cruise ships, as sideline "entertainment."

J.W. told the board he wanted to discuss the Lake Tahoe issue "within the family." Bill read the signal from his father and said that he might need to cut off his talks with Parks if the board was considering a no-casino rule. "I do not want to be embarrassed in my negotiations with Mr. Parks, who is an honorable man, if the board might later reject a reasonable proposal on ethical grounds," he said.[10]

It was a rare time that J.W.'s objections were a relief to his son, and the Tahoe plans were dropped. "Dad didn't want us to go into gambling with a hotel casino, and I didn't either," Bill said. It was a new line of business that not only had no appeal for him but might well be the ruination of the company he was proud to lead. He spelled out this deeply held opinion in his 1997 book, *The Spirit to Serve*:

"The gambling and lodging businesses are completely different. The two might often be found in one building, but their operations—right down to the way their books are kept—have little in common. The result, I think, is that one has to give way to the other. I've watched many Marriott competitors go so far down the road into gambling that their original business, lodging, has become a secondary thought. Their attention has been diverted away from what was once their core business. Given our presence in and love of lodging, I couldn't see allowing the company to be pulled in a direction that would do short shrift to what we do best."[11]

Bill had no problem when it came to promoting wholesome entertainment more in line with his values, and that included the Church-owned Polynesian Cultural Center (PCC) on the Hawaiian island of Oahu. Latter-day Saint missionaries first went to Hawaii in the mid-1800s and from there spread out to other Polynesian islands. With a substantial presence in the Pacific, Church leaders became concerned that vibrant Polynesian cultures and traditions were disappearing. The Church had opened the Church College of Hawaii (later remained BYU–Hawaii) on Oahu and had another concern about the ability of Latter-day Saint Polynesians to afford the tuition and travel expenses.

Thus was born the PCC adjacent to the college—a unique tourist attraction preserving the culture of Polynesia and providing jobs for students in an otherwise sleepy corner of Oahu. Running the nonprofit operation was an unpaid board headed by one of the Church's Apostles, Marvin J. Ashton, who invited Bill to serve on the board in 1977.

When Bill joined the board, the PCC had just become the number-one paid tourist attraction in Hawaii, due to an ambitious expansion from fifteen to forty-two acres. Among the improvements was a new, 2,500-seat Pacific Theater hosting a ninety-minute evening spectacular, "Invitation to Paradise," with more than 150 cast members, most of them students. The show was so popular that reservations had to be made months in advance.

Bill found one area in need of an improvement he was uniquely qualified to provide—food service. He shared his own expertise and loaned Marriott restaurant experts to consult with the PCC. Some PCC employees got Marriott management training in Washington, D.C., and Bill included the PCC and the adjacent college in Marriott purchasing deals for everything from kitchen equipment to cleaning supplies.

Service on the PCC board was demanding for Bill. Ten hours flying time was required each way to the meetings in Hawaii, and he would often take a red-eye flight to get back to business in D.C. Each board meeting included a Sunday devotional service. Bill remembered one beautiful Sunday driving from his hotel to the devotional. He stopped to let a foursome of golfers in their carts cross the road. "I remarked to those who were in the car with me how much I would have liked to have been in that Sunday morning foursome, but I knew I would feel better about myself if I did my duty and went to church as I was supposed to do—and I did—and I didn't have to suffer a nagging conscience because I wasn't where I was supposed to be."

In his first year on the PCC board, Bill multitasked by scouting Hawaiian hotel sites. He found that while Waikiki was saturated with hotels, the outer islands offered tantalizing opportunities. He partnered with Amfac Corp. to build a resort hotel along the Kaanapali Beach of western Maui. The hotel—Marriott's one-hundredth—opened in January 1982. Typical of his travel schedule, Bill arrived ten days before the grand opening to host the PCC board for two days of meetings at the hotel. Then he flew to Tokyo, Hong Kong, and Singapore, where he signed up $20 million in new airline catering business. When he returned to Hawaii, Donna and his parents were there to join him for the grand-opening festivities.

J.W. was amazed at how much ground his son covered and at all the work Bill accomplished on the trip. But, as was typical, J.W. recorded his admiration in his journal rather than in person to Bill. He wrote: "Bill phoned from his room. He is leaving 8 a.m. tomorrow for Washington. A great man. Did very well here and has promoted the hotel in a marvelous way. Very proud of him—his character, family and business success. *It is he who has put the Marriott name around the world.*"[12]

The PCC was not Bill's only voluntary service to his Church during those years. He also served five years as a counselor to Washington D.C. Stake President Ralph Mecham. Presided over by a president and two counselors, the stake was an ecclesiastical umbrella over multiple congregations attended by about 4,000 Latter-day Saints who primarily lived in D.C. and Montgomery County, Maryland. As the Latter-day Saint population in D.C. grew, the stake expanded to twelve congregations during Bill's tenure. President Mecham's term of service ended in December 1982, and, to Bill's chagrin, President Spencer W. Kimball chose him to be the new stake president, a position he would hold for eight years.

As Bill's responsibilities multiplied, J.W. eased more into semi-retirement. He and Allie spent more than three months every year at Camelback, from late December to April. An outdoorsman who loved the West, J.W. flourished under the desert sun or atop a horse at Camelback. Bill was happy to escape his father's criticism while his parents were in Arizona. J.W. compensated by turning his perfectionism on the staff at Camelback and across the street at the Mountain Shadows resort, which Bill bought in 1981, the sole purchase to survive the Del Webb negotiations.

Perhaps more than any other Marriott property, J.W. treated Camelback as his personal fiefdom. When there, the aging restaurateur couldn't help but meddle in the affairs of food. Once when Bill was preparing to address a gathering of Marriott general managers, he called J.W. at Camelback to ask him for input. J.W. complained about the pancakes. "They are cooking them ahead and putting them on the steam table, and they get soggy and you can't eat them. Tell the general managers to cook the pancakes to order and don't ever put them on the steam table!"

"Are you kidding me?" Bill responded. "These are sophisticated GMs from around the world. They want to learn about the latest technology and marketing trends. So what do you really want me to tell them?"

"Tell them to cook the pancakes to order and don't put them on the steam table, as they get soggy and you can't eat them. That's all I have to say." Then J.W. hung up.

Steve Hart, the manager of Camelback's Chaparral Restaurant, recalled a busy Sunday night when an influx of conventioneers lined up outside the restaurant. Hart noticed J.W. and Allie making their way to the head of the line. J.W. said he and Allie just wanted a bowl of Camelback's famous chicken soup, the Sunday night special.

Less than fifteen minutes after the Marriotts were seated, while the line of conventioneers was still out the door, Hart found J.W. at his elbow asking him to come take a seat at their table. "'Gosh, Mr. Marriott, we're really busy right now,' I said. He said, 'No, I think you need to have a seat.' We sat down and he said, 'Have some soup.' So I grabbed the bowl. . . . He gave me a spoon. The soup was cold as hell. He said, 'Holy smokes, Steve, what's going on?' He never cursed. He never, never, never, never lost his composure. But he started in about the checklist that must not have been followed. There was no excuse for cold soup."

After about an hour, Allie sweetly patted Hart's hand and asked him to have a bellman escort her back to her room. "'You're going to be here for a little while longer," she knowingly smiled at Hart.

J.W. was just getting started. "I was sitting there like a disciple listening to every word over and over," Hart said. "For two hours and fifteen minutes, he repeated the same story a dozen times about how he'd entrusted this part of his business to me and that he counts on me to make sure that everything is absolutely perfect all the time. He knew exactly what he was doing. He knew from that point on that there would never be anything less than a perfect cup of soup that was served out of any hotel that Steve Hart ever had anything to do with. He was never cross about it, and finally, he got that most adorable smile on his face and he said, 'Let's have some dessert.' He wanted to say that he really thought I was an okay guy, that I was worth keeping by the fact that we could have one piece of cherry pie and one piece of rhubarb à la mode together."

For Hart, it was a lesson in how the Marriotts operated. "They will invest that kind of time in a young Turk restaurant manager just to make sure that I will never have a cold bowl of soup that's ever served in any of my hotels. It's precisely this attention to every detail that has made Marriott so successful."

At Camelback, J.W., Allie, Bill, and Donna were surrounded by an interesting group of friends and family, many of them wealthy businesspeople and Hollywood celebrities. One of the most interesting friendships was with film star Charles Boyer and his wife, Pat. The French-born Boyer was the "Great Lover" of the silver screen, starring in more than eighty films between 1920 and 1976. In real life he had only one true love, the British-born Patricia, his wife of forty-two years. In the same year of his last film (1976), when the couple was living in Geneva, Charles was informed by doctors that Pat was in advanced stages of liver and colon cancer. Anxious to make her final days worry free, he made the doctors swear they would not tell his wife of her fatal illness.

Ailing himself, Charles persuaded Pat almost overnight to move to Arizona, where the climate would be good for his health. They checked into Camelback Inn in November 1976 and called on the Marriotts, with whom they hit it off immediately. Allie helped Pat shop for new clothes because everything had been left behind in Geneva in their rush to move to Phoenix. Though the Boyers were Catholics, Pat enjoyed reading the Book of Mormon that the Marriotts gave her. Pat and Charles died within two days of each other in Phoenix in August 1978.

There was also the Marriotts' three-decades-long friendship with the reclusive millionaire Nelson Davis and his wife, Eloise. Davis invested in nickel mining, auto sales, real estate, paint and varnish manufacturing, trucking, and highway paving. "A smart, ruthless fellow—a financial genius. Good habits—doesn't drink or smoke but loves money," J.W. observed in his 1955 journal.[13] Davis once invited the Marriotts to stay in his palatial estate north of Toronto, which included a private eighteen-hole golf course on which J.W. played a few rounds. After they returned to their own Garfield Street residence, J.W. concluded: "It is good to be home. Ours is a humble cottage compared to Nelson's, but there is love here and that is all that is important. Allie has made it a real home."[14]

The Davises were a continual reminder of the lifestyle the Marriotts could have afforded but did not want. Davis bought the Phoenix home of *Time* magazine publisher Henry Luce and his wife, Clare Booth Luce, and spent hundreds of thousands of dollars renovating it. "It's more like a museum than it is a home," J.W. noted after his first visit. "He has priceless things in it from all over the world. When we came home [to the Camelback casita], we said we wouldn't trade our little cottage here for his big house with all the fabulous things in it."[15]

Bill and his father shared the same values. *People* magazine observed contemporaneously that Bill "places family and friends above fortune. [He] disdains the trappings of wealth. His brick home looks like a condensed version of a Marriott hotel, done in pink and green colonial style. He drives himself to work in a two-year-old Cadillac and flies coach, except for long trips."[16]

Often asked about what it means to be wealthy, Bill cites a Chinese philosopher who once said a rich man can only eat so much. He concludes: "I believe money should only be a means to an end. If we do good with it, help those in need, provide an opportunity for others to have some of the good things in life, contribute to worthy causes, do things that make others happy, then money is a great blessing. Otherwise, if we are selfish, it becomes a curse and provides no happiness for anyone."

CHAPTER 15

FULL SPEED AHEAD

There were two words to which Bill Marriott had an aversion. Marriott executives jokingly referred to them as the company's curse words, the "S" and "V" words, *strategy* and *vision*. Time and again, journalists asked Bill, "What is your vision for the company?" His good humor would temporarily diminish. "I am not going to give you a lofty vision statement—I'm not into that," he responded once. "I work by gut instinct, and that has been more often right than wrong. I see myself as a tactical leader, not a visionary. I serve one customer at a time and build hotels one brick at a time. That's the way I am."

He was perturbed enough by the repeated question that he asked a consultant, "What is strategy?" That consultant was his friend Mitt Romney, CEO of Bain Consulting. Romney's definition of strategy was, "Anything that's important to your business." Bill liked that. "That's the way I look at strategy," he said. "It's what is important to our business—delivering to our customer, taking care of [employees], making sure they have a good experience, that they're motivated, that they enjoy their work, that they take care of the customer and have an opportunity to grow and develop and advance."

A few years after he became company president, Bill hired a corporate strategic planner, but the department remained a corporate backwater with little influence. Bill continued to look at opportunities on a case-by-case basis. But that changed—primarily because of the company treasurer, Gary Wilson. According to Bill, "Gary came to me and said, 'I want planning.' I said, 'Fine. We don't do any.'" Then Bill allowed Wilson to hire a consultant, Tom Curren, to fill the gap. It was Wilson and Curren who came up with something that was revolutionary for the entire hospitality industry in the early 1980s—limited-service, moderately priced hotels.

At the time, American hotels and motels offered about two million rooms falling into four pricing categories: "luxury" or "boutique" (which included Camelback), "high class" (which was Marriott's main tier), "moderate," and "budget." It was the "moderate" tier that most tempted Bill. It was often called the "Holiday Inn segment," and it was ripe for a Marriott entry. Moderately priced hotels were a backwater of dubious quality. Bill wanted to offer the Marriott reputation for first-class lodging without the full-service convention and restaurant experience.

Bill hired Don Washburn as the team leader, and Washburn hit the road to scout the competition. He discovered, "There was no consistency of image in these hotels. Their properties were dilapidated in many areas. They were facing a demand for hotel rooms that was in excess of the supply. Since they didn't need to fight for business, they were not eager to spend any money upgrading them."

Washburn sketched the first designs for Marriott while riding a bus in Dallas. He reflected on a visit to the Four Seasons Hotel in Houston: "I walked into the lobby and immediately saw this beautifully landscaped courtyard of flowers, shrubbery, and lawn. I'd seen a few other courtyards like this, and it always gave the hotel a country club sort of feel, a residential feel. Holiday Inns had institutional courtyards, but they filled them with swimming pools, so it wasn't the same feel." Thus was born the central design of what would become Courtyard by Marriott.

Part of that process required a new financial model that would allow the team to refine the concept by trading off various kinds of investments, Curren explained. "For example, if we wanted to make the room six inches wider, that was equivalent to 50 cents on the room rate. Customers wanted security, especially the business*women* who were becoming an increasing factor in the workforce. If we provided additional security by having a twenty-four-hour guard service instead of a one-shift guard, that added 20 cents to the room rate. Customers also wanted the feel of a *fresh* room. That meant replacing the 'soft goods'—bedspreads, sheets, and the like—on a four-year cycle rather than a six-year cycle. Well, that added 37 cents to the room rate. So we were incessantly faced with tradeoffs. Which would be better? Fresh bedspreads, an extra guard, or a wider room?"[1]

Then there was the unique design of the room itself, whose success in the end turned on the placement of the lamps.

From the inspection tours of competitors, and from extensive surveys with potential business customers, Washburn's team decided they needed, somehow, to create three distinct areas for business travelers in the room—a place to work, a place to relax, and a place to sleep. Typical twelve-by-seventeen-foot or twelve-by-eighteen-foot hotel rooms of that era had one or two beds, nightstands, and a small desk—which did not allow for the superior room Marriott needed to compete with the established, franchised chains.

To create what *was* needed, Washburn's designers needed another foot in the width. "We had to do it in thirteen feet because anything wider made the room too expensive," Curren explained. The best way to achieve the three-area feel was to angle the bed or beds differently. "But when we turned the bed, there was no room for a nightstand. So then we asked, why do we need a nightstand? Well, to put a lamp on it. Why don't we do a wall-mounted lamp sconce? A&C warned us, 'Bill will never allow a wall-mounted lamp because they break off. They're too high maintenance.' So we went searching for a sturdier wall lamp and I met with Bill, holding my breath. I told him, 'If we can wall mount the lamp, we can turn the bed and create the separate rooms for our targeted business traveler and penetrate the Holiday Inn segment with the best room and become the best and most diverse lodging company in the world—*if* we wall-mount the lamps. He approved the lamps."

At a cost of several million dollars, the Courtyard project incubated for three years, which was unprecedented at Marriott. The majority of Marriott managers and employees had no hint of the Courtyard project, which had been conducted on a need-to-know basis. When the concept was presented to the board in May 1982, J.W. did not speak up, but it was evident to Bill that his father was skeptical.

Washburn's team had secretly built several model Courtyard rooms within the Gaithersburg Marriott in Maryland, and Bill asked Washburn to give J.W. and Allie a tour. They were polite, but firm: "I don't understand why you're doing this. Why put more square footage in the room? Why make them wider? Why turn the bed like this? Nobody cares about the bed being like this." Washburn tried to answer their questions. J.W. remained unconvinced, but Allie decided it made sense, and told him so. Later, when the board called for a decision, J.W. was the last to vote. "I'll vote for it, but I hate this idea."

Atlanta was a booming market and the best incubator for Courtyard by Marriott. The first hotel was under construction by September 1982, and still the plans did not leak to the public. When Bill made the announcement rolling out Courtyard in early June 1983, competitors were stunned. Within hours, Marriott stock hit a new high of $75 a share. Courtyard became an unqualified success story for Marriott. Every one of five test-market Courtyards had a higher occupancy rate than was projected, and thus were more profitable than expected. Bill went all in—building 100 Courtyards in the next five years.

The success caused a paradigm shift at Marriott, not only

The Courtyard venture was a big success.

encouraging out-of-the-box thinking but verifying the economic value of long-term study and research before jumping into any new business.

It also prompted a revolution within the hotel industry, whose CEOs were now prodded into looking beyond their own market segment to others. "Courtyard was the first venture by a full-service hotel company to diversify into a different tier," observed Marriott executive Brad Bryan. "This was huge. This was a big decision by Bill Marriott, and a big win. Not incidentally, it was yet another example of how fortunate the company was to have Bill at the helm, and not the Chairman. Remember, J.W. opposed Courtyard."

Having made a year-round success of Camelback in Arizona, Bill turned his sights on Palm Springs and Rancho Mirage in southern California. He was enthusiastic about a resort condominium project when he sat down with Bill Bone of Sunrise Corporation in 1975 to discuss a joint venture. Bone's contribution was to be a twenty-seven-hole golf course, along with most of the equity for development of twenty-six acres adjacent to the golf course in Rancho Mirage. Over the next two years, costs rose by more than $2 million, and Marriott was forced to put up half of the equity.

Reading between the lines of the Executive Committee minutes in October 1977, it was apparent that J.W. was fit to be tied about the ballooning project. He wanted it canceled, but Marriott had already committed to Bone and had spent $1 million in the planning phase. "How could you negotiate such a long-term contract without including a rejection clause?" J.W. was right about that oversight, and Treasurer Gary Wilson apologized and admitted his mistake. "Mr. Chairman, it will never happen again," he promised. Bill defended Wilson and informed J.W. that the best option was to move ahead with the project. Hesitantly, J.W. joined the unanimous vote to build Rancho Las Palmas.

Bob Hope, who was completing a mansion on a hill nearby, agreed to cut the ribbon for the February 1979 grand opening. He did it with a hard-hitting golf drive. The resort was an instant success, and in 1987 Bill would open a second resort in nearby Palm Desert, the Marriott Desert Springs Resort & Spa, for which son-in-law Ron Harrison would be tapped as the first resident manager.

Bill was on the road much of the time during this period. In his view, scouting sites and inspecting hotels were pivotal uses of his time and leadership. In the first six months of 1982, he kept meticulous track of every flight and found he had flown a total of 106,000 miles. He recalled once flying into Miami and learning that the Marco Island hotel might be for sale. He immediately rented a car and drove to the resort, then drove to Tampa to check out another site. Marriott bought Marco and built in Tampa. "I figured that was a pretty good day—two hotels in one day," Bill said.

Unexpected events on the trips kept travel interesting but not necessarily enjoyable. For example, when Bill flew Senator Strom Thurmond of South Carolina to the opening of Marriott's Hilton Head hotel, the elderly senator lobbied during the whole flight to put his young wife on the company's board of directors. More than once the senior senator said, "My wife should be on your board. She's really pretty!" Bill later laughed about that. "He was dead serious, so I said, 'Well, I'll think about it.' Of course, it never happened."

Most of the time, Bill flew commercial. At a time when other CEOs were purchasing company jets, Bill didn't feel it was worth the expense. Occasionally, he used a charter Lear jet company on an as-needed basis—that is, until an unusual incident during an inspection trip to the New Orleans Marriott. The charter pilot went barhopping in the French Quarter and was jailed for public drunkenness. Afraid to call his boss, the pilot made his one allowed call to the customer, Bill, at one a.m. "I went out and bailed him out of jail, which I never should have done," Bill said. "I should have let him sit in jail." The owner was called, the pilot was fired, and another pilot was sent for Bill's return trip. Bill then changed charter companies.

The worst trip of that era was for the opening of the Denver City Center Marriott. As Bill was leaving the plane, he reached deep into the closet for hanging bags and dislocated his left shoulder. He was rushed to a hospital, where doctors worked for three hours before they could put the shoulder back in place. He left the hospital in time to get to the hotel and speak to the employees the evening before the opening ceremony. "Then I went to bed."

Unlike his father, Bill was not a big fan of Hollywood celebrity events, personally preferring, for example, the groundbreaking for the Houston Medical Center Marriott, when he was able to spend time with pioneering heart surgeon Dr. Michael DeBakey and former Texas Governor John Connally. He also got a kick out of the twenty-two circus elephants who were part of the Long Island Marriott opening.

Still, the closer his hotels were to Los Angeles, the more necessarily star-studded his hotel events became in order to attract wider press coverage. At the Rancho Las Palmas opening, Cary Grant made a rare appearance. Hollywood stars were also frequently on hand for Santa

Barbara Biltmore events after Marriott acquired that storied hotel. The 747-room Anaheim Marriott hotel opening was especially memorable. As guns blazed in the streets, a horse-drawn stagecoach rolled up to the hotel's front door, and out stepped legendary Western film star Gene Autry.

"Is this Tombstone, Roy?" Autry asked as Roy Rogers clambered out of the stagecoach.

"I don't think so," Rogers laughed.

"Well, after the hundreds of films you've made, Roy, and the hundreds of films I've made, I think we got the payroll here OK," Autry continued.

The two proceeded to cut the ribbon with a hot branding iron, and then they burned an "M" for Marriott into a big wooden key. As Bill watched, he could not help but remember that a quarter century before, he was offered the management of the new Disneyland hotel in Anaheim and turned it down.[2]

There were four hotels opened during this time that were particularly important to the Marriott family. First was the Bethesda (Maryland) Marriott on the outskirts of Washington, which was nearly a decade in the making. After the hotel opened in mid-1979, the Marriott family frequently gathered at the hotel. The Kona Kai restaurant was a favorite of J.W.'s.

Until 1981, Marriott did not have a hotel within the District of Columbia. That changed when Ulysses "Blackie" Auger, proprietor of the well-known "Blackie's House of Beef," proposed a joint-venture hotel above and around his restaurant on 22nd and M Streets. That first D.C. hotel's progress was marred by two controversies. Workers erected an illuminated red-and-white Marriott sign on top of the building. After several weeks of local protests calling it "an eyesore," the D.C. zoning board rescinded approval for the large sign, claiming that the original permit had been a clerical error. Then, at the March 1981

Among the honored guests at the grand opening of the Salt Lake City Marriott were (left to right) Church leaders Ezra Taft Benson, N. Eldon Tanner, Spencer W. Kimball, and Marion G. Romney, along with Salt Lake City Mayor Ted Wilson.

grand opening, fifty labor-union demonstrators marched and shouted outside the hotel protesting Marriott's long-standing nonunion policy.

For many years, Bill had wanted to have a hotel in downtown Boston. For Marriott's twelfth hotel, he had built in the less-expensive suburb of Newton. But by the late 1970s, he was ready to move downtown. Mayor Kevin White provided the best opportunity when he held a design competition among hotel developers hoping to build on the city's prime waterfront site close to historic Faneuil Hall. Marriott won the contest and built the Marriott Long Wharf Hotel, with every room providing panoramic views of Boston Harbor.

The most emotional opening, at least for J.W., was the October 1981 Salt Lake City Marriott. Both he and Bill always planned to build in Salt Lake but were averse to competing directly with the premier downtown hotel, the Church-owned Hotel Utah. That reluctance was overcome when Bill found an ideal site close to Temple Square and was encouraged by Church leaders to build there. Many Marriott relatives were on hand for the grand opening in their home away from home. The evening reception with 3,000 guests was nothing short of overwhelming. "We were pushed and shoved by every one of our old friends and relatives. It was not fun and we were glad when it was over," Bill confessed. But his parents relished the evening. "All the people we had ever known were at [this] beautiful party," Allie wrote.[3] "Couldn't move for friends crowding around to say hello—have never seen so many people under one roof that I knew." Bill had seldom seen his father so happy. He said, "A lot of [Church leaders] came to honor my dad. I remember him being so proud that his name was on a beautiful Salt Lake City building near the temple."

As the hotel division was booming, three divisions were limping along: dinner houses, theme parks, and Sun Line cruises. In a restaurant industry wracked by escalating costs and overpriced meals, the Marriott dinner houses, by virtue of their limited menus, inexpensive extras, and reasonable overhead, offered dining bargains wrapped in a high-class atmosphere. By mid-1978, it was evident that profits were declining, with only a slight possibility of improvement. Bill told the executive committee of the board that it was time to sell, and he had two interested buyers. J.W., who always believed any Marriott restaurant could be turned around, opposed the sale but reluctantly agreed to it in the end.

Though the Great America theme parks in Santa Clara, California, and Gurnee, Illinois, were profitable, the margin began decreasing in the late 1970s because of the increased costs of capital improvements (multimillion-dollar thrill rides), foul weather (long periods of rain in Gurnee), and advertising campaigns combined with heavy discounts.

Santa Clara park attendance was also hit hard after a tragic accident on the "Willard's Whizzer" roller coaster killed a thirteen-year-old boy in March 1980. Largely because of Bill's compassionate response to the family, the company was never sued over the accident. But the press was not satisfied. Reporters pushed the federal Consumer Product

Safety Commission to use the Great America accident as a test case for federal regulation of thrill rides. So CPSC, for the first time, fined a company for alleged safety problems. Like the rest of the park industry, Marriott didn't recognize CPSC's jurisdiction, a position that Bill continued to maintain even after paying the $70,000 fine. The showdown prompted a final congressional resolution the following year against CPSC. The new federal law declared that the states, not the federal government, had regulatory authority over amusement parks and carnival rides.[4]

In the end, theme parks were simply not a good fit for Marriott. Both were sold in 1984 for $215.5 million.

Marriott's Sun Line cruises got off to a stuttering start because of an oil embargo, a recession, and a war in Cyprus. When the aftereffects of those challenges receded, Bill tried flexible itineraries and new routes to increase business. One summer Marriott even moved the *Stella Maris,* which was the smallest of the line, to the Great Lakes via the St. Lawrence Seaway for freshwater cruises. At the end of the summer, the *Maris* sailed up the Potomac River, navigating the fifteen-foot-deep channel off Hains Point to dock at "Port Washington." The 300-foot cruise ship was an unforgettable sight for Washingtonians, whose city had not been an origin point for cruises for at least fifteen years.

At the same time, Marriott tried to end the division's hemorrhaging losses by selling off the ships one by one, but the deals fell through. So Bill turned to his friend Fred Malek for help. Having supported Richard Nixon's presidential campaign, Malek was first made deputy undersecretary of Health, Education and Welfare and then appointed special assistant to the president, where he earned a reputation as Nixon's hatchet man, firing presidential hangers-on who became excess baggage.

After Nixon's second inauguration, Malek was promoted to be deputy director of the Office of Management and Budget. He never got involved in the illegal Watergate activities, so he survived Nixon's resignation. But the Maleks were anxious to leave Washington, so he resigned with no clear plan for what he might do next. In one of his last days in office, he had a White House lunch with Bill, which had been arranged by their mutual friend Jon Huntsman. "I was looking for a senior executive, and Jon convinced me that I could develop Malek into a star for Marriott," Bill recalled.

Bill urged Malek to stay in Washington while he searched elsewhere for a job. In the meantime, Bill hired him to consult on the Sun Line problem. That led to a permanent job with Marriott. Malek's most important advice about Sun Line was to convert the *Stella Polaris* into a dockside hotel. A Kuwaiti company offered to partner with Marriott to refurbish the ship, tow it to Kuwait, and plant it in a beach. The conversion cost $4 million.

Malek succeeded in moving Sun Line from red to black ink, but there was still no potential for healthy profits, so Marriott finally sold the ships at a loss. Bill summarized: "We spent fifteen years trying to make a go of it before finally getting out. We had felt confident that we could pull it off. Weren't cruise ships essentially just floating hotels? Wrong! Sun Line provided our first major lesson about the dangers of getting into a completely unfamiliar business. That lesson served me well, as mistakes often do."

Not one executive at Marriott could match Bill as CEO or was ever considered a possible successor in the 1970s and 1980s, which made the Marriott board of directors nervous. Across the country, most CEOs were required by their boards to have a succession plan in place in the event of their injury, resignation, or death, but Bill deflected such concerns.

The Marriott board was particularly worried when in 1982 Bill participated in a risky powerboat race up the Mississippi River. More than a century earlier, the first 1,027-mile New Orleans-to-St. Louis race had pitted two stern-wheelers against each other—the *Robert E. Lee* and the *Natchez*. The *Lee* won the 1870 race, steaming into St.

Louis three days, eighteen hours, and fourteen minutes after it left New Orleans. The *Natchez* arrived six and a half hours later in what historians regard as the most famous race in the river's history.[5]

More than a thousand record-challenging attempts had been made over the next century, with only twelve of them being successful. The most recent record had been set at twenty-six hours and fifty minutes in 1972. Larry Smith, the founder and designer of Scarab powerboats, thought one of his outboards could beat the record, so he approached veteran racer Michael Reagan, considered one of the top five powerboat racers in the world, to be the team leader and primary driver. Reagan was the oldest son of President Ronald Reagan.

Michael Reagan was leery of using his celebrity in a stunt race to promote Scarab, so he redesigned the event as a fund-raising effort for the U.S. Olympic Committee. Reagan signed up corporate sponsors, with Anheuser-Busch being the most energetic and generous. As a result, Reagan named the diesel craft *Bud Light.* Reagan invited speedboat enthusiast Bill Marriott to join the team as one of the alternate drivers.

When Bill mentioned it to Marriott board members, they were quietly alarmed. They knew it was impossible to forbid Bill to race. But when they expressed qualms, he made a persuasive case. The event was good for the Marriott corporate image, and the kickoff benefit luncheon featuring Vice President George Bush would be held at the New Orleans Marriott. Best of all, President Reagan himself had agreed to host a benefit dinner at the end of the race at Marriott's downtown St. Louis Pavilion Hotel. A compromise was finally reached between Bill and the board: he would race only part of the route and get off at Vicksburg, Mississippi.

A week before the race, the diesel engine in the *Bud Light* was unable to run more than thirty miles without a mechanical problem. Reagan ordered two more boats as insurance. He would drive the lead boat, a new thirty-eight-foot Scarab with 3,500 horsepower, which

Bill prepares for the big race.

could take its speed up to 95 miles per hour. The questionable *Bud Light*, with its 600-horsepower engine capable of speeds up to 60 miles an hour, became the *Bud Light II*, with Bill and Larry Smith alternately at the helm. A third boat, slightly slower, was to follow with mechanics and spare parts. Reagan's plan was to be driving whichever of the three boats arrived in St. Louis first.

Bill spent the day before the race opening the Albuquerque Marriott. The following morning, on July 21, 1982, he flew to New Orleans, where he joined Vice President Bush and brewery baron August Busch for the benefit luncheon at the Marriott. They left the luncheon early to board the boats and prepare for what was dubbed "The Assault on the Mississippi." Bill, Larry Smith, and Tom George shared the driving on the *Bud Light II*. From four to ten-thirty p.m., as darkness fell, Bill drove the speedboat upriver for 343 miles at speeds in excess of 55 miles per hour, dodging barge traffic, tugboats, and debris. "It was really a great thrill. After we left Baton Rouge and almost until we got to Vicksburg, we didn't see a single house. It was pure wilderness, and it was just delightful. The settlers discovered it 300 years ago, and here it was—clear, calm, and almost blue," he said. One of his fondest memories was passing the *Delta Queen*, one of the last running overnight excursion paddle-wheelers. "It is a beautiful boat, and everyone was on the deck cheering and waving."

Bill's last two hours at the helm were in darkness. The radar and half the boat lights were not working by that time. "It was like being in a black closet with sort of a pale light in front of it from the buoys. There were several barges we almost ran into; once, we found ourselves in the middle of three barges, two going one way and one going the other way. We lost sight of the buoys and were completely off course. The pilot became disoriented and we almost ran aground more than once. It became quite dangerous."

Not long before Bill pulled into the Vicksburg refueling stop, the boat struck a log, which caused some damage. The following morning, because of an unrelated mechanical problem, the boat had to be towed back to New Orleans, and, for Bill, the race was over. He took a helicopter upriver scouting for Mike Reagan's boat, eventually flying on to St. Louis. Bill was on hand with President Reagan and a cheering crowd when Mike Reagan sped beneath the St. Louis Gateway Arch, setting a new record of twenty-five hours and seven minutes.

That evening, the mood was jubilant at the St. Louis Marriott Pavilion as President Reagan presided over the benefit dinner honoring August Busch. Security was so tight that at first Bill was denied entrance to his own hotel's reception room. Anheuser-Busch had hired twenty-four off-duty St. Louis police officers as additional protection for the brewery's CEO, and one of those guards refused to let Bill in. He went to another door and was waved through by the Secret Service, who knew him on sight. The next morning, Bill and Donna joined the president's motorcade to the airport and flew on Air Force One with the Reagans back to Washington.

As thrilling as a flight with the president was, it paled in comparison to Bill's memory of his hours at the helm of the speedboat. When the *Washington Post* profiled Bill two months later, the reporter noted that "an uncharacteristic passion crept into Marriott's soft voice as he relived the adventure." Bill was quoted as saying: "That trip was more fun than anything I've done in years. I thought, as I was driving that boat, 'Not only am I doing something I like to do, but I am also trying to achieve something. I'm moving toward a goal. I'm not out for a joy ride in a boat riding around in a circle. I'm headed from Point A to Point B in an attempt to get there faster than anybody else has ever done it before.'"

The reporter concluded with this insight: "Huck Finn lay on his back and looked up at the stars as he drifted down the Mississippi on a raft. But leisurely voyages of self-discovery are not the Marriott style. It is characteristic that Bill Marriott raced up the river in a test of speed and endurance fortified by the knowledge that his trip had 'a purpose.'"[6]

A year later, Bill was in another long-distance Scarab speedboat race, this time with his son John, challenging the Northwest Passage from Seattle to Juneau. Scarab's president, Larry Smith, wanted to demonstrate that his V-bottom hulls were as good as or better than the catamarans that were taking over offshore racing. According to *Powerboat* magazine: "After some gentle prodding, hotel magnate Bill Marriott and his son John agreed to handle the driving chores on the specially-prepared 34-foot Scarab."[7] For two days, Smith and the Marriotts raced up the Alaskan shoreline, averaging 50 miles per hour. There had been one new requirement imposed by Marriott's board of directors for this Northwest Passage run, after they had realized just how dangerous the last part of Bill's Mississippi River race in the dark had been. The rule was this: no night racing. That wasn't a problem in the "land of the midnight sun."

As with his powerboat racing hobby, Bill went full speed ahead with his business, which made him very different from his father. Bill's success did not ease J.W.'s growing fears. When he was asked to write his life history for a Marriott family genealogy project in 1980, J.W. praised his son for "developing a great organization and expanding the business," and then added, "but the business expansion of the '70s was too much." He conjectured that Bill's zealous business pace might have contributed to the four heart attacks J.W. had experienced in the previous decade.[8]

The differences between the two, as well as J.W.'s frustration with aging, came to a boiling point in 1980 when J.W. wrote the most critical entries about his son in his journal while the whole family was vacationing at the lake. "Couldn't sleep," he wrote. "Thinking of Bill's and my relationship. Can't talk business with him. Everything is personal. He won't listen to me on anything, so I have to go around him to staff. Very disturbing to both of us and makes for a very bad feeling. I would resign from the Board but must have something to do, and he needs my advice. He is travelling too fast in the face of a serious recession."[9]

The next morning, J.W. walked to Bill's house on the lake and "gave him the business." Bill did not take it well. J.W. went back to his own house and penned the most bitter remarks about his two sons he had ever committed to paper. "Bill would rather I go," J.W. complained. "I'm glad I didn't give him my Washington home. I gave him and Dick everything else [including] control of the business—and they totally disregard me. If Bill were a [better] businessman, that would let me out. But he is a dreamer, a spender, a plunger. He disregards all the economic signs. . . . Well, what's the use? It sure doesn't pay to give your sons everything and then let them kick you around."[10]

On the third morning, after Bill had gone back to D.C., a sheepish J.W. wrote: "I got over my madness." Nevertheless, he still called Bill at the Bethesda headquarters and "listed all his big mistakes and policies."[11]

When Marriott forged ahead with plans to build a $300-million hotel on Times Square in New York City, it precipitated another tempestuous row. J.W.'s biggest frustration at the time was that everyone on the board, many of whom J.W. had appointed, always voted with Bill. "I had a big argument with Bill, but he said I can't stop him and he is right—without a lot of trouble," J.W. recorded. "He said if I didn't like it to resign and sell my stock. My remarks were not writable. I came home and was sick." J.W. and Allie had invited Bill and his family over for dinner, but he had Allie cancel it.

Late that evening, J.W. recorded, "Bill called and we made up. I said I put him in the driver's seat and I guess I would have to let him drive. But no money or company was worth breaking up the family."[12]

To his father, Bill may have seemed fearless in business, but that was not the truth. What drove Bill was the company's 20-20 mantra. He had pledged to stockholders that he would grow the company 20 percent each year, and add another 20 percent return on equity. The larger the company grew, the more difficult it was to achieve that growth without taking increasing risks. Thus, less than a year after the 1980 father-son eruptions, Bill went ahead with plans for a new $200-million hotel in Atlanta and another $300 million in acquisitions. He did not make those decisions easily, as his father seemed to think, and each one took a toll on him.

"The pressure is very heavy," Bill confided in a journal entry in 1981. "I'm not sure how long I will hold up."[13]

CHAPTER 16

THE GUNSLINGERS

Gary Wilson did more in the 1980s than anyone except Bill himself to propel Marriott into the stratosphere. And not far behind Wilson's contribution was that of his protégé, Al Checchi. Wilson was hired first, as Marriott treasurer. In early 1975, when the company was beginning the roughest year in its history to date, Bill had instituted a hiring freeze, but Wilson dipped under the CEO's radar to hire his longtime friend Al Checchi to work on a project. For a few months, Bill didn't know about the new employee. Checchi recalled, "At the River Road headquarters, we all ate at the same cafeteria. Every time Bill Marriott showed up, Gary would signal me and I'd go hide." But it's not easy to keep company secrets from Bill, and once he found out about Checchi, he accepted him.

Everything changed for the better during that recession when Wilson and Checchi brokered the sale of the Lincolnshire resort in Illinois to Prudential Insurance for $27 million. "That was the beginning of turning ourselves into a major real-estate developer, but with a firm commitment not to retain the real estate," Bill noted. "Why wait around for others to build hotels and ask us to manage them when we could construct them, sell them, and keep long-term management contracts? Why wait to be invited to the dance when we could build the ballroom and hire the orchestra ourselves?"

Wilson was put in charge of hotel development deals. Checchi was tasked to raise outside money for a new hotel in downtown Chicago and an expansion of the New Orleans Marriott. He didn't hesitate to accept the challenge, but he did so with a gut feeling that it was a "suicide mission." Checchi explained: "Since failure was inevitable in the midst of recession, inflation, and high interest rates, and since I apparently was judged expendable, I was given the challenge of financing and developing what would be two of the largest real-estate projects to be undertaken in America" at the time.

The Chicago hotel, the first new convention hotel built in that city since 1927, would rise forty-five stories and boast 1,214 rooms, making it the tallest hotel ever built in the Midwest. When completed, the expansion of the New Orleans Marriott made it, at 1,354 rooms, the largest in the Marriott chain and the biggest hotel in New Orleans.

Securing the financial backing was almost impossible. "I was doing these things for the first time, and I was running a little scared," Checchi said. But he was determined to prove himself to Bill. He successfully completed the task by, in some cases, bullying his way into investors' offices.

The sales of the Lincolnshire and Chicago hotels, along with the New Orleans expansion funding, were the beginning of a financial revolution at Marriott. "For the first fifty years of our existence, we had what could be called a 'bean-counter' mentality toward finance. Property leases and traditional mortgages were pretty much the extent of our financial universe," Bill recalled. "As long as we were leasing and building small facilities like restaurants, our simple financing approach worked very well. But by the mid-1970s, when we were trying to move into the big leagues, the formula was holding us back—especially on the lodging side, where huge mortgages not only limited the number of hotels we could build but put a real strain on what we could show in the way of returns to our shareholders."

In early 1977, Bill was driving to Richmond, Virginia, with Wilson and Checchi when Wilson asked, "Do you have a few minutes to listen to what Al has to say about a new way to sell?" Bill listened as Wilson continued: "The problem is that our best vehicle for growth is hotels, but we can't build more than a couple dozen because of the capital it ties up. Besides, it takes ten to twelve years for a hotel to pay back its investment, and we can't wait that long if we want to hit our 20 percent annual growth target. Al has a way around that."

Checchi recited how Conrad Hilton had pioneered the management contract idea in the 1950s when the only way he could expand overseas was to find foreign investors. But those contracts did not pay well. Checchi suggested selling a bundle of hotels below their book value in trade for healthy management contracts on those hotels. The cash from the sale would be used to build more hotels. The plan had some complicated twists to assure uninterrupted growth in corporate earnings to please the stockholders.

"I'm not a sophisticated financial person, but I understood Al reasonably well," Bill recalled, and he approved the concept. Wilson and Checchi bundled seven older Marriott hotels—Twin Bridges, Dallas, Los Angeles, Philadelphia, Miami, Newport Beach, and St. Louis—and sought a buyer for at least $100 million. Equitable, the nation's third-largest insurance firm, eventually agreed to pay $119 million. But getting Equitable to agree turned out to be far easier than getting J.W. to sign off on it. "Dad didn't like borrowing to build the hotels, but once we had them, he hated the idea of selling them and giving up all the valuable real estate we had. It was hard to convince him that with the very strong management contracts we had crafted, we would have almost as much cash flow as we would have had if we retained ownership of the hotels," Bill noted.

On May 9, 1977, Bill and Checchi went to J.W.'s house and laid

Allie and Billy in 1936.

The Marriott family, around 1950. Bill (standing), Dick, J.W., and Allie.

The historic mansion at Fairfield Farm in Virginia.

Christmas 1954 at Fairfield Farm with the Eisenhowers. Ezra Taft Benson is on the left.

Hot Sauce

Published twice
a month for
the employees of
Marriott-Hot Shoppes, Inc.
and their families

THE MARRIOTT-HOT SHOPPES FAMILY NEWSPAPER

OUR COMPANY'S 38TH YEAR   DEC. 1, 1964   Circulation 10,00

J. W. MARRIOTT JR., ELECTED PRESIDENT

J. Willard Marriott   J. W. Marriott, Jr.

One of the Youngest Chief Executives

Born in Washington, D.C., J. W. Marriott, Jr., at 32, ranks as one of the youngest chief executives of major corporations in the nation.

Educated at St. Alban's School in the nation's capital and the University of Utah, where he majored in banking and finance, Mr. Marriott, Jr. has been active in the business since 1950, when he started working in the Salt Lake City shoppe while attending college.

After graduation, he served 18 months in the Navy Supply Corps as ship service officer aboard the the aircraft carrier USS Randolph.

Mr. Marriott, Jr. became a full-time member of the company in 1956, working in the Store Operations Department. In late 1956, he took over supervision of the Marriott Twin Bridges Motor Hotel.

Later, under his leadership in the Motor Hotel Division, a long-range expansion program saw the Marriott Motor Hotel sales increase more than tenfold since 1957. During these years, Mr. Marriott, Jr. planned and developed the company's specialty food services—the Sirloin & Saddle Restaurants, the Sirloin Inns, the Fairfield Inns, the Kona Kai Polynesian Restaurant and the Windjammer Club.

The past year, in which he served as executive vice president, Marriott-Hot Shoppes experienced a record year in both sales and profits. Sales during the year totalled $84.7 million, and profits showed a 31 percent gain, to $3.1 million.

Mr. Marriott, Jr. is a member of the greater National Capital Committee of the Washington Board of Trade, the American Management Association, Sigma Chi Fraternity, the Board of Directors of the Better Business Bureau and the Columbia Country Club.

He and his wife, the former Donna Garff, and their three children live in Kenwood, Maryland.

J. Willard Marriott Makes Announcement

J. W. Marriott, Jr., executive vice president of Marriott-Hot Shoppes, Inc., has been elected president of this company, succeeding his father who founded Hot Shoppes nearly 38 years ago.

J. Willard Marriott, in turning over the presidency of Marriott-Hot Shoppes to his oldest son, will remain active in the company as chairman of the Board of Directors.

In announcing the board's election of J. W. Marriott, Jr. as Marriott-Hot Shoppes' president, Mr. Marriott said:

"For nearly four decades, I have headed our company's operations, and—with the help of many dedicated, talented people—I have been privileged to see the business grow from a small rootbeer stand to a major national chain with annual sales which now approaching the $90 million level.

"I feel it is my responsibility to shareholders to turn over the active management of the company to a younger man.

"Our Board of Directors feel that the outstanding job done by J. W. Marriott, Jr., both as executive vice president of Marriott-Hot Shoppes and as president of our Marriott Motor Hotels Division has qualified him to assume the responsibilities of president of the corporation. However, I expect to be around for a long time as chairman of the board to assist in every way I can to be helpful to the continued growth and development of our company."

Mr. Marriott, Jr. headed up the Marriott Motor Hotel Division for seven years, and was promoted executive vice president of the company last January.

Marriott newspaper article announcing Bill Marriott's election as president of the company in 1964.

The extended Marriott family, around 1964.

Dale Evans and Roy Rogers join Bill to open the first Roy Rogers restaurant in 1968.

Bill and Donna and their four children.

Celebrating the opening of Marriott's 100th hotel, in Maui.

With President Ronald Reagan aboard Air Force One in 1982.

With former president Gerald Ford at opening of Rancho Las Palmas Marriott in 1987.

Bill and Donna with President George H. W. Bush and his wife, Barbara, at the inaugural ball in January 19

Bill and Dick with former president Jimmy Carter at the 1992 Democratic National Convention.

This iconic portrait of J.W. and Bill hung in Marriott lobbies for many years.

The boathouse in flames after Bill's boat exploded with him aboard.

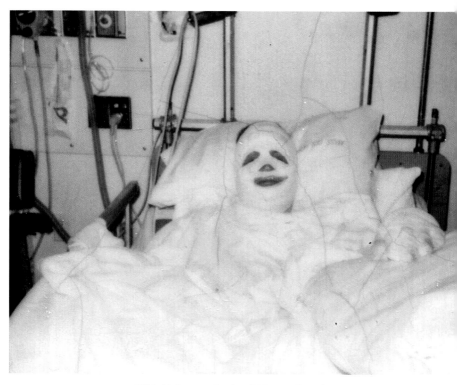

Bill in his "mummy bandages" following the explosion.

Bill beside a plaque at Camelback honoring his father.

Bill and Donna at President Bill Clinton's inaugural ball in 1993 with Coretta Scott King,
with whom Bill worked closely for the successful creation of a national memorial in Washington, D.C.

9/11: The Marriott World Trade Center hotel is shown shortly before the World Trade Center buildings collapsed. As the south tower fell, it sliced the Marriott Hotel in half. Fourteen firemen and a Marriott guest were coming down stairwell at the time. Less than half an hour later, the north tower collapsed and demolished the rest of the Marriott.

The crash of the second tower crushed the stairwell down to the third floor, but, miraculously, the survivors had just made it to the second-floor stairwell, which allowed them all to crawl out to safety.

Bill with President George W. Bush.

At this March 11, 2009, White House meeting with Barack Obama, Bill led the effort that successfully persuaded the newly elected president to make a strong statement the following day in favor of business travel to off-site locations for important meetings. This was pivotal in beginning a reverse of the devastating economic effects of the housing mortgage crisis on the hospitality industry.

Bill cements Marriott's partnership with Nickelodeon by getting slimed.

Bill celebrating his sixty-fifth birthday at Camelback in 1997.

The Marriott family in 2011.

Bill and Donna.

out the Equitable deal. They took two hours to explain it to him. Three days later, it was raised at a board meeting, and J.W. objected. Twelve days after that, Bill and Checchi again went to J.W.'s home and spent two and a half hours explaining the deal. The day after that, Checchi returned to confer with J.W. yet again.

On the evening of June 8, Checchi was asked back to the senior Marriott's home to go over the numbers for hours. The next morning at an Executive Committee meeting, J.W. said he had "a natural aversion to selling real estate in an inflation economy." Five days after that, J.W. had a heated exchange with Al Checchi about selling hotels. Two days after that, Checchi was summoned to the senior Marriott home and underwent another two and a half hours of grilling. J.W. "is very upset about it," Allie recorded.

And so it went. On August 24, the Equitable "agreement in principle" to buy the seven hotels was publicly announced, and the financial community responded positively. J.W. continued to oppose even as the details were worked out over the next ten months. The owners of the land under the Miami and Newport Beach hotels refused to assign leases to Equitable, so they were dropped from the deal. On June 20, 1978, the $92-million deal for five hotels was ready for the final Executive Committee vote.

The meeting seemed never-ending to Bill as his father filibustered. Finally, after J.W. said he was not going to change his mind, the vote was taken, and every committee member but him voted yes. For his part, Gary Wilson respected J.W. and sympathized a bit with him. "He started the company and made a great contribution. I understood the old man's mentality because my father was the same way. They lived through the Depression. [J.W.] was irrational about debt. Plus, he wanted the company to stay in the restaurant business instead of hotels, and that's why we stayed with restaurants for too long."

Wilson was a rare non-family eyewitness to the battles between J.W. and Bill. "It would be an intellectual argument at first. I'd be on

Bill's side and so would [Allie]. She was a mom, but she also knew which way the company should go. [J.W.] was very lucky that he had Bill as his son, but he wasn't often happy about it."

Then Wilson noted how bad it could get when Allie was not there to restrain her husband. "I saw enormous struggles between the father and the son behind the scenes. The old man was tough as hell, a beat-on-the-table type, and Bill doesn't do that—so his dad would just verbally [try to] intimidate his son. It was terrible. He'd do it in front of me. I mean, it was embarrassing. Half the time, I crawled out of the room. Bill fought hard—we all fought hard against the old man because we all knew which way the company should go."

Wall Street supported the Equitable deal when it was signed in July 1978. Security analysts universally praised the "creativity" and "brilliance" of the deal. No hotel company had ever sold multiple hotels while retaining seventy-five-year, lucrative management contracts. Bill explained to reporters: "Our objective is to get into a position in which we can develop a pipeline—building new hotels, operating them for a while to establish a track record, and then selling them and operating them under a management/lease contract."[1]

At the end of 1978, after the Equitable deal closed, more than half of the company's 17,000 rooms were managed by Marriott for other owners. By the end of 1981, Marriott owned only a third of the hotels it operated. The Marriott management contract revolution was off to a roaring start, and the company was flush with cash.

In January 1979, Gary Wilson moved up to CFO and Al Checchi was promoted to treasurer. The mentor and his protégé were now in place to do the most good. Wilson's first move as CFO was so stunning it rocked Wall Street and inevitably spawned many imitators. The fact that Bill agreed to the idea was a genuine act of courage that Checchi still regards as a "bet-your-company" decision.

Wilson and his financial team, including top strategic planner Tom Curren, had been considering for months what to do with all

Gary Wilson.

the cash coming in from hotel sales. Bill asked for a strategic plan for the use of the money. One of the recommendations was to buy up as much undervalued Marriott stock as feasible in the open market. Bill agreed, authorizing repurchase of five million shares of Marriott stock. By November, Wilson had accomplished the objective for the bargain price of $70 million.

Wilson wanted to double down on the stock repurchase program, and he made a pitch at the January 1980 board meeting. Knowing the massive risk Bill was on the verge of taking, Checchi tried to lighten the mood. In Bill's private copy of the presentation, he included a picture of Bill taken at the Seattle hotel opening, sitting in a canoe floating in a swimming pool, wearing a Native American headdress. The caption read: "What? Me worry?"

Wilson offered four alternatives to the board: "internal expansion," paying cash dividends, acquiring more businesses (Wilson suggested that Marriott could double in size by acquiring the ailing Walt Disney Company), or buying back more company stock. Wilson maintained that the latter was the best use of the money. Bill had been briefed beforehand on what Wilson would recommend, and he backed the stock purchase. Both J.W. and Allie were absent because of illness. When the presentation was over, the board gave unanimous consent to the stock purchase plan.

"What Bill approved would amount to the largest share buyback in American corporate history," recalled Checchi. On January 29, 1980, the company announced a tender offer for up to 10.6 million shares of its common stock at $23.50 a share. By the time the offer expired a month later, on February 28, tenders for 7.5 million shares were accepted and paid for. Bill came back to the board and asked for authorization to buy on the open market the additional three million shares not purchased during the tender offer's time limit. J.W. was present for this board discussion, and he vehemently argued against the whole idea of buying back stock. But when he saw which way the wind was blowing, he and Allie abstained from the vote, which was otherwise unanimous. "He was crushed to be outvoted," Allie recorded.

It turned out to be an unnecessary tempest in a teapot. Just five days after the board meeting, Bill voluntarily shut down the repurchase program because Marriott stock had risen so much it then exceeded the "bargain" price Marriott had been paying. When it was over, the investment world was surprised to realize that in less than a year the Marriott company had bought back 12.5 million of its own shares—or one-third of the company's common stock.

A historic precedent was set, and the Marriott move began to have a hidden but seismic impact on the corporate finance world as well as on the company itself. At the annual meeting held two months after the stock repurchase, Bill spoke to the stockholders in terms that went against everything his conservative father believed about debt. "In a time of high inflation, our company should maintain a prudent level of debt. Not only is long-term debt repayable in cheaper dollars, but interest on debt is tax deductible. This makes debt the cheapest form of capital available to us."

One of Wilson's lieutenants at the time, John Dasburg, maintained that what Wilson dreamed up, and Bill implemented, changed the way American corporations operated. "That major stock repurchase was very novel at the time in the American corporate environment. It may be a bit arcane to some people, but it sure as hell is important. Gary took something that was an important financial concept and made it acceptable and pragmatic in corporate America."

Making history was all well and good, but what pleased Bill the most was the result. By 1985, the same share the company had bought for $20 was, after stock splits, worth $200 per share. Thus, the best investment Marriott ever made was in itself.

• • •

Bill's family "no-big-shots-here" mantra went with him to the office, where he asked people to check their egos at his door. His belief in humility was a core value that emanated from his religious upbringing. Debbie said her father never liked arrogance in employees, and then she qualified it: "He doesn't like people who are dumb and arrogant. If they are smart and arrogant, he can deal with that."

Bill's style was to run his company by consensus. Longtime chairman of the National Geographic Society Gilbert M. Grosvenor, who knew Bill as a child and also served on the Marriott board, said that, unlike so many CEOs, Bill "just doesn't have a big ego, so he's got an unusual style based on management by persuasion, not power."[2]

Bill often harked back to the Christmas of 1954 when he had felt empowered by Dwight D. Eisenhower because the president had asked him, "What do *you* think?"

"I became a great believer in that phrase, and I've used it ever since. 'What do you think?' It works wonders! This more active version of listening is a particularly important skill for high-level leaders—like presidents and CEOs—who, by their lofty positions, often intimidate junior staff."

He routinely employed the listening technique during company business meetings. "When you open your ears, you open your mind, too. So, for example, I found it was vital not to signal that I've come to my own conclusions too early in a meeting. The less I say, the less I sway the discussion. I'd rather have people feel comfortable suggesting wild-eyed arguments or pie-in-the-sky concepts than take the chance that someone is holding back a good idea because they're picking up signals that I've already come to a decision."

Bill honed the attribute of decisiveness, recognizing that it had been one of his dad's challenges. "My father had a very hard time making decisions. He was raised in a family of eight kids who were noisy, opinionated, and just loved to argue. Dad took debate in college. I used to tell him, 'You'd rather argue than play golf or go fishing.' I won't drag stuff out. A lot of CEOs want stuff analyzed to death and they never do anything, and I think that's a terrible failure."

Bill considered yes-men who always agreed with him to be, in effect, disloyal. But one meeting Checchi described illustrates how people didn't feel entirely comfortable about standing up to the boss. Division heads had gathered to discuss a proposal that they all knew Bill liked, but they didn't. Before Bill joined the meeting, the executives passed the time grousing about what a terrible idea it was. When Bill arrived, he clapped his hands together happily and asked, "How's my project looking?"

"Well, Bill, it's looking good—really good," the assembled executives chimed in, at least everybody except the most junior executive, Checchi, who had not opened his mouth. Bill turned to him and asked his golden question, "You haven't said anything. What do you think?"

"I proceeded to rattle off all the reasons why the project was a disaster in the making—the same reasons that everyone around the table had been airing just minutes before Bill came in," Checchi said. The room went silent. Bill paused and frowned, and then exclaimed, "You know, you're absolutely right. Kill it!" And then he walked out of the room.

Marriott could not have achieved the extraordinary growth in hotels it did in the 1980s without the fortuitous confluence of events and people that occurred in 1981. By that time, a typical hotel's institutional money sources—the major insurance companies and pension funds—were drying up. Interest rates had soared so high that those traditional investors were backing away, or demanding a bigger piece of the pie than Marriott could afford to share.

Both Bill and Gary Wilson saw a ray of financial sunshine when Ronald Reagan was elected president in 1980. Believing Reagan was firmly committed to enacting tax cuts, Bill and Wilson hired John Dasburg, a partner with the accounting firm KPMG Peat Marwick, as the new vice president of tax. Thus, Marriott would be poised to take swift advantage of tax changes.

Using Reagan's mandate from the voters, two Republican leaders, Congressman Jack Kemp of New York and Senator William Roth of Delaware, coauthored the Economic Recovery Tax Act (ERTA), which was passed by Congress in August 1981. Only a month after President Reagan signed it into law, Wilson appeared before the Marriott board and unveiled his big new idea—limited partnership syndications formed to buy Marriott hotels.

He explained to the board that "the major insurance companies to whom we have looked in the past have not been willing to enter into long-term leases or management contracts on terms acceptable to the company. The proposed hotel limited partnership is an alternate source of financing. Under this proposal, a publicly owned limited partnership [LP] would be formed to develop certain Marriott hotel properties, [which would be] under a long-term management agreement" with Marriott.

What made this so appealing to private investors were the new

ERTA tax benefits that made the unique syndication a tax shelter. Wilson listed a few disadvantages, the worst being that the limited partners, not Marriott, would reap the benefits from future resales of any of the hotels. But Wilson advised that Marriott executives or board members would be allowed to invest in the LPs. "Our investment bankers believe that significant participation by officers and directors—particularly members of the Marriott family—would give added credibility to the partnership and assist us in better marketing the offering."[3]

Bill led the way to unanimous consent for Wilson to work out the details. For their first effort, called the Potomac Hotel Limited Partnership, Wilson put together an offering of eleven hotels. Five were already in operation, three were under construction, and three were only in the planning stage. The mix of hotel development was intended to be a template for future LPs, if this one succeeded.

The greatest attraction of limited partnerships to investors, especially those in higher income tax brackets, was the tax breaks. When Wilson first ran the numbers and reported back to the board in November, it looked like every dollar an investor put into an LP would bring five dollars in tax deductions. By the time Marriott was ready to file the proposed LP with the Securities and Exchange Commission, Wilson determined the benefit was even greater—an 8.7-to-1 ratio, instead of 5 to 1. Someone who invested the minimum of $10,000 in the Potomac LP would receive $87,000 in tax shelter deductions over the next fifteen years.[4] Once again, as with the stock repurchase program, when this new financing vehicle became public in January 1982, it generated substantial excitement throughout the industry.[5]

"Marriott Corp. has created an unprecedented plan to finance expansion of its hotel business by selling tax shelters to the public," wrote chief financial writer Jerry Knight of the *Washington Post.*[6] "Tax shelter sales are a common method of raising money for real estate ventures, but the Marriott deal [is] the first time a major corporation has [done it]." The *New York Times* agreed: "Marriott is a financial innovator, with such twists as the recent public syndication, an industry first [and] a clever use of financing."[7] Steven Rockwell, an analyst with Alex. Brown & Sons Inc., was quoted in the *Times* article as calling the idea "masterful." John Lanahah of Laventhol & Horwath, an accounting and consulting firm specializing in lodging, said, "Marriott is certainly the most aggressive and visible in the industry [with its] unusual financing techniques."[8] In the six months following Marriott's LP announcement, another L&H official informed *Forbes* that "several other chains are already beating down our door asking for help in setting up similar deals."[9]

The Chesapeake Hotel Limited Partnership became the second syndication, a nine-hotel offering that sold out quickly in 1984. With two under his belt, Bill went all out with LP financing. "I believe there were nineteen of them between 1982 and 1990, when the last one closed," recalled Assistant General Counsel Bill Kafes. "The total amount raised was in the billions of dollars. That was the financing vehicle for much of our hotel development all through the 1980s, which was the most rapid period of Marriott hotel development."

Gary Wilson's reputation was one of bluntness, arrogance, and intellectual intimidation. But, on the plus side, he had a laserlike command of detail second only to Bill's, a loyalty to the company, and a willingness to be convinced by logical argument. He had one unrelenting opponent at the company—Jack Graves, the longtime head of Architecture and Construction (A&C). It was Graves who dubbed Wilson "The Armadillo" because you could try to run over him, but the well-armored Wilson would never stop crossing your road.

Like Graves, many within the company feared that CEO Bill Marriott had become so entranced with "deal makers" like Wilson and Checchi that his appreciation of the "operators" who made up the core of the company would inevitably diminish. Their fears were unfounded. Bill was and is an operations man. Both Bill and Gary knew that every one of their team's better deals depended upon the success of the company's superior operators. "My philosophy of management is that no company can do well if it is not balanced between operations, finance, and marketing," observed Wilson. "If you have any company that's skewed in one direction or the other, it's not going to be successful. You try for a balance among the three. We (Marriott) became strong financially (because) we clearly were a strong operator."

Even longtime Marriott hotel operator Bus Ryan reluctantly recognized that, though they were often personally abrasive, these fast-talking, high-flying deal makers were a necessary evil for Marriott. "Deal makers don't care what they say to people. They don't care what people say to them. They're made with a certain amount of armor. They don't let little things bother them. That's a gift they have. They can sit at a table with somebody and say something that's totally off the wall with somebody just to test them. They know how to handle those kinds of things. They end up making the deal and shaking hands. So a certain amount of arrogance is healthy in those things. You can't be a good deal maker without being a gunslinger, and we needed these gunslingers."[10]

One trouble with gunslingers is that they usually move to another town when no more challenges are left in the town for them. Bill knew it would be impossible to keep his best deal makers forever. "People like Gary and Al are so smart they get very easily bored," he said. "They come in here and get all excited. They want to run out and grow real fast by buying something. But they don't want to mess with the nitty gritty. Yet this is the heart and soul of what made our company. It is brick by brick, inch by inch, step by step, hotel by hotel."

Checchi was the first to give notice, but Wilson quickly replaced him with another bright star, Stephen Bollenbach, who had a background in finance, real estate, and the savings and loan industry. To the company's "operators," Bollenbach was a breath of fresh air. In a four-year stint with Marriott, he helped facilitate big changes, including the growth of yet another company franchise—airport restaurants and gift shops.

At the same time as Bill began carving out a lucrative hotel chain from his father's restaurant company, Chuck Feeney founded Duty Free Shoppers Group (DFS) in Hong Kong. The concept was simple: offer high-end items free of import taxes to trans-Atlantic airline travelers who had a refueling stopover between Europe and North America.

DFS became the global pioneer of the duty-free concept in airports and other tourist locations. It was most lucrative in Asia, where cognac, cigarettes, jewelry, and other luxury items could be marked up more than 300 percent. DFS profits exploded after 1964, when Japan lifted the postwar foreign travel ban on its citizens. Flush with cash from two decades of saving, Japanese tourists immediately showed a voracious appetite for American goods, especially if they didn't have to pay taxes on them.

Eventually, other companies, including Host International, began challenging DFS's dominance. Then came a business shootout in 1980, which changed the future of not only DFS and Host but also Marriott. DFS's lease had expired at the Honolulu Airport that year, so Hawaii's Department of Transportation put the lease up for bid. The winner would get the prime shop site next to Japan Airlines' gates and a downtown duty-free store.

DFS bid $165 million and expected to win; no significant competitor had been detected. With victory assured, Chuck Feeney flew to Honolulu for the bid postings. Then, an unexpected bid went up on the board—from Host International for $246 million—and Host won the lease.

Always a fierce competitor, DFS quickly set out to emasculate Host in Hawaii before its operations could begin. DFS raised the salaries of its Japanese-speaking staff so Host couldn't poach them, and upped its commissions to travel agents, tour guides, and taxi drivers to make sure they stayed loyal to DFS. Host was beaten even before its shops opened in January 1981. In less than nine months, Host lost $25 million. Its stock plummeted. Smelling blood in the water, DFS offered to buy the limping Host, and Howard Varner, CEO of Host, agreed in principle. When Bill was tipped off about the agreement, he jumped into the fray.

Bill and Host had been talking merger for years. Host operated airport food services, gift shops, fast-food restaurants, and specialty dinner houses, including fifteen that it had purchased from Marriott.

Two concurrent events had increased Bill's interest in acquiring Host. Eight months before, he had purchased airport terminal concessions from AMFAC Inc. in Anchorage, Las Vegas, and Albuquerque. Three months after that, the Professional Air Traffic Controllers (PATCO) began an illegal strike. As federal employees, the 13,000 air traffic controllers had contractually sworn never to strike. The new president, Ronald Reagan, ordered them back to work. They were given forty-eight hours to return. Any employee who didn't would be fired and banned from federal civil service for life. Only 10 percent—about 1,300—returned to work. The immediate impact was a temporary 50 percent cut in available airline flights, which significantly affected Marriott's In-Flite catering income.[11]

But Bill soon discovered something unexpected: business at his airport terminal restaurants and concessions, including the recent AMFAC acquisitions, boomed so much that it covered In-Flite's losses. Travelers came to the airport earlier, had longer layovers, and thus spent more money at terminal concessions. Bill told *Forbes:* "If we don't get them on the plane, we'll get them in the airport. If your flight is delayed by two hours because of the air traffic controllers' strike, you're a lot more likely to stop for a drink or something to eat than if it's on time." The Host acquisition was a way to defend against the ups and downs of the airline catering business.[12]

Bill needed board approval for the acquisition, and his father the chairman was vehemently opposed. While Bill was looking at hotel

262

sites in Mexico, J.W. convened a special board meeting to settle the Host matter. Bill joined the meeting by phone. The board went against J.W. and agreed that Bill could offer up to $30 for each Host share. What Bill didn't know was that Varner had gone back to DFS and cut a deal for $29.25 a share. When Bill found out that Host was not even going to allow him to make a counteroffer, he was furious. Varner refused to take his phone calls, so Bill began playing hardball. "We got on the phone to Hong Kong advising DFS we were going to fight in court if necessary, charging them with *tortious interference*," a term for illegally interfering with a contract. "Signals began coming back through the lawyers that they might be interested in a three-way deal."

Meanwhile, J.W. had worked himself into a frenzy about the deal. On Monday, November 30, 1981, he met with Bill to try to stop it. "I made a mistake visiting with Billy," he wrote after the meeting. "He wants the world and I hope he can handle it!" In the afternoon, his heart began beating irregularly, and Allie assumed her husband was about to have another heart attack. Fueled by fear, she called Bill. "I talked to Billy and said I hoped we were dead before we went bankrupt," she wrote in her journal.[13]

Bankruptcy was not in the cards. No matter what Bill did, J.W. and Allie were set as multimillionaires for the rest of their lives, so Bill might have brushed off his mother's remark, except for the harshness of her tone. So he got mad instead. "Billy blew up," she recounted. "He said, 'This is the damndest, dumbest thing I've ever heard.'"

Allie was taken aback. "He was mad at me. It's the first time he's ever been mad at me."

They made up the next morning. That same morning, Host's Howard Varner finally called and said he would meet with Bill and DFS the following day in New York City.

The summit held in a Manhattan skyscraper on December 2, 1981, was an all-day battle. "It was maybe the toughest business day of my life," Bill wrote.[14] Marriott agreed to pay $31 a share for Host and to sell DFS the Host duty-free operations at the Los Angeles and JFK (New York) airports. Bill also agreed that DFS could purchase 875,000 shares of Host.

Bill made it back to D.C. in time for Donna's big National Symphony fund-raising night with its annual ball. It was a glittering, white-tie affair, and he could enjoy himself with the grueling negotiations behind him. At the end of the evening, according to his journal, "Dad actually congratulated me on the Host deal. He seemed real pleased."

The Host acquisition turned out to be one of the best bargains Bill ever made. "Everybody says acquisitions are very risky, and they are. Most of them don't work, and that's true. But this one was a barn burner," Bill said. "In fact, it may have been the best acquisition that ever took place in our industry up to that point. The timing was perfect. We bought the company when they were in trouble, so we got it at a fair price. They had a lot of restaurants that we didn't want, so we sold off all the restaurants. Then we took the airport business, and there was a huge amount of air traffic growth. So we caught it on the upswing when the air traffic growth was strong and we had a great run. Without them, we would never have gotten our 20 percent growth in earnings at that time."

• • •

Marriott had come a long way since President Harry Truman had stopped to eat at a Hot Shoppe restaurant on the way back to the White House after his 1949 inauguration, but there were still Hot Shoppes in the greater D.C. area. Many of them had been closed in the late 1970s, but by the mid-1980s, Marriott still operated twenty-two Hot Shoppe cafeterias and seven restaurants. Most of the survivors served neighborhoods with a need for bargain prices and family fare, which earned a loyal base of elderly customers. Some Hot Shoppes were exceptional moneymakers, but they would never be a significant profit-making division of Marriott. Any profit is good profit in business, but Bill always had to consider how much valuable management time, including his own, went into nursing along divisions that had limited growth potential.

The Big Boy chain increasingly began to fit into that category. Big Boy had been a consistent profit center since Bill bought the chain in 1967, and it had been pivotal in helping the company weather the recession of the mid-1970s. Bill's team, headed by his brother Dick, had turned it into the nation's number-one coffeehouse chain. By 1981, the company owned and operated 195 Big Boy coffee shops and fifteen Big Boy Jrs. In addition, Marriott franchised another 941 Big Boys. When Marriott purchased the company, Bill knew there was a looming problem. Its founder, Bob Wian, had been so anxious to expand his concept across the country in the early days that he had made some bad franchise deals that Bill couldn't get around.

The Roy Rogers fast-food chain, wholly owned by Marriott, had brighter prospects for expansion. Bill knew the best way to grow the chain was by purchasing other fast-food restaurants and rebranding them as Roy Rogers restaurants, which he did as quickly as possible. An important key to success in the fast-food business was national advertising, which for Marriott was cost effective only if Marriott had a big market share. It didn't pay to run expensive TV ads if Marriott had only a smattering of restaurants. The company could either build more restaurants from scratch—the most expensive and time-consuming option—or buy and rebrand existing restaurants. The best opportunity for the latter was acquisition of the Gino's hamburger chain, with 466 restaurants on the East Coast.

Bill went to the board with a proposal to buy the Gino's empire for $100 million. That included restaurants under several brand names, such as KFC. A worried J.W. responded with a barrage of questions. In the end, he abstained from the vote, and, for only the second time, Allie voted against Bill.

At the annual stockholders' meeting in 1983, Bill reported that the deal "has gone better than planned." The bottom line came in under $49 million. The results of the Gino's purchase were not as spectacular as Host had been, but it was a solid and highly profitable move, leapfrogging Roy Rogers several notches higher up the hamburger hierarchy.

• • •

There was one idea—a really big idea—that Bill's top gunslinger, Gary Wilson, had begun pushing in the late 1970s: that Marriott should buy the Disney company. After Walt Disney died in 1966, "the company was brain-dead for years," Wilson said. "Like most entrepreneurs, Walt wasn't lucky enough to have a son like Bill Marriott. He surrounded himself with guys who never grew. So after he died, they kept asking, 'What would Walt do?' It was the wrong question. Walt would likely have changed with the times, but they couldn't."

When Gary first raised the prospect of a Disney acquisition, "Bill looked at me like I was nuts, because Disney was two or three times bigger than we were back then." Finally, in late 1980, Bill relented, having been impressed by Wilson's persistence and confidence in the idea. He gave a cautious yellow light to proceed with a detailed review of the prospect.

What Wilson needed was inside information from the notoriously tight-lipped organization. He thought of a Trojan horse—negotiate with Disney for a new Marriott Orlando hotel, and thereby learn the company's inner workings. In February, Wilson and Bill flew to Los Angeles and met with Disney CEO Cardon Walker, who initially dismissed the idea of another hotel. By the end of the meeting, Walker grudgingly agreed to continue discussions. He ended up killing the project, but during the negotiations, Wilson had seen inside Disney's financials and had proved to Bill that Marriott could dramatically improve Disney profits by simply raising theme park admission prices and expanding hotel capacity. What worried Bill, though, was Disney's moribund film division. At the time, Disney hadn't produced a blockbuster in years, and Marriott had no one with the expertise to turn that around.

The project would require a $2.5-billion loan to bankroll the acquisition, and Disney wasn't for sale. Bill didn't want to be involved in a hostile takeover; it wasn't his style. But he gave Wilson one last hope in late 1983—if a buyer could be found for a spun-off Disney film division, Bill would take a run at buying Disney. No buyer could be found for that portion, and after three years Bill put an end to the plan.

In February 1984, corporate raider Saul Steinberg took advantage of the golden opportunity Wilson had discerned. After secretly buying more than 6 percent of Disney stock, he announced his plan to buy up to 25 percent of the shares, which put Disney "in play." Ironically, at that point, the main thing that saved Disney from a hostile takeover was the Marriott connection. Because Checchi had been part of Wilson's team looking at the Disney acquisition, he knew all the details and persuaded his new employers, Bass Brothers Enterprises, to put together a complicated subsidiary-related plan that made it too expensive for Steinberg to continue his bid.

As the largest shareholders, Bass Brothers then became the new *de facto* owners of Disney. At that point, Checchi went to Wilson and offered Marriott a great deal. Bass Brothers would sell its Disney shares at a reasonable price, and Marriott could finally own Disney. Wilson managed to put together $2 billion in financing for the deal and took his proposal to the finance committee of the Marriott board.

But Bill's heart wasn't in it. Following Bill's lead, the committee decided to pass on Disney. Wilson was greatly disheartened. "I'd been there for ten years and done almost everything I wanted to do—and everything Bill wanted me to do. But when he turned it down, I didn't harbor any ill feelings."

Checchi and Bass Brothers found another buyer, who ended up

recruiting the chief of Paramount Pictures, Michael Eisner, as the new Disney CEO. With that brilliant hire, Wilson decided to take one last run at Disney. He revived the Marriott offer to manage Disney's three hotels at the two parks, as well as build and operate new ones. For a while, Eisner and Bill both entertained the idea of the partnership. Bill knew the possibility of a deal with Disney was important to Wilson, who was clearly getting bored at Marriott. Bill's hope of somehow keeping Wilson engaged is the only explanation for why, at the same time, he made a bid to own a major railroad company. "It was Gary's idea," Bill said. "Gary wanted to leave the company, but he wanted to stay involved. So he wanted me to partner up with him and the Bass Brothers to buy Conrail."

Consolidated Rail Corporation was created by the federal government in the early 1970s to take over the routes of bankrupt Penn Central and six other bankrupt rail companies. Congress authorized the sale in 1981, but it took three years to put it on the auction block. Interested parties were invited to submit bids by midnight, June 18, 1984. Out of the fourteen bids, the most unexpected, for $1 billion, came from venture partners Bill and Dick Marriott, the Bass Brothers, and Gary Wilson. It would be a personal investment for the group, not a corporate acquisition.

Norfolk Southern Railroad eventually won the bid, however, and Bill was relieved about losing. "It was the dumbest thing I ever looked at. What do I know about railroads?" Congress eventually canceled the deal and instead "sold" Conrail to investor-shareholders via the New York Stock Exchange for more than $1.6 billion.

Shortly after Bill lost the Conrail bid, Michael Eisner called Wilson with an offer he couldn't refuse. Eisner wanted him as the new CFO of Disney. Wilson accepted and left Marriott in August 1985. Years later, at a social event, a curious Eisner made his way over to Bill. Both knew that despite Eisner's movie-making prowess, it was Wilson and the groundwork at Marriott that had given Disney the boost it needed when Eisner became CEO. Eisner asked why Bill hadn't bought Disney when Wilson originally proposed it.

"Because I didn't know there was a Michael Eisner around who could run the movie division," Bill responded. "I had to make my decision before you were hired, and I knew I couldn't run it. I don't know how to make movies or animated cartoons. I don't know what sells and what doesn't sell. I had no feel for the entertainment business."

Bill subsequently summarized his final thoughts about this "missed opportunity" in the 1997 book he coauthored with Kathi Ann Brown, *The Spirit to Serve:* "The Disney question is a fine example of an opportunity that came and went, never to return. It's also a good illustration of what I think is [a key] rule of decision-making: Don't waste time regretting, revisiting, or ruminating over what might have been. Have there been moments when I've wondered what might have happened if Marriott had acquired Disney? Sure. But I made peace with the decision years ago. The making peace part is important in decision-making. If you spend time going over the what-ifs of every decision you make, you do nothing but waste time that could otherwise be going into exploring new opportunities."[15]

CHAPTER 17

THE CHAIRMAN'S GRAND EXIT

For Chairman J. Willard Marriott, his last year, 1985, began with an accidental milk spill, which resulted in a trip to the hospital.

On New Year's Eve, J.W. spilled some milk, and when he stooped over to clean it up, he fainted and fell, wrenching his back. The back pain prompted him to go to Georgetown Hospital on New Year's morning, where exams determined that he had experienced a heart episode. He was hospitalized for nine days until the doctors felt it was safe for him to go home.

On January 22, J.W. and Allie flew to their Camelback desert home for a three-month getaway. During that time, J.W.'s strength waxed and waned as he entertained a string of visitors from Church leaders to grandchildren to Roy Rogers. He found time to grouse about quality-control issues at the resort, including railing at the restaurant manager for an hour. "He knows nothing," J.W. fumed. Nevertheless, that manager and every other supervisor of the resort gathered to say good-bye to J.W. and Allie the morning of April 19. It was the last time J.W. would see Camelback.

That spring, there were final moments in the spotlight for J.W. On May 1, he and Allie flew to Wayne, Pennsylvania, and were met by their friend Bob Hope. He drove J.W. in a golf cart across the parade grounds of the Valley Forge Military Academy to the grandstand, where J.W. enjoyed the thirty-minute parade that the 650 cadets put on for him, complete with horses and cannons. Hope then presented J.W. with the "5-Star Civilian Award." Four days later, he received an honorary doctorate from George Washington University.

May and June were a great time to visit his beloved Fairfield Farm, fussing as usual about its upkeep and hiring a new manager. Accident-prone Allie, who wasn't as fond of the farm as her husband was, tripped over a neighbor's dog and fell flat on a cement floor, injuring her back. June 25 was the last day Willard Marriott spent on the farm that reminded him so much of his childhood. His oldest friend and first Hot Shoppes business partner, Hugh Colton, had come to Washington for a family wedding, and he had asked to spend a day at the farm.

The previous January, when J.W. had been hospitalized with heart failure, Colton had sent him a letter full of memories. "As you know, for more than one-half a century, you have been the best friend I have ever had," he wrote. "I well remember our trips to the Yellowstone . . . and your good marksmanship in killing elk, deer, and even a bear. Also, your skill in catching big trout on Jenny's Lake. My memory also runs to the ruggedness of the high and beautiful [Uinta Mountains in Utah] when you nursed broken ribs for days, along the Skyline Trail. I also recall how you saved our lives with your rowing skill going down the turbulent Yampa River. . . . When I think of the fun times we have had together, my regret is that youth could not be perpetuated."

Both old cowboys knew they were near the end of the trail during the reunion at Fairfield Farm that June. "We sang old songs—well, Mr. Marriott and I sang while Grandpa listened and once in a while joined in," recalled granddaughter Carolyn Colton, who joined the two friends that day. "The love and admiration each felt for the other was contagious. Even though they didn't say it when they shook hands goodbye, I felt Grandpa was saying, 'I love you and I don't think I'll see you again.'"[1]

There were four places J.W. referred to as "heaven on earth." By

July 1, when Bill put him on a chartered jet from Washington to New Hampshire, J.W. had unknowingly said good-bye to three of them—the farm in Virginia, the "Jackrabbit Casa" at Camelback, and the house on Garfield Street. J.W. and Allie were happily traveling to their fourth "heaven" on the shore of Lake Winnipesaukee.

Only a few weeks earlier, the extended family had gathered for a dinner to celebrate J.W. and Allie's fifty-eighth wedding anniversary. The family sensed that their patriarch was more mellow than usual. "In the last year, he seemed to be a little more at peace with himself, and more at peace with what Bill was doing at the company, even though he still didn't agree with the debt the company took on," Donna recalled. There were some evidences of this as he and Allie settled in for a summer at the lake.

The first night, Bill and Donna invited his parents to a family dinner. Instead of criticizing Bill's expenditure on his classic car hobby, J.W. looked over what he called "the new old cars" and pronounced them "beautiful."

The "old" J.W., however, erupted on the Fourth of July with his own kind of fireworks. Dick had hired a crew to tear down dozens of trees at the end of the family's pasture so he would have more clearance for the landings and takeoffs of his new ultralight plane. When J.W. went for a walk that holiday morning, he discovered that the trees were missing. "Looked at what Dick has done to our pasture to make an airport with hangar for plane," he recorded. "Am writing him—no airplanes!" Father and son had a talk before the family barbecue that evening, and the tempest passed. Dick didn't need his father's permission to clear the land. It had been deeded to him and Bill in the mid-1960s.

The pasture-clearing incident was minor compared to the last stand J.W. planned against his son Bill at what would be his final board meeting, which was to be held on August 1 in Boston. For months, J.W. had been marshaling his arguments to halt Bill's secret negotiations to acquire the once-dominant Howard Johnson lodging and food-service chain. He saw the August board meeting as his last chance to put a stop to it, so he spent the night before the meeting listing reasons that the acquisition should not go forward.

Ironically, J.W. could have taken credit for the acquisition; he had first proposed a merger between Hot Shoppes and Howard Johnson restaurants in 1947. Those merger talks went on for almost two decades. J.W. could not close the deal before Howard Johnson Sr. died in 1972. "Neither of them could ever agree who would be in charge of the new company," Bill laughed in recollection.

At its peak in the mid-1960s, the Howard Johnson empire—colloquially known as HoJo—was the largest restaurant chain in the United States. Instead of reinvesting in the business by upgrading and remodeling its restaurants and lodges, Johnson Jr. sat on the profits. The chain began to rot from within. It was bought in 1980 by Imperial Group, a London-based tobacco, food, and beer conglomerate. After HoJo barely broke even in the first half of 1984, Imperial decided it was time to unload it. Bill was interested in the turnpike restaurants but not the brand—and not the hotels. His plan was to sell those. The best restaurant sites would be converted to Big Boys or Roy Rogers, and the rest would be sold.

In March 1985, Bill joined a half dozen other bidders for HoJo. Imperial announced that the winning bidder would be revealed on May 15. The day before, J.W. begged Bill to pull out. Bill vehemently refused, but he did lower his bid because HoJo had just recorded a $9.9-million loss. Imperial said it would not agree to the lower price.

When it came to business, Bill could show a lot of patience. Time and again, he simply waited until he got what he wanted. Over the next month, the competition narrowed, and Imperial invited Bill to the table again. J.W. knew the August 1 board meeting was his last chance to stop the acquisition.

All the directors were present when J.W. called the meeting to order at nine-thirty a.m. at the Copley Place Marriott in Boston. J.W. lobbed a volley of questions and objections about the quality of HoJo's operations. Dick, who had spearheaded the deal, replied that Marriott was not buying the operations; it was buying the properties and would quickly sell the ones it didn't want. J.W. expressed doubt about whether that could be done. Sensing the vote was going against him, J.W. finally questioned the cost of converting HoJo restaurants to Marriott brands, but Dick told him a conversion would be half the price of building from scratch.

J.W. called for a vote, announcing that his was a definitive "No." He polled the board, and each in turn voted in favor of Bill and Dick's deal, until it came to Allie. She was between a rock and a hard place for the last time. A "no" vote would please her husband, while a "yes" vote would favor her sons. She abstained. Judging from J.W.'s journal entries and accounts of family members, when he returned to Lake Winnipesaukee after the board meeting, he seemed resolved and peaceful, as if he sensed that he had only a short time left to savor life. That meeting turned out to be the lion's last roar.

When death came calling for eighty-four-year-old John Willard Marriott, Sr., that summer, it was neither unexpected nor unwelcome. The previous summer, he had been sitting on the porch at the lake home when he suddenly felt dizzy, stood up, and then fell onto the lawn. He spent twenty days at Boston's Massachusetts General Hospital, where tests determined that he had had a cardiac "incident" but not a full-scale heart attack. J.W. didn't care what they called it; he knew what had happened. "I felt like I died," he told Bill. "It was a sweet, wonderful experience for me. I am not afraid of death anymore."

J.W. had never been afraid of much, and certainly not of death. Once when he and Bill were on a morning flight to New York, the plane flew into a thunderstorm. J.W. slept through it until a particularly violent jolt awakened him. He looked over at Bill, who was terrified. "What's the matter with you, Bill?"

"It's apparent to me that in a few moments, we will surely die," said Bill.

J.W. replied, "Don't you know that dying is one of the great experiences of life?" And then he went back to sleep.

Like most Latter-day Saints, who believe life is eternal, J.W. knew he had an appointment with death, and he also was certain that life would go on after death. He had missed a few of his "appointments." He had come close to dying from Hodgkin's disease in 1933 and believed that healing priesthood blessings had saved him. He had escaped death twice in 1967—the first time when he suffered a heart attack and the second time when a blood vessel burst in his brain. Exceptional medical treatment was aided by the same spiritual system that had always sustained J.W.: his own faith, the ministrations of his "chief nurse," Allie, the faith and prayers of family and friends, and healing blessings.

Over a twelve-day period in 1975, J.W. had suffered three heart attacks that should have taken him down for good. During that period, sixteen-year-old grandson Stephen was on his knees with impressive frequency, earnestly pleading with God to save his grandfather's life. "I still remember praying to let him live at least ten more years—enough for him to see me go on a mission, get married and have a child," Stephen wrote. "My wish and prayer were granted" exactly to the year.[2]

When J.W. returned to the lake from the board meeting in Boston, he was greeted as something of a conquering hero by his family. The fact that he had lost the Howard Johnson vote was irrelevant to them. Instead, they were cheered by the clean bill of health he had been given during an examination at Massachusetts General Hospital. Pleased that their patriarch would be around a while longer, they gathered in the field adjacent to their lakeshore homes and waved as J.W. and Allie's helicopter hovered, then landed in the pasture at three p.m. Thursday.

Privately, J.W. was not so sure he was as fit as his physician had suggested. On Friday, he ventured out to hit a "bucket of balls with Bill." But after knocking a few of them around, he was too tired to continue. On Saturday, he took the boat out for a trip around Rattlesnake Island, but he almost fainted at the wheel, and so he turned back.

J.W. on horseback in 1985.

On Sunday, August 11, he was able to make it to church meetings at the new Wolfeboro chapel he had helped fund, which was scheduled for an official dedication in two weeks. J.W. enjoyed hearing Dick's wife, Nancy, sing on the program, and he joined her later at a Protestant church where she also sometimes shared her talent. That afternoon, J.W. asked Nancy, "Do you know 'Abide With Me; 'Tis Eventide'?"

"Yes," she said, noting the catch in his throat.

"Will you sing it at my funeral?" he asked.[3]

J.W. and Allie went to Bill's house for dinner in the early evening on that Sunday. Probably because of the religious meetings he had attended, J.W. was more sober than usual, and he did something that was entirely unexpected—he hugged Bill with a strong embrace, telling him he loved him and expressing how proud he was of his grown-up boy. Bill was taken aback; he had not heard such sentiments from his father in a long time.

. . .

When the sun rose over Lake Winnipesaukee on Tuesday, August 13, 1985, it was evident this was going to be a beautiful day. J.W. had pancakes for breakfast and helped plan the family cookout. Then he took a nap while Bill took the younger family members on a long boat ride.

By the time the boaters got back and walked to J.W.'s summer house, Grandpa was up and, as usual, ordering around his longtime chauffeur—the ebullient jack-of-all-trades and barbecue chef for the day, Cornelius "Mack" McNeil. Before the hamburgers were cooked, J.W. wanted everyone to gather on his porch for a family photo. "Take the picture of us, Mack," J.W. directed, but McNeil had another idea and asked a caretaker to take the photo. "You always told me I was a member of the family," McNeil said. "How can I take a family picture and I ain't in it?"

After the first photo, McNeil stepped off the porch to take over the photographer duties. When he put the viewfinder up to his eye, he saw a fishbowl-shaped light around J.W.'s head. He lowered the camera to check it, and J.W. asked what the holdup was. McNeil didn't answer. "When I put the camera back up again, I saw that aura again. It was a glow. I wouldn't lie to you. I remember just like it was yesterday," he recalled, quietly weeping more than twenty-five years later. "Something was going on here and I knew it." At the time, he kept it to himself.

After the blessing on the food was offered, and the family was chowing down on hamburgers and baked beans, J.W. got to his favorite part—the sweet New Hampshire corn on the cob that had been purchased fresh that day. When he was about to eat a second piece, he looked over at the cob on Bill's plate and remarked that it wasn't as good a piece as the one he had in his hands. "Here, take this one, Bill," he said. J.W. had never done that before.

About seven-thirty p.m., J.W. got up and walked into the house to his recliner with its window view of the shimmering lake. Before eight p.m., he began feeling some discomfort in his chest and sent the cook to bring Mack and Allie into the house. They applied the oxygen inhaler and gave him nitroglycerin pills. Bill joined them in time to see J.W. take his last breath, peacefully, without complaint.

An ambulance was summoned, and first responders attempted to revive J.W. on the way to the hospital, but it was too late. When Allie returned home after the ambulance left, McNeil was there to meet her. "Mack, Mr. Marriott is gone," she said.

"Mrs. Marriott, I know it. Mr. Marriott died in this house. He didn't die in the hospital."

Debbie agreed. "Grandpa had died, but his spirit was still in the room," she said later. "It was really interesting to look at the body that the EMTs were working on. That was not my grandpa. Grandpa was in the room, but he wasn't in that body. The thing I remember most clearly was that he was still the same person, same personality, same sense of humor, and that he loved us and his death had nothing to do with us. It was his time to go."

When Bill returned from the hospital, he sat at his father's desk and began the funeral preparations. Given the likely number of mourners, Bill knew that the funeral had to be held at the largest Latter-day Saint facility in Washington, which was the stake center adjacent to the temple site. As the stake president, it would fall to him to conduct the meeting, if he could keep his composure. That evening, Bill decided to put his grief in abeyance until he had conducted the funeral with a dignity that would honor his father.

As he made plans, he read a note in his father's handwriting, apparently scribbled the night before after he had watched a movie on TV that featured a famous old song. "The best things in life are free," J.W. had written, by way of affirmation. "The moon belongs to everyone; it shines just for you and me."

Bill called his closest friends in the Church's leadership and learned that three Apostles, Elders Gordon B. Hinckley, Ezra Taft Benson, and Boyd K. Packer, would attend the funeral. All three agreed to speak. Bill also asked Dr. Billy Graham, the most famous preacher in the world, to offer remarks. The choice of the next speaker was a surprise to everyone, even himself. Former President Richard Nixon called Allie to express his condolences, then asked Bill if he could attend the funeral, if his presence wouldn't be a distraction. Nixon had resigned in disgrace eleven years earlier and usually kept a low profile. Of course he should come, Bill said. In fact, "Would you consider speaking at the funeral?"

Between Wednesday and the funeral on Saturday, condolence calls, letters, and telegrams poured in by the hundreds. J.W.'s death was front-page news across the country. In a rare tribute for a nonpolitician's death, the *Washington Post* devoted an editorial to his passing, seeing it as an end-of-an-era event: "Pardon us for taking a slightly parochial view of J. Willard Marriott when we point out that with him died another bit of small-town Washington. A community's merchants give it much of its character. And the quality of its individual businesses reflects the quality of those who are responsible for them." The city's "warm recollection of the Hot Shoppes institution is a tribute to Marriott. For many years, his little chain of restaurants helped give this capital something of the flavor of a courteous, pleasant, overgrown village before he became a towering business figure and the city also went on to bigger things."[4]

From a vacation at his California ranch, President Ronald Reagan told reporters that J.W. had been "a living example of the American dream." In spite of his rise "from modest beginnings [to] become one of the world's most successful and respected businessmen, he never lost the value of honesty, decency and hard work, instilled in him as a youth. He built an enterprise and raised a family, both of which are models for us all." The president also sent a private letter to Allie, which concluded: "May our Lord comfort you with warm memories of your life together."[5]

Vice President George Bush called Bill and offered sympathy. Former President Gerald Ford sent a handwritten note from Rancho Mirage calling J.W. "a person of greatness. . . . I will forever be grateful for his many kindnesses and loyal support while I was President."[6]

Former governor and presidential candidate George Romney told the press: "For me the world will never be the same. He was a magnificent individual and friend and was so well-balanced in every way." Romney's son, Willard Mitt Romney, wrote to his "Aunt Allie": "I have looked to Uncle Bill as a model since I was old enough to know that I was named for him. . . . I remember the ranch, Uncle Bill as a tall, lanky smiling cowboy. . . . I warm at the thought of his humor and twinkle. . . . It was the character, integrity, fairness [and] loyalty [that] makes him so worthy of respect and emulation. . . . I love him, and look forward till we meet again at Jesus' feet."[7]

Bill and the Marriott family received more than 640 condolence notes, telegrams, and letters, which his secretary recorded on a list that covered twenty-five pages. The king of Saudi Arabia sent Bill his best wishes, as did Coretta Scott King, Supreme Court Chief Justice Warren Burger, and Dr. Robert Schuller, the popular preacher of Los Angeles's Crystal Cathedral.

In the end, the tribute Bill considered to have the most reassuring eternal significance came from the President of The Church of Jesus Christ of Latter-day Saints, Spencer W. Kimball, who wrote that J.W. "was a man whose accomplishments in business and industry provided an unparalleled example of integrity. Even greater than these accomplishments was his devotion to his God, his family and his country. . . . We rejoice in the knowledge of his life, so well-lived, and a posterity devoted to the same principles which made him such a remarkable man."[8]

Hundreds attended the viewing at the funeral home on Friday, where the flowers filled four rooms. Allie had asked Ellie Colton—wife of Sterling, Bill's longtime friend and the company's General Counsel—to arrange the funeral flowers in the stake center to look like an English garden. The Coltons worked until two a.m. Saturday arranging cuttings from dogwood and magnolia trees, along with a profusion of floral arrangements.

The family asked another friend, internationally famous columnist Jack Anderson, to act as chief usher for the funeral. His job was to stand at the chapel's front entrance and direct distinguished guests to the seats reserved for them. More than a few were anxious about what might happen if he and Nixon interacted, considering Anderson had once been Nixon's archenemy in the media. "Nixon strode up to me to get his instructions, not paying attention," Anderson recalled. "Then we made eye contact. When he recognized me, his face contorted into that old 'hunted adversary' expression. 'Hrrumph,' he growled, and walked away."[9]

There had been a similar Cold War between George Romney and Nixon. Though Romney had served as a cabinet secretary under Nixon, he and his family were convinced Nixon had broken promises he had made to Romney during the 1967–68 presidential campaign, and that Nixon had lied to Romney about the president's involvement in the Watergate scandal. Romney had not given Nixon the time of day for a decade, which is what made the funeral photo of Nixon and Romney, with Billy Graham acting as mediator, so rich with history. The spirit of the funeral program for their mutual friend was so powerful that the two old political warriors buried the hatchet. "The whole experience softened my feeling toward Richard Nixon and for the first time since I left the Cabinet we are going to have a visit. I had never wanted to see him before," Romney wrote Bill.[10]

At 10:50 a.m., at the stake center and at a satellite temple visitors' center location, more than 2,500 congregants all stood as Dick and Donna escorted Allie to the first pew, facing her husband's red-rose-draped coffin. With his penchant for punctuality, stake president Bill Marriott began the meeting promptly at 11:00 a.m.

Bill had assigned himself to be the first speaker, the sole family member to offer remarks. "I've often said that the best decision I ever made in my life was to select my parents," he began. "I feel as if a giant redwood has gone and left a great space in the forest. . . . His greatness was his goodness, his deep love of the Lord, his earnest study of the scriptures and his strong testimony that God lives and that there is life beyond the grave."

Distinguished funeral guests and speakers, including (left to right) President Ezra Taft Benson, Bill Marriott, Elder Boyd K. Packer, President Gordon B. Hinckley, the Reverend Billy Graham, former president Richard Nixon, Mark Evans Austad, Governor George Romney, Ken Garff, and Richard Marriott.

Bill kept his talk short, thanking everyone for the support they had shown the family. "I loved my dad and I will miss him greatly," he concluded.

Billy Graham came next: "The Apostle Paul once said that we are not to be slothful in business. No one can ever accuse [J.W.] of being slothful or lazy. He never believed in the forty-hour week for himself. He worked sixty and seventy hours a week. . . . He showed how you could build a great business with honesty and integrity and make a profit. . . . Now we say as the French do, 'Au revoir,' till we meet again, because we will."

Some in the congregation nervously fidgeted when the next speaker, former president Nixon, came to the pulpit. No one knew what to expect. Any tension was quickly dispelled as he spoke in a folksy, personal manner about his friend. He spoke for twelve minutes without notes. J.W. was "a nice guy who finished first," Nixon declared. He quoted Sophocles: "One must wait until the evening to see how splendid the day has been." Then he described J.W.'s last day of life at the lake. "I think all of us can be thankful today that in the evening of his life, he could look back and say, 'How splendid the day has been!'"

Nixon and Graham had to leave right after the funeral. They shared a limousine to the airport and then flew on to New York together, still talking about the powerful spirit of the funeral after they landed. "Words cannot express the impact your family, friends, and especially the service, made on me Saturday," Dr. Graham wrote Bill. "The deep spiritual content made a lasting impression on me. As a matter of fact, I told George and Barbara Bush that it was one of the greatest services I had ever attended."[11]

The funeral procession to Parklawn Cemetery in Rockville, Maryland, was two miles long. Dozens of white-gloved police officers blocked intersections until the full procession passed. Flowers lined the entire route inside the cemetery. At the graveside, George Romney delivered the dedicatory prayer. Bill had introduced Romney as "a good friend for sixty years," and Romney lamented in a letter to Bill a few days later: "As you probably know, while your father had many close personal friends, I had only one, and none really close, now that he has departed temporarily."

Romney and other out-of-town visitors—about 250 mourners altogether—were invited to join the family for lunch at the Bethesda Marriott Kona Kai restaurant. Just as Allie had done for many decades when J.W. had been too busy or ill to write in his journal, it was left to her to write that evening's entry: "It's all over, and his wonderful life will be a wonderful memory."[12]

CHAPTER 18

THE REFINER'S FIRE

Bill Marriott was alone at the top of his company, and never before had the responsibility of its future weighed so heavily. He had good employees and a superior management team, but in the first two weeks of that fateful August 1985, he lost three important players upon whom he'd come to depend—his father, his brother, and Gary Wilson.

Technically, Wilson was the CFO until September 3, but he had already moved to Los Angeles, having been hired by Michael Eisner as Disney's new CFO. Wilson and Al Checchi (who had left three years earlier) had been the financial wizards who—through inventive limited partnerships, stock buybacks, and other creative maneuvers—had been critical to Marriott's growth. J.W. never fully trusted Gary's financial wizardry, which hadn't made Gary appreciative of the obstreperous Chairman.

The funeral, however, changed Wilson's view of the formerly fearsome man. In a note to Bill, he said, "Unfortunately for me, I saw The Chairman principally from an adversarial business vantage point and not as the wonderful family man that he obviously was. I know you had disagreements with The Chairman over company matters but, unlike the rest of us, you saw the warm, religious family man that he really was. . . . He lived a fine life and his final day was truly wonderful, with his entire family present. May God rest his soul."[1]

Wilson had been a front-row witness to the ongoing bouts between father and son, and he had stayed firmly in Bill's corner, supplying the encouragement and strategy needed to win the struggle for the company's future. Now the final bell had rung, and the seemingly endless contest between the company's founder and its builder was over. Yet, in all those years, Bill never doubted that his father wanted the best for him, even if they didn't agree on what that was.

J.W.'s death took away the friction for Bill, according to Donna. "Bill was always on edge knowing that no matter what he did, his dad might not approve. Now that was gone." Yet the responsibility he felt for the company and its employees weighed heavy. For two decades since becoming president, Bill had worked sixty to eighty hours a week, sacrificing time, family, and health, to grow the company. Over those years, Marriott had grown from four hotels to 144; from 9,600 employees to 140,000; from annual revenue of $84 million to more than $4 billion.[2] He could not stop, and Donna well knew it: "He could have just been out there fooling around with his cars or his boats, and say, 'Well, I've got enough money. I don't need to make any more.' But he's just not that kind of person."

What Bill had not entirely expected was his brother Dick's decision to resign from daily work at the company. Shortly after their father's burial, feeling that the chains of filial obligation had diminished, Dick met with Bill. "I am not interested in running the restaurants anymore," he said. "I did it because Dad wanted me to. You're CEO; I don't ever want to be CEO. I love you, and I support you. I will help you in any way I can, but I don't want to be tied down to a desk here anymore."

With that, Dick stepped back. No formal resignation was ever tendered or accepted. Dick spent fewer hours at headquarters and company events, but he had never spent as many hours as Bill had anyway, so there was little change there. He remained on the Marriott board of directors and was promoted to vice chairman, but he had no regular assignment other than to attend meetings and advise Bill. Thus, on the day of J.W.'s funeral, the Marriott family's generational legacy with the company, so key to its corporate culture and success, had gone from three to one. The future rested primarily on Bill's shoulders.

Bill never begrudged Dick his decision. He knew that sibling rivalry had torn many small and large family companies apart, and Dick had never challenged him. Instead, in the past and future, Dick unstintingly believed in and praised Bill's leadership. "He's been very loyal to me," Bill said. "There's never been a bit of conflict between us. He's just as loyal and wonderful a brother as you can possibly ever have."

The day after the funeral, a Sunday, Bill's course seemed set. Only then could he begin to deeply consider the loss. After church meetings that day, Allie called her sons and asked them if they would come over and give her a priesthood blessing to help her find peace. Seated in a chair, Allie asked Bill to be "voice," meaning that it was his responsibility to seek inspiration for the words of comfort and blessing that God would have him say. Such a blessing always begins with the recipient's full name. As they all closed their eyes in prayer, Dick and Bill put their hands on Allie's head. "Alice Sheets Marriott . . ." Bill began, almost in a whisper. And then he began to weep.

Many of the Marriotts returned to Lake Winnipesaukee during the week after the funeral. Their guests included John's future wife, Angela Cooper, and Elder Boyd K. Packer, who was staying to dedicate the new Latter-day Saint chapel in Wolfeboro on Sunday, August 25. On Saturday morning Bill got up early to prepare his speedboat to give Elder Packer a tour of the lake; the fifteen-year-old Donzi was sometimes temperamental. The sky was clear, and the weather was already getting humid, but Bill was chilled and had his woolen sweater on. What was most different about that morning was the still air.

Bill began filling one of the boat's tanks with gas about nine-thirty a.m. The family compound was just stirring. Elder Packer was finishing breakfast in Allie's home. Ron and Debbie were at their home getting their five-year-old twins ready for the boat ride. David was still asleep in his parents' house. John was telling his mother about another migraine headache that was plaguing him. His girlfriend Angie was taking a shower in a guest bedroom. In another guest room were Roger and Kathy Maxwell. Roger was the golf pro at Camelback Inn and had become quite close with J.W. and Allie during their months-long annual stays in Arizona.

Maxwell wandered out of the house onto the lawn. He was less than a hundred feet from the boathouse, where he could make out the shape of Bill pumping gas. At the controls of the boat, Bill was unaware that, in the still air, gas fumes were accumulating on the deck around his legs. Nor could he have known that the ignition switch would prove faulty and nearly fatal.

About 9:40 a.m., intending to check the gas gauge needle, Bill turned the ignition key. Suddenly there was an explosion that shook the windows and frames of all the nearby homes. Maxwell saw a fireball immediately engulf Bill, and he assumed it was the end of his boss. Incredibly, inside the boat, Bill was still conscious, staring at his pants and hands on fire. Instead of succumbing to immediate shock, he heard a loud voice: "Get out of the boat." Still aflame, he managed to jump off the back of the boat into the cold water. He made his way around the back of the boathouse to the beach.

When John heard the explosion, he knew exactly what it was. He raced out the door past Maxwell, who was still frozen in place. Angie heard the explosion from the shower. She threw on some clothes, ripped the sheets off the bed, soaked them in water from the shower, and ran to the beach where John was helping Bill crawl onto the shore.

Angie was incredibly calm as she tended to Bill. "I know you don't know me that well, but we're going to have to take your clothes off," she told him in a steady voice. As he groaned from the pain, she pulled off the heavy, wet V-neck wool sweater that had protected his torso but now threatened to do more damage, as it still retained enormous heat. Some of his hair and all of his eyebrows and eyelashes had been burned off. His polyester golf pants had mostly burned off, leaving only a few ragged remnants around his belt.

In what would be significant for Bill and his family, his knee-length garments, special underclothing worn by temple-attending Latter-day Saints and considered sacred, had not been singed or burned, fully protecting his upper legs in a miraculous manner. While his lower legs were badly burned, Angie could see that his hands had suffered the worst, having turned white and bloodless, with skin hanging off them like inverted gloves. She carefully wrapped his burned flesh in cold, wet sheets and towels. Angie and Donna helped Bill into the family station wagon, which could make it to Huggins Hospital in Wolfeboro faster than the ambulance could make the round-trip.

The Marriott fire was the largest blaze ever seen on the shores of Lake Winnipesaukee to anyone's memory. The firefighters faced a raging inferno fueled by gas, wood, and plastic, not only at Bill's boathouse but also at the neighbor's—a classic $500,000 boathouse from the 1920s that went up in flames. The fire increased as secondary explosions went off. Boating sightseers came from far and near to watch the blaze. Bill's boathouse was a smoking ruin. The Donzi and the yellow speedboat moored with it both burned down to the waterline and sank. The total damage was estimated at nearly $1 million.

At the small hospital, the doctors and nurses knew they were not up to the task ahead. A helicopter was called to take Bill to Massachusetts General Hospital in Boston. While they waited, Elder Packer and Dick gave him a priesthood blessing. In it, Packer remarkably promised there would be no long-term repercussions, not even scarring on Bill's face. The recovery would not be easy, but this tragedy had occurred "for a wise (divine) purpose."

Before the helicopter arrived, the Huggins Hospital medical team made a serious mistake. Bill had lost a lot of fluids by the time he got to hospital, and nurses had correctly started him on IVs to bring up those levels. But, in their haste, they hadn't warmed the bags. When the medics from Boston arrived, Bill's temperature had dropped to 89 degrees and he was in danger of dying from hypothermia.

After the helicopter took off, Donna returned to the lake house with Allie and Elder Packer. He would remain at the lake for the chapel dedication on Sunday.

Bill was fortunate that Mass General's burn unit was run by Dr. John F. Burke, who assigned himself to Bill's case. Burke had an international reputation for a series of innovations in the treatment of burn victims. His most stellar achievement was to co-invent the world's first viable artificial skin—an amalgam of shark cartilage, cow tissue, and plastic—which is known today as Integra and has saved the lives of countless burn victims since its creation in 1981.[3]

Within minutes of Bill's arrival at Mass General, Dr. Burke ordered a series of life-preserving procedures for him. A thorough examination of Bill's lungs determined that, miraculously, they were not damaged. Next, Bill was tethered to at least two IVs, one of them pumping liters of a saline solution into his arm, and the other infusing him with a high-protein, high-calorie, high-carbohydrate liquid. The team washed Bill's burns in a silver nitrate solution, which caused a black stain over his body, and then treated the burns with Silvadene cream. Then Bill was wrapped almost completely in gauze bandages, leaving only his eyes, nose, and mouth uncovered. By the time Donna and Debbie arrived at the hospital, Bill had undergone all these procedures. His appearance was alarming. Entirely wrapped in the bandages, he lay abnormally still, eyes filled with concern and body tethered to tubes. But he could still joke.

Debbie decided to preserve his new "mummy look" with a Polaroid picture, and she showed it to him. As Bill looked at it for a minute, he couldn't help but think about what a horrendous year 1985 had been for his family. Then Debbie saw a faint and familiar twinkle come into her dad's eyes. He spoke in a halting, raspy voice: "Hey, Donna. Let's put this on our Christmas card this year with the caption: '1985 was a hell of a year for us. We hope next year is better for you!'"

Bill didn't see the first public Marriott bulletins to news outlets. Spokesman Al Rankin understated the severity of the injuries; the company expected him to be released from the hospital "in a few days." The only accurate part of the statement was that, "all things considered, he's in good spirits."[4]

The Marriott stock price had dipped only slightly when J.W. had died less than two weeks earlier, mainly because savvy investors knew that Bill had been running the company for two decades. But when news of Bill's brush with death was reported, there was a more distinct downturn in price. The stock stabilized after a few days as Rankin kept reassuring nervous investors that Bill would soon be back to work.

Bill underwent isograft skin surgery by Dr. Burke, which meant grafting healthy tissue onto the wounds. Dr. Burke never used his own artificial skin creation unless the patient was so extensively burned that there was not enough of the patient's own skin to graft. But the doctor did something unexpected to save Bill's hands. "He used super glue to attach hooks—like those from a lady's dress—to my fingernails," Bill explained. "He then used ping pong paddles with dress hooks at the top. Then, he stretched my hands flat across the paddles and used rubber bands to attach the hooks on my fingers to the hooks on the paddles. . . . I had paddles for hands for over a week in the hospital."[5]

The body of a burn victim contracts upon itself, and Dr. Burke's invention saved Bill from having clawlike hands for the rest of his life. Hospitals now routinely use splints, skintight Jobst garments, and extensive physical therapy to stretch contracting limbs, but in the mid-1980s, what Burke did with the Ping-Pong paddles was ingenious.

During Bill's sixteen-day stay at Mass General, Donna discouraged visitors except immediate family. After a few days, she let John and

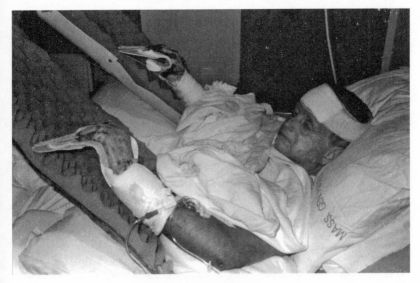

Bill's painful recovery.

David visit. "It was overwhelming," John recalled. "They tell you he's doing okay, but it's hard to separate that from what you're seeing—your father looking like charred beefsteak." His younger brother, David, vomited on seeing his dad's condition. "The whole thing was just upsetting, and I ended up running into the bathroom of his room and throwing up all over the place."

Dr. Burke dropped by often to check on Bill, and the two men quickly bonded. On Bill's second day in the hospital, President Ronald Reagan called from the White House to check on him. Dr. Burke ribbed Bill about it. "What the hell is he calling you for?" Burke said. "Doesn't the president have anything better to do than talking to you?"

At the hospital, Bill was taught a dissociative technique of pain management. The doctor asked him to think about the times when he felt most relaxed. Easy, Bill responded, when he was at the wheel of his boat on the lake, the sun overhead, and smooth water racing by him. He found that particular visualization an effective way to distance his mind from his pain-racked body.

291

A very low point at the hospital for Bill, which came after he had been there about a week, had nothing to do with his continuous pain. It was the day Dick called with bad news. Allie had had a serious accident. She was stepping off the back porch of the lake house to feed her golden retriever, Rusty, when she fell over the dog and broke her pelvis. Dick was going to drive her home to Washington, D.C., to recuperate. "Here I was laid up in Mass General for burns," Bill recalled. "Dad had died the week before. Now Mom had broken her pelvis. At this point, Dick was the only one walking around."

Stephen was visiting from Phoenix at that time and wrote in his journal: "Dad is all right. He is in a lot of pain. He has lost about 20 pounds and he's very weak. He has also aged. However, the doctor said he is healing well." Stephen found his dad remarkable, never complaining about the accident or the pain. He refused to break down. But it was from Bill's deep well of empathy that, upon hearing the news of his mother's accident, he finally wept for just a moment. Stephen recorded with admiration: "The only time I really saw Dad cry was while we were together in the hospital and he learned that Grandma Marriott fell and broke her pelvis. And then, he wasn't crying for himself."[6]

When Bill hit the two-week mark at Mass General, he had had enough. "I can't really stand this anymore," he confided to Donna. "The smell in this burn unit is so bad. People are moaning and groaning and crying out in pain. I'm not getting any sleep. I've got to go home."

Donna approached Dr. Burke, and he consented to the release on two conditions: that Donna learn how to change the dressings, and that Bill return every week to Mass General for physical therapy and progress checks. Nurse Donna was a quick study, and Bill was released into her care on the sixteenth day. To play it safe, they drove to the lake house to try the new arrangement for a few days before venturing farther from the hospital.

Donna steeled herself for the pain she knew she inflicted on Bill every few hours when she changed the dressings. The process involved boiling saltwater first, and then using wet gauze on the old dressings so removing them would not pull off new skin. After applying cream, she redressed them—the hands, the two calves, and the graft site on his hip. (His face had been flash-burned—like a bad sunburn—and was mostly healed by the time he was discharged from the hospital.)

Bill and Donna had been home only a week when a setback occurred. Having been cooped up for so long, Bill was trying to do more things around the house than he should. On his way to the basement, he collapsed and fell down the stairs, dislocating his shoulder and ripping open at least one of his hand grafts. He shouted for help, and John rushed to his aid. John found his dad a few steps from the bottom of the stairs with his shoulder dangling, one hand bleeding, and appearing physically spent. John knew he couldn't lift his father up the stairs alone in that condition, so, besides bandaging his hand, he would have to put the shoulder back in its socket.

A memory from seventh grade came to John's mind. The family was at Camelback for the Christmas holidays, and Bill had driven John and Stephen to Flagstaff for some skiing. Since he didn't ski, Bill was walking up the side of the slope to watch his sons, when he slipped on an icy patch and dislocated a shoulder. John and a member of the ski patrol skied to his side and popped the shoulder back into place.

Sitting on the stairs, John needed Bill to relax his muscles. He called to his mother to bring Valium. She brought one. "He needs three," John said, and sent her back to the medicine cabinet. Then, when Bill was feeling no pain, John popped his shoulder back into place. After that, it took half an hour to boost Bill up the stairs. "John was there when I needed him," Bill recounted with emotion the following March at the wedding luncheon for Angie and John. "John was there and carried me to the top of the stairs, helped me get my shoulder back in place, and got me back to bed. That was a moment of closeness and tenderness that I will never forget."

The fall had torn the graft on one of Bill's fingers, so he and Donna flew to Boston the next day, where Dr. Burke grafted some of Bill's skin that had been kept in the hospital freezer. After that incident, Bill tried not to overdo again. Donna rarely left Bill's side during the four-plus months when he recuperated. She counseled him through the natural depression that afflicts burn victims. She traveled with him to Boston, where he repeatedly endured pain as the therapist bent his fingers again and again so they would retain full range of motion. She continued to change the bandages at the five sites, day after day, hundreds of times. "There were days when I didn't know how I was going to get David to school and back because I was so tired from taking care of Bill," she recalled. Occasionally, she accepted help from others for the grocery shopping and cooking, but not to change Bill's bandages. The family could have afforded in-home nursing care, so why didn't Donna opt for that? "I guess," she said, "if you love somebody enough, you do what you can to take care of them. I just felt it was what I needed to do. Things like that make you closer."

Stephen saw the recovery process up close and had his own thoughts. "I really have great parents," he wrote during an October visit home. "Neither of them has complained this whole year despite the setbacks and trials. [Mom is] rarely to bed before 12:00 a.m., and she's up early to help Dad. She's tired, exhausted even, but she doesn't complain. My love and respect has increased greatly for my parents. They are valiant."

Except for attending the grand opening of the New York Marriott Marquis in October 1985, Bill did not return to work full-time until the following January. He waited until he could fully dress himself and tie his own shoes. That month, he left on his first long-distance business trip to California. Donna was suffering from a bad cold as they said good-bye.

By the next night, when Bill called her from the West Coast, Donna couldn't talk; she could barely breathe. He hung up and called the family doctor, who rushed over to see her. After a quick examination, he was alarmed. "Find somebody to take care of David," the doctor ordered. "I'm taking you to the hospital now."

In Donna's view, she had been so worn out from the four months of care and stress that her body finally crashed with a potentially fatal disease. The diagnosis was bacterial epiglottitis, a disease in which bacteria infects and swells the epiglottis to the point that every time the afflicted person swallows, the air passage closes and he or she can't breathe. Donna was hooked up to IVs of steroids and antibiotics to reduce the swelling. Bill took the next available flight home and went straight to the hospital when he landed. It was his turn to be the caretaker.

After three or four days, when she was on the mend, Donna checked herself out of the hospital. Epiglottitis might have been the illness that killed George Washington, but it was not going to take down Donna Garff Marriott—not if she had anything to say about it. And she did.

Bill and Donna left the hospital hand in hand, both resolute and optimistic that, despite its rough beginning, 1986 was going to be a better year for them.

CHAPTER 19

THE JEWEL BOX

Billy Marriott was eight years old when he first set foot on New York City's Times Square in 1940. He and his parents were on their way by car from Washington, D.C., to a summer vacation in Maine when J.W. decided to treat the family to a night at the luxurious Hotel Astor on Times Square.

When Billy strode through the doors into the grand lobby with its twenty-one-foot-high colonnade of marble and gold, the Hotel Astor was the most popular meeting place on Broadway. In the center of the lobby was an ornate clock under which couples often met, and which was featured in a Judy Garland movie, *The Clock*. At the time of the Marriotts' visit, the hotel was the temporary residence of several of the rich and famous, including Charles Lindbergh, Will Rogers, and Arturo Toscanini.

Times Square never lost its allure for Bill, who returned two decades later in 1960 in the hope of opening a hotel there. At the time, he was chief of Marriott's "Hotel Division," overseeing a grand total of two hotels. He was thinking about buying the historic twenty-five-story Times Tower, built in 1904 as the headquarters of the fledgling *New York Times*. Though the building was still owned by the *Times* in 1960, the newspaper had moved its offices elsewhere.

At the time, J.W. was a board member of the American Motors Corporation, and he had worked closely with AMC President George Romney on a proposed partnership to buy or build a hotel in the Times Square area. An AMC executive suggested renovating the Times Tower instead of building from scratch. Bill worked up the figures, and it looked like it could be done. But the deal subsequently died because of poor handling by Marriott executive Milt Barlow and also because the deal's biggest champion, George Romney, left American Motors in 1962 to become Michigan's governor.

A decade later, the whole area was in sorry shape. The Hotel Astor had closed its doors in 1967. Prostitutes, drug dealers, and drunks took over after dark, and theatergoers would hurry out of the area after the shows. Hoping to turn around two decades of decay, Mayor John Lindsay approached Atlanta architect-developer John Portman about building a new hotel on Times Square. Portman had designed the first eye-popping hotel atrium in Atlanta, which had jump-started the Hyatt hotel chain. He put an option on Times Square property but could find no one willing to bankroll a luxury hotel in the seedy neighborhood. He gave up in 1975. That year, J.W. and Allie visited Times Square and could not believe how bad it had become. Wrote Allie that night: "Terrible neighborhood now. Trashy pornographic stores & peep shows."[1]

Three years later, Mayor Ed Koch lobbied Portman to return to the project, even though it had already been dubbed "Portman's Folly" by critics. Koch arranged tax incentives and a federal redevelopment grant, so Portman agreed to try again, but by mid-1979, the projected cost of construction was $200 million, and no one was interested in funding Portman and his folly. A year after that, along came Bill Marriott, who strongly believed that Portman's hotel could not only make a profit but also begin a revival of the wonderful Times Square of his youth.

Portman and Marriott had been competitors for more than a decade by the time they sat down to discuss a potential partnership in

New York City. Just two years before, in 1978, the two men had dueled over rights to build a hotel two blocks from the White House. Bill won and built the hotel, which he named simply the J.W. Marriott. It became the company's flagship. When he heard Portman needed a partner for a hotel on Times Square, Bill was all in. From the outset of the negotiations, Portman said he wanted the Marriott brand on two hotels—Times Square and a second Atlanta hotel. Bill took it to the Marriott board.

In the seventeen years since he had become president of the company, Bill had rarely failed to receive a unanimous vote from the board for every project he recommended. His father had often harangued him and vocally opposed him even at the board level, but when J.W. could see that every director—each of whom he (J.W.) had handpicked— was in favor of Bill's proposal, he would usually cast a vote in favor or abstain. The vote at the February 1981 board meeting was a notable exception.

Bill showed the board plans for a fifty-one-story hotel on Times Square with nearly 1,900 rooms. J.W. voiced strong opposition, saying there were too many other capital expenses facing the company at the time. When the vote was taken, J.W. was the only negative vote. Even Allie voted yes. "I opposed taking $300 million hotel on Times Square, but Bill got his way," J.W. lamented in his journal before privately conceding that it would be "a beautiful hotel—greatest in America."[2]

Four months later, with relatively little debate, the whole board also signed off on the $190-million, 1,800-room Atlanta hotel partnership with Portman.

The Times Square project soon entered rough waters. Litigation over the fate of the historic Morosco and Helen Hayes theaters on the property, combined with other delays, drove the price up to $322.5 million, making it the most expensive hotel being constructed in the United States. That brought the project back to the Marriott board, where J.W. had another chance to protest. For the first time ever, when the vote was called, *both* J.W. and Allie voted against the project. Bill wrote in his journal, "It is disappointing to have them go against me."[3]

Not one to give up easily, J.W. sent his son a handwritten seven-point memo two weeks later, signed "Mother & Dad," asking him to reconsider the project. The hotel was too expensive, he said, the neighborhood was "disreputable," and the trade unions were likely to interfere in a nonunion project. "Why gamble?" J.W. asked, adding that the premium Marriott hotels in Atlanta and Boston "plus all others" should be enough. J.W. surprisingly closed with a conciliatory reference to himself and Allie: "Bill—maybe we can't see far enough?"[4]

Ironically, it was J.W.'s obsession with artificial grass that finally pushed Bill over the edge on the Times Square deal.

J.W. would have covered every Marriott concrete surface with Astroturf if he could have. All of the company's general hotel managers had been subjected to his Astroturf lectures ad nauseam, and perhaps no one more than Steve Hart, general manager of Camelback. "He wanted every pool deck and every outdoor deck—just about every piece of concrete we had—covered with Astroturf. He loved the wonderful fresh green color and texture of the covering." One night, after an executive meeting at Camelback, J.W. got a devilish look in his eye when he turned to Hart and said, "Steve, there's something we haven't Astroturfed yet." He reached into a bag and pulled out a toupee made out of Astroturf, and Hart obligingly put it on.

It was Bill who got the brunt of J.W.'s Astroturf fixation. "Dad was constantly after me to use large quantities. He even checked Astroturf prices on a near-weekly basis at the country hardware store not far from the family farm in Virginia. He would walk into the office on Monday morning, quote the latest price, and wait expectantly for me to jump at the chance to buy in bulk at the store's low rate, which was about half our procurement price. If we bought it in the country, he pointed out, we could use twice as much. The Astroturf update became a predictable part of our weekly ritual."

On June 19, 1982, Bill was in his office, mulling over the last-minute details of the Times Square hotel deal, when the phone rang on his desk. It was the landowner, reminding Bill that his option to buy the site would expire in six hours. After that, the new sales price was likely to be much higher.

Then another phone lit up. It was the general contractor, reporting that he could not secure a "no-strike" clause in the construction contract.

Then, a third line lit up. It was the mayor's office, calling to get confirmation that Marriott was going forward with the deal.

The fourth caller was J.W.: "When are you going to put Astroturf on the balconies of the Twin Bridges hotel?"

"Just when you might think I would have been most dismayed to have to listen to yet another lecture on the merits of Astroturf, I was in fact relieved," Bill recalled. "My father's simple, down-to-earth question about fake grass had the effect of bringing me down to earth, too, reminding me of the company's real priorities—attention to detail and looking after our customers' comfort."

The call from J.W. crystallized Bill's thinking, and he told the other three callers that the hotel was a go. He wrote in his journal that evening: "I finally decided to go ahead with the new hotel based on the vitality of the new convention center, and the lack of competition in NYC for a truly first-class convention hotel."[5] The final price would be $500 million. "It was probably the biggest and toughest decision I ever had to make."[6]

Portman and Bill shook hands over the Times Square project after signing the final contracts on July 2, 1982. As much as anything Bill had done, this was his "bet-the-farm" move, and it was a pivot point in Marriott company history. If the half-billion-dollar venture failed for any reason, the negative reaction of shareholders and investment analysts would be harmful to the company. Positive assessments from that sector had always been based on faith in Bill's business savvy. If he slipped on this big, very public decision, that confidence would seriously erode.

For such a historic event, the hotel still had no name. Bill and Portman met in October and decided on New York Marriott Marquis. Their Atlanta joint venture would be called the Atlanta Marriott Marquis. As Portman explained to the press, this would distinguish the two hotels as a "new class of hotel," and the Marquis title would be given to future Portman-Marriott hotels, should there be any. The signing of the deal did not mean the hotel was a slam dunk. Before Marriott came aboard, Portman had worked out $150 million in loans, but that wasn't enough. No one had as much faith in the future of Times Square as Bill did, and, in the end, he was willing to put his own money on the line.

When insurance companies and banks could not be found to buy hotels Marriott was building, Gary Wilson had used the "limited partnership" option, which provided significant tax advantages to investors. The LP plan worked easily for the Atlanta Marriott Marquis, and in that case the idea was so popular that investors had to be turned away. For the New York Marriott Marquis hotel, Wilson put together an initial consortium of twenty-three institutional investors. Nearly $100 million in additional funding came from a partnership of Portman and Marriott, but Marriott had to supply 89 percent of it. At the eleventh hour, Bill turned to his brother Dick, who never failed him when Bill asked for his support. The two of them then reached out to Gary Wilson, Butch Cash, and Fred Malek to join them in a partnership taking on 39 percent of the equity, leaving the corporation with 50 percent. They agreed, and the hotel went forward because Bill's loyal brother and three executives backed his play with their own money.

With the funding in place, the challenges continued. "Never have we built a hotel which has been more difficult to design and build," Bill said at the "topping-out" ceremony in October 1984. "Bringing building materials to this site and erecting them is a challenge, perhaps

Construction proceeds on the New York Marriott Marquis.

only surpassed by the building of the pyramids years ago." That was not mere hyperbole; besides the mind-boggling logistics of building a skyscraper in the middle of Manhattan, there was also the frustration of dealing with construction trade unions, a portion of which were thought to be controlled by organized crime syndicates.

Jack Graves, then head of Marriott's Architectural and Construction Division, said, "I had been in construction all my life. I thought I knew everything there was to know about building a hotel until I got to New York, and they took me to school. It was all the unknown elements involved there. It was like swimming in cement."

Portman was even pithier at the topping-out press conference: "Had I known about the problems before we started, I would have left town on the next bus." When an effusive Mayor Ed Koch declared during the ceremony that the hotel "is the largest human creation since ancient Egypt and the pyramids," Portman wryly muttered: "Pharaoh had an easier time than I had."[7]

During the three-year construction, the contractors had to deal with many of Manhattan's obstacles—including heavy traffic, the inability to store materials nearby, and a myriad of other issues. When they began blasting the sixty-foot hole for the foundation, the work could not be done during matinee performances at nearby theaters. Later, when the steel structure began to rise, ironworkers had to move from the west side to the east side if they were using noisy air-driven torque wrenches during matinee hours. Materials had to be trucked in at night to avoid rush hour.[8]

Two Manhattan concrete contractors had a union-supported near-monopoly, and they charged about $82 a cubic yard, which was then $30 to $35 a yard higher than in nearby Westchester County or Staten Island. When Marriott's contractor tried to work around it by installing precast concrete floor slabs, the Teamsters Union brought construction to a halt with a wildcat strike—one of a dozen or more that slowed the project down. In that case, a court ordered the union members back to work.

A massive mistake by the contractor's primary out-of-state steel provider—sending steel that was too short—delayed the project almost eight months. Also causing extra delay and cost, Teamsters Local 282 required the contractor to freight the steel to New Jersey instead of directly to New York, so it could be unloaded there, then reloaded onto trucks that were driven by Teamsters into the city.

None of this was news to state and federal investigators, including the Federal Bureau of Investigation and the President's Commission on Organized Crime, which had long been investigating corruption in the New York construction business. Graves had been warned that there were "four Mafia families" tied to the workers on the job. The news was sufficiently intimidating that Graves found the project management the "most dangerous" he had ever overseen. At one point, when Bill appeared on NBC's *Today Show* and was critical of Manhattan union tactics, Graves said he got a call from a reputed crime figure asking him who was feeding Bill these disparaging reports on the union. The next thing he knew, the FBI phoned Graves and asked him to come to their office and tell everything he knew. He dodged the request because he had no firsthand knowledge of Mafia involvement.

Bill also had no firsthand knowledge of that, but he believed that pro-union vandals did everything they could to make sure union workers racked up overtime as the project was near completion. In the summer of 1985, vandals ripped vinyl off walls, poured cement down toilets, yanked electrical wiring out of walls, and flooded bathtubs. "We put on guards, but the guards just turned their backs," Bill said. "They just knew they had us over a barrel because we had to get the hotel opened. We had conventions coming in, and we had a commitment to get most of the hotel open." The company had to pay more than $12 million in overtime due to vandalism.

The hotel had its "soft" opening while Bill was still undergoing burn treatments at Massachusetts General Hospital. Guests were so wowed by the hotel's airy heights, bright lights, and thousands of polished surfaces that, early on, they nicknamed the hotel the "Jewel Box." The Marquis had the largest ballroom in Manhattan, a two-level penthouse suite complete with a grand piano and breathtaking views, and the city's first revolving rooftop restaurant. For the "soft" opening, fewer than one-third of the rooms were ready. The contractor had countered the vandalism by cannibalizing from partially finished rooms to make sure those 500 were available.

The grand opening of the New York Marriott Marquis, Marriott's 147th hotel, occurred one month later during a weeklong extravaganza beginning October 7. The theme for that event was "The Best of Times." The irony of that theme was not lost on Bill, who had been going through his "worst of times." He probably should not have attended the affair, since his burns and skin grafts had not yet healed.

The video record of his appearance reveals a man still in pain, with both hands bandaged and shaking at times. Rabbi Arthur Schneier, a Holocaust survivor, offered a prayer at the ceremony, thanking God for Bill's miraculous survival.

When Bill was introduced as the last speaker, it was pointed out that just the previous week he had become "the second chairman in the company's fifty-eight-year history." Bill began by recounting the wonder of his first boyhood visit to Times Square. Now, years later, "being here today to preside at the opening of this hotel, to participate in it, is one of the greatest days of my life," he continued. "My mother wanted to come too, [but] she fell, broke her pelvis, and was not able to be here either." Glancing at his brother Dick, seated nearby, he offered a tender aside: "There are only two of us in the family, Richard."

In the quiet days and weeks following the grand opening, Bill stayed home in Bethesda to recover from his burns and regain full use of his hands. He had plenty of time to worry about whether the New York Marriott Marquis had been too risky a venture.

He was comforted somewhat by the fact that, before the grand opening, his marketing team had already booked 1.2 million room reservations through 1995, representing $900 million in revenue, which was the largest piece of forward business any of Marriott's hotels had ever booked. An industry rule of thumb was that, to break even, a hotel room should generate $1 a night for every $1,000 in construction costs. The *New York Times* pointed out that "the Marquis will have to charge $220 a night, a rate seen only at top New York hotels like the Helmsley Palace, the Pierre and the Waldorf-Astoria, which are in far more attractive neighborhoods."[9]

But it was an act of faith that paid off. In less than a decade, the Marquis was the most profitable hotel in the whole Marriott system, and it has remained so into the twenty-first century.

• • •

If Bill Marriott had an archrival in the hotel industry of the 1980s, it was Darryl Hartley-Leonard, the British-born hotelier who started at Hyatt Hotels as a desk clerk in 1964 and rose to become the chain's president at the age of forty in 1986. In an interview with the *Chicago Tribune*, Hartley-Leonard, who was fourteen years Bill's junior, confessed: "I can't bear the thought of losing our edge, but in some ways I see it already has happened. I wake up every morning and there's this great weight of Marriott hanging over my head."

Only Marriott and Hyatt recorded occupancy rates above 70 percent. Together, the two companies had built more quality hotels in the previous decade than the rest of their competitors combined. Marriott was the larger of the two, managing 150 hotels; Hyatt had 80. Marriott's hotel revenue was $1.9 billion, while Hyatt was not far behind, at $1.65 billion.

Bill had a healthy respect for Hyatt because of their mutually strenuous efforts to achieve high standards. The two companies kept a close eye on each other's innovations. However, Hartley-Leonard was usually slower on the draw than the more farsighted and flexible Bill Marriott. One example was Marriott Honored Guest Awards, the frequent-guest program Bill rolled out in 1983.

"We were the first ones really to start a frequent-stay program in the hotel business," Bill recalled. "Holiday Inn had one before we did, but it was very small and ineffective. We really went all out for it. My gut told me that it would work." In trade publications, Marriott's was called the "preferred lodging awards program," and intuitively added perks like redemption of points for discounts with airline, cruise, car rental, and other partners.

Hartley-Leonard called Bill when the company announced the program and warned him, "You're making a big mistake. You can't give away this stuff. You're crazy. I will bury you in advertising!" Four years later, a sheepish Hartley-Leonard finally had to begin Hyatt's own frequent-guest program. "By the time Darryl woke up after we got that four-year jump on them, we were so far ahead he couldn't catch us," Bill said.

In the mid-1980s, Bill foresaw that because of the aggressive expansion by all the chains, major cities would be overbuilt with full-service hotels by the end of the decade. Alternatives for lodging growth were needed, and the Courtyard concept was only a partial solution. Another idea was smaller full-service hotels designed for suburban markets. Internally, as Marriott studied it for a year, the potential new product was referred to as "baby Marriott" or "mini-Marriott." Hartley-Leonard came to the same conclusion about a new area for growth and was designing mini-Hyatts at the same time. He won the race to complete the first compact hotel in 1988, but Bill was not perturbed. When Marriott opened its first compact hotel a month later at Peachtree Corners in Atlanta, Bill was confident that he had come up with the better product for the bottom line. Compact Marriotts were soon proliferating at a steady pace. Because Hyatts were more costly, and financing became more difficult to obtain, they were unable to keep up with Marriott.

The editor of *Lodging Hospitality* concluded in 1986 that while Bill Marriott lacked the charisma, visibility, and good looks of his fellow hotel giants, "he is the smartest man in the lodging industry today. When it comes to innovation, growth and profitability, the Marriott Corporation is, in my opinion, unmatched by any other chain or lodging organization." A major reason for this success, the analyst determined, was that, unlike the others, Bill did not "shoot first and ask questions later. Marriott prefers to sit back in the weeds, analyze and test extensively before launching a new product or a marketing program." As an example, he pointed out, while other chains "jumped on the all-suites bandwagon," Bill waited until he could design the best product to make the most money.[10]

Not until Holiday Inn unveiled a new generation of all-suite hotels called Embassy Suites in 1983 did Bill feel it was time to enter that market. His Marriott Suites hotels would feature separate living rooms and bedrooms; each suite would also have a large work desk, two televisions, a wet bar, and a refrigerator. The suites would appeal to business travelers seeking an upscale, residential atmosphere, and to families seeking two rooms for the price of one.

All-suite hotels promised a higher profit margin than the mini-Marriotts or Courtyards. Full-service prices could be charged for rooms that cost less to build, and all-suite hotels could be operated with fewer employees. As with the Marquis, Courtyard, and compact hotel prototypes, the location for the first Marriott Suites was Atlanta. Bill presided over the March 1987 opening even as another half dozen Marriott Suites were being designed and constructed in California, Arizona, and Illinois.

With the Suites concept off to a strong start, Marriott strategic planner Tom Curren urged Bill to look closely at possible entry into the economy-lodging segment, which was then defined as hotels under $40 per night. The competitors fell into three categories. There were the independent, "mom-and-pop" units, which had 28 percent of the market; traditional chains such as Holiday Inn, Best Western, and Ramada, with 34 percent; and "new generation" chains such as La Quinta, Comfort Inn, Days Inn, and Red Roof, with 38 percent. Because American travelers could likely support more than 500,000 economy hotel rooms, there was plenty of room for Marriott.

Bill authorized $50 million to design and produce the first ten units, which were to be called Fairfield Inns, a trademark Marriott already owned. J.W. had opened several specialty restaurants under that name in the 1960s. It was a reference to the family's beloved Fairfield Farm in Hume, Virginia.

Where to put the first Fairfield Inn? Atlanta, of course. "It was always a good place to begin," Bill said. He flew to Atlanta in December 1987 to personally launch the first Fairfield Inn at the airport. By the chain's second year, the travel-industry experts in the annual *Business*

Travel News survey ranked Fairfield Inn as the best economy-lodging chain. At the same time, the Inns achieved higher-than-expected occupancy rates and profit ratios. By 1990, Marriott had seventy-five Fairfield Inns in twenty-five states.

When the original Fairfield Inn opened, the *Washington Post* observed that Marriott had all-suite hotels charging $100 and up a night; traditional full-service hotels at $80 per night; Courtyards at $60; and this new budget offering at about $40 a night. "This gives the company hotels in every segment of the market."[11] Not quite; there was yet another segment Bill coveted. For this segment, a golden opportunity virtually fell into his lap, allowing Marriott to become the overnight leader.

Jack DeBoer was the pioneer of the "extended-stay" lodging concept with his Residence Inns starting in 1975. His decision to add a free breakfast would later become an industry standard. Along the way, he added a partner, Holiday Inns, but then decided to buy them out of the partnership. He needed money to do that, and he turned to Marriott in 1987.

Marriott was already designing its own extended-stay product, but Marriott executive John Dasburg felt that buying was better than building, so he and Bill were open to a partnership with DeBoer or an outright purchase of Residence Inns. DeBoer needed $50 million quickly to pay off Holiday Inns, so he asked Marriott for a loan and promised to either sell the company to Marriott or pay back the loan in six months. It was an offer the company couldn't refuse. The money was loaned, and Dasburg cut the Residence Inn acquisition deal for $120 million in cash and assumption of $143 million of the company's debts. Holiday Inn management was stunned by the announcement of the sale. Residence Inn by Marriott was now the runaway leader in the extended-stay market, with ninety-two company-owned and franchised hotels, and another fourteen under construction.

DeBoer then turned around and created a new extended-stay

concept, Summerfield Suites, at the high end of the market with rates near $100 per night. The first was opened in 1988, and after several years it was sold to Hyatt. Darryl Hartley-Leonard had belatedly decided Hyatt should be in the extended-stay market too, and Summerfield was his buy-in. He regretted again falling behind his archrival Marriott but was fairly sanguine about the setback. "We had developed an arrogant attitude at Hyatt," he said. "And then Bill Marriott came along and just stomped all over us, and we learned a very valuable lesson. Just because the rest of the world tells you how great you are, doesn't mean someone else can't come along and outdo you. We have fought now for years to regain our position. It's healthy to have a competitor who just frustrates the hell out of you and keeps you on your toes."[12]

• • •

If Bill had not become president of Marriott in the mid-1960s, J.W. probably would have stayed primarily with what he knew— the food and beverage business, with its narrow profit margins. The company would have engaged in limited risk and achieved moderate growth, possibly struggling in the 1970s from the fast-food challenge of McDonald's and other chains that were the death knell of many family restaurants. But, in spite of his runaway success with hotels, Bill still embraced the food sector, too, by taking great risks with swift expansion and major acquisitions.

"Industrial feeding" was little noted and mostly unheralded at Marriott for four decades, but in a mere eighteen months in the mid-1980s, Bill, Executive Vice President Butch Cash, and CFO John Dasburg transformed it into a behemoth that was number one in the world. J.W. began an "industrial feeding" program in 1943 when Hot Shoppes took over the Naval Communications Annex Cafeteria in Washington, D.C. After the war, J.W. picked up contracts for cafeterias in non-defense industrial plants and other government agencies. Then

J.W. moved into the health-care food field in the 1950s with D.C.-area hospitals.

Because most of the contracts were short-term, and businesses sometimes went back to self-catering, the small department grew slowly. When Bill became Hot Shoppes' president in 1964, there were only twenty-three clients. He formed a new "Food Services Management (FSM)" division, but the business remained stagnant. Bill still sensed there was potential, so he hired more salespeople and recruited Daniel Altobello to run the division. Under his leadership, Marriott invested in new cafeterias in trade for longer-term contracts, particularly at universities.

Institutional food service wasn't a glamorous business, and it wasn't a big business at Marriott yet, so it received little attention from Bill. His interest began to grow in the mid-1980s when Gary Wilson advised him to get out of the theme park, cruise ship, and restaurant businesses and focus on hotels and food service. But the prospect of food-service acquisitions was far riskier than any of Bill's previous purchases. "When we bought a hotel or a restaurant company, we were buying assets," explained executive Bill Shaw. "But if we bought a food service company all we were buying was a filing cabinet full of accounts that could be canceled after we acquired the company. So, naturally, Bill and many of us had a lot of concern."

The first dip into FSM acquisition waters was the purchase of Gladieux Corp., with 100 accounts and facilities at seven airports. It also had twenty-four turnpike restaurants, which, when added to the converted Howard Johnson toll-road restaurants, turned Marriott's highway division into the largest in the world. Next, Marriott bought another industrial food business, Service Systems, Inc. The two acquisitions turned Marriott's FSM division into a nationwide business with 1,400 clients in forty-five states—more than tripling its number of employees to 28,000. "It also gave Food Service Management critical mass at Marriott, transforming the division in just a few months from almost a footnote to the company's second-largest business [after hotels] in sales revenue," added John Dasburg.

Marriott's new $615 million in annual food-service revenue had also pole-vaulted FSM to the number-three position within the industry. Only ARA Services ($800 million) and Saga Corporation ($700 million) were ahead of Marriott. In business, Bill was always driven to be number one. That meant he had to acquire either ARA or Saga. An ARA acquisition was nearly impossible because its top executives had just taken the company private. Saga, however, was a different story.

Saga had been founded in New York by three Hobart College seniors who persuaded the administration to let them run a dining hall at the school. They soon expanded to other colleges, and then to business and health-care food service, just as Marriott had done. Bill had met the founders more than once and thought, "Saga was a first-rate operation. My father liked them and I liked them. We were always interested in acquiring them." But Saga wasn't interested in being acquired. That changed by the beginning of 1986. On the face of it, Saga was a robust company, but internally it was torn by dissension between the CEO, Charles Lynch, who fancied himself as a turnaround artist, and a board that didn't see the need for a turnaround.

Marriott saw an opening, but as chairman of the Saga board, Lynch had packed it with people who would not welcome a takeover. That meant Bill would have to engineer a hostile takeover, which was not in his nature. The board authorized Bill to open negotiations, and he flew to Menlo Park, California, to meet Lynch. It was Bill's hope that he could convince Lynch to agree to a friendly merger, but Lynch had his back up. When Bill offered $30.50 a share, or $366 million, Lynch said he thought it was "too low" but he would present it to the board. They agreed to sell to someone, but not to Bill at that price.

Less than a week later, Bill raised the offer to $34 a share, for a total of $425 million. At that point, Saga solicited other bidders. Assessing the competition, the Marriott board raised its limit to $39.50 a share, or $716 million—the most expensive acquisition in Marriott history. But rather than risk being outbid, Bill kept the offer in his pocket until the hour that the Saga board was meeting to pick a winner. It was after the bidding deadline when Bill picked up the phone and interrupted the meeting with a call to Lynch.

"Hello, Charlie, this is Bill," he began as Lynch put him on the speakerphone at the board meeting. "I have a couple of questions about your process."

"Go ahead, Bill," Lynch cautiously responded.

"Does the highest bidder win?"

"Yes," Lynch agreed.

"If we submit the highest bid right now, are we the winner?"

Lynch asked him to hold a minute, and muted the phone.

There was silence for five or more minutes. When Lynch came back, they could hear emotion in his voice.

"Yes," he affirmed. "If you give us a number now, and it's the highest number, you win."

"It's $39.50, Charlie," Bill said.

After that, there was total silence for a few moments, no doubt as Lynch counted the heads around the table.

"Well, Bill, you now own Saga Corporation."

The Saga deal vaulted Marriott to the top as the largest food-service contractor in the world. When Saga's approximately 920 accounts were added to the Gladieux and Service Systems accounts, as well as Marriott's own contracts, FSM soared past ARA Services, the previous leader. It also made Marriott the largest public company in the D.C. area, surpassing Martin Marietta.

CHAPTER 20

THE FLAGSHIP AND FLEET EXPANSION

Bill Marriott learned from his father the philosophy of Management by Walking Around (MBWA). J.W. began the practice of regularly inspecting the restaurants of his Hot Shoppes chain, giving Bill boyhood memories of trailing behind on those property tours. He grew up believing firmly in MBWA and embraced it wholeheartedly, even when the company expanded to hundreds of facilities in the 1980s.

In a television and magazine advertising campaign that made his face famous, Bill proclaimed: "I have to make sure we do things right. After all, it's my name on the door." His advertising agency, Ogilvy & Mather, pressed the usually shy CEO to be the spokesperson. "They wanted to provide a face—let people know there's somebody named Marriott who's concerned with customers. There's no Mr. Hyatt, Mr. Sheraton, or Mr. Ramada," Bill said.

Nation's Business hailed him as "a modern-day Gulliver" who logged an average of 150,000 air miles a year to maintain face-to-face contact with the managers and employees of his far-flung business empire. In a typical year, Bill visited more than 100 of his hotels, 75 competitors' hotels, dozens of airline kitchens, and at least 100 of his food-service outlets. He was away from home at least 180 days every year.[1]

Many other CEOs thought Bill was crazy to try to keep up such a pace. "A lot of them like to go to industry meetings; they like to mingle with other CEOs," Bill said. "They think that they can learn a lot more by hanging around with other CEOs than they can by hanging around with their own people? Two-thirds of my best ideas come from visiting our operations. I gain a lot more than I give."

"You will not walk through a lobby and find a piece of paper or anything on the floor if Bill's around on a tour," recalled Marriott executive Dan Altobello. "We checked out a Hyatt hotel once, and Bill bent over and picked up a gum wrapper. 'You should leave it there—this is a competitor's hotel,' I said. He said, 'Habit, habit, habit.'" Indeed, the *Washington Post* concluded that if there were "a true Marriott corporate symbol, it would be an executive reaching for litter."[2] Since most of Bill's hotel inspections were anticipated by the staff, he learned to pack a small can of paint remover in his suitcase, just in case he brushed against a surface freshly painted for him.

As grueling as his schedule was, Bill lamented in a 1986 talk that he could not visit more properties that year and would only be able to "shake hands with maybe 15,000 employees throughout the company, only seven and a half percent of our work force."[3] But he also needed to be at headquarters for important meetings, spend quality time with his family, and fulfill his Church assignments.

During this period of unprecedented corporate expansion, Bill was president of the Washington D.C. Stake of The Church of Jesus Christ of Latter-day Saints. It was a volunteer position, but equivalent to being the archbishop of a Catholic diocese. Why would a busy CEO willingly take on such a responsibility? He explained it in a 1989 speech to a Church gathering: "If I have been successful in business, it is because of the help the Church has given me. If I have been successful as a husband and father, it's because of the Church. It has been the greatest influence in my life. I owe all I have to the Church."[4]

Bill had been called to be the eighth president of the Washington D.C. Stake on December 12, 1982. He was president for eight years, including the time he was recovering from his burns. As the Latter-day Saint population in the D.C. area grew, and even after several wards spun off to other stakes, Bill's flock grew to 3,143 members in eight congregations within Montgomery County, Maryland, and the District of Columbia.

Latter-day Saint stakes operate by a plethora of leadership meetings, and Bill was a master at conducting them. He was never late. He always brought an agenda, and when that was covered, the meeting was over. Twice a year, Bill flew to Salt Lake City to attend the Church's general conference, which included special training sessions for stake presidents. He also attended board meetings for the Church-run Polynesian Cultural Center in Salt Lake City and Hawaii. And he was assigned to the Church's Public Communications Advisory Council, which met regularly to discuss ways to improve the image of the Church. There were literally hundreds of meetings over the eight years, ranging from local lay leadership to the top of the Church hierarchy.

Occasionally, Bill had to convene a "disciplinary council." If a member committed a grievous sin—adultery, apostasy, a felony— the stake president invited him or her to a meeting to examine the person's worthiness for continued membership in the Church. Excommunication might result from the council. Bill never rushed those meetings, letting everyone talk who might be impacted by the outcome. The same was true for any of the one-on-one counseling sessions he held with individual members in need.

Bill's private files are full of letters from stake members who attested to his kindness to them and told how it had changed their lives. "Bill loved working with the members individually and helping them," observed Marriott lawyer and fellow Latter-day Saint Steve West. "Instead of making financial and business goals at the company, it was a whole different thing where he could see their personal growth and achievement—and gain great joy from it."

The Washington D.C. Stake had hundreds of people on the

membership rolls who had drifted away from the Church. He challenged bishops of the individual congregations in the stake to visit every inactive member within six months. If they needed help, he went along with them. He also focused his efforts on young people, making sure that they had mentors in each ward and bishops who would be more inclined to counsel rebellious teenagers than to discipline them. The stake presidency also came up with a shadow leadership program for teens, making them responsible for organizing their own programs and activities.

In everything he did as stake president, Bill professed his faith in Jesus Christ. "Jesus never performed a selfish act," he said. "Everything that he did was done for us. His love for us knows no bounds. He is the personification of love, the author of mercy, the prince of peace. . . . Civilizations rise, dominate the world, and crumble into dust. But Jesus Christ is eternal. He remains the same, and only in Him can we find refuge and strength. . . . He will be with us in the fiery furnace and the deep pit. He will accompany us to the hospital room, the funeral home, the gravesite. He will be our captain on a rough voyage and will be the eternal light which we may see, and the eternal warmth which we may feel."

While Bill sprinkled his talks with references to heroic figures from history, he never included himself in that company. He lived by the code he established for his family: "No big shots here." Instead, he endeared himself to stake members with self-deprecating remarks about his own imperfections, as in the following personal stories he shared:

—"The last time my wife and I had a serious argument was several years ago, when she had carefully baked three dozen cookies for a church [gathering] and I had sneaked into the kitchen and eaten some of them. She had committed to show up with thirty-six cookies. Now she didn't have that many and we had to leave in ten minutes. She became upset with me and I with her. How silly it was on my part to have eaten the cookies and started the argument in the first place."

—"Too often I find I am dictating to my children, telling them what to do instead of listening to them. My three married children frequently remind me that when they were small and all yelling at once, I would say: 'If you don't shut up, I'll give you something to cry about!' . . . How unlike the Savior I had behaved in each instance. I always tried to do better."

—"One night we were almost through dinner when our child David, who was three years old, opened the ketchup bottle to put some on his hamburger. I noticed that the entire bottle of Heinz Finest ketchup had just covered David's hamburger and most of his plate. I let out a big yell: 'David, watch what you're doing!' He looked up with a twinkle in his eye and said, 'I'm just a little boy. I'm sorry. Please don't yell at me.' Well, Donna and I began to laugh. We laughed with David until we were weary. The next night when David spilled his milk, I didn't say a word. We parents must step back from the furious pace for a while, and really look at our children. There is so much to enjoy. The Lord only made one of each. There are no copies, and even tomorrow each one will be different from today."

Among Bill's most memorable sermons were those focusing on adversity, especially after he had gone through his own "refiner's fire" in 1985. "In April my wife Donna's only brother took his life and left behind a lovely wife and three children. My father passed away in August. Ten days later I almost lost my life in a severe boat explosion. I was in the hospital for sixteen days and underwent extensive surgery for my burns. A week after I went into the hospital, my mother fell and broke her pelvis. I was in one hospital; Mother was in another. It was then that I remembered my father's prophetic words when I was little and didn't want to go to Sunday School: 'You'd better learn to love the Lord and serve Him because someday you're really going to need Him.' That time had obviously come. I have truly learned that adversity strikes everyone, but the blessings of our Father in Heaven can bring us through the most difficult circumstances."

One of Bill's great joys as a stake president was the beginning of a long friendship with a fellow stake president from Frankfurt, Germany, named Dieter Uchtdorf. The two first met on business, not Church business. Uchtdorf was Lufthansa Airline's "chief pilot" and senior vice president of flight operations. As such, Uchtdorf was in charge of the airline's food service, which was one reason Dieter wanted to meet Bill. The second was that Dieter wanted to meet one of his personal heroes. As a high-level German official, Uchtdorf was often in meetings with European airline chiefs who would quiz him about being a Latter-day Saint, a Christian religion they viewed with suspicion. Dropping the highly regarded Marriott name was one way of setting them straight.

"I would explain that we had a worldwide, respected church," Uchtdorf said. "Then I'd say, 'Do you know Bill Marriott of the hotel chain?' 'Yes, yes, I've heard of him. He's a good man, a fine business-man.' They were very positive because Bill has always represented the values and principles of the Church in a very humble, down-to-earth, perfect way. There was never a risk of embarrassment taking Bill as the example of Mormon values."

It was not until April 1988 that the two finally met—during the Church's semiannual general conference in Salt Lake City. They sched-uled a Saturday night dinner at the Salt Lake City Marriott to see if they could come to terms on a business deal.

Over dinner, "Bill was very friendly and we talked about every-thing," Uchtdorf recalled. "He is a quiet person, very quiet, and he has a good sense of humor—a cool one." Dieter discovered that Bill was an avid reader of books about or by Winston Churchill and about World War II, so Uchtdorf was pleased to answer questions about his growing-up years in wartime Germany, his escape from East Germany, and his religious conversion. Then they got down to business.

"As a Lufthansa guy, I wanted to have consistent, high-quality ca-tering on my planes, and I knew Marriott would be a great partner to do that. I also wanted a good deal for our crews to stay in Marriott hotels. We already had several contracts with them for Lufthansa flights out of the U.S., but I wanted more. He was tough, and I was tough.

He offered some good hotel deals, but some of his numbers for catering our flights in Europe were high, so we didn't agree on everything." Face-to-face, each earned respect from and for the other.

"I will never forget that night," Dieter reflected. After their dinner, they attended a session of the Church conference together. "That was so unique for me. In Germany, I was not used to having my business partners being [Latter-day Saints]. So I was deeply impressed to do business negotiations with a wonderful businessman who knew what he wanted, and then go with him to the [conference]. That was very special."

On other occasions, especially after Dieter Uchtdorf became an Apostle of the Church and later a member of the First Presidency, he was upset to hear occasional criticism of Bill from fellow Latter-day Saints because of a solitary but necessary aspect of the Marriott business. "They will say to me, 'If he's a Mormon, why does he serve alcohol?' I have to laugh at this. They usually don't know that at Lufthansa, I was responsible for buying all the wine and all the cigarettes we sold on board. That was part of my business, just as it is for Bill. Some criticized [golf star] Johnny Miller because he played golf on Sunday, or [star NFL quarterback] Steve Young because he played football on Sunday. We should not split hairs on these things. We should be more understanding—more merciful, really—with each other."[5]

Elder Boyd K. Packer, the Apostle who was at Lake Winnipesaukee the day of Bill's boat explosion, and the one who released Bill as stake president in 1990, later summed up Bill's commitment to the Church: "He would do anything the Lord asked him to do. When I needed something—like helping the Church with his political, diplomatic, and other foreign connections—I got him on the phone and then he did it. I've known a few prominent men in the same kind of position whose membership in the Church kind of fades in the background. Not Bill Marriott. He is front and steady for the Lord's Church."

During those years he served as stake president, Bill's corporate responsibilities never cut him a break: hotels were built, he launched a variety of product lines, he faced his own mortality, and he beat back financial ruin, all while juggling family and Church responsibilities.

Of course, Bill couldn't have managed the Church workload without the help of a large stake leadership organization that included two counselors, a twelve-member high council, seven clerks and secretaries, the presidencies of six auxiliary organizations, two patriarchs, and, of course, a half dozen bishops and their "staffs" of more than 100 volunteer member-leaders. No one was paid to perform his or her service.

Among those helpers was Phyllis Hester, who juggled Bill's Church appointments so they would mesh with his corporate schedule. Hester's "day job" was as a secretary to Geico CEO Jack Byrne, whom she described as "the total opposite of the very organized Mr. Marriott." Whenever Byrne ran into Bill at business events, he bragged about his Latter-day Saint secretary: "I couldn't find my watch without Phyllis Hester."

Sensing Hester was ready for a change after her husband died, Bill offered her a job at Marriott to become his assistant. While longtime secretary Mary Harne filled Bill's primary secretarial needs, Phyllis was given the responsibility for Bill's schedule. She quickly discovered his calendar was so full it was impossible to accommodate all the requests for his time. "Getting time on his schedule is always like getting blood out of a turnip!" she remarked.

When Harne retired after years of faithful service, Phyllis moved into the gatekeeper's position just outside Bill's office. For the next two decades and counting, she has been his Girl Friday, coordinating not only his corporate and Church work, but also some private Marriott family events.

"If Phyllis wasn't here at the office, I don't know if I would be," Bill said. "She is terrific. She has always been kind and helpful to everyone who calls my office, and she seems to always be in the office—long before eight a.m. and long after five p.m. She eats lunch at her desk in spite of my efforts to get her out and have a nice meal. I could

Phyllis Hester.

never—*never*—have done my jobs at work and in the Church without her tremendous help and support."[6]

Adds his daughter Debbie: "Phyllis has one of the hardest jobs in the world—taking care of my dad! For decades she has been getting him where he needs to go, and on time. In a world of iPhones and iPads, she is his own self-declared 'smartphone,' typing out the daily schedule that he keeps in his pocket. In this way—and many more—she is always close to his heart. In fact, she is so near and dear to all of my family that she has become a part of our family."[7]

• • •

Airline catering began taking Bill on a wild roller-coaster ride, and he wondered if he should be in that business anymore, even though Marriott was the undisputed leader. He reflected on the time when his father had invited Bill, then a college student, to join him at a sales meeting with George T. Baker, the autocratic president of National Airlines. Baker was an intimidating figure. He didn't believe in serving his passengers food, but he had hired Marriott a few years earlier to run his headquarters employee lunchroom in Miami. J.W. heard that Baker was about to drop Marriott and operate the cafeteria in-house.

It was an unforgettable meeting for Bill, notable for its hostility, brevity, and lessons learned. Though J.W. was not cowed, Bill was taken aback by Baker, a big man with a bulldog jaw and a buccaneer swagger. Baker confirmed that he was going to end the contract with Marriott and run the cafeteria at a lower cost by buying inferior food. "That would be a mistake," J.W. responded. "The quality of the food that your employees eat will do a lot for their morale. If they feel better about where they work, they will do a better job."

"Nonsense!" Baker countered. "Anybody can cook hamburgers and French fries—what do I care? Frankly, I've got so many union problems that I just don't give a damn if the employees like the food or not. They'll take what I serve them."

At that point, "my father said if he truly felt that way, Mr. Baker should do his own food service—and we left. My dad was glad to walk away from that contract," Bill recalled.

The lesson Bill learned was that if Marriott could not provide quality food service, even in the face of cost-cutting, there was no point in doing it. This was the ongoing conundrum in the airline catering business. Marriott In-Flite served dozens of airlines, and each one had its own menus, which changed from month to month. Some airlines insisted that Marriott buy from specific vendors, such as Delta's requirement that all its steaks must be purchased from a Texas wholesaler. During airfare wars, when "no-frills" service was popular, meals were downsized to snacks, which required the same labor and delivery costs but had to be done at a reduced price.

Excellence could not happen unless the airline valued good customer service, and that was usually out of Marriott's control. Airline presidents concentrated on rates and routes, with little understanding of airline food. Bill visited with one airline CEO who said he wasn't happy with Marriott's food service.

"Do you eat breakfast or dinner most frequently?" Bill asked.

"Well, I've never actually tried a meal," the CEO responded.

"How do you know it's bad?"

"The flight attendants tell me," he answered. Bill found out it was a single flight attendant who had made the comment to the CEO, and Bill tracked her down.

"What's the problem with our food?" he asked.

"Oh, no big problem. I mean, every now and then the cake is dry."

"Anything else?" Bill probed.

"Well, once the pilot said he didn't like a serving."

"How long ago?"

"Last year sometime," she said.

On another occasion, Bill advised one director of catering to use canned instead of bottled soft drinks for safety reasons. "Mind your own business!" the man retorted.

One exception to the rule was Frank Borman, the astronaut turned CEO of Eastern Airlines. Bill and Borman had much in common. Both were modest men. Bill had no corporate jet, lived in an understated house, and bought his suits off the rack twice a year. When a *People* magazine reporter spotted him in a Halston sports jacket and remarked on it, Bill was surprised. He didn't know. "My wife got it for me because she said it doesn't wrinkle."[8] Similarly, Borman never let the astronaut hype go to his head. He lived as simply as did Bill and complained about the waste of company limos and jets. Both men were workaholics who collected information and ideas from their people, then made decisions and stuck to them. Both also firmly believed in "Management by Walking Around." Borman asserted, "I don't want many people between me and the baggage handler."

Upgrading food service was high on Borman's list. At the time, Marriott had some but not all of Eastern's business. Borman invited Bill to fly to Miami for a Friday morning meeting. The night before, he called Bill and said, "I don't like the idea that we're tied up with all of these other caterers. You guys do the best job, so make me a proposal to take over as much of our airline catering as you can. Give me a list of all the stations that you want."

Stunned, Bill asked if he could call back in fifteen minutes. "Then I frantically got on the phone with all of my people to put this dream list together," he recalled. "Frank tentatively agreed to the whole list over the phone." The next morning, the two men signed the deal, and Marriott took over a dozen Eastern airports overnight. The biggest coup was Atlanta, which was then the second-busiest airport in the world. Based on the Eastern contract, Bill built a large kitchen there, and other airlines switched to Marriott in Atlanta.

For nearly four decades, the airlines had been part of a government-controlled industry. No major airline went out of business during that period of regulation. It was a comfortable situation that allowed vendors like Marriott In-Flite to make money with dependable airline contractors. That all changed in October 1978, when the Jimmy Carter administration deregulated the industry.

In the beginning, Marriott In-Flite profits were increased because of the profusion of new airlines and routes. But when things began to settle, catering took a downturn. Bargain upstarts offered no food service, and the big airlines fought back by cutting fares and food. Eastern cancelled contracts with Marriott at four airports. Eventually Borman was forced out, and Marriott's biggest contract shrank. Marriott's competitors began making bargain-basement bids for contracts that wiped out profit margins. Braniff Airlines went bankrupt owing Marriott $6 million. Bill signed a deal with Continental Airlines only to have the airline declare bankruptcy a month later.

Bill's best move was to make Fred Malek head of the In-Flite division. The former White House official had proven to be a gifted manager at Marriott, and he kept In-Flite afloat during those rocky years. When Bill promoted Malek to executive vice president in 1982, he tapped Dan Altobello to be the new chief of In-Flite. Nerves of steel and a willingness to take risks were critical, qualities both Bill and Altobello had in spades.

The highs often outweighed the lows. For example, there was the loan of Marriott's hydraulic lift trucks to the U.S. Air Force to lift wounded soldiers into military aircraft after the 1983 invasion of Grenada, and the opportunity to cater all the flights for Pope John Paul II and his entourage during his 1987 tour of the United States. There were also the acquisitions of several competitors' kitchens. And in 1989 In-Flite won the first joint-venture contract between the Soviet Union and a Western food-service company, catering Aeroflot flights out of Moscow. The deal was widely hailed as a significant milestone of Mikhail Gorbachev's nascent glasnost strategy.

Marriott was able to hold its position as the world's largest airline caterer. Thus, even though Bill's hotel empire was growing rapidly during the 1980s, the company's most ubiquitous "advertisements" were the hundreds of In-Flite trucks emblazoned with Marriott's logo loading food carts onto airplanes at airports across America. At its peak, Marriott In-Flite serviced more than 150 airlines from more than 100 flight kitchens at forty-two U.S. and thirty-eight foreign airports— which produced annual revenue of $800 million.

Given all that, how could Bill decide in late 1988 that he was going to sell this golden goose? The answer is as simple as a number: $4 billion. It was the total revenue possible if Marriott owned all the airline-catering business in the world. Marriott already had nearly a quarter of the global market. Even if Bill won half of the business, the cap of $4 billion was simply not enough to make it worth his while. It was too low for the kind of growth to which he had committed his company.

Bill had a sentimental attachment to the business he had poured so many years and so much heart into, but that was tempered when Altobello and a group of In-Flite senior managers offered to take it off his hands. When former Marriott executive Fred Malek learned that Altobello wanted to spin off In-Flite, he enthusiastically signed on to make it happen. The new company would be called CaterAir Inc. Among other investors, Altobello would own 36 percent and Malek 33 percent. The sale resulted in a $231-million profit for Marriott.

"Bill sold it—and we bought it—at its peak," recalled Altobello. "He maximized his value out of it. The first three years after the buyout, we made great profits and Bill looked like a fool for selling the business. But then, the second three years, when the catering business went downhill, Bill looked like a genius for selling the business. This goes to prove the point at which Bill is a master: Timing is everything."

• • •

While Marriott launched new hotel concepts in the economy and moderate price ranges, at the same time, the company continued to expand the fleet with convention and luxury hotels. The New York Marriott Marquis opened soon after J.W.'s passing, but before that, the flagship JW Marriott Hotel in Washington, D.C., opened in 1984, a year before J.W.'s death. That downtown Washington project had begun as an urban renewal idea and had taken almost six years to come to fruition. Bill had not been the city's first choice. Atlanta developer John Portman was the front-runner, but the city fathers balked at his design and asked Bill to enter the competition.

The proposed convention hotel would be the first major hotel development in what was still a "war zone" after the race riots of the late 1960s. It was Bill's hometown, but he was initially reluctant to wade in. The historic resonance of the location—14th Street and Pennsylvania Avenue—persuaded him to take a chance. "It was along that famous parade route that I watched every inaugural parade beginning with Roosevelt. I witnessed the funeral processions of Presidents Roosevelt and Kennedy," Bill recalled. "Our first A&W root beer stand was located on 14th Street, as was our first Hot Shoppe restaurant and our corporate offices until the early 1940s."

Bill won the competition with Portman in large part because he agreed to build his hotel around the iconic National Theatre, which Portman was proposing to tear down. Bill had astutely pledged more than $4 million for renovations of the theater. Construction began, and when it came time to put up the "Future site of . . ." sign on the lot, Bill had a surprise for his father. On one of the happiest days for father and son, Bill drove J.W. to 14th and Pennsylvania and pointed out the sign.

"Do you see your name up there?"

"What do you mean?" J.W. responded. Then he saw it. The sign said, "JW Marriott Hotel at National Place."

"Why didn't you tell me?" J.W. said quietly.

"Well, I figured we ought to name it for you since you founded the business up this street a few blocks. I'm planning to create a new luxury brand of JW Marriotts around the world in your honor, and it seemed right that this would be the first."

Besides its name, another tip-off that this hotel was going to be a special place for the Marriott family was that it did not technically have a "grand opening" with the bells and whistles Marriott was known for. Instead, attendees were invited to the "dedication" of the hotel on May 24, 1984.

It was an emotional event for the family. It included a twenty-minute video with personal tributes to J.W. from Bob Hope, Billy Graham, President Gerald Ford, and others. J.W. was nearly speechless. "I couldn't use my written speech. It had all been said, so I clowned around for ten minutes without notes," he recorded in his journal. His off-the-cuff speech was a hit, however: "We are not just building buildings at Marriott. We are building people. We are trying to impress upon our people the value of fairness and how much opportunity a young man or young woman has for growth with us if they have good habits and live right." Bill then presented J.W. with a 242-foot-long card containing the signatures and well wishes of thousands of Marriott employees in the D.C. area.

J.W. died a year later. Two years after that, at the D.C. hotel, Bill presented the first J. Willard Marriott Awards of Excellence to fourteen employees from throughout the company who distinguished themselves through exemplary performance. On the back of the medals were the words: "Character, Dedication, Ideals, Effort, Perseverance, Achievement." The first recipient was Allie.

Many important events were held at the new hotel. The most publicized was an assist to the December 1987 Reagan-Gorbachev summit, which marked the signing of the treaty eliminating U.S. and Soviet medium-range and shorter-range nuclear missiles. Seven thousand journalists and their crews from more than 100 countries converged on the capital for the three-day summit. In a last-minute search for a place to brief the press, the State Department asked Bill to turn the hotel's grand ballroom into an operations center for the media.

Bill chose not to hang around, instead flying to Atlanta for the opening of the company's first Fairfield Inn. Then he was off to Phoenix to bid for airport terminal facilities. "We all have to make choices in how we use our time," he informed the Phoenix officials. "This week, the White House has taken over our JW Marriott Hotel in Washington as press headquarters for the summit. My wife and I were invited to the State Department today for a luncheon with [the Gorbachevs], but I preferred to be in Phoenix for this presentation. I didn't tell my wife about the luncheon invitation," he laughed.[9]

Bill was simply not interested in the spotlight. A single paragraph—headlined "An Ordinary Guy"—appeared in *Business Travel News* before the summit. It illustrated this aspect of his character: "It was a busy Tuesday at the JW Marriott Hotel here on Pennsylvania Avenue. The flagship of the Marriott chain was packed to the gills with delegates attending [conferences] and various other business meetings. At the hotel's popular National Cafe, the line of would-be diners waiting for a luncheon table stretched back into the lobby. Near the end of the line, one gentleman waited patiently. When his turn finally came and the hostess asked his name, there was a shocked look of surprise and recognition: Marriott, table for one. It was Chairman Bill Marriott, sampling the wares and waiting in line like an ordinary guest for a table."[10]

Bill didn't like the label *pioneer*. When others referred to him as one, he would often respond wryly: "My definition of a pioneer is a guy with an arrow in his back and his face in the mud. We're not pioneers." His goal was "not to waste a lot of time and money trying to do it a different way than anybody else," explained Marriott hotel executive Bus Ryan. "Our corporate charter did not include innovation. We were going to take a new concept that was out there and do it better than anybody else."

The truth was somewhere in the middle. Marriott was at the forefront of the first large motor hotels; Marriott was the leader in suburban and airport hotels; Marriott was the first to have nonsmoking floors and concierge floors; Marriott came up with preregistration and express checkout services; and Marriott put frequent-guest programs on the map, along with partnerships with airlines and car-rental companies.

It was also Bill's vision beginning in the 1950s to garner business through meetings, conferences, and conventions at his suburban hotels. By the end of 1985, he had big hotels in the top five convention cities and a dozen others. Bill didn't always have to build a mega-hotel to attract large conventions. In Miami and San Antonio he linked his hotels with each other and with competitors' hotels to create convention-worthy complexes.

One location Bill did not court at first was Orlando, Florida. "I may be dead wrong," he told the *Miami News*, "but I have a feeling the Disney area will be saturated to a point where few of the operators will make any money."[11] A decade later, however, Bill foresaw that Orlando was going to be a major convention city, and he changed his mind. He would be the first to put Orlando on the large-convention map with construction of a spectacular 1,500-room hotel just five minutes from

The Desert Springs resort in Palm Springs.

Disney's EPCOT Center. It appeared on the horizon, a pink mono-lith surrounded by an eighteen-hole championship golf course. When Marriott's Orlando World Center resort opened in May 1986, it was the largest hotel in Florida. Once again, in spite of his verbal disparagement of pioneering, Bill had been the first non-Disney hotel operator on the scene to go big.

In 1983, Bill got a foothold in London, where he bought the classy little Europa Hotel on Grosvenor Square, and in Paris, where he bought the Prince Charles de Gaulle Hotel. Back in the States, he secured two choice locations in the Los Angeles area—San Fernando Valley and Century City. The latter was one of Bill's more exclusive and expensive projects, and he named it JW Marriott at Century City. The grand opening in June 1988 was a star-studded charity event on behalf of the Children's Miracle Network.

One property that took Bill's breath away was the company's second resort in the Palm Springs area. Sunrise Corp., the developer of Marriott's Rancho Las Palmas resort, came to Bill in 1982 and said it was time to work on a second project, since Marriott had proven that the desert could support year-round resorts. Bill agreed and put his team to work. They developed a plan for the largest resort in California, a $134-million complex stretching over 240 acres in Palm Desert. In addition to 892 rooms, there would be water everywhere—twenty-three acres of lakes and waterways, including a sandy swimming beach and a river that ran into the lobby so boats could carry guests to their rooms and restaurants.

The grand opening in February 1987 raised $1.2 million for the Bob Hope Cultural Center. Guests included Gerald and Betty Ford, Gene Autry, Willie Shoemaker, Don Drysdale, Ginger Rogers, and many other notables. Wayne Newton brought his Las Vegas act. "I realize this show is cheaper than a room here," he quipped.

Debbie's fondest memories happened away from that glamour, seeing her father's joy as Desert Springs was being developed. "He was so proud of it all. I remember him saying once, in a quiet moment as we surveyed the work in progress, 'You know, this is what makes my job worth it. I just love this!' And that was only one little teeny piece of the big empire he was building."

CHAPTER 21

SEISMIC TREMORS

Bill began 1988 with a wreath-laying, a prayer, and a sermon of hope in Atlanta. Since Dr. Martin Luther King Jr.'s assassination, Bill and the Marriott corporation had contributed significantly to the Southern Christian Leadership Conference and Coretta Scott King's efforts to build the King Center for Nonviolent Social Change. "We had a huge African-American presence in our company," Bill explained. "I felt one way we could support those good people was to support the King family's work."

For many years, the nation's media have praised Marriott's exceptional diversity initiatives, not only hiring and promoting women and minorities but also making sure a certain percentage of its subcontracting has gone to minority-owned business. A "Committee for Excellence" was created to regularly update the Marriott board as to the progress achieved regarding Marriott's ambitious diversity goals. Also, although Bill always deferred using personal names for anything other than his father and others, he finally agreed in 2004 to an exception. Having created a singular companywide diversity award as part of its annual awards program, Bill was honored to have it called the "J. Willard Marriott, Jr., Diversity Excellence Award."

That same commitment was evident over the years in his personal friendship and support of King family initiatives, particularly the foundation for a national King memorial in D.C., which involved more than two decades of planning, fund-raising, and construction. Bill was a major contributor and as such was an honored guest at the foundation's programs, including the 2011 dedication. But few moments could emotionally top the occasion when Coretta King called Bill in January 1988 and invited him to deliver a short sermon in Atlanta at the twentieth annual ecumenical service since her husband's assassination.

Bill joined the family for the wreath-laying at the gravesite a few yards from the Ebenezer Baptist Church where King, his father, and his grandfather had all been pastors. Then hundreds of friends and family members packed into the church for the program. "'Only when it is dark enough can you see the stars,'" Bill began, quoting King from the sermon he gave in Memphis the day before his assassination. "Certainly, over the years, the Reverend King was well acquainted with the darkness of night. Yet no matter how dark it was, he taught people to bury their weapons in order to win their battles and to beat their swords into plowshares. He taught that the power of love could conquer oppression. That was the beauty of the man—his life was laced with confrontation, but his response was powered by love, not hatred. . . . It was a vision founded on faith and the belief that we should always remember what God has done."

The church program was followed by lunch, after which Bill joined the group on that rainy afternoon to walk in a parade along downtown Atlanta's Peachtree Street. Among the marchers were several presidential candidates, reminding Bill that the presidential campaign was already in full swing, which meant he was about to lose his reliable number two, Fred Malek, who was taking a leave of absence to chair the Republican National Convention.

This exacerbated a short but painful episode at Marriott that insiders called the "Twin Towers Situation" long before terrorists destroyed the real thing in New York City. The moniker referred to two top executives—Butch Cash and John Dasburg—whose ambitions and intense competition were unhealthy for the company and its CEO.

Francis W. "Butch" Cash joined Marriott as controller and chief accounting officer in 1973. Cash was not fond of his chosen profession. Instead, he saw himself as a leader with gifts beyond crunching numbers, and Bill agreed. In time, Cash was moved out of the finance department and appointed head of various departments in other areas.

After a decade with the company, Cash was promoted to executive vice president in charge of the Big Boy and Roy Rogers chains, the Host airport businesses, contracted food services, and the initial phase of the Courtyard development. In Bill's view, Cash had earned those opportunities, but things began to go awry because of his expanding ambitions.

When Bill told In-Flite chief Dan Altobello that his division might be put under Cash, Altobello balked. "Because I had extraordinary respect for Bill, I told him I would tolerate Butch. But I also gave Bill a piece of my mind. 'Every time Cash asks you for more power, you give it to him. And, trust me, what he wants is your job, and so you cannot satisfy him.'"

Cash became concerned in early 1987 when Bill indicated that it was probably time to get out of the Big Boy business, whose faulty franchise rules had thwarted every effort to expand it. Butch countered with a bold proposal: instead of dumping Big Boy, why not buy Denny's and roll the Big Boys and maybe Roy Rogers into that chain? With 1,200 restaurants, Denny's was the largest chain in the country; Marriott's Big Boy system was second with 900. If a top executive came up with a reasonable idea, Bill's management philosophy was to allow the person to proceed. So he gave Cash the green light.

Cash began negotiations with Denny's by offering $880 million, the highest amount Bill had authorized. When the Marriott-Denny's negotiations were announced, Marriott stock fell. Echoing Bill's own private thoughts, securities analysts saw the drop as a backlash against more acquisitions after Marriott had already bought Saga, Host, and Howard Johnson's. Moody's Investor Service hinted that it might downgrade Marriott's debt rating—restricting the company's ability to borrow money at favorable rates.

Marriott financial experts took a closer look at Denny's books and realized that the company was not worth $880 million. The board told Cash to drop the offer to $854 million. Denny's responded by calling off the deal; it later sold to another buyer for $843 million. "What went right, what went wrong and why?" asked *Nation's Restaurant News,* after editor Charles Bernstein conducted an investigation into the strange outcome. Bernstein concluded that Cash was "highly respected" and had Bill's total confidence, but that the merger had failed because Bill himself didn't do the deal. A high-level Denny's source was quoted in the article: "Chief executives only deal with other chief executives in this business."[1]

The prospect of a Denny's merger had filled Bill with a growing unease over the acquisition and over Cash's ability to handle a new restaurant chain. "I never wanted Denny's," Bill recalled. "Butch wanted Denny's, which would make him the King of Restaurants at Marriott. It seemed to me to be a power move."

The other half of the Twin Towers, John Dasburg, was hired in 1980 to be Marriott's tax expert. He was a brilliant rising star, eccentric and a loner. When Gary Wilson left to become Disney's CFO, Dasburg was promoted to replace him as CFO. In that post, he played a major role in the acquisitions of Howard Johnson's, Saga, and Residence Inn. Cash and Dasburg were collegial associates, if not friends, who had worked well together on the Saga acquisition and other projects, but that didn't last.

Fred Malek's impending departure would leave a big hole in the company's leadership. Bill took it as an opportunity to reorganize the company into two operating units—a service group and a lodging group headed, respectively, by Butch Cash and John Dasburg. Cash continued his responsibility for all the food-service groups and added airline catering to his duties. Dasburg was put in charge of all lodging except Courtyard, which Cash retained. In essence, Bill would now have two number twos.

Each man had been given stewardship over half the company. The *Washington Post* opined that it might be a sign Cash or Dasburg, both younger than Bill, would succeed him as president one day.[2] It was as if the two thoroughbreds were waiting at the starting line for a race that must be won at any cost, even if it meant trampling Marriott's convivial corporate culture and Bill's peace of mind.

Cash was the first of the two to miscalculate. Two months after the failed Denny's negotiations, Bill sat down with Cash and concluded that the Big Boy operation was not going to work out. The board soon transferred the franchise rights for the whole Big Boy Family Restaurant system to one of its bigger franchisees. Then Marriott became a franchisee itself with the 208 company-operated Big Boys. Cash had an idea to use those units to develop a new national chain of Marriott family restaurants. Appreciating Cash's enthusiasm and commitment, Bill agreed.

Cash put the new concept on a fast track, shortening the study phase to a few months. Playing on Bill's love for his mother, Cash named the new restaurant "Allie's." San Diego became the test market, with fifteen Big Boys converted to Allie's restaurants at a cost of $320,000 apiece. The first two opened in June 1988, and customer counts and sales were substantially higher than they had been at the Big Boys. Two months later, Cash pushed for the $85-million acquisition of two more restaurant chains—Bickford's and Wag's—to convert them to Allie's. Marriott executive Jim Sullivan said the hoopla and energy Cash put into his new venture was out of proportion to Marriott's overall profile. And there was a problem hidden in the hype. "Butch's plan was to get as many customers as possible through the doors to get used to the new restaurant," explained Sullivan. "So he practically gave the food away. He got huge volumes of sales, the highest in the industry on the West Coast, but we made no money on it. At the time he began increasing the price to make profits, diners were bound to go elsewhere."

On the lodging side, John Dasburg was on the same fast track, overextending the company to the point that it ultimately threatened Marriott's continued existence. CFO Bill Shaw tried to raise red flags on a few of Dasburg's hotel development plans, but Dasburg rolled over him. "John really believed strongly that we should go ahead with this aggressive building," Shaw said. "I'm sure the idea of outshining Butch had something to do with it."

At the end of 1986, Bill knew that the hotel industry would soon reach a supply-and-demand imbalance. In 1981, Marriott had shown the way to finance a hotel through tax-sheltered limited partnerships, and the rest of the top lodging firms had jumped on the train, making an oversupply of rooms in many American cities inevitable. The 1986 Tax Reform Act, which ended investment real estate tax benefits, should have prevented the coming lodging crisis, but it didn't.

At the time, few in the press, the industry, or on Wall Street questioned Marriott's unusually aggressive hotel building, even in that constricting environment. Since Marriott was considered the gold standard, the company was able to continue selling restructured limited partnerships (LPs) until 1990. Without the tax benefit, Marriott had to guarantee investors a cash return. New hotels take several years to turn a good profit, so Marriott offered to forego some of its management fees and even to loan investors (as a second mortgage) enough to service mortgage debt if the hotel profits lagged. With the new LP structuring, Marriott sold a phenomenal $1.4 billion of its hotel properties in the first eighteen months after the tax law changed.

Around the same time, new light emerged from the Land of the Rising Sun. Japan was in the middle of a financial boom that had its bankers looking for American real estate and companies to buy. Between 1985 and 1990, Japanese companies raised $638 billion in new capital through the stock market alone. The boom precipitated Japan's biggest spending spree since 1945, and Marriott was a beneficiary.

Nikko Hotels, a subsidiary of Japan Airlines, was the first big buyer from the Far East. It made an unsolicited $175-million offer for Marriott's prestigious Essex House on Central Park, which Bill accepted, mainly because at the time the New York Marriott Marquis just blocks from the Essex was nearly finished. As Marriott had acquired the Essex years before for $28.6 million, this represented a stunning $146-million profit. Not long after the Essex sale, three major Japanese banks invested more than $300 million for a refinance of the new Marriott Marquis.

Dasburg suggested that it would be a good idea to list Marriott on the Tokyo Stock Exchange as a way to cement growing relationships, which the board approved in 1987. Several deals followed with Japanese investors, including the purchase of the JW Marriott at Century City for $83.5 million and the ownership syndication of twenty-three Residence Inn hotels for $131.5 million.

Those financing deals buttressed Dasburg's belief that if Marriott built it, investors would come. As with the Allie's restaurants, though, there was a fly in the ointment. The development and sales of hotels were based on Dasburg's inflated projections of future returns. But Dasburg's manipulations became a costly blind spot for Bill, which he admitted in his 1997 book, *The Spirit to Serve*. Dasburg's "reassuring eloquence overcame my gut feeling that the company ought to have exercised more caution. His arguments for continuing to build hotels in spite of [an oversupply and] signs of recession were so smooth, so reasonable, so apparently logical that I let myself believe everything would be fine. What I learned, of course, was that just because someone is a polished speaker or presenter doesn't mean that his or her ideas are always right."[3]

Ex-Marriott treasurer Steve Bollenbach suspected Dasburg was leading Bill down the garden path when he heard Dasburg speak at a lodging industry conference. Bollenbach had left the company when Dasburg was made CFO instead of him. Almost immediately, Bollenbach had been offered the CFO post at Holiday Inn. Bollenbach recalled that at the conference all the buzz was about overbuilding, "and somebody asked John, 'Is Marriott going to overbuild?' He said, 'Marriott is so powerful we can build through any cycle.' I was sitting there thinking, 'Is this the most arrogant statement I've ever heard? Probably.' Now, did John believe what he was saying? I have no idea."

The Twin Towers rivalry between Cash and Dasburg was the backdrop for key corporate missteps during this time. Bill would go home after work and share his frustrations with Donna. "Bill doesn't like friction," she said. "He wants to keep communication open, but that wasn't happening. Butch and John were doing things to try to undermine each other." Increasingly Bill could see that neither man was suited to be president of Marriott.

As the rivalry escalated at the end of 1988, tragedy struck. Dasburg's six-year-old daughter was killed in a school-bus accident. In the wake of that tragedy, Dasburg sought solace by immersing himself even more in his job, including redoubling his rivalry with Cash, which did not bode well for the company in the critical year of 1989.

The Marriott family began the year with a celebration of the election of President George H.W. Bush. Having been both financial and ideological backers of Bush, they watched the inaugural parade from the JW Marriott on Pennsylvania Avenue and attended one of the inaugural balls. A month later, Bill traveled to Hong Kong to open Marriott's first hotel in the Far East.

This "first" was not without its hiccups. The *New York Times* reported that Marriott's decision to put employees on a five-day work

Marriott's first hotel in Asia.

week had angered the competition in a city where most people were expected to work six days.[4] The company was ostracized from the Hong Kong Hotels Association, and the general manager was banned from talking to employees of local restaurants (for fear of "poaching") and was shunned at business gatherings, where most lodging executives refused to even shake hands with him.

Bill was furious, but he stuck to his standard employee practice. "I am quite surprised by the reaction," he observed to a *South China Morning Post* reporter. "Hong Kong is a bastion of free enterprise and to me free enterprise means free to compete, free to make your own decisions, free to make mistakes. We are coming into an extremely tight labor market situation here, and not going to change our way of doing business."[5] Employees from other hotels flooded Marriott with applications. Bill found that the hardworking Chinese weren't attracted by having an extra day off; they saw it as an opportunity to find better part-time work with the paired two days.

When Bill returned from Hong Kong, Cash reported on his profitable food-service operations in airports and on toll roads. One of his newest departments was showing promise as well. Marriott partnered with Nashville-based Corporate Child Care, Inc., to develop and manage day-care facilities at work sites. Six centers had been established, and there were 100 prospects on the horizon among FSM's corporate and health-care clients. Another new operation, facilities management, was also going gangbusters. Marriott had fallen into this line of work when the Saga acquisition included a 20 percent share in a small firm specializing in housekeeping, industrial plant operations, and maintenance for hospitals and schools. Sensing a new market, Bill also bought a major provider of housekeeping, maintenance, and laundry services with more than 600 contracts.

On the good news-bad news front, Marriott's senior-living facility offerings were popular, but the tremendous demand on the company's capital was a drag on profits. In the early 1980s, Bill recalled, "I told our people, 'We've got to get into the health-care business. This is going to be a big, big business, and we've got skills to apply.'" His parents were in their eighties, and he became interested in the plight of the aging population and how they could experience good care while retaining their independence and dignity.

Traditional nursing homes had a terrible reputation. Bill thought Marriott could build first-class facilities and make a profit. The first two projects for the new Marriott division, Senior Living Services (SLS), were "endowment" concepts, meaning that residents paid a large dollar amount up front to be taken care of until death. Retired army officers joined with Marriott to build "The Fairfax" in Fort Belvoir, Virginia. Haverford College near Philadelphia partnered with the company to develop "The Quadrangle" for its retired alumni and faculty. Both opened in mid-1989. Marriott also acquired the Villa Valencia retirement complex in Laguna Hills, California, and Basic American Retirement Communities, which had management contracts for eight communities. SLS was moving ahead with three more communities: "The Colonnades" in Charlottesville, Virginia; "The Jefferson" in Arlington, Virginia; and "Bedford Court" in Silver Spring, Maryland. The last was named after the English county that Bill's ancestor Elizabeth Stewart Marriott came from. Additionally, a new line of "Brighton Gardens," which had both independent and assisted-living housing, was planned for older Americans of modest means.

As positive as all this sounded when Cash was reporting to Bill in early 1989, SLS was still unprofitable and was going to eat up $110 million in capital that year alone.

Cash's new Allie's restaurant chain was also struggling, which put two of Marriott's biggest enterprises, Big Boy and Roy Rogers, in doubt. The previous November, Bill had initiated "Project Sparrow," an internal confidential review of all Marriott operations. Early word was that the analysis would recommend disposing of the restaurant chains and airline catering. They were profitable, but their growth was too slow to fit the Marriott paradigm. In the midst of such uncertainty, Cash ramped up his rivalry with Dasburg to prove to Bill that it was Cash who deserved to be the next president of Marriott.

Neither of the Twin Towers seemed to realize that their internal warfare was stressing Bill to a breaking point. Dasburg recalled that his disagreements with Cash had their core in the men's competing views of where Marriott should go. "He ran half the company and I ran half the company," Dasburg said, "and the two of us had a vastly different view of what the future of Marriott ought to look like. I wanted to split Marriott into two companies." Cash disagreed. Bill recalled that he talked with Dasburg about separating the company but never seriously considered it.

As an active Latter-day Saint, Cash might have thought that gave him an edge over Dasburg. Although Bill appreciated Cash's faithful

Church service, it was Cash's ability to sell himself to the CEO that mattered. "He was always working on convincing me that he was doing a good job. He sold me, and I missed it. I had blinders because I liked him personally, and I thought he was pretty sharp. But after he was promoted to run half the company, he got carried away with himself and started making some bad decisions. He became very difficult. Even when he was talking with me, he would say, 'My company'—'In my company, we do it this way.' That was not the attitude of a team player. He was always pushing me for more money and responsibility. He wanted to be CEO."

The competition was a strain on morale at corporate headquarters. "Both of these men were bright, capable, hands-on managers, but instead of taking care of each other and those who worked for and with them—a key tenet of our teamwork-based culture—they let personal priorities get the upper hand," Bill reflected. "In the process, they destroyed a great deal of goodwill, wasted energy, and upset a lot of people, including me."

In-Flite Services chief Dan Altobello was above the fray because he was on his way out to become CEO of the split-off CaterAir. He said, "Dasburg and Cash got into this company warfare and other idiots in the company took sides. I did not, but I did go to see Bill at his home and suggest: 'Why don't you just fire both of them? You are working too damn hard! It will be easier for you if you just throw them out.'" Altobello thought the rivalry was a contributor to Bill's first heart attack on October 2, 1989.

Bill was on his way to New York for his first full meeting of his newest obligation—the General Motors Corp. board of directors. Rather than flying, he decided to take the train and catch up on his reading during the three-hour trip. The night before had been an uneasy one. He awoke at three a.m. with chest pains, took some aspirin, and knew he wouldn't get back to sleep. The pain subsided, "So I went down and rode my stationary bicycle for ten minutes and nothing happened. The pain didn't come back and I was fine," he recalled. He arrived at the office at six a.m. and worked until after nine a.m. Then he left for Union Station to catch the ten a.m. Amtrak Metroliner to Manhattan. Delayed by traffic, when he reached the station he asked his driver, Bracey Bullock, to stick around for ten minutes in case he missed the train.

Bill's chest was burning as he settled into his seat. Then he heard a voice tell him, "Get off the train." It was the same voice that had told him four years earlier, when he was literally on fire, to "Get off the boat." For the second time, Bill obeyed.

Bracey, who was still outside with the car, raced his boss to Georgetown University Hospital, where tests showed Bill had experienced a heart attack. A cardiologist performed a balloon angioplasty. Bill was fifty-seven, a decade younger than J.W. had been when he'd had his first heart attack. Family and friends had little doubt that the Twin Towers feud was in part to blame, but Bill was reluctant to agree. "I had been the walking stereotype of the workaholic executive—too little exercise and rest, too much work, and too many heavy dinners too late at night," he said. "Obviously, the infighting at the office was stressful—very stressful. I agree that the Twin Towers, so to speak, had something to do with it."

After a week in the hospital, Bill was on a therapeutic treadmill when he suffered his second heart attack. Doctors performed a second angioplasty, and Bill was released after two weeks in the hospital. He had been home less than a day when his world was rocked once again with unsettling news from the opening day of his much-awaited San Francisco Marriott hotel.

The morning and afternoon festivities and ribbon cutting went off without a hitch. Then, at 5:04 p.m., the hotel began to move. It was October 17, 1989, the day of San Francisco's worst earthquake since 1906. During the temblor's fifteen seconds, terror filled the city. Homes and buildings in the Marina District collapsed, as did sections of the two-level Interstate 880 in west Oakland, and the San Francisco–Oakland Bay Bridge.

At the new Marriott hotel, the glass crystals in the chandeliers of the ballroom fell like a hailstorm. The glassware above the bar of the thirty-ninth-floor View Lounge crashed to the floor. (The lone glass that survived was later displayed in the lobby under a plaque stating: "Shaken and Stirred.") Guests rushed down the stairwell to the lobby, expecting to find it in ruins. But because the hotel had been built to meet modern earthquake standards, it fared better than many buildings in the city. The staff shepherded the guests into the Golden Gate Ballroom, where they would spend the night on makeshift bedding. Many San Franciscans who could not make it home found refuge in the hotel.[6]

Bill was relieved that the hotel had escaped significant damage, but he knew that a tremendous amount of money would be lost from cancellations of conventioneers who had booked the hotel in its first weeks. He also remained concerned that Dasburg had been unable to sell the $300-million hotel before it opened. That was too much debt for the company to carry for a single project. In less than a year, when the company was in the midst of an unthinkable crisis, the *Washington Post* would refer to that day in San Francisco as "a bad omen" for Marriott.[7]

Out of the hospital, Bill began an exercise regimen that included walks and supervised workouts on a treadmill and a bicycle. He knew he had to travel less on business. Dick came out of his semi-retirement to fill in. "The most important thing is that somebody with the Marriott name is out there," Dick said at the time. "You won't find a better friend or a more loyal brother than Dick," Bill said.

In a tribute to Dick a couple of years later, which was both rollicking and touching, Bill tied a number of Dick's attributes to his middle initial, "E"—such as Eating. "'Let's eat' has been a clarion call of Dick's for as long as I can remember," Bill said. "A few years ago he invited me to shop a few competitive fast-food units in Phoenix. After the twelfth restaurant and twenty-fifth meal, I was searching in vain for the Rolaids and Dick was pressing on for the next twelve joints. Last week he stopped by to visit my mother and, after his second Reuben sandwich, he ate a whole rice pudding. Mother complained that she was only able to get two mouthfuls before the entire bowl had disappeared."

His younger brother was also notably Efficient. "Dick is one of the most efficient time managers I have ever seen. He knows how to get things done and do them fast. His fine performance these past years is a result of his ability to make decisions and take fast action. He is super fast in everything he does. He has a natural ability to build and fix broken things and does not waste time doing it."

Dick was singularly Economic in his personal expenditures, as their parents had been. "Dick has the bucks because he doesn't spend them," Bill remarked. "If there is a less expensive way to do it, Dick can find it. He's an outstanding businessman and really knows how to save his money. A few years ago, I complimented him on his new suit—it was beautiful. He informed me that it just came in from Uniforms for You, the company's uniform supplier, and was really not very expensive since it was made from the same material as our waiters' jackets in the Sirloin & Saddle restaurant."

He was also the epitome of Endophasia, Bill added, which "is a medical term meaning internal speech with no audio vocalization. My dad often called Dick the 'silent one.' After I returned from a two-week business trip with him where Dick and I went all the way around the world together, Donna asked what we had discussed. I said we talked about the business a little—and, oh yes, Dick looked at Hong Kong harbor from the hotel room and said, 'Look at all those boats.' I was at a loss to find out what else he had said during the two weeks since Dick doesn't like to talk a lot!"

Finally, Bill said, Dick was an example of Empathy, Effort, and Elocution. "During my health problems, Dick has been empathetic with frequent hospital visits, home visits, and phone calls. Always concerned, always caring—as I've canceled trips and he has put forth the effort to make them for me. As I've canceled speeches he has energized his great elocution skills and made over a dozen speeches that I've had to cancel."

In short, Bill concluded, "my brother's personal pursuit of excellence in everything he does is amazing. Because of this, he has enhanced and enriched our lives by his loyalty, his love for this business, and his love and concern for all of us (in the family)."[8]

While Dick was out on the lecture circuit covering for his ailing brother in the fall of 1989, the difficult Twin Towers episode ended when one of the two men, John Dasburg, resigned.

In the months before Bill's heart attacks, Dasburg had been pushing hard for permission to build more Courtyards, Fairfields, and Residence Inns. Bill was uncomfortable with the debt that would entail. When Bill found out that Dasburg had forged ahead with several hotel projects that Bill hadn't fully approved, he was ready to grant Cash's request to be made chief operating officer, a new position at the company. A few days after that, Dasburg stormed into his office and said, "I'll never work for Butch!"

Then Dasburg went to Cliff Ehrlich, senior vice president for human relations, and announced, "I can't work for the same company as Butch Cash so I'm quitting." Ehrlich immediately called Bill at home and asked, "What do you want me to do?" Bill's answer was firm: "Accept it."

The next morning, Dasburg called Bill and said he had had a change of heart, and could he come back? "No, you quit," Bill said. And that was it, the end of the Twin Towers, after nineteen months of turmoil at the top of the company.

The hardest work Bill Marriott put into his recovery from the heart attacks was to not work. What unsettled him the most during that time was a persistent sense that a storm was coming for the company. "It was not easy to face the fact that three decades of sixteen-hour days on the job had put me in the very position I most wanted to avoid: not being at the helm if we hit rough seas."

Bill finally returned to work in mid-November, six weeks after the first heart attack. During that recovery period, Marriott's board of directors expressed deep concern that Bill had not yet chosen a successor. One board member asked Bill at a meeting, "All right, Mr. Marriott, on the way back from the cemetery after burying you, what do you want us to do?" Bill's three sons were too young and inexperienced to replace him; Dick was not interested. So the board settled on Chief Financial Officer Bill Shaw as the best possible successor.

In the meantime, Bill Marriott needed to build up his strength by staying at home as much as possible. Thus, he missed the grand opening of the five-hundredth Marriott hotel, this one in Warsaw, Poland.

The company had identified Poland and Hungary as the two most likely places for Marriott to crack as the Soviet Union was crumbling. Five thousand Poles flooded Marriott's Warsaw recruitment office to apply for jobs, lured by the higher pay and the opportunity to learn Western business and service practices. General Manager Haile Aguilar decided to "grow his own staff" from applicants untainted by prior hotel experience. He turned down all but three applicants with hotel résumés, believing "that the lack of a profit motive and more than 40 years of state control had deadened the notion of service in most Warsaw hotels."[9]

Instead, he said, "We looked for young people with big smiles who spoke English and were willing to work. The ones who held the most intelligent conversations in interviews were made managers." Twenty of those hires were sent to Boston for Western hospitality training, and they assisted in hiring the rest of the staff. So, a former teacher was soon carrying bags, a plumber became a kitchen steward, a computer technician patrolled the halls as a security officer, a dental technician carried trays in the coffee shop, and so on. Transforming Eastern Bloc workers into Western service personnel was daunting. In the first week, five employees were fired for drinking on the job and two for theft. Many had to be coached about their personal hygiene.

Still, Marriott's high standards were evident from the first day the hotel opened in Warsaw to great fanfare. *Hotels* magazine called it "The Miracle on Chalubinskiego Street."[10] Dick flew to Warsaw to represent the Marriott family at the opening. When Bill Tiefel initially saw the 1,000-person list of other invitees, he protested to GM Aguilar. "I said, 'It's too many people. It's going to be a mob scene!' His reply was, 'I invited everybody who was in (Communist) power when we started to make our deal here. I invited everybody in power (in the Solidarity government) today. And I also invited everybody that I think is going to be in power next week. So I have three times as many politicians as I need.' You know what? He was right."

Exactly two weeks later, the Berlin Wall fell. It was an unforgettable symbol of the end of the Cold War and an opening of the Eastern Bloc to the West. "We just opened a hotel in Warsaw," CFO Shaw noted at a press conference. "Some say that was the most planned stroke of genius in history, but we've been working on that for five years. Neither Mr. Marriott nor the rest of us had any idea that Poland was going to turn its back on Communism so totally as it has, but that hotel has positioned us well with other East European countries, whose representatives attended that opening and were tremendously impressed. They want Marriotts in their cities because they do not have good hotel accommodations, and because they *must have* foreign capital now."[11]

The future was bright for Marriott in what had been so recently known as the Warsaw Pact countries. Meanwhile, in Western Europe, Marriott was also expanding with Courtyards in the United Kingdom and hotels in West Germany.

The day in November that Bill returned to work after his heart attack marked the twenty-fifth anniversary of his promotion to president of what was then called Marriott-Hot Shoppes Inc. Over those twenty-five years, he had racked up an extraordinary annual compound growth rate of approximately 20 percent each year in sales, net income, earnings per share, and stock price. Annual sales had gone from $84 million to nearly $8 billion.

Marriott had also become the tenth-largest employer in the United States, with 230,000 employees—compared to 9,600 in Bill's first year as president. Aside from bringing Marriott to the number-one spot in terminal, turnpike, airline catering, and contracted food-service businesses, Bill had multiplied the number of hotels the company managed from four in 1964 to 534 at the end of 1989.

Having been raised by his father to believe that "success is never final," Bill felt a big change was needed. At a New York City securities analyst meeting on December 18, 1989, he announced a "major restructuring of Marriott corporation." The spin-off of the airline catering division had been finalized, and Marriott would be selling its fast-food restaurant chains. "Our family's name is over the doors, so deciding to exit our two oldest businesses—restaurants and airline catering—has been a difficult and an emotional choice," Bill said.

Only the twelve Hot Shoppes in the D.C. area, the last of the company's original 1927 product, would be retained. Marriott would still keep its foot in the door of food service with more than 4,000 restaurants in its hotels, at fifty-one airport terminals, along fourteen interstate highways, and in institutional feeding operations.

"As we move into the 1990s, we want to sharpen Marriott's focus on mega-markets in lodging and contract services," Bill said. "We plan to double our number of hotels to 1,000 properties by the mid-1990s, and one-third of these new hotels are already in our pipeline."

Two days after the big announcement, Bill woke up to a 3:30 a.m. phone call. American troops had invaded Panama, and the Marriott Caesar Park hotel was surrounded by hostile forces that had raided the hotel and taken away hostages to an unknown fate. Under the code name "Operation Just Cause," President Bush had ordered 27,000 American troops to launch an attack at midnight aimed at unseating and capturing General Manuel Antonio Noriega. Resident manager Daniel Sarria was in charge of the skeleton hotel staff.

A half hour after the invasion began, a dozen of Noriega's paramilitary battalions raced through the front and back doors of the hotel armed with rocket launchers, Uzis, AK-47s, and M-16 rifles. They fired a few shots for effect as they herded eighty guests into the lobby and ordered them to lie facedown on the floor and put their hands behind their heads. "We're being invaded, so we're taking hostages," said the man who appeared to be their leader. After the soldiers checked passports, twelve foreigners, including three journalists and four other Americans, were taken away.[12]

Soldiers surrounded Sarria when they learned he was the manager and demanded the keys to the rooms of all the American guests. When he refused, he and two American journalists were tossed into the back of a pickup truck and driven away. Sarria was released after a couple of hours, and he walked through the dangerous streets back to the hotel, where he continued to take care of the guests. He had some of the Americans don employee uniforms and hid others in laundry hampers and industrial washing machines.[13]

American troops had higher military priorities than the hotel, but, by evening, the pleas of Bill and American broadcast news officials finally had an effect. Secretary of Defense Dick Cheney and Secretary of State James Baker knew that Bill was a political supporter and friend of the president, so his problem carried extra weight. After most of the military targets had been secured, ninety U.S. paratroopers braved three hours of firefights to cover the two-mile distance to the hotel. They secured the hotel at midnight, ending a day of terror. The following morning, "the paratroopers piled 110 guests and hotel workers into two Marriott airport food service trucks and we barreled down the road under fire," recounted a rescued Associated Press reporter.[14]

All the hostages were eventually released unharmed. With a .30-caliber machine gun set up facing the main entry, American soldiers occupied the hotel for fifteen days, enjoying accommodations in the most luxurious suites on the fifteenth floor. They were welcome to that and more, as far as Bill was concerned.

. . .

For many years, it had been the Marriott family's tradition to fly to Acapulco the day after Christmas and stay in the vacation home Bill and Donna owned. "We were supposed to go to Acapulco, but we decided to scrub that plan," Bill recalled. Donna insisted: "You've got this heart problem. We're not going to Mexico. We're going to Florida." So they flew to Fort Lauderdale and checked into the Marriott Harbor Beach Resort hotel, which had opened five years earlier.

Although he occasionally experienced chest pains, the morning of the second day at Harbor Beach, Bill was exercising on the stationary bike when the pain became severe enough to warrant a trip to the hospital. "They couldn't find anything wrong with me and sent me back to the hotel," he said. In the evening, Bill and Donna went to a movie.

While they were away, a regional Marriott executive slipped a note under the couple's hotel suite door. It said: "If you have any heart problems, call this cardiologist. He's a good friend of mine."

Less than half an hour after returning from the movie, Bill was nearly bowled over with extreme chest pains. Gasping, he called the cardiologist and left a brief message: "It's Bill Marriott. I think I'm having a heart attack. Call me back." The doctor called within ten seconds and instructed Bill to meet him at the Florida Medical Center. Bill had only one blocked artery, but it was the left anterior descending (LAD), a condition doctors call "the widowmaker" because it's the one that causes the biggest heart attacks. Bill needed a bypass and he couldn't be moved.

"I will never forget that lonely, sleepless night," Bill told a church audience the following spring. "It has been said the Lord will indeed accompany us to the hospital room and we must have total faith in

Him to do what He knows is best. I thought a lot about my past deeds—some were good and some fell short. . . . I wondered whether or not I would truly qualify to enter the presence of our Lord. Would I pass the judgment bar, or fail?"[15]

After a relatively sleepless night, his spirits were lifted at 5:30 a.m. when two nineteen-year-old Latter-day Saint missionaries whom he didn't know entered the room. One of the hotel's executives had thoughtfully contacted the mission president to request a visit by the elders, who gave Bill a priesthood blessing. "That blessing helped give me the faith, courage, and strength I needed. I felt their humble, strong spirit as they uttered the simple blessing."

He was then operated on by a surgeon he did not meet until ten days later. When Bill woke up, "the nurse said, 'Well, *Mr. Cash,* how are you feeling?' I couldn't talk because I had a respirator down my throat, but I thought, 'Have I died and gone someplace else?'" For privacy and security reasons, Donna had provided the hospital with an alias—Ronald Cash—for her husband.

A few days into Bill's hospitalization, close friend Ralph Hardy flew to Florida for a visit. He teased Bill about going ahead with the bypass at the unfamiliar hospital. When Hardy had faced open-heart surgery in Salt Lake City, Bill had said, "I'll set it all up at Mayo or Mass General. Those are the only places you should go." Ralph had declined the offer, and the surgery had gone just fine. Now, Hardy said, "You're in an even smaller hospital than I was, which none of us has ever heard of. And you didn't even know the doctor who did your open-heart surgery!"

After two weeks in the Florida hospital, Bill returned home. Little did he know, as he was wrapping up this difficult year, what challenges were awaiting just around the corner.

CHAPTER 22

"WHAT HAVE I DONE?"

There has seldom been a financial boom equal to the one that occurred in Japan between 1985 and 1989. Real-estate prices more than doubled throughout the country, pushing tiny condominiums to sell for more than $1 million in downtown Tokyo. From the beginning of 1985 to the Tokyo stock market's peak on the last day of 1989, the value of shares traded was roughly $3.2 trillion—a bubble not seen previously except on Wall Street just before the 1929 stock-market crash.

Japanese investors were flush with cash and went abroad for the largest spending spree of their history, with America as their shopping mecca. They snapped up hotels and other real estate in Guam and Hawaii, then moved on to California, where they acquired one-fourth of the state's bank assets. Nearly every large new office building constructed in Los Angeles was owned by Japanese investors, as were a few major Hollywood studios.[1]

Obsessed with golf, but having few golf courses available on their home islands in which to invest, Japanese investors gobbled up American golf courses at almost any asking price. One Tokyo tycoon paid $831 million for the famous Pebble Beach golf courses.[2] All in all, according to the *New York Times*, "Japanese companies spent $77 billion on real estate in the United States, buying everything [during the boom] from the former Exxon Building to Rockefeller Center. No price was too high for the Japanese who were confident in the long-term value of the office buildings, hotels, golf courses and shopping centers."[3]

Some of that money went to Marriott. After the American institutional investors, such as insurance companies, dropped out of hotel buying, and after the 1986 tax law change, which made limited partnerships harder to sell, "Japan became the last buyer," Bill recalled. "They were buying everything in sight, and they were paying great prices. Why? Real-estate values in Tokyo were so astronomical that they looked at real estate in cities like Los Angeles and Chicago and New York and said to themselves, 'These values are less than ten percent of what we're paying in Tokyo. Americans don't understand real estate. We do.'"

"Once you reached an agreement, they didn't get as hung up on all the legal stuff as American investors," then-CFO Bill Shaw added. "They were in for the long term. They were trying to build relationships with us, so they accepted lower initial returns on the deals than American competitors, so we did business with them, and it was very good business."[4]

The first deals were pivotal refinancing deals: the New York Marriott Marquis in 1986 and seven hotels refinanced by Mitsui in 1987. A year after that, as part of the Los Angeles buying binge, Sumitomo—the world's largest bank in total assets—paid $83.5 million for the new JW Marriott at Century City. Then Sanwa Bank, the world's fifth-largest, financed the $131.5-million syndication of twenty-three Residence Inn hotels. In September 1989, Adachi financed the $400-million syndication of nine Marriott hotels in Europe. Two months after that, Mitsui Trust Bank signed a $112-million, exclusively Japanese, limited-partnership deal for four all-suite Marriott hotels.

The Japanese relationship that Bill worked the hardest to secure was with Nomura Securities International. It was the largest and most profitable financial institution in the world, managing assets of more than $430 billion. During meetings in Japan, in California, and at Marriott's Maryland headquarters, Nomura expressed interest in a variety of Marriott hotel purchases as well as the Marriott retirement communities. Nomura first paid $196 million to refinance the Atlanta Marriott Marquis. Then, in April 1990, Nomura agreed to purchase the San Francisco Marriott for $330 million. It was a big debt Bill was anxious to get off Marriott's books, so he was elated. Although the Tokyo stock market had been declining since the first of the year, "it didn't seem to bother Nomura because they were so big," Bill said. "I had no reason to believe they would not close the deal."

Marriott was the world's largest operator of hotel rooms, primarily because of the development explosion in the late 1980s, which resulted in nearly two Marriott hotels opening every week. The company built and opened ninety hotels in 1988, another eighty-eight in 1989, and another one hundred in 1990—at which point they were managing 639 hotels. Marriott became one of America's top ten real-estate developers. One out of every four hotels built in America was a Marriott.

That kind of growth produced a dangerous hubris within the company ranks—the idea that if they built a hotel, they could always sell it and retain a lucrative management contract. Top executives felt invincible. TV commentator Daniel Schorr even suggested that the way for President Ronald Reagan to balance the budget would be to "sell the White House to the Marriott corporation" so they could manage it for a profit.[5]

Failure was unthinkable in the general corporate culture, but Bill was growing concerned. During a ceremony at Camelback celebrating Marriott's rapid growth, Bill realized that "I wasn't entirely comfortable with what I was seeing and hearing. What if the market dried up? But everyone else in the room seemed to be so bullish and positive about our business that I set my worry aside and joined in the celebration. After all, every sign at the time was positive. Our hotels were filling up as fast as they could be finished, and capital was plentiful. Why not just keep going?"

The biggest issue was the company's debt load. At the end of 1986, Marriott's debt-to-equity ratio was 1.7 to 1, meaning that the company owed $1.70 for every $1 in assets. Considering 2-to-1 a good ratio, Wall Street analysts were very comfortable with Marriott's bottom line. But by early 1990, the debt-to-equity ratio was 7.4 to 1, which made Wall Street analysts nervous. Marriott's long-term debt had climbed to $3.3 billion, which cost the company at least $300 million a year in interest. If the company made a profit lower than its annual interest payments, it would be on the edge of bankruptcy.

One bright light was the growth of the company's golfing ventures, which prompted Bill to create a new Marriott Golf Division in April 1990. Since developing its first golf course at Camelback twenty years earlier, the company had constructed fifteen more resort courses in the U.S. and Bermuda. Marriott was the country's largest golf-course operator, with 800,000 rounds being played on its courses annually.

Heading the new golf division was Roger Maxwell, the company's first pro and golf shop operator at Camelback. Maxwell negotiated with golf legend Jack Nicklaus, who wanted Marriott to manage fifteen public golf courses he was planning to build. Bill flew to Florida to meet with the "Golden Bear" himself. Entering Nicklaus's Palm Beach office, Bill spotted a hand-embroidered pillow that, according to the *Miami Herald,* "shattered any misconceptions that Nicklaus was just another dumb jock." It read: "Happiness is a positive cash flow."[6]

On the home front, when Bill ramped up his work schedule after his heart attacks, Donna urged him to get additional office help. Their son John, who had been working at headquarters in strategic planning, marketing, and financial planning, was made Bill's executive assistant on a temporary basis to help reduce the load.

Shortly after the stock market crashed on Black Monday, October 19, 1987, a *Forbes* writer had visited Bill in his office and found him surprisingly calm about the situation. He noticed several seascapes on the office walls by Depression-era British artist Montague Dawson. Bill's favorite was a majestic ship plowing through a storm-tossed sea. "We're in uncharted waters," Bill reflected, looking at the painting. "But we've always been able to come through recessions and continue to grow. The chances are that the next downturn, whenever it comes, will prove no different."[7]

But it was proving very different by late spring 1990, as Marriott stock dropped to $22 a share—a 52-week low. "Lodging is overbuilt, the real-estate business is in the tank, and financial markets are tight. The challenges are great. However, we have been through down cycles in the past and have emerged successfully," Bill reassured his senior managers.[8]

Bill wasn't as sanguine as he appeared, however, and his concerns began to crop up in his public remarks. He was not usually a fan of modern art, but he agreed to head a fund-raiser for the privately held Phillips Collection museum in downtown D.C. He found himself absorbed with a painting by surrealist Joan Miro called *The Red Sun*. He told a crowd at the event, "My interpretation of this painting is that of a person whose head and heart are detached from the body with the stomach in turmoil—a portrait of the end of the day for a CEO in these times."[9]

There was also a reference in a speech to his marketing managers regarding the lightning victory of General Douglas MacArthur at Inchon, North Korea: "MacArthur was blinded by his astounding victory. He became more arrogant than ever and wound up being fired by President Truman. The Chinese would not have entered the war if he had not pushed so far forward to the Chinese border and provoked their counterattack. General MacArthur's arrogance cost him his job and cost America thousands of lives in the prolonged Korean War," he concluded. His message to Marriott's marketers was, beware arrogance.

"We cannot let it blind us to the current climate. This is a real competitive war we are in."[10]

Having foreseen the oversupply of hotel rooms years before, Bill began shutting down full-service hotel development in 1988, with the San Francisco Marriott being the last big one built. However, believing that Americans would always use moderate and economy hotels, even in a recession, Marriott did not begin curtailing Courtyard, Residence Inn, and Fairfield Inn development until April 1990. At that time, Marriott cut the projected construction budget for 1991 from $1.2 billion to $900 million. The company also laid off forty headquarters employees, an almost unheard-of move for Marriott.

In July, the Japanese came to the rescue and bought fifty Fairfield Inns. But Nomura was still dragging its heels on closing the agreed-upon deal to buy the San Francisco Marriott. Bill took off for a much-needed vacation at Lake Winnipesaukee and returned home just as war broke out in the Middle East.

On August 2, 1990, Iraqi despot Saddam Hussein invaded and occupied Kuwait with 100,000 troops. Oil prices skyrocketed, and American troops entered the conflict.

Within a few weeks, the Tokyo Stock Exchange crashed. The Japanese had been referring to their real-estate and capital boom as *Baburu Keizai* (The Bubble Economy). They knew all bubbles burst, but no one predicted how spectacular the crash would be. Tokyo was the world's largest financial market at the end of 1989, but it fell behind New York in August 1990 and kept on free-falling. Occasionally, it would rebound a little in what one security analyst called a *dead-cat bounce:* "Even a falling dead cat will bounce, but not far and not for long." A stunning $2.25 trillion of Japanese capital vanished in just nine months.[11]

America was already in a recession, but these factors deepened it. Most lodging companies were already in serious trouble, and that was made much worse by swiftly declining tourist and business travel and the Tokyo exchange crash. In all, more than 300 hotels went broke in 1990. "I feel like an architect watching Rome burn," lamented Hyatt chief Darryl Hartley-Leonard.[12]

Bill recalled: "We got hit with three things back-to-back that were out of our control—the real-estate recession, the Gulf War, and the Japanese crash." September began the first of many dark months for CEO Bill Marriott. There was a very real possibility that the company would not survive.

On September 18, the nation's second-largest hotel company, Prime Motor Inns, Inc., filed for bankruptcy. "The idea of Marriott and bankruptcy had never been said in the same breath until Prime Motor Inns went broke," Bill said. "We were doing the same things they were. We were building and selling properties. We were overleveraged like they were. We couldn't sell our hotels just like they couldn't. Everybody was saying, 'Marriott's going to be next.'"

Bill went through a reassessment of where the company stood, considering as well whether he was up to the challenge. "Do I have enough to get through this?" he recalled asking himself. "Am I going to push myself into this thing and get done what needs to be done? Is my health going to hold up, or am I going to have another heart attack?"

On Monday morning, September 24, Bill convened a meeting with his top executives. Mincing no words, he said, "We're in very bad shape financially. If we don't work together, I don't know whether we'll be able to make payroll in a month. This is the most serious situation this company has ever had, and we may wind up going out of business. We have to stop building. We have to cut costs wherever we can. We have to freeze salaries for everyone but the hourly workers, who can least afford it. We have to cut some of our salaries, including mine. We have to put off annual bonuses. And we have to lay off more employees in a couple of divisions. I'm not happy about any of this. I'm sure you aren't either. But we have to do this if we're going to survive. We have to do this together, or we will fall together. I personally believe we will come through this and rise together."

That afternoon, Standard & Poor's (S&P) credit rating agency announced that Marriott was being placed on their CreditWatch "with negative implications." On Tuesday, the second of the Big Three rating agencies, Moody's Investors Service Inc., said it was reviewing Marriott's long-term debt with an eye to lowering its A- rating.

Attempting to halt any further slide, Bill went public that afternoon with his austerity plan. On Thursday, the company issued its third-quarter profits report, revealing a 57 percent drop compared to the previous year. Bill announced a further cut in Marriott's projected capital expenditures in 1991 to $650 million, compared to $1.3 billion in 1990. Marriott shares dropped to $8.37½ in the first week of October. That meant the market value of the company had fallen from $3.98 billion to $861 million in less than a year.

To make matters worse, short sellers descended on Marriott en masse, like a flock of vultures.

Short selling is a legal way for investors to benefit from a *decline* in a stock's price. Essentially, they *borrow* the stock, wait for it to lose value, and then buy the stock at a lower price, turning the shares over to the lender and pocketing the difference. For example: a short seller borrows 1,000 shares of Marriott stock at $10 a share from an investor pool, promising to pay the lender or replace the shares in a certain amount of time—say, thirty days. If the stock drops to $5 a share in that time, he buys 1,000 shares for $5,000, signs them over to the lender, and pockets the $5,000 profit. (Of course, if the stock goes up in those thirty days, the short seller stands to lose a bundle of money.)

The same speculators who made tens of millions of dollars selling Prime Motor Inns short began concentrating on Marriott. "By late September these market bears have had a field day with Marriott, selling its stock short with a vengeance," a business magazine noted. According to New York Stock Exchange data, Marriott had become one of the top five targets of short sellers. An unhealthy 14 percent of its shares was sold short against an exchange average of less than one percent.

The best way the short sellers could make high profits was to tear down the Marriott image at every turn. "These people have a huge vested interest in spreading rumors on the market," explained Shaw. "They were really hitting us hard in the press because they wanted us to go down. We were getting a lot of bad reports from the hue and cry they were stirring up like Chicken Little: 'Marriott is going to go bankrupt! Marriott is going bankrupt! Marriott is falling!'"

Bill urged calm in an October 5 letter to his management team. Still, the company continued to slide in public perception. Four days after Bill's encouraging letter to executives, Duff & Phelps became the first rating agency to downgrade Marriott's credit rating. The other two, S&P and Moody's, soon followed. Marriott debt was still considered investment grade (not "junk" status), but the triple punch signaled the possibility of worse things to come.

The only thing that could sink the company in a single day was looming on the horizon. During the crisis, Bill had to draw down the entire $1.7-billion credit line he had obtained earlier from a three-bank partnership. The drawdown produced a new $1.7-billion loan, called a "revolver," meaning the banks had to decide by October 18 whether they were going to roll it over or call for the full debt to be repaid. If they thought the company was going to fail, they might call in the debt and expect to recover pennies on the dollar.

While Bill was in Mexico, presiding over the opening of hotels in Cancun and Puerto Vallarta, the banks agreed to renew the loan. CFO Bill Shaw said the only reason the banks did that in the midst of a full-blown recession was "because of the good will Bill Marriott himself had developed with those bankers over the years—and the faith they had in him personally."

At this same time, Bill was released as longtime president of the

Church's Washington D.C. Stake. His farewell remarks focused on the importance of developing "spiritual reserves of faith" as well as "financial reserves sufficient to give you a cushion that will allow you to come through whatever economic storms you can foresee. As we continue to strengthen our spiritual and financial reserves we will develop a more positive mental attitude and more confidence in our own abilities to deal with any crisis that confronts us. Most importantly, a positive mental outlook comes from a sure knowledge that we are all sons and daughters of God. If we believe this we will also believe in His abiding love for us and His strength in helping us through tough times."[13]

Then he was off to Japan with Bill Shaw for make-or-break meetings with Japanese investors—especially Nomura, in order to discuss the delayed completion of the big-ticket $330-million San Francisco hotel deal.

"If we'd have had San Francisco open in April instead of October of 1989, we'd have been okay," Bill said. "The next spring, it was still for sale, and we had good offers from New York banks, but Nomura beat their pricing." Throughout the summer, Shaw received reassurances that the Nomura deal was still on. As the crisis escalated in the fall, the incomplete Nomura–San Francisco deal became the media's preferred symbol of proof that Marriott had lost its mojo and was failing. Hence the trip to Tokyo to salvage the deal and the company's image with it.

"Bill didn't want to go," Shaw recalled. "He never liked to negotiate, because he doesn't like conflict. But this was worse because it was so important. Both of us were frustrated by the inscrutability of the Japanese, but he was willing to go because it was time to sit down and force the issue: 'Is this going to happen or is it not going to happen?'"

Bill and Donna arrived in Tokyo on Saturday, November 3. On Monday, Donna flew to Hong Kong, where Debbie, Ron, and their five children were living and Ron was managing the Hong Kong Marriott. Bill was now free to make the rounds with CFO Bill Shaw to "Lenders Receptions" and private meetings with various potential buyers. Shaw recalled, "They weren't real direct when we talked with them. They would always say 'maybe' about this deal or that. They wouldn't say, 'Not very likely' or 'This will be difficult.' We tried to understand and finally realized what they were really telling us was that, with the stock-market crash, Japan was only committing money to Japanese assets. It became Japan for Japan: 'We're going to take care of our own.'"

Then came the last meeting, with Nomura. "It was so frustrating," Bill said. "I couldn't tell what they were thinking and what they were planning on doing. They had become so slow to move in any direction. There was no clear signal that they were going to stop the San Francisco deal. But there was no signal we were going to close it soon. Since this came after the lukewarm talk with all the other Japanese investors, it was the final straw. I felt it was the final straw for Marriott."

He flew to Hong Kong to join his family, and they all went out on a boat in the middle of Victoria Harbor. "We were showing Bill and Donna the harbor and the beautiful skyline," said Ron. "But he wasn't talking. He was more detached and introverted than he had ever been. He had the weight of the world on his shoulders. He was thinking about all those investors and shareholders, small and large. He was thinking about his 230,000 employees. Were they going to have a job in six months? Was their pension going to be wiped out? Everybody was relying on him, and he felt it."

Bill shared the depths of his anguish with Debbie during that trip. She recalled, "Dad was lying on the couch in his room because of jet lag. He was so tired. I was worried about him. I thought he was going to have another heart attack because he was worrying so much."

Debbie started to say something, and her father began to cry. "As an adult, I have only seen my Dad cry like that once, and it was gut-wrenching. Between the tears, he said, 'I don't know what to do. I could lose the business.' Grandpa had always lectured him about keeping the company out of debt. He was thinking about that, because, after more tears, he said, 'I have disappointed my father so much. I am losing the company. He's up there looking at me right now and I've let him down.' And then he asked a heartbreaking question, 'What have I done?'"

• • •

The massive Marriott hotel-building machine had ground to an abrupt halt in September 1990. Shaw said the decision to put on the brakes was a bold one. "I don't think many people at the top of many companies could stop like we did that month. It was a great credit to Bill that he did so. Some of our own executives complained privately he had gone too far—that he had overreacted. But he was close enough to the details of our business to know it had to be done."

Bill's edict was unequivocal: if a project hadn't broken ground, it was put on hold. There were attempts to move some dirt around to simulate a ground breaking, but that didn't get past Bill. "He checked every project to see if somebody was fudging it," said Shaw. "Nobody with a favorite project they were trying to continue after the ban got anything by him." Hotels that were nearly finished—all but the interior work—were allowed to continue, but other construction projects were boarded up.

Two unfinished full-service hotels—in Gaithersburg, Maryland, and Crystal City, Virginia—were frozen in place. The *Washington Post* reported that the two construction sites displayed "all the architectural panache of postwar Baghdad."[14] Just as stark were the steel skeleton towers of The Jefferson, the senior-living community in Arlington, Virginia. By the time the companywide construction halt was called, the two twenty-story towers were one-third finished. The company had already received 2,205 refundable deposits of $1,000 each from enthusiastic seniors, including Shaw's own mother. Marriott executive Brian Swinton assigned a lone security guard to protect the project with a unique secondary task: "I asked him to go around the site every day or so and bang on something with a hammer so we could keep our construction permit active."

The mandate came from the top to run a much leaner operation without compromising quality. That meant reducing excess inventories and finding extra cash wherever it might be. In flush times, the measures would have been nickel-and-dime stuff, but now they were crucial. For example, Bill found out that Host airport restaurants were routinely keeping a couple thousand dollars in their cash drawers overnight. Shaw directed that cash go to the bank at the end of the day, where it would draw interest and be used for other expenses. Bill calculated, "We had hundreds of these restaurants, so we picked up millions of dollars doing stuff like that. We just found cash all over the place. . . . It forced us to discipline ourselves." This "cash sweep" alone resulted in a savings of working capital by more than $100 million in the first few months of the crisis.

Another cost-saving move was to freeze or reduce the salaries of Marriott's middle and top managers. Hourly workers, such as waitstaff and housekeepers, who could ill afford a cut in their salaries, were exempt. To set an example for the people at the top, Bill took a pay cut of 27 percent. Approximately 1,100 senior executives had their pay frozen for a year. Annual bonuses were delayed forty-five days, and some executives (including Bill) didn't get them at all. Middle managers had their salaries frozen for six months. Other administrative and clerical employees saw a three-month freeze. Surprisingly, there was little complaining, according to Bill.

In his corporate book, *The Spirit to Serve,* Bill described the most difficult measures as the layoffs in the hotel-development offices when there were no longer any hotels to develop: "We had been developing about 100 new hotels a year in the latter half of the 1980s. There truly was nothing comparable in the American hotel industry, or most other industries, for that matter.

"Almost overnight, we had to close down the assembly line.

Marriott had never in its 63-year history faced the prospect of letting go of two entire departments. . . . The cornerstone of our corporate culture has always been: 'Take care of your employees, and they'll take care of your customers.' Laying off a substantial number of people who had worked hard to contribute to our success felt like a betrayal of that philosophy."[15]

The A&C Division was slashed from 1,200 to 200 employees. Recalled Jack Graves, A&C's highly effective chief for many years: "This was the worst time of my life, terminating all these people. But I saw it through. The last man I fired was myself. There was no need for an executive vice president to manage nothing, so I retired."

Bill was deeply and personally involved in this wrenching part of the crisis. "Dad *hated* downsizing," said Debbie. "This was real grief for these people losing their jobs—good people, loyal people, people whom he had known for a long time. It just killed him to do that. Someone would come into his office and say, 'I've loved working for you for seventeen years, and now I'm out?' The whole thing was awful."

To mitigate the pain, Marriott poured money into generous severance benefits, as well as an employment service, helping with résumés, job searches, and interview coaching. When the bloodletting was finally over in late 1991, the company had placed more than 90 percent of its laid-off workers who had not taken early retirement. In hindsight, construction head Graves said the dark days ended up being "the best time for Marriott because it gave everybody a chance to reflect on where we were going and where we had been. We became a better, more lean and more efficient company for the long haul."

While the cash conservation and cost-cutting measures helped, Bill continued his search for asset buyers and new financing sources. He approached at least one unusual source—the Coca-Cola Company—and expertly manipulated the competition between Coke and Pepsi to his advantage. The two cola companies regularly engaged in pitched battle for corporate contracts. Marriott had been a loyal twenty-year customer of Coca-Cola, serving Coke and not Pepsi at its restaurants in 639 hotels, at its airport and thruway restaurants, and for 2,300 food-service accounts in hospital and university cafeterias. Bill figured it was time to call in a favor. His request to Coke for help was unusual, but it was an expansion of a hidden cola company practice of providing "marketing allowances" in the form of large cash advances to its best customers.

"I called Coke and I said, 'We're going to make it but we really need cash. Are you guys willing to step up and help us?'" Bill recalled. Coke's senior vice president Charles S. Frenette derided the request in an internal company memo, saying Bill was asking Coke to become a banker. A few days after the request, Bill was notified that Coke wouldn't help, which became a cold-shoulder decision Coke has regretted for decades.

Somebody tipped off Pepsi CEO Wayne Calloway about the Marriott-Coke dustup, and Calloway saw a big opening for Pepsi. Bill recalled that just two days after Coke's refusal to help, Calloway "called and asked me, 'How much do you need?' I said, 'At least $50 million.' He said, 'You've got it, but we want your business.' I agreed."

Marriott was quiet about the deal, but it leaked to the press, and Bill didn't mind. He was furious with Coke, and the public message was abundantly clear—Coca-Cola didn't view loyalty as a two-way street. "So every time Coke has come back trying to get our business, I've said, 'Good-bye, guys.' Pepsi got it all," Bill said.

In spite of small victories such as the Pepsi deal, the financial crisis was keeping Bill awake at night. Donna feared the stress would bring on another heart attack. "I had never seen him so distraught and disappointed with himself. He wished he was smarter and could have foreseen everything. He told me, 'Somebody might take us over and I'd be out.' You don't know what's going to happen to a company in a takeover, and he could see all the good people he felt responsible for getting fired. He really thought it might be all over."

Bill had reason to be worried about a hostile takeover. In 1984 and again in 1989, the board had rewritten the corporate charter to include so-called "poison pill" provisions to prevent a takeover. One of the reasons for the board's regular multimillion-share buyback of Marriott stock was to prevent anyone else from accumulating enough to seize control of the company. The fact that the Marriott family owned a quarter of the stock also was a healthy deterrent to corporate raiders.

But by November 1990, the company was vulnerable to moves by any determined corporate raider with a pile of cash. Richard Rainwater, the financial genius who had made the Bass family billions, called Bill and said he was considering "taking a position" in Marriott with the stock at such a low price. Bill politely told Rainwater to back off, and he did; he was not interested in a hostile takeover.

Another call came from Charles Brady, the brains behind the spectacular growth of the Atlanta-based Invesco investment firm, which was then managing $21 billion in stocks and bonds for more than 200 clients. Invesco wanted to buy a substantial amount of Marriott stock, but before he filed the SEC report signaling this intent, Brady wanted to assure Bill that he wanted no more than 15 percent of Marriott and would not expect a seat on the board. The board said no, and Brady stepped away.

A third foray was made by an old friend. Gary Wilson flew from California in mid-November and met with Bill. He explained that he and Al Checchi had put together a group that wanted to buy into Marriott in a big way. Ever the deal-maker, he undoubtedly thought he could help Bill at the same time as he helped himself. Bill was offended, however. "Instead of coming in and saying, 'What can I do to help you?' he came in and said, effectively, 'Do you mind if I profit off of your misfortune?'" As soon as Bill told Gary his overture was unwelcome, Gary backed off, and the two remained friends.

While Bill had been able to swiftly deflect all suitors, the most fearful challenge occurred the following January, 1991, when the stock was selling at $10.50 a share. A Malaysian group offered a substantial loan to Marriott, which could quickly be converted to Marriott stock at the group's discretion. The company was Genting Group, a global resort and casino operator with pockets deep enough to make a raid on Marriott. Shaw knew the loan offer was a ruse to attempt a takeover, and he declined. The group left unsatisfied, and Shaw hoped that would be the end of it; it wasn't.

Two days later, one of the company's lawyers called and reported that they would file with the SEC that they were going to buy Marriott stock, possibly more than 20 percent. "Bill and I knew this was a hostile takeover attempt, and a serious one," Shaw recalled. The group most likely intended to turn Marriott into a gaming company, selling off other lucrative parts of the corporation. The most certain way to stop them was to drive the stock price up to the point where it would be too expensive for Genting—or anyone else—to take a run at Marriott.

Bill and Shaw redoubled their efforts to find additional loans on reasonable terms. "I'd never been through anything like that in my life. We spent day after day, night after night with the banks," Shaw recalled. "The banks were always willing to lend us more money. But they would have loaded the loans with requirements and restrictions. It would have been like working for somebody else. To Bill, agreeing to those kinds of loans was equivalent to losing his company, because it would mean losing his flexibility to run it."

A few friends tried to help Bill get a fair loan—including Jon Huntsman, who was serving on the board of a major U.S. bank. "I think it was the scariest time of Bill's life," Huntsman observed. "My company was going through a tough time as well during that recession, but I wasn't as worried about losing the company because I had started the company. It's worse if you're Bill Marriott and possibly losing the business your father founded. He pulled every lever he could possibly pull. I went to bat for Bill with the bank where I was a major voice on the board, but it did no good. They were convinced the Marriott corporation was going down, and didn't want to rescue a sinking ship."

Finally, at the end of January, a three-bank consortium led by Citibank offered a $400-million credit line at reasonable rates, with an initial bridge loan of $150 million. The banks recognized Marriott had a liquidity problem, not a solvency issue. It was a huge vote of confidence and proved to be the turning point for the company. The credit line was announced on February 1, and it met with universal acclaim on Wall Street. Marriott was one of the heaviest-traded stocks on the New York Stock Exchange that day, swiftly rising 26.9 percent, to $13 a share.

There was still a hard road ahead, but Bill suspected correctly that the worst was finally behind him. He had been in the fight of his life and was bloodied. "In the military, the million-dollar wound is the one that gets you a Purple Heart and sends you home. It's not bad enough to kill you," reflected former Marriott executive Mike Hostage. "When Bill went through this, it probably seemed like the wounds were going to be fatal. Instead, he got through with a Purple Heart. What doesn't kill you makes you stronger."

CHAPTER 23

THE GREAT DIVIDE

Donna constantly feared that her husband would break under the pressure of the company's financial crisis. He was exercising regularly, but his blood pressure was rising and his stress level, in her view, was off the charts. The memory of J.W.'s strong opinions shook Bill's confidence and caused him to second-guess every major decision. "Again and again, my husband would raise the question at home: 'What would my father think of me?'" Donna recalled.

No one had been tougher on Bill than his father about avoiding debt. General Counsel Sterling Colton witnessed it up close at board meetings. "Every board meeting [J.W.] delivered a lecture on the evils of debt. I can still hear him. It was every meeting where he was very critical of Bill in front of the board members. Bill would take it, but it was hard on him. Then, five years after his father was gone and we started to go under, both Bill and I could hear his father say: 'I told you so!'"

As forcefully as she could, Donna urged Bill to get help for his stress, and he learned some coping skills from Dr. Stephen Hersh, a clinical professor of psychiatry at George Washington University, who became a close family friend.

But the best medicine for Bill was getting the company on a more even keel because of the $400-million credit line. As it turned out,

Marriott never had to draw on it. Buyers were found for the Marriott-owned Big Boy and Howard Johnson's restaurants. Marriott's employee profit-sharing trust showed solidarity by buying five Courtyards. CFO Bill Shaw sold $62 million of the time-share division's "receivables." And, through Shaw's patient work, the Tokyo-based Nomura group finally came through with a helpful mortgage for the San Francisco Marriott, which better positioned it for its subsequent sale.

Despite the positive gains, the company still had a long way to go. During this time of financial struggle, the negative press continued to weigh heavily on Bill. The worst of it was the April 1991 cover story in *Regardie's,* a Washington business magazine named after its mercurial founder, Bill Regardie. Writer Keith Girard drove home the idea that Bill was past his prime: "Today, at 57, he's a lion in winter; his health is questionable and his management talent is suspect. Which raises a nagging question: Does the chairman have the strength to rise again?" The cover featured an unflattering photo of Bill with the headline, "What the Hell Happened to Marriott?"[1]

The article received little notice outside D.C. because, by the time it was published, the information was stale. To meet the April publication deadline, Girard had to finish the final draft in early January, weeks before the $400-million credit line had turned the perception of the company around. A few months later, Bill ran into Regardie himself and buttonholed him. At the time, the magazine's advertising revenue was dropping. Still stinging from the article, Bill warned the publisher: "When you go out of business, I am going to run a full-page ad in the *Washington Post* with your picture on it and it's going to say, 'What the Hell Happened to Regardie's?'" The magazine folded at the end of the following year. Bill never bought that ad, but decades later he summarized the episode with evident pride: "*Regardie's* took that awful picture of me and put it on the cover, and I'm still going strong while *Regardie's* went broke."

In spite of the company's crisis, Bill's stature in the business community was substantial. The U.S. Chamber of Commerce had asked him to be their chairman a few years before, which he had declined because of his busy schedule. That recognition from the business community meant that when Bill called for a jump start to the economy a week after the launch of the ground war against Saddam Hussein in Iraq (Operation Desert Storm), important business and political leaders listened. He issued a clarion call for an aggressive response to the crisis at a 1991 dinner meeting of President George H. W. Bush's Business Roundtable:

"As we [corporations] stay home and ignore calling on our customers or attending meetings or seeing our people, trade is languishing, unemployment is rising, and sales are dropping," Bill said. "The domino effect is cascading throughout our consumer ranks and could throw us into the worst recession of our lives. Presidents of airlines tell me that if this continues, all the world's airlines will be bankrupt in six months. For those who have restricted travel, I urge reconsideration. If our economy falls apart because of this war, Saddam will have won a major victory in spite of his certain defeat on the battlefield."[2]

Among the first to step up to the challenge was First Lady Barbara Bush, who flew on a commercial plane on Valentine's Day from D.C. to Indianapolis for a veterans' hospital visit. "People basically were afraid to travel because they thought Iraqi terrorists would blow up the airplanes," Bill recalled. "So we got Barbara Bush to take that flight to prove to the American public that it was safe to fly. She commented to me, 'Isn't it the silliest thing you've ever heard? That if I fly on an airplane it proves they are *all* safe?' But she was willing to do it, and it really helped."

Bill followed up by forging a coalition of fifty travel-industry competitors that put up $6 million for a six-week national advertising campaign. "We're going to be telling people that you can't remember those wonderful vacations if you don't take them," Bill said. "And we're going to tell business people you can't do business by fax machine. They've got to get out and press the flesh."[3]

Meanwhile, Marriott had been supportive of the war effort in various ways. Many of the hotels and restaurants offered free breakfasts for military families, put together care packages for the soldiers serving abroad, and hosted frequent blood drives. President Bush personally praised the corporation's efforts, especially when the Cairo Marriott became his "Cairo White House" during a visit to forge a broad military coalition.[4]

America was in an ebullient mood when the Gulf War ended, and Marriott was a significant part of that celebration. The JW Marriott Hotel in D.C. became the headquarters for the national festivities culminating in the June 8, 1991, victory parade, and the company made a substantial donation to the cost of the parade. In addition, area Marriott hotels gave free rooms to visiting family members of the 373 American troops killed in the conflict.

Still flush from that feeling of victory, Bill and Donna moved into a new home two weeks later. They had lived in the same modest four-bedroom, two-story colonial house in the Kenwood subdivision for thirty-five years. Despite the Marriotts' increasing wealth over the years, there were several reasons why they did not trade up to a bigger home. One was that Bill never wanted his children to think they were "big shots." Explained daughter Debbie: "My father never made us feel like we had any money or that we were more special or more wealthy than anybody else. The house we lived in was the best way to underline that."

A second reason he stayed was that, as a Church leader, he knew a mansion might intimidate those whom he counseled on spiritual and secular matters, especially members who experienced personal financial difficulties.

A third reason was that he knew his father would give him grief if he bought a bigger house. J.W. had always thought even the Kenwood home was too much. "His dad was furious with Bill when we bought the home in Kenwood in 1956," Donna recalled. "He wanted us to go into a small starter house."

Bill didn't seriously consider buying or building a new home until after his father died in 1985. When he helped his mother clean out his father's closets, a new resolve began to grow, which he relayed to Debbie: "Grandpa worked so hard and he had so much money, but he hadn't bought a new suit in ten years. He had a few nice watches that people gave him, and lots of cowboy boots, but that was it. The air conditioning doesn't work in his house, the plumbing is crummy, and the plaster is falling off the walls. I don't want to be like that. While I don't want to be materialistic, I want to enjoy what I've worked for. It's time to have a nice new house."

A year and a half after J.W. died, Bill and Donna paid $500,000 for a lot in Potomac, Maryland, overlooking a wooded ravine and the Avenel Golf Course (where the Kemper Open professional golf tournament was then played). Bill was intimately involved in every aspect of the Georgian-style brick home construction. Over the next four years, Bill and Donna spent $8.7 million on the home's design, construction, furnishings, and art. The most unusual feature was a detached garage for Bill's private museum of classic cars. The $2.8-million sale of his 1956 Ferrari 410 Sport, which he had bought for $275,000 a few years before, helped pay for the house.

On June 26, 1991, Bill, Donna, and David moved into their new 15,000-square-foot home. Two months later, their Kenwood house sold for $862,500 to the country of Sweden, which used it as a diplomatic residence. That was an $800,000 profit from Bill's original purchase price, but he couldn't help regretting the sale of Marriott stock to buy it in the first place. Those shares would have been worth roughly $25 million when the house sold. Laughing ruefully, Bill allowed, "I made a bad deal."

By the end of 1991, Marriott had become a different company. Necessity required Bill to move away from hotel development to acquisition of troubled hotels. "Tough times provide many good opportunities for strong companies," he advised senior executives at the beginning of the crisis. "There are many undervalued hotels for sale and we need to look out for them." At least half a dozen hotels were acquired. In each case, sales improved significantly under the Marriott brand. Bill also focused on taking over management contracts from competitors, a process called "flag changing." At least sixteen properties kept their owners but changed their flags to Marriott during the crisis.

While he was buying struggling hotels, Bill made serious headway in reducing the company's debt by selling properties, too. The most reluctant sale for Bill was the 170-room Prince Charles de Gaulle Hotel in Paris. To get Sheraton to buy five other Marriotts, Bill had to throw in his Paris crown jewel. It would be five years before a Marriott hotel again opened for business in Paris.

Despite Marriott's having cut its multibillion-dollar debt by half, the weight of the remainder was still a drag. In a speech at George Washington University, Bill declared that the Marriott mantra of 20 percent annual growth was history. "The quest for growth in EPS [Earnings per Share] had been my goal for the twenty-seven years I have been president. We had only one recession year [1975] when we did not increase EPS. Otherwise, our annual growth averaged 20 percent. We thought it could go on forever. But no tree grows to the sky. We knew we had to change our way of operating."[5]

The change agent came in the person of Steve Bollenbach. Since Bollenbach had resigned as treasurer of Marriott in 1986, he had turned around the fortunes of two major hotel companies. Bill knew Bollenbach would return to Marriott only for the CFO slot, so he offered Shaw a promotion to open up the job. Shaw would replace Butch Cash as president of the Services Group. Cash had been a positive performer at the company for years before overreaching ambition had led him into the destructive "Twin Towers" competition. It was time for him to go. Cash subsequently became CEO of the Red Roof Inn chain.

With the stage set for further corporate evolution at the beginning of 1992, Bill was happy to have weathered the storms of 1990 and 1991. In moments of private and public reflection, he acknowledged with humble gratitude the blessings God had showered upon him and his family during that time. "The only way you can keep your sanity in trying times is to know that you have a family who supports you and sustains you and a church that is a bedrock foundation," he said.

The second coming of Steve Bollenbach to the Marriott corporation was not seen as the arrival of a savior. Nevertheless, it was he who devised the idea that would change the company forever, and for the better.

His résumé included a stint as CFO of the struggling Holiday Corp. The first day he reported to work there, he discovered that Donald Trump "had decided to take over the company and fire all of the management because he felt they were a bunch of idiots," Bollenbach recalled.[6] He fended off the takeover by adding so many loans to the Holiday Corp.'s debt that it was no longer a tempting target for Trump.

To float the sinking Holiday Inn ship, he sold the majority of the company to Bass PLC, the British brewing giant, for $2.2 billion. He spun off the rest of the company—the lucrative casino hotels under the Harrah's name, and its newer hotel brands, Embassy Suites, Hampton Inn, and Homewood Suites—into a new company named Promus.

Considering that Bollenbach was once a business adversary, it was more than a little ironic that in 1990 the nearly bankrupt Donald Trump was forced by his creditors to beg Bollenbach to come to work for him and rescue the Trump organization. Always up for a new challenge, Bollenbach agreed. Over the next two years, through debt-for-equity swaps and the sale of Trump's flagging real-estate and casino assets, Bollenbach saved the future U.S. president from bankruptcy.[7]

Bill Shaw, who had kept in close touch with Bollenbach over the years, asked him if he would leave Trump for Marriott, and he did.

Bollenbach reported to work on March 2, 1992, and was surprised with changes that the financial crisis had wrought upon the once-thriving company he had left six years before. "It was the most demoralized place you can imagine; it was like a morgue. People were going around moaning, 'We're broke!'" But in Bollenbach's eyes, they were overreacting, probably because of the stagnant value of their own stock options. Sure, the stock was on life support, but Bollenbach felt that the company had begun a significant turnaround, and the problems were fixable. In retrospect, he observed that his optimism may have come from the lifesaving mission he had completed at his last job. "I'd been working on Donald Trump's problems and knew what real financial problems were about."

A month into the job, Bollenbach gave Bill a list of objectives. In hindsight, the most important item was #7: "Revise Marriott story."

"We had a short-term story, which was that we had to sell the real estate that was holding back our earnings," Bill explained. "We were besieged by calls from security analysts who only wanted to know if we had sold any real estate that day. We said, 'Hey, we have more to tell than that,' but they wouldn't listen. Steve felt we were focusing too much on the sale of real estate, and he wanted to get us off that. I agreed."

Bollenbach suggested that the new story should be, "It's really a good time to own these hotels because they're good hotels." Marriott was not going to get rid of any of its premium properties at fire-sale prices, no matter how depressed the market got. In the meantime, Bollenbach needed to extend the maturity of Marriott's various loans, so he quickly moved ahead with Bill Shaw's plan to sell bonds. The first $200-million lot was for twenty-year bonds, and the second $200-million sale was for ten-year bonds. Bond sales include a large document called an "indenture," which is full of restrictions on the company selling the bonds. The fewer restrictions, the higher the interest rate offered. For these bonds, Marriott offered higher interest because the indenture was less restrictive.

Bollenbach expected that he would have to put on the usual road shows before the sales, which were traveling presentations to potential investors in New York City and elsewhere. "But the bond market had gotten very hot, particularly for Marriott bonds," Bollenbach discovered as he began calling investment bankers to broker the sales. One told him to forget the dog-and-pony shows and just let his bank sell each lot over the phone. He agreed, and on April 22 and 29, $400 million of Marriott bonds sold in less than forty-five minutes over the phone on each day.

Though the bond sales were an incredible success, they didn't rate even a mention in the financial press. Marriott stock, at about $16 a share, remained stagnant. "The stock market was saying, 'So what?' There was no press and no uptick. It was just a big yawn," Bollenbach recalled.[8] So it was time to totally concentrate on the one line in his objectives memo that Bill had highlighted: "We will need to adopt a different approach to creating shareholder value." It resonated with Bill because that was precisely his job as CEO—to enhance shareholder value.

Three days after the last bond sale, Bollenbach and his wife headed north for a weekend at their Connecticut home. That Saturday, May 2, Bollenbach mused over the core issue—the dual nature of Marriott's business, which confused investors. Was it a real-estate company or a management-service company? Then he hit on The Big Idea: Split the company into those two parts. That would be his way to revise the Marriott story.

The plan he worked out that weekend was unique. Companies with divergent missions typically split up via leveraged buyouts, hostile takeovers, spin-offs, and sales of unwanted assets—like Marriott's own sale of its airline catering division several years before. But no one had split a company in two without involving a third-party buyer. This time, there would be no sale; there would be no new owner, just two Marriott companies.

In Bollenbach's shorthand notes that weekend, the old company, which he dubbed "RealCo," would become a real-estate-only company (including the hotels Marriott owned) and would also retain all the debt associated with those assets. "NewCo," the spin-off, would be a nearly debt-free entity focused entirely on management services of hotels, food services, and other operations. Bill could be CEO of NewCo, where he would be free to grow the management side. Bollenbach himself could well be CEO of the "weaker" sister, the debt-laden RealCo. He foresaw that once the real estate market turned around in a few years, RealCo would become one of America's top five hotel-owning firms.

The connection between the two companies would be vital for the health of both, so Bollenbach's plan outlined a series of administrative and other services they would share, including the same headquarters building. But the core staff of each would be separate, as would the boards of directors. He felt Bill should be chairman of the NewCo board and hoped younger brother Dick would agree to be chairman of RealCo. The split would be accomplished with a special two-for-one dividend to stockholders. For the shares they had in RealCo—which was the planned survivor of the old Marriott corporation—they would receive the same amount of shares in NewCo.

The plan was elegantly simple in principle, but extremely complex and formidable to achieve. Consent would be needed from many players, including the board of directors and then the shareholders. General Counsel Sterling Colton's team would also have the monumental task of seeking approval from the Securities and Exchange Commission, the Internal Revenue Service, all the partners in the limited partnerships, all the landlords of leased sites, and a whole array of others. It was mind-boggling for Bollenbach to conceive that all the obstacles he foresaw might be overcome, but he was determined to try.

His first concern was the recently sold bonds. Did the fine print forbid such a corporate split? When he returned to the office Monday morning, his first call was to Colton's best expert on the subject, William Kafes, who told him that the bondholders had no protective covenant that would prevent a company split. Bollenbach had not come up with the idea until after the bond sale, so there had been no obligation to warn the bond buyers. Still, those who had bought bonds in a diversified company would not be happy to find their bonds attached to a debt-laden real-estate-only company.

Bill immediately saw the exciting prospects of such a split and was enthusiastic, but he confessed to Bollenbach that he didn't understand how it would work legally or financially. He told Bollenbach to make sure the Marriott legal team was in the loop, and to meet individually with every board member before the issue came to a vote. The company had no obligation to bondholders other than to pay annual interest on time and pay the principal when it was due. But an active secondary market, in which the bonds could be resold, would be adversely affected by such a split. Having anticipated the bondholders' resistance, Bollenbach pledged that as the plan evolved, more would be done to manage their concerns.

Bollenbach had to come up with a code name for the project to keep it from leaking. In a moment of admittedly "sick humor," Treasurer Matt Hart suggested "Project Bhopal," after a 1984 toxic chemical plant explosion in India. Hart was thinking about the reaction the bondholders would have, but Bollenbach was not amused.[9] Someone else suggested "Chariot" because it rhymed with Marriott, and Bollenbach adopted it.

Marriott executives were divided into two teams to advocate for RealCo and NewCo, to make sure each company got its due. It soon became evident that the "fairness" issue to bondholders would require a major revision of the plan. RealCo needed another revenue stream beyond the debt-laden real estate. So NewCo team members moved Marriott's toll-road businesses to the RealCo side. But RealCo team members said that wasn't enough. They wanted Marriott's Host airport terminal restaurants and gift shops, too. Reluctantly, the NewCo team agreed. At that point, RealCo received its final name, Host Marriott. NewCo was given the name Marriott International (MI).

The historic transformation of Marriott nearly fell apart when financial consultants hired by Marriott, the James D. Wolfensohn

Stock certificates showing the split companies.

investment banking firm, concluded that the current plans would not produce two thriving companies. The solution was for MI to give Host a $600-million line of credit. Then the other shoe dropped. Board member Dr. Thomas Piper, a senior associate dean at Harvard Business School, had just finished editing a book on business ethics. He was concerned that the bondholders might view the Marriott split as somehow unethical. Piper solved his problem by resigning from the board on September 29.

On October 4, the rest of the board voted unanimously in favor of the split. The following day, before an overflowing crowd of media and security analysts at the New York Marriott Marquis, Bill announced that, subject to shareholder approval the following year, the

Marriott corporation would cease to exist; it would become two separate companies.

As expected, some bondholders expressed outrage, which dropped the bonds' trading value by about 10 percent. Bill had been advised this would happen in the short term, but they would soon return to the par value. Meanwhile, the stock market was electrified. In an otherwise down day on the market, heavy trading in Marriott stock drove the share price up 12 percent, to $19.25. Bollenbach's bold plan thus got the most positive first-day review from the only constituency to whom he had fiduciary responsibility.

The *Washington Post* neatly put the split in perspective: "That Marriott needed a radical pick-me-up is one of the few things about Project Chariot that people agree on. It represents, in effect, the blueprint for the third incarnation of one of the great Horatio Alger stories of the 20th century."[10]

Bollenbach warned Bill time and again that once the split was announced, the bond traders would probably set the dogs loose on him. In the end, "It was worse than Bill expected," Bollenbach observed. "In fact, it was even worse than I expected."

The first hit occurred on the day of the announcement. Moody's Investor Service immediately downgraded Marriott bonds from "investment grade" to what the industry refers to as "junk" status. Bond traders panicked and began selling. The value of the bonds in the resale market dropped from 110 percent of their original sale price the previous Friday to 80 percent on Monday. Marriott had plenty of money to pay the principal and interest promised to the original bond buyers. No one was going to get less than they had bargained for, if they bought and held those bonds to maturity. But for those who had purchased the Marriott bonds hoping to resell them for a profit in the secondary market, their bubble had burst in a big way that day.

The first two bondholder lawsuits against Marriott were filed in federal court in Baltimore a week after the announcement. This triggered a media pile-on like Bill had never known before or since. Some in the company began to jokingly refer to Project Chariot as "Chariot of Fire." *Newsday* financial columnist Allan Sloan wasted no time launching an attack. "The folks at Marriott Corp. go out of their way to act classy," he began. "The company's chairman, J. Willard Marriott Jr., is a pillar of the business establishment. The company has nice hotels and a nice, upscale image. But this oh-so-classy operation is trying to pull off an incredibly tacky deal to enrich the Marriott family and other stockholders at the expense of Marriott bondholders. This is the kind of thing you expect from financial wheeler-dealers. It's not the kind of fancy financial footwork you're supposed to get from mainstream types like Bill Marriott."[11]

In the financial media, terms such as *opportunistic, predatory, slick, brazen, fiasco,* and *disaster* were applied to the company's plan and to Bill personally. He bore the attacks with outward equanimity. "The 61-year-old chief executive of Marriott Corp. has endured gale-force contempt," the *Washington Post* observed. "Lawsuits against him and his Bethesda company have come whistling in like Scud missiles. One group of angry investors threatened to organize a boycott of the company's hotels. The verbal abuse has been nearly constant. 'Someone called me the scuzz of the earth last week,' Marriott noted, though he seemed more bored than annoyed by the hostility."[12]

The more savvy members of the financial press saw through the outrage to the nuts and bolts of the law. Marriott's only obligation was to pay the principal and interest promised in the bond contract. If a bondholder had hoped to make more money by reselling the bonds at a profit, that was not Marriott's responsibility. Marriott's obligation to its stockholders was paramount and very different from bondholders. Shareholders expect to trade up, and it was Marriott's job to run a healthy enough company that its shares continue to increase in value, but that isn't stated in writing. With bondholders, the company has a legal contract, called an indenture, that guarantees annual interest payback. In the case of the Marriott bond sale, the indenture was less restrictive, meaning the company had more leeway, but the bond buyers also got better interest rates.

At the December 3 board meeting, Arne Sorenson, of the law firm Latham & Watkins, briefed the board on eight lawsuits filed against Marriott in Baltimore's federal and circuit courts. He would represent Marriott in the suits and was confident about an eventual settlement. This marked the first appearance at Marriott of Sorenson, who was destined to become the company's third CEO and its first non-Marriott-family chief. No one in that meeting could have predicted such an unlikely turn of events.

The majority of the bondholders were represented in court by Goldman Sachs. A smaller, more hostile group was led by PPM America Inc., a subsidiary of a large British insurance company. In March 1993, Marriott and the Goldman Sachs group reached a settlement in which Marriott offered to pay bondholders one percentage point more in interest on their bonds.

That left a bad taste as far as board member Harry Vincent was concerned. "The bondholders extorted money from the company by insisting that we buy them off, which we did," he complained privately. The smaller PPM group refused to settle. Ironically, at the same time, the bonds in the secondary market had recovered in price nearly to their presplit level.

In July 1993, 85 percent of the stockholders voted in favor of the split as a "special dividend," giving them one share of each company for every Marriott share they currently owned. The following October 8, after the IRS finally ruled the dividend would be tax-free, Marriott split into the two companies. The increased shareholder value exceeded all expectations. Just before the split had been announced the year before, Marriott stock was trading at $17.12½ a share. The combined price of the two new Marriott companies on opening day was $33.37½ per share—a remarkable 95 percent increase in the otherwise sluggish market.

Clearly, the markets had rewarded Marriott for its big surprise, but the PPM lawsuit alleging fraud remained. Some even suggested that there was a greater expectation of probity from the bondholders because Bill was a Latter-day Saint, and that hurt him personally. But the dark cloud had a silver lining, in Bill's view, and that was his increasingly close association with the chief attorney for the defense, Arne (pronounced "Arnie") Sorenson.

Two years after the first suit was filed, Judge Alexander Harvey began the jury trial in the U.S. District Court of Maryland in Baltimore on September 26, 1994. At the heart of the case was the bondholders' accusation that Marriott had violated federal securities laws and defrauded the bondholders by failing to disclose the pending split of the company before the bonds were sold. The bondholders were claiming $18 million in actual losses and also asking punitive damages. To win, they had to prove that Marriott executives knew before the bond sales that they were going to separate the company.

Bill was called to the stand on October 4, the second week of the trial. In spite of the stress leading up to his testimony, he was cool and implacable. PPM's attorney Larry Kill tried to imply that the split had been concocted by the Marriott family so they could enrich themselves. "That benefited you and your family, did it not?" Kill asked.

"It benefited all 65,000 shareholders," Bill replied.

But, Kill said, the Marriott family alone had seen a $47-million gain in its stock in just one day—the day of the announcement. "I don't know what it was," Bill replied. "I never looked at it."

It was this kind of attack that most upset Bollenbach. Months after the split was announced, he told *Lodging* magazine: "The thing I regretted about this transaction is when people made personal criticisms of Bill, because they didn't have a way of understanding the man. . . . There was the criticism that this was some kind of financial maneuver to increase his wealth. This guy could care less about that. He started out following his father around to root beer stands and making hamburgers when he was nine years old and worked right through three heart attacks. This is his life. He's not going to sell his stock. From Bill's point of view, he's not going to sell his stock for $5 or $50. What's important to him is he's got a company that can grow, that he can provide job opportunities for his people and he can deliver good services."[13]

In his testimony, Bollenbach was equally dismissive when Kill asked him to defend the bonus Marriott paid him for devising and carrying out the split. He acknowledged that after the split he received a compensation package that included 1.5 million shares of stock to be doled out over five years. "It's likely to be a lot of money," Bollenbach said.

"About $6.4 million," Kill said.

"I hope it will be more," Bollenbach smiled, ruining Kill's attempt to shame him.

When Bill came off the stand, the message he left with the jury was straightforward: He didn't think about splitting the company until after the bond sale; he had no legal obligation to disclose the idea to bondholders or anyone else while it was a work in progress; and he had insisted the company do everything within its power to protect the bondholders and pay them back.

Even as he was harangued by Kill with charges of self-enrichment, Bill managed to slip something in that hurt PPM's case. The jury was not supposed to know that most of the bondholders, including PPM itself, had already sold their bonds for a profit before the trial began, which undercut their claims for damages. Bill quickly let the jury know this before Kill could cut him off.

In his closing statement, Sorenson asked, "What is this case about? It's about whether these large sophisticated institutional investors should be allowed to come into this court and get something they did not pay for."

While the jury was deliberating, Bill unexpectedly had to fly to

Salt Lake City with Donna to deliver a eulogy at the funeral of her father, Royal Garff. Donna's sister Joanne and her husband, Ray Hart, joined him in the hotel room as Bill prepared his remarks, and they recalled how distracting the pending jury verdict was to him. He paced the room, fearing the impact the verdict would have on his company's reputation and future. Bill said to Ray Hart, "Today, when this phone call comes, I may not have a Marriott hotel business. This thing may take us down."

Hart decided to leave the hotel room at one point to walk to the nearby temple. Part of tradition in Latter-day Saint temples is to conduct group prayers for those needing consolation or help. Hart put Bill's name on the daily prayer roll and returned to the hotel to tell him. "That's the only thing I could think of that I could do to help you," he told Bill. Within an hour, the phone rang.

After two years of legal wrangling, three weeks of trial, and fourteen hours of jury deliberation, the jurors sent a note to Judge Harvey. They were hopelessly deadlocked. Judge Harvey declared a mistrial.

Both sides asked the judge to decide the case himself rather than start a new trial. On January 25, 1995, Judge Harvey did just that. He dismissed the case against Marriott, saying the bondholders had not proved any of their claims. Rather than waste more money on legal fees, presuming PPM would try to appeal to a higher court, Marriott settled with PPM for a token $1.25 million on March 4, 1996.

One week after that final settlement, Arne Sorenson began his career at Marriott International. Bill had been so impressed with Sorenson that he had lobbied his trial lawyer for more than a year to work for the lodging company. Sorenson's surprising rise at Marriott began with him spending a few months in the General Counsel's office before moving to business development and then becoming CFO after only two years on the job. "He's such a quick study and mastered a number of things that people take decades to do in a few short years," Bill said. "I saw a bright future for him at Marriott."[14]

CHAPTER 24

PUTTIN' ON THE RITZ AND RENAISSANCE

At the same time as he was retooling his own company for future growth, Bill Marriott was doing the same for General Motors. He did this as an activist member of the board of directors that engineered a coup to save America's largest company.

Founded in the early 1900s, GM became the world's number-one auto manufacturer in the post–World War II years, when its American market share exceeded 50 percent. But GM sat on its success for two decades while its market share slowly diminished. The company seemed totally unprepared for the challenge of Japanese compact cars. In 1982, before Bill joined the GM board, he said in a speech that a key reason GM was sliding was that the company wasn't listening to its customers or employees. One GM board member, Ross Perot, resigned in frustration, saying that trying to change GM was like "teaching an elephant to tap-dance."[1]

When GM Chairman Roger Smith asked Bill to join the board in August 1989, Bill was both honored and intrigued. His son John summarized Bill's acceptance in this way: "He couldn't say no. My dad loves cars and this was a chance to see up close how America's biggest company worked—or didn't work, as the case turned out to be."

GM was not just an American behemoth; it was the world's largest manufacturing company, with 775,000 employees. In 1988, GM's sales reached $110 billion and included a record $4.9 billion profit. But a closer examination by Bill revealed systemic weaknesses. Most of that profit had been made by its nonauto businesses. Smith seemed relatively unconcerned about GM's declining U.S. auto sales, and nominated like-minded GM executive Robert Stempel to succeed him as chairman and CEO in 1990.

A trio of board members—Bill Marriott, former Procter & Gamble CEO John Smale, and former Secretary of Labor Ann McLaughlin—began meeting secretly to plot an insurrection. The trio carefully drew in other outside directors, and by the time the board met in April 1992, the revolutionaries were the majority. At that meeting, the board stripped Stempel of his chairmanship of the board's executive committee and put him on probation. The board then chose John F. "Jack" Smith, Jr., as the new president. Smith had been instrumental in studying and borrowing Japanese auto-manufacturing practices and applying them to GM's European operations, putting them on an increasingly profitable upswing.

Stempel failed to use his probationary period well. Bill summarized: "We told Bob Stempel we didn't think he had a good team of managers. He defended his team and was unwilling to make any hard choices. No matter how hard we pleaded and confronted him, he refused to act. He ended up going down with his team. In eighty years, GM had never fired a chairman, but we fired Bob Stempel because it was necessary to save GM."

Not only did they fire Stempel, but the board voted in director Smale as the new chairman, stunning the business world with the unprecedented election of a non-GM executive as chairman. The *New York Times* predicted the board's revolutionary action would have serious "reverberations far beyond Detroit. [This] awakening of the once sleepy G.M. board will redefine the cozy relationship that often exists between the nation's top executives and the hand-picked members of their boards." The *Washington Post* agreed, quoting an expert: "When the chairman of the largest industrial company in the world gets fired for nonperformance, that reverberates through every executive suite in the country."[2]

With Stempel out, Jack Smith was promoted from president to CEO. He radically shook up the company, focusing on the core auto business and decentralizing GM's management structure to encourage innovation. For the first time in four years, GM made a profit ($2.5 billion) in 1993. Smith continued the company's upward trajectory for the next decade, and Bill remained on the board at Smith's request until 2002.

The GM experience was additional evidence to Bill that complacency was the archenemy of success. "Success breeds failure unless deliberate steps are taken to avoid it. We know that the results of not changing are continual decline and eventual disappearance from the marketplace," Bill said in one speech.[3] He was testing that principle as his new company, Marriott International (MI), began business in October 1993. With the separation from the "original" company (re-titled Host Marriott), Bill knew his employees were nervous and unsettled, wondering what their future would be. So he made the rounds of the company with a series of pep talks.

Released from the shackles of real-estate ownership, which was now with Host Marriott, Bill envisioned unparalleled growth for MI with assistance from hotel conversions and franchising. It had taken him thirty-nine years to expand from the company's first hotel to its 1,000th. When the 1,000th hotel opened in Lihue, Kauai, in 1995, Bill said he was intent on doubling that number over the next five years; "2,000 by 2000" became MI's goal, even though many thought he was reaching too far.

Bill still believed that quality was more important than quantity, so he instituted a companywide TQM (Total Quality Management) program and stuck to its guiding principles into the new millennium.

When it came to serving customers, Marriott conducted continuous guest surveys, which produced surprising results.

"We have always assumed that being friendly and nice was a major competitive advantage, but business travelers say 'no,'" he explained in one speech. "Of course, we know that if we weren't nice, they wouldn't come back. But nice is not enough for our core business customers." Bill summarized the opinion of business travelers: "We are not travelers excited about being away from home. We are on the road to get the job done so treat us that way. If we needed 'nice,' we'd send our mothers. And our needs are changing rapidly, so if you want our business, you'd better change fast too."[4]

Critical among those changes were registration improvements. Bill had opened Marriott's worldwide reservation center in Omaha in 1971, which became the largest single-site reservation operation in U.S. hotel history. In 1990, Marriott opened a second reservation center in Salt Lake City. Along the way, the company constantly invested in more efficient computer programs for automated reservations.

Over the years, Bill found that the majority of guest complaints involved the speed of checkin and checkout. With the latter, Marriott was the pioneer of express checkout in the 1980s. "We found that slow checkout was a major problem, so we put the bill under the door at four a.m. When they check out, all they have to do is sign the bill and hand it to a clerk. Complaints were cut in half," Bill said.

In 1991, the company instituted the "First Ten" program to speed up check-in as well. "A customer's first ten minutes at a hotel set the tone for their entire visit," Bill explained. "Nobody likes to wait in line, especially hotel guests who have been in lines for airplanes and rental cars all day. They don't like to be handed off from the doorman to a bellman to a busy front desk clerk and back to a bellman. With 'First Ten,' we preregistered guests through their credit cards when they made their reservation, and then met them at the front door with their key." Just as with express checkout, this Marriott preregistration practice hailed by the *New York Times* soon became an industry standard.[5]

In the 1990s, no one exemplified Marriott service better than Albert "Smitty" Smith, the Atlanta Marriott Marquis concierge captain. He specialized in catering to sports teams, making them loyal Marriott customers. "Smitty knows every coach and player and what they like, even a sportscaster who wanted his English muffins burned black," Bill explained. His biggest challenge came when a Hilton opened up nearby, offering half-price rates and causing many sports teams to switch hotels. "But whenever a team stayed at the Hilton, Smitty would find out when the team was arriving. Then he would wait in the lobby of the Hilton for the team's arrival."

Once, Smitty greeted the Dodgers and their manager Tommy Lasorda when they arrived at the competitor hotel. "Smitty, it's great to see you—do you work for Hilton now?" Lasorda queried.

"No, Coach," Smitty replied, "I'm still at the Marriott, but I just wanted to come over and welcome you to Atlanta. Also, I know that after every game you order a double cheeseburger, onion rings, and strawberry milkshake. Since you have a game tonight, it could go into extra innings, and room service closes at eleven p.m. at the Hilton. So I'm going to bring up your special order from the Marriott."

Taken aback, Lasorda asked, "That's awful nice, Smitty, but why would you do such a thing?"

"Well, Coach, because I want you to know that even though you can't afford to stay at the Marriott anymore, we still love you!"

Bill reported that "with this attitude, Smitty was able to bring every single sports team back to the Marriott because he cared!"

Along the way, the veteran bellman was promoted to concierge, where he became so appreciated by Atlanta's leading lights that they made sure when the International Olympic Committee (IOC) visited Atlanta in 1987, they stayed at the Marriott Marquis and experienced the Smitty touch. When Atlanta won the bid for the centennial

Olympics, the *Atlanta Journal* and even IOC President Juan Antonio Samaranch acknowledged that Smitty was second only to the Atlanta Olympic Committee in closing the deal with the IOC. And Samaranch designated the Marriott Marquis the official IOC host hotel.[6]

That may have also had something to do with the "lucky chestnut" talisman Samaranch carried around with him. During a stay at the hotel, Samaranch called the manager frantically to say that he thought he had left the chestnut on his room-service tray. The director of room service climbed into the kitchen dumpster to look for it—a task made more difficult by the fact that he didn't know what a chestnut looked like. He found it and returned it to the grateful Samaranch. Then came another call the next morning. He had left the chestnut on the room-service tray again. So, again, the manager went dumpster diving to retrieve it. Bill told the story to an employee conference and concluded, "To our customers, let me say, 'We may not be able to pull your chestnuts out of the fire, but we will go into the dumpster for you!' Every time."[7]

As Bill moved aggressively toward the goal of 2,000 MI hotels by the year 2000, he worked hand in hand with Host Marriott's CEO, Steve Bollenbach. Though he was a first-time CEO, the 52-year-old Bollenbach did not always dance to Bill's tune, but they were in agreement more often than they disagreed.

Any serious criticism of Bollenbach as architect of the controversial Marriott corporation split was forgotten after he had been on the job only a year. Shareholders and security analysts loved him. One calculated that if he was a company, and a shareholder invested in him in 1982 when he worked for Marriott the first time, then followed him from job to job until he became CEO of Host, the "Bollenbach stock" would have increased 1,300 percent in just a decade.[8]

Host Marriott necessarily developed a different personality from Marriott International. It had less bureaucracy, by virtue of fewer people, and those people made quicker decisions. The biggest disagreement Bollenbach had with Bill was about Host's potential acquisition of Circus Circus, the Las Vegas casino company. Bollenbach had solid experience with gaming operations. When he was CFO at Holiday Inn, he had expanded their Harrah's gambling empire. He raised the Circus Circus proposal with Bill, who said he wanted to think about it for a couple of days and discuss it with his brother. A few days passed, and he met with Bollenbach again.

"I've thought a lot about this, and I understand that it's a good deal," Bill said. "You're the CEO of Host, so if you want to do it, you should go ahead and do it." Then the other shoe dropped: "But if you do go ahead, I will resign [as a director of Host] and sell my stock. And so will my brother."

Bollenbach was not caught entirely by surprise. He knew Bill had avoided casino operations at all his hotels except when he had been required to include them in partnerships with governments, as in Egypt. "Since I was the CEO of Host," he said, "I had to consider, 'Would we be better served being in the gaming business but losing the close affiliation with Marriott International?' There was no question it was more important to have that connection with Marriott International. So we passed up the deal. I respected that Bill had considered it seriously and was prepared to let it happen—he just wouldn't personally be a part of it."

A bigger deal, which Bill easily approved in 1995, was the spin-off of the terminal and thruway business from Host Marriott. Bollenbach engineered the restructuring with the same deftness he had applied to the Host-MI split. The $1-billion food-service and concessions business had been an odd fit for Host; it was added only in an attempt to appease bondholders. As it turned out, it didn't matter to the stockholders, so it was again apparent to both Bill and Bollenbach that if they spun it off, the predicted stock value of the two companies would once again be greater than its value with Host Marriott alone.

Thus was created a new, independent entity known as Host

Marriott Services (HMS), with Bill Shaw as chairman of the board. In less than a year, the combined stock value of Host Marriott and HMS was, indeed, greater than if it had not been spun off. And Host Marriott was finally the exclusive hotel-owning real-estate company first envisioned.

When Bollenbach became CEO of Host Marriott, there was casual betting at Marriott headquarters about how long he would stay. The biggest money was on five years, when his stock options would vest and make him quite wealthy. To his own surprise, the restless Bollenbach didn't even make it two years.

In 1995, Disney's Michael Eisner called and proposed that Bollenbach become the troubled company's CFO, and he accepted. Bill wished Bollenbach well publicly, but privately predicted that he wouldn't stick around at Disney for long. After ten impressive months on the job, during which he engineered the $19-billion acquisition of Capital Cities/ABC Inc., Bollenbach accepted another offer he couldn't refuse. Barron Hilton asked him to become the hotel company's first non-Hilton CEO, where he stayed for a decade.

• • •

One of the little-known facts about the Marriott hotel empire is that the Ritz-Carlton chain is a highly profitable and integral part of it. The company's 1995 Ritz acquisition coup happened because Bill had a bright star—Jim Sullivan—who was able to seize the opportunity when the perfect timing arrived, and who possessed the extraordinary skills to pull off the complex deal.

Swiss hotelier César Ritz founded the chain in the 1890s, most notably with the Paris Ritz and a Carlton as well as a Ritz hotel in London. He was known as "the king of hoteliers and hotelier to kings." Among the famous people who preferred his hotels was Ernest Hemingway, who declared: "When I dream of afterlife in heaven, the action always takes place in the Paris Ritz." By the time Irving Berlin penned his famous song "Puttin' on the Ritz," the word *ritzy* had become an adjective meaning fashionable, luxurious, or elegant.

In 1983, restaurateur William B. Johnson bought the Ritz-Carlton Boston, which included rights to the name in North America. Johnson founded The Ritz-Carlton Hotel Company and put his trademark on thirty-one hotels. But in late 1994, he was in serious financial trouble. Former Marriott executive Fred Malek tried to put together a consortium of investors to buy out Johnson, but he failed.

Meanwhile, acquisition of Ritz-Carlton wasn't in the realm of possibilities for Bill or Jim Sullivan, Marriott's vice president of Mergers, Acquisitions and Development. Jim was temporarily sidelined with tremendous grief over the back-to-back deaths of his oldest daughter, Patricia, and his father.

Though he was still on leave, Sullivan decided to go ahead with his friendly quarterly get-together with former Marriott executive Fred Malek, who had provided an invaluable assist with Marriott's earlier Residence Inn acquisition. Of that fateful February 1995 lunch, Sullivan recalled: "We spent a very nice two hours talking about my family, about his business and any deals that might be going on. I was putting my coat on when he said, 'By the way, you're not interested in Ritz-Carlton, are you?' I took my coat off and said, 'I've tried to buy that one or two times, but Bill Johnson won't even talk to me.' Fred smiled and said, 'Well, he needs financial help now.'"

Ritz-Carlton had been hammered by the 1990–91 recession, and Johnson had a $60-million debt coming due. Sullivan jumped on the information. Without telling Bill, he flew to Atlanta on a Sunday to have dinner with Johnson, who candidly revealed that if he didn't get $60 million by Friday, the Ritz-Carlton Company would be in default. By the end of the meal, the two had a verbal agreement for a Marriott acquisition that would include paying the debt.

Sullivan called Bill at home that night. "I'm in Atlanta, and I

Marriott acquired Ritz-Carlton beginning in 1995.

just shook hands with Bill Johnson to buy the Ritz-Carlton Hotel Company."

"What?" Bill came back.

Sullivan outlined the terms, and Bill promised to put thirty Marriott people on the first flight to Atlanta Monday to make it happen in a deal that would include Malek and his group of investors. The negotiations leaked to the press, and Marriott stock jumped.

"This is one of the most significant developments in the hotel industry in the last decade," said Joseph J. Doyle, a market analyst. "You have the best hotel management company in the world buying what is arguably the classiest luxury brand in the world." Added a Kidder, Peabody & Co. analyst who followed Marriott: "You're combining Marriott Corp., which is known for lean management and profitability, with Ritz, a company that is known for excellent service—but not for making money. When you put the two together, you potentially come out with one chain that has both exceptional quality and profitability."[9]

Marriott bought 49 percent of the Ritz-Carlton management company, with an option to buy the remaining 51 percent in three years.

One problem was that four Ritz-Carltons—in New York City, Houston, Aspen, and Washington, D.C.—were owned by Saudi Sheik Abdul Aziz al-Ibraham, brother-in-law of King Fahd, who was scrimping on funds for repair and upgrade. Worse, Aziz had filed a $250-million suit in the U.S. District Court in Manhattan against Ritz-Carlton, alleging mismanagement. Although Marriott was still just a minority owner, Bill wanted the suit settled as soon as possible.

For that he turned to litigator Rick Hoffman. It was clear early on that Judge John S. Martin was unhappy with the sheik. At one hearing, Martin realized the sheik in the court was not even Aziz. "Wait a minute, you're not the sheik I subpoenaed?" the judge demanded. "No, your honor, he's in Saudi Arabia. He's very busy." According to Sullivan, "The judge went ballistic. He said, 'What am I? Chocolate chips? *I'm* busy. The next time I send a subpoena, you have that son of a bitch in my court or we'll extradite him and put him in jail!'"

The secret to winning the case turned out to be simple: attorney Hoffman advised Bill that Aziz's four hotels were not good ones, and the Ritz-Carlton brand would be better off without them. Ritz-Carlton declared the sheik to be in breach of contract because of delinquent fee payments. At midnight on Friday, August 1, 1997, a note was placed under the door of every guest in those hotels informing them that they were no longer staying at a Ritz. Cancellations poured in, particularly from brides-to-be who had wanted to be married at the Ritz. Without the name, it was just another hotel.

Sullivan and Hoffman were also the point men for negotiations with Egyptian businessman Mohamed al-Fayed for better access to the Ritz name. Fayed owned the Paris Ritz, which included ownership of the Ritz name, and Marriott wanted a long-term license on the name outside North America. Fayed's outsized ego got in the way of negotiations. To sweeten the deal, Sullivan proposed that Marriott could manage the hotel Fayed was building in London. But Fayed wanted Marriott to build the hotel, pay him £50 million, and manage it for free. "Why would we ever do something like that?" Sullivan sputtered. "Because then you could tell the world you have me as your partner," Fayed responded.

The stalemate continued until the tragedy that rocked the world. Fayed's son Dodi and Princess Diana died in a car crash on August 31, 1997, when they sped away from the Paris Ritz to escape the paparazzi. The subdued Mohamed al-Fayed soon let Sullivan know that he would come to terms with Marriott if Bill himself flew to Paris to sign the deal. When Bill and Sullivan arrived at the Paris Ritz, Fayed announced that he had changed his mind again. Patience paid off, though, and Hoffman was later able to negotiate favorable terms for international Ritz trademark rights.

In Bill's view, "The determination to acquire the Ritz-Carlton management company was probably the quickest major decision that we ever made, but it was one of the best. We had been thinking about getting into the luxury tier of lodging beyond our own JW Marriott hotels, and this opportunity was right on target."

•   •   •

On a Tuesday in February 1996, Bill received a call he never expected to get. A producer at the *60 Minutes* TV show wanted to schedule an interview with their grand inquisitor Mike Wallace to talk about Bill's religious beliefs as part of a larger segment on The Church of Jesus Christ of Latter-day Saints. Bill had two days to prepare.

Wallace's reputation was formidable. At seventy-seven years old, he was "the king of TV's ambush interviews." No American television newsman was more feared. The *New York Times* called him "the scourge of *60 Minutes*." He flame-broiled presidents, badgered world leaders, and interrogated both criminals and CEOs with equal fervor. In fact, a prosperous cottage industry of well-paid public-relations experts had expanded to offer high-priced training programs for corporate chiefs about to face "Mean Mike" Wallace.

For more than two decades, there were two "white whales" that Wallace tried to harpoon for an interview—the Pope and the President of The Church of Jesus Christ of Latter-day Saints. The men filling those positions had repeatedly refused his requests for years, until, in 1995, Gordon B. Hinckley became the fifteenth President of the Church.

President Hinckley knew there was no greater opportunity—or risk—than appearing on *60 Minutes,* the most-watched television show in America. In late 1995, he turned the tables and invited Wallace to meet him for a lunch at New York's Harvard Club to discuss a possible interview. Wallace wrote that he was "totally unprepared for a cordial, even a sunny greeting. . . . His bespectacled eyes literally twinkled as he good-naturedly allowed that it sounded like an appealing notion [to appear on *60 Minutes*]."[10]

If President Hinckley had agreed, Bill could hardly refuse to be part of that segment. He would not have worried so much during the two days between the request and his own interview if it had been about the hotel business. But the focus of the interview was his faith. "I had no time to prepare," he recalled. "Obviously, they didn't send the questions in advance. I could only get on my knees and pray to my Father in Heaven and ask for His guidance."

When Bill arrived at his office, where the interview was to take place, it had been turned upside down by the film crew. Furniture was pushed aside. Wallace had claimed Bill's comfortable desk chair, and Bill was directed to a hard, straight-back chair and wired with a microphone. Still, when the interview began, an unexpected peace settled over him.

> WALLACE: Why does the church come first in your life? Is it God, is it Jesus, is it Gordon B. Hinckley—what is it?
>
> MR. MARRIOTT: It is our strong belief that we know why we're here, we know where we came from,

and we know where we are going. We are taught from a very early age to develop a strong belief and strong testimony of the divinity of our church.

WALLACE: What is there in Mormonism that gives Mormons the desire, the willingness to work hard and develop that kind of a reputation?

MR. MARRIOTT: We realize we are on the earth to perfect ourselves as much we can, to develop our talents, to improve and to make something of ourselves. My father . . . had demanding church assignments when he was building his business from nothing. The church always came first in his life and it comes first in mine. Families and church are our priorities.

WALLACE: Young Joseph Smith—fourteen years old—upstate New York and God and Jesus come to see him? Do you believe that?

MR. MARRIOTT: Yes!

WALLACE: Why did they choose him and what did they say?

MR. MARRIOTT: The Father said, "This is my son, hear him." The Savior told him that in answer to his prayer looking for the right church that he should join none of the churches on the earth but that things would be revealed to him in which he would be involved in reestablishing the church of Jesus Christ on this earth.

And so it went for forty-five minutes. Though his questions were tough and incisive, Wallace was always respectful. As the cameras were packed away, Wallace told Bill he had his own questions about an afterlife. He told Bill that he never had gotten over the grief of losing his oldest son, Peter, who had fallen to his death during a hike in Greece thirty-four years earlier. "I don't know where he is and I don't know if I'll ever see him again. I wish I had your faith that I would see him again."

The biggest problem in agreeing to a *60 Minutes* interview was that the interviewee had no control over how the footage would be edited. The producers could make anyone look like a saint or a fool. The show aired on Easter Sunday evening, April 7. As the Marriotts and thirty-five million other Americans gathered around their televisions, they watched President Hinckley deftly handle Wallace's questions. Then, to Bill's delight, *60 Minutes* aired his own testimony about Joseph Smith after this Wallace voice-over introduction: "You'd expect the head of the church to believe it, but so does Bill Marriott, chief of the Marriott hotel chain, a hardheaded businessman, and he's a Mormon."

The most potentially uncomfortable question Wallace asked Bill was about his underwear. Temple-worthy Latter-day Saints wear special undergarments to remind them of their covenants with God, much in the manner of orthodox Jews, whose knotted tassels remind them of God's commandments.

> WALLACE (Voice-over): Mormons know that some outsiders think they are weird. Why? Well, for one thing, devout Mormons wear sacred undergarments for protection from harm—cotton undershirts with undershorts that reach to their knees.
>
> (Question) Do you wear the sacred undergarments?
>
> MR. MARRIOTT: Yes, I do. And I can tell you, they do protect you from harm.
>
> WALLACE: Really?
>
> MR. MARRIOTT: I was in a very serious boat accident. The boat was on fire. I was on fire. I was burned. My pants were burned right off me. I was not burned above my knee. Where the garment was, I was not burned.

WALLACE: And you believe it was the sacred undergarments?

MR. MARRIOTT: Yes, I do, particularly on my legs because my—my pants were gone. My undergarments were not singed.

When Bill offered those unhesitant comments during the interview, he felt this was fulfillment of the blessing he had been given after the accident, which said he had been preserved "for a wise purpose." Of course, there were *many* purposes for Bill's continued life, including his service in the Church and his leadership of his family and company. But when Wallace asked him that question in the interview, he felt that the purpose had been fulfilled. The terrible accident had allowed him to testify on national television about the tender mercies of God and the validity of the priesthood of his church.

Positive reaction poured in to Bill and the Church after the show aired. Some responses were moving, including a letter sent to a Church leader from an ex-Mormon who was prompted in part by "the testimony of Bill Marriott on *60 Minutes*" to rejoin the Church.[11]

At the following October general conference of the Church, President Hinckley publicly thanked Bill and the two other prominent Latter-day Saints, Senator Orrin Hatch and NFL quarterback Steve Young, who had also appeared on the *60 Minutes* program. President Hinckley concluded it had been a great risk for all of them and was not "an enjoyable experience" for any one of them. But, "as Paul said to Festus and Agrippa, 'This thing [the Christian church] was not done in a corner' (Acts 26:26). We have something that this world needs to hear about, and these interviews afford an opportunity to give voice to that."[12]

• • •

In the summer of 1992, Bill's son-in-law Ron Harrison was promoted to a headquarters position as vice president of financial planning and analysis. With the launch of the new Marriott International in late 1993, Bill asked Ron to focus on the long view for the company. Ron formed two competing teams of the company's best and brightest to come up with the first drafts of Marriott's future strategy. When the Red and Blue teams turned in their assessments, Ron convened the "Plum Team" to merge their best ideas.

In late 1994, he presented the sobering Plum Team report to Bill and other executives. Their conclusion was that the company was not prepared for the future. The team identified trends that required immediate attention, highlighting the need for Marriott International to become truly international. The formerly Communist Eastern Bloc of Europe was poised to embrace the free market. And the biggest emerging markets in the world were China, South Africa, Indochina, Mexico, India, Poland, Brazil, Argentina, South Korea, and Turkey. However, according to the report, MI may have had *international* in its name, but it was only "a domestic company, doing business internationally with some of its lodging products. New businesses are always conceived and developed domestically. [Our] products and services are not positioned where future economic growth will occur."[13]

The Plum Team's conclusions were no surprise to Bill. The truth was that few at Marriott were comfortable with going global. They didn't have the expertise in different cultures and languages. Relatively minor capital had been put into hotels in Mexico, Europe, the Middle East, and Hong Kong. When Jim Sullivan joined Marriott in 1991 as chief of International Development, he thought the title was almost laughable. The company was struggling to survive; there wasn't any money for hotels abroad. Hence, in 1992, he counted it a major victory when the strong relationship he and Bill developed with the Canadian Scott's Hospitality led to a major initiative in the United Kingdom. In short order, Scott's Hospitality opened ten Courtyard by Marriott hotels in the U.K.; most of them were converted from Holiday Inns.

Several years later, Sullivan returned from a London lodging conference with an even better prospect. He had connected with David Thomas of the diverse British hospitality company Whitbread, and they had talked well into the night about the potential of a Whitbread-Marriott alliance. Whitbread had been founded as a London brewery in 1742 and was a multibillion-dollar company with pubs, restaurants, budget hotels, and leisure operations. Whitbread then bought out Scott's Hospitality's Marriott franchise and signed a deal in 1995 to develop dozens of Marriott hotels in the U.K.[14]

In a speech to assembled Whitbread executives, Bill noted that David Thomas "is fond of pointing out that the heritage of Whitbread predates the U.S. Declaration of Independence, while the heritage of Marriott is just short of seventy years—but we do share common values. Among these are strong family involvement, attention to the bottom line, and a commitment to our customers, our associates, and outstanding quality."[15]

The Whitbread alliance was a good start for Marriott's globalization efforts, but it wasn't where the company most needed to go.

Once the Plum Team finished its work, Ron Harrison led another group, the Jade Team, to focus on opportunities in the Far East. The team's most important conclusion was that Marriott must acquire management contracts for an already-established Asian hotel chain to jumpstart its growth there. Sullivan and Bill agreed and felt the best acquisition would be the Renaissance Hotel Group (RHG), owned by the ultrawealthy Cheng family of Hong Kong. Henry Cheng had divided his hotel empire into two companies, much as Marriott had—a real-estate holding company and a separate management company (RHG).

Marriott approached the Chengs about a possible merger with the management company in mid-1996, but they shut the door firmly in Sullivan's face. They were not for sale. Then, in late December, Henry Cheng changed his mind. He secretly engaged in negotiations with a new chain called Doubletree. On New Year's Day 1997, Bill was reading the business section of the *New York Times* when he came upon the unexpected news on page 61 that Doubletree and RHG were making a deal. He assigned Arne Sorenson, now senior vice president of business development, to see if Marriott could make a better one.

And so, Sorenson became the point man in the acquisition, which was privately considered to have less than a 40 percent chance of succeeding. But Arne went all out; he had been with Marriott only nine months, and this was a major opportunity to prove that Bill's faith in the former litigator was justified. Even so, it was stunning that Arne pulled off the biggest deal in the company's history in just forty-nine days.

The RHG board was required to review Marriott's offer in early January because they were a public company and the shareholders had not yet voted on the Doubletree deal. As it turned out, not only did Marriott outbid Doubletree, but so did Starwood and Wyndham hotel groups. Bass, the British parent of Holiday Inn, was making inquiries as well.[16] At a critical point in late January, Arne advised Bill that the pair should meet with Cheng in Hong Kong in order to advance negotiations. Bill's Chinese-speaking son-in-law, Ron Harrison, was recruited to provide assistance on the trip.[17]

The trio met Dr. Henry K.S. Cheng in his unostentatious high-rise office. The usually taciturn forty-nine-year-old Henry was welcoming but not warm at first. "He was kind of quiet, even though he was personable. But considering his business was worth billions and he was such a big player in Hong Kong, he didn't carry himself with much arrogance," Sorenson recalled.

The meeting turned decidedly friendly when Bill reviewed the similarities between their company's histories and cultures. Bill pointed out that both he and Henry were the sons of founders. Both of them, though, had changed the origin of the companies into more profitable enterprises—in Bill's case, from Hot Shoppes restaurants to hotels, and in Henry's, from jewelry shops to hotel and infrastructure development.

Bill scored important points in the overseas meeting, and then it was up to Arne to carry the ball back in America. Normally, the seller is enthusiastic about sharing company information with a prospective buyer, but with an offer already on the table, Henry told Arne, "Here's what we're going to show you. It's not all you asked for, but if you're interested, make a proposal by [a certain date]."

Sorenson's best case was that Marriott would be much better at managing the Renaissance group hotels than Henry would—or any of the competing bidders. The *average* occupancy of a Marriott-run hotel was then 78 percent, while RHG could only achieve a 67 percent occupancy. In addition, Arne said the strategic alliance for the future would be invaluable with Cheng to advise MI on future expansion in Asia. With Bill's consent, he invited Henry to join the Marriott board, and the offer proved as pleasing to Cheng as it was unexpected.

When Arne and Henry sat down for a third meeting—this time in Palm Springs, California, on Monday, February 17—Cheng told him he believed RHG and Marriott were "a perfect fit." But he insisted Marriott increase its $29 per share offer to $30 a share. Arne thought it was too high, and, in any event, he had no authority to proceed further. A bit disconsolate, he drove back to his Renaissance hotel room in Los Angeles and called Bill with the bad news.

After Arne briefed the CEO, Bill asked, "What do you think we should do, Arne?"

"I think we should go to $29.50 but no further. I've worked hard on this deal, but I'm ready to walk away," Sorenson responded.

There was a notable pause and then a response that Arne has not forgotten: "You know, Arne," Bill said, "this is a billion-dollar deal, so the only difference between $29.50 and $30 is $15 million. Why do you want to risk it for 50 cents? Give him 30 bucks a share. Let's get this deal done!"

Arne quickly called Henry at Palm Springs. "All right, 30 bucks a share." Henry's one-word response was about as enthusiastic as Arne ever heard from him: "Okay!"

Bill called an emergency board meeting at 3:30 p.m. EST, which was 12:30 p.m. in California. All nine board members were located and connected by conference call to vote on three matters: a $30-per-share cash tender offer for RHG stock, an increase to MI's bank credit line to $1.9 billion to help pay for the deal, and a seat on the board for Dr. Cheng. All three proposals were unanimously approved, and, after Doubletree declined to raise its bid, the Renaissance-Marriott deal was signed that afternoon.

The next day, Tuesday, February 18, Bill was grinning from ear to ear as he announced the $947-million deal to a packed press conference. "It's a big price," he laughed, but it was also a very big boost for Marriott. The company's management portfolio was expanded by 150 hotels and three new brands—Renaissance, New World, and Ramada International. "With the addition of these outstanding brands, we will immediately reach customers in 40 new markets including Russia, China, Japan, India, Italy and Turkey. We will more than double our presence outside of the United States."[18]

Wall Street analysts were unanimous: RHG was an ideal marriage for Marriott. Heavy trading in the market pushed the Marriott stock price ever upward.

The day after the Marriott-Renaissance announcement, China's longtime Communist leader Deng Xiaoping died. Four months later, on July 1, 1997, the long-awaited event known as "the Handover" occurred: Hong Kong officially became part of China again. Though "the Handover" had been feared by market analysts for years, it was fairly uneventful. There was no Chinese nationalization of any Hong Kong business. There were no new regulations and no rapacious new taxation by the Chinese government. At the same time, China itself began expanding its adjacent mainland zones of Western-style free trade.

The prospect of enormous future growth for Marriott International was thus insured. As Bill declared without a hint of hyperbole or refutation at the press conference: "We are now a *global* hotel company."

CHAPTER 25

YOU'D BETTER
BE RUNNING

Bill's father had long dreamed of going on an African safari, partly because of the early 1960s encouragement of friend and former Eisenhower administration budget chief Maurice Stans. The friends finally made firm plans for a 1966 safari, only to have J.W. change his mind—deciding to take Allie to the Holy Land instead. A second safari plan was also canceled, and J.W. never went. But, what the father was not able to do, the son did.

Bill's family was growing, and he realized he needed to find a place to "get away from it all" and take the whole family. He came up with a plan for the safari in Africa about which his father had once dreamed.

Because of Stephen's health and disabilities, he and his family had to decline, but the rest of the family was enthusiastic about the prospect. Debbie and Ron Harrison joined the group with their five children; John and Angie joined with their three; and newlyweds David and Carrie completed the group. The clan met up in Nairobi, Kenya, spending the first night at the famous Norfolk Hotel, which had hosted Ernest Hemingway, Teddy Roosevelt, and other notables. The next day, a private charter plane flew them to Lewa Downs in Kenya's Northern Frontier District, and the safari was on.

The most exciting thirty minutes of the trip—at least for Bill and the boys—occurred as they watched a thin female cheetah with two hungry cubs hunt a gazelle. As John recorded in his trip journal, "The chase only lasted about 10 seconds as she ran, weaved, and pounced on her prey, which would be enough food for her and her cubs for the next few days. She carried the gazelle to a nearby tree. We sat and watched—some in amazement, others in a bit of disgust—as the dead animal was slowly devoured by the cats. Interestingly, she showed the cubs how to move the stomach to the side so as not to open it and create a smell that would attract other animals."[1]

Bill saw a metaphor in the hunt: "Every morning in Africa, a gazelle wakes up. It knows it must run faster than the fastest lion or it will be killed. Every morning a lion wakes up. It knows it must outrun the slowest gazelle or it will starve to death. It doesn't matter whether you are a lion or a gazelle; when the sun comes up, you'd better be running."

Besides family retreats, Bill also found rare respite in his car collection, which began with a Lamborghini.

In 1967, while in Rome to acquire a European catering business, Bill dropped in at a Lamborghini dealership, where a salesman convinced him to take a ride in the demonstrator Miura model. It was one of only three handmade prototypes Lamborghini produced, and it had been driven 1,000 miles. Bill hung onto his seat while the car raced through the capital's narrow and winding streets at eighty miles an hour. He was sold. Because it was used and a prototype, Bill got it at a bargain price of $12,000. Only 761 Miuras were ever produced, so, as time went on, Bill's Miura, which became the oldest surviving model, increased exponentially in value.[2] Bill kept the car at Camelback Inn for many years and finally sold it to John.

The Lamborghini Miura was the first collectible car Bill ever purchased, and it was another decade before he bought a second one, which he did with an eye to delighting his father. During World War II, J.W. had driven his family around in one of the first automatic transmission vehicles, a '41 Cadillac 60. As they rode around, young

Bill often heard his father complain that he should have bought the top-of-the-line 60S or "Special," which had a glass divider between the front and back seats, almost like a limousine. In 1979, Bill found one, bought it on the spot for $8,000, and drove to White Post Restorations in Virginia for a makeover.

Mechanic Skip Hurt recognized junk when he saw it. "I wanted very badly to tell Mr. Marriott, 'You don't want to restore this car,'" but the owner of the shop intervened, and the work went ahead. Over the next year, Bill enjoyed going out to White Post on weekends to check on the restoration progress. He and Hurt became good friends.

Before the Cadillac project was done, Bill read that a 1936 Mercedes Benz 500K Roadster had sold at auction in Los Angeles for $400,000, making it the most expensive passenger car in the world. He hunted for a similar one, locating a 1934 500K in a barn in Cologne, Germany. For $155,000, Bill purchased the unique car, which had been owned in the 1930s by Hitler's race-car driver Manfred von Brauchitsch. Word of the purchase price and the restoration that followed stirred great excitement among auto collectors across America.

Meanwhile, the restoration of the Cadillac Special was finished, and Bill proudly drove the car to J.W.'s house to show it off and to give it to him as a present. But J.W. had recently bought a new Cadillac Seville. He took one look at the vintage car in the driveway and said, "What the hell is that?"

"That's the 60 Special you always wanted. It's yours," Bill said.

J.W. said nothing and closed the front door, so Bill drove the Cadillac home. Soon after, it won its first auto show in Winchester, Virginia, and Bill's pride of ownership was renewed.

When restoration of the $155,000 Mercedes was finished, it easily won its first national Concours d'Elegance at Pebble Beach, California, with judges including famous photographer Ansel Adams. The cost of restoration totaled $228,000. The mechanic, Skip, felt his boss at White Post had charged too much, so he quit. When Bill found out about the principled decision, he offered Skip a job to be his mechanic and caretaker at the New Hampshire summer home. Bill never blamed White Post. He could afford to be gracious, since he ended up with an excellent mechanic and lifetime friend, not to mention a beautifully restored '34 Mercedes with a value reaching nearly $3 million.[3]

Bill's fascination with cars is a family trait—one that nearly killed his son David. In the predawn hours of a frigid winter morning in 1993, David "borrowed" his father's Ferrari Testarossa for a quick spin. The joyride ended when he lost control of the car going more than 100 miles an hour on a wet curve in the road and slid sideways into a concrete pylon. It was a wake-up call for the nineteen-year-old, who had struggled with school and gravitated toward a crowd of fast friends and fast cars.

The red Ferrari was a late-model vehicle, not one of Bill's museum pieces. An ambulance took David to the hospital, where John quickly joined him. David had been diagnosed with a broken clavicle. When Bill and Donna, who had been out of town, were unexpectedly met by John at the airport, they knew something was wrong. "What did David do now?" Bill instinctively asked.

They went straight to the hospital. "I woke up from the anesthesia, and there were my parents standing over me," David recalled. Bill spoke just four words: "I'm glad you're alive." Then he turned around and left the room. "My mom is definitely the more compassionate one," David observed. "Quite honestly, I'm amazed that he handled it as well as he did, given the way he was raised by his own father, who had a real temper."

David was then at the age when he had to decide whether to commit to serve a two-year mission for his church. "His attitude toward the Church was one of indifference," Bill recounted in a subsequent speech to a group of Latter-day Saint youth. "He attended Church meetings reluctantly, and when he did, he assumed the head-on-the-bench-in-front-of-him position—where he slept. His mother and I became more

The red Ferrari after David's near-fatal accident.

frustrated each day. The harder we tried to force David into Church activity, the more he resisted."[4]

So it was something of a victory for Bill when, a week after the accident, David agreed to go on a mission. The accident had been life-threatening, but David's mission to England turned out to be life-changing. His parents had long prayed for a miracle, and they got it. "In retrospect," David later said, "I honestly feel that the reason I had that accident was to get me on a mission." He gave this response to a *Washington Post* reporter's question: "The mission was a phenomenal experience for me. It was the first time in my life, as a young 19-year-old, that I really looked outside myself. It taught me how to work and to think about others' interests and needs above mine. It taught me how to be grateful."[5]

Though Bill can afford many things, he is not a self-indulgent man. His house is large, but not showy. He doesn't have a yacht, and he has rarely partied with the rich and famous. Cars are the primary exception to his modest lifestyle. In the mid-1980s, when Bill was still a little touchy about the "indulgence," he told a reporter that his antique sports cars were mostly investments. That made him feel better about splurging on his hobby, and in the early years he really believed they represented a major investment.

Evidence of his initial intention is found in a handwritten note in 1979 to his personal financial assistant, Carolyn Cullers.[6] It was dated just a few days after he bought the Cadillac Special 60. "Please talk to Arthur Andersen [the accounting firm] about my investing in Classic automobiles. Can I depreciate them? Can I set up a company to own them and charge off the repair and storage expenses? How can I handle this Hobby as inexpensively as possible?" Bill dropped the idea after his accountants advised that for tax reasons the proposed business would require him regularly to sell off the cars.

Bill has sold a few cars over the years for a substantial profit. Once, though, he bought back a car he had previously sold. He first bought this particular 1957 Ferrari TRC in 1983 for $135,000 and sold it seven years later for $1.5 million. "Mr. Marriott likes cars that look fast even while they're sitting still. And he always loved that TRC 500 because he thinks it is the prettiest sports racer ever built," explained auto restorer David Carte. "So he bought the same car back [in 1997] for $910,000, which was substantially less than he had sold it for seven years before."

When *Forbes* asked Bill why he collected the cars, he answered with a question: "Why do people get hooked on art? It's the same thing."[7] Bill sees little difference between himself and those who buy an original Rembrandt or Monet. The classic car designers and builders were masters in their own right, creating rolling works of art. To Bill, they are his Renoirs of the Road.

Nostalgia also significantly drives Bill's collection, as it does for many other collectors who tend to buy the cars they admired in their youth. An example of this in Bill's collection is his 1951 Cadillac Allard

J2 Roadster. While in college at the University of Utah, he saw Bill Pollack finish first at Pebble Beach in the Allard. When the same car came up for sale in 1996, Bill didn't hesitate to buy it.

After the Lamborghini Miura, the Cadillac 60S, and the '34 Mercedes, Bill went all Italian. Over the next four years, he bought six Ferraris, three of which were Spyders, including the California model that the 1986 film *Ferris Bueller's Day Off* made one of the most desired in the world. Over a four-month period, Bill paid $400,000 in total for the '59 California Spyder, '67 Spyder 275, and '71 Daytona Spyder. They are currently valued collectively at more than $9 million, but Bill will not sell them, preferring to save them for his children.

Once he had acquired all the Ferraris he wanted, he looked around for something equally exciting. During a visit with a Beverly Hills collector, Bill discovered several French models sometimes called "Paris gowns on wheels" because of their exceptional designs. He soon bought a trio of 1938 French showstoppers: a Delahaye 135 MS Roadster with a unique, sculpted dragonfly hood ornament, and a pair of Talbot-Lagos, one of them the T150-C-SS Teardrop Coupe with its pioneering streamline design.

His collection eventually expanded to an eclectic mix including a '57 Cadillac Fleetwood Brougham, a '59 Corvette Scaglietti Coupe, a '48 Buick Roadmaster convertible, and a '36 Voisin Saliot Cabriolet. Many in his collection are valued in the millions of dollars, including a 1960 Aston Martin DBGT Coupe ($3 million) and a 1954 Maserati A6 GCS Coupe ($5 million).

In spite of his expensive hobby, the fact that Bill remains well grounded was evident in an interview with a South Carolina magazine when he served as the honorary chair of Hilton Head's 2007 Concours d'Elegance. Most of the questions were about his passion for vintage races, but the last question took Bill off guard. "For what would you most like to be remembered?" the reporter asked. "That is a hard question," Bill responded. "I think that I would like to be remembered for helping people, that I have been able to give many people the opportunity to achieve their ambitions."[8]

When Bill turned sixty-five years old—a traditional retirement age—he was not ready to give up on the mission of "helping people" through his growing empire, even though at that age it was not uncommon for people to confuse the graying Bill with his late father. One newspaper reporter asked him to describe what it was like opening his first root beer stand in 1927. "I know this is a tough business, but I'm not quite that old!" he replied.

A portrait of J.W. and Bill in nearly every hotel lobby occasionally prompts confusion between father and son, with many assuming the older gentleman in the picture is Bill. "I really like that picture of you and your son," a stranger told him. "I hear he's doing a great job." Bill got used to it. "When they say, 'I hear your son is doing a better job than you are,' I smile and say, 'Absolutely!'"

For the Marriott board, Bill's age was no joking matter. Since the early 1980s, a contingent of the board led by Harry Vincent had consistently pressed Bill to groom a successor. When Bill became president at the age of thirty-two, the Hot Shoppes company was much smaller and less complex than the international conglomerate he had built since then. In the early '80s, all three of his sons were in their late twenties or younger. They were many years away from being ready to stand at the helm of the large corporation.

"Bill was very reluctant to choose a successor who was not a member of his family," Vincent recalled. "He finally named Bill Shaw, who was then the CFO, but we forced him to do it. And he said he would not be comfortable with it until after Shaw gained some operational experience." In 1992, to accommodate the return of Steve Bollenbach, Shaw was shifted from CFO to head the nonlodging half of the company, where he gained that operational experience.

Bill said of Shaw, "I've never met a more honest man. Plus, he's a tireless worker and wonderful contributor who rarely ever loses his cool." One of the greatest evidences of that came the day in 1994 when the two Bills traveled to South Bend, Indiana, for a football game that pitted their respective teams—Catholic Notre Dame and Latter-day Saint BYU—against each other. The press called it a "holy war." Not only did BYU hold the Fighting Irish to the fewest points Notre Dame had scored at home in almost a decade, but BYU won, knocking Notre Dame out of the national rankings. "I can't imagine a more difficult situation than to sit next to me at that football game and see BYU defeat the Fighting Irish for the first time ever. He didn't even say 'Damn!'" Bill laughed.

Far more important was the coolness and competence Shaw exhibited during the company's financial crisis. In a later tribute, Bill said: "If I could pick someone to be alone on a desert island with, it would be Bill Shaw. I know. I've been there with him. 1990–91 were the most difficult years of my career. Bill Shaw's leadership saved the day." When Bill offered Shaw a modest raise during that period, "Instead of being delighted, he was somewhat embarrassed and—I must say this had certainly never happened to me before—he turned me down." A year later, Shaw actively recruited Steve Bollenbach to come to work for Marriott, even though it might put his own job on the line. "He has always put the company and not himself first," Bill said.[9]

Shaw was very much on Bill's mind in early 1997. At that point, Bill had been the Marriott president for thirty-three years, CEO for twenty-five, and chairman for twelve. He was ready to give up the lesser of the three titles—president—and Shaw was just the man to be the company's first non-Marriott president. In February, Bill announced the fifty-one-year-old Shaw's promotion to president and chief operating officer. Shaw was under no illusions about who was still boss.

Bill tried to delegate more to Shaw, but it wasn't easy. Bill said he would stop going to budget meetings so Shaw could run them. Bill skipped one meeting and stewed at home while it was going on. Shaw told him to come back, and it was business as usual.

Besides Shaw's promotion and the Renaissance acquisition, the corporation's seventieth-anniversary year of 1997 was also notable for the publication of Bill's first book, *The Spirit to Serve: Marriott's Way*. The impetus for the book had come from his public communications department, which felt that a new Marriott book was overdue. J.W.'s biography, *Marriott: The J. Willard Marriott Story*, was two decades old. It was a rags-to-riches tale of a restaurateur. But in the twenty years since, Marriott had been radically transformed into an international conglomerate. It was time for an update, and Bill approved the corporate project as part of the seventieth-anniversary celebration.

In late 1995, a husband-and-wife team of oral historians, G. Wesley and Marian Johnson, conducted a series of interviews with Bill and seventeen other top Marriott executives. By spring 1996, the company hired a writer, Virginia-based Kathi Ann Brown, to craft the book Bill envisioned. The Brown and Johnson interviews comprised a behind-the-scenes look at the company's successes and missteps along the way. Few of those interviews were used for the final book because, before the writing began, Bill changed the emphasis from a biography to a promotional vehicle for Marriott International.

Published by HarperBusiness in the fall of 1997, the book received fair reviews. The universal theme of the reviews was that Bill Marriott deserved his place as one of America's best and most-admired CEOs, but his "magic formula" for success was nearly impossible to describe in depth. Since he had no illusions that the book would be a bestseller, Bill was happy with the result. "What I like the most is celebrating our employees, and having them get excited about what they're doing," he later explained.[10] *The Spirit to Serve* did that in spades. "I've said again and again that our associates are number one," he wrote in the book. "It won't hurt to say it one more time. Without the hard work and dedication of our team, Marriott wouldn't exist. Period."

Less than three months into Shaw's presidency, Bill agreed with his suggestion to jettison one of the company's oldest businesses—contract food services. The division had started in 1943 when Hot Shoppes Inc. contracted to run a United States Navy cafeteria. When the Food Services Management division merged with Saga Corporation in 1986, Marriott became the number-one private contract feeding operation in the country. FSM grew to include facilities management, child care, and other offshoot services. The name was changed to Food Service and Management and subsequently to Marriott Management Services (MMS).

MMS was a substantial help during the 1990–91 crisis, when its contracts provided the company with vital cash flow while hotel occupancy floundered. But the long-term prospect was not bright for MMS, in Bill's view. It was a low-margin food-service business whose growth could be accelerated significantly only by acquisition. Even though MMS contributed about 30 percent of Marriott's overall $10.2 billion revenue in 1995, it accounted for only one-sixth of its profit. It would never be as profitable as hotel management.

In late 1996, a French investment bank approached Shaw on behalf of the Sodexho Alliance about buying MMS. Sodexho was the dominant food-service outfit in Europe and had begun to make inroads into the U.S. market. After a series of acquisitions, Sodexho was number four in America while Marriott was still number one. If Marriott agreed to sell, Sodexho would become the number-one food-service contractor in the world. In September 1997, the Marriott board approved the sale—a four-year process of joint ownership with an option for Sodexho to buy out Marriott in 2001, which it did, for about $3 billion. Less gratifying, however, was a related shareholder vote, which became the only one Bill lost in his storied career.

During the merger-mania decade of the 1980s, many companies adopted a dual-class stock position, which involved giving existing stockholders more votes with "super voting stock" so future corporate raiders buying one-vote stock shares could not prevail as easily in a hostile takeover attempt. Long-term investors in a company, such as owners and employees, appreciated the extra power it gave them. But institutional investors sometimes opposed the idea because it was better for them to get the windfall of cash that came with takeovers.

In the Sodexho deal, Bill saw an opportunity to try the dual-class concept and further protect Marriott from a hostile takeover. Because the Sodexho deal was technically a merger rather than an outright sale, it required that Marriott International be dissolved and reborn in the blink of an eye as a "new" Marriott International that included Sodexho.

The company proposed that existing stockholders be given two shares of the new Marriott for every one share of the old Marriott. And that extra share would come with ten votes instead of one. The monetary value of the share would not be more, only the "super" power times ten of the shareholder when casting votes. This had to be approved by the SEC and a majority of the company's shareholders, which Bill was confident would happen.

As expected, a number of Marriott's institutional investors, such as pension funds, opposed the proposal. Collectively, however, the institutional opponents owned only 1 percent of the stock. The Marriott family, which accounted for one-fifth of the shares, would vote for the dual-class restructuring. So the victory or defeat would be decided by small investors—the individual shareholders, who, by this plan, would each be gifted an additional share and ten votes for every share of stock they currently held.

If a man is known by his enemies, Bill Marriott could hardly have had a more ignominious one than the proposal's chief opponent, Edward T. Hanley, the iron-fisted leader of the 250,000-member Hotel & Restaurant Employees International Union. For nearly three years, the U.S. Senate Permanent Subcommittee on Investigations had focused on Hanley, uncovering allegations of rampant corruption at the top of the union.[11] Hanley considered Bill Marriott an archenemy. Every new hotel the company built or managed was another reason for Hanley's anger because Marriott ran nonunion hotels. The company was able to resist unionization using a simple strategy: it treated employees well, created solutions for their valid complaints, and, most important, paid them better salaries and benefits than any unionized hotel could offer. Marriott employees also didn't have to pay union dues.

Hanley's animus against Bill and Marriott International was so great that even though Hanley's union was being monitored by the Justice Department, he still went after Bill. Hanley and the union pulled out all the stops to oppose the dual-class initiative. Their first move was to buy thirty-five shares of Marriott International so they could force the company to allow them to send protest information to their fellow shareholders. Their inaccurate and scary circulars hit a large group of individual shareholders (many of them elderly) like well-targeted grenades.

Never before had anyone opposed a Marriott management proposal to the shareholders in such a dramatic manner, and that alone created doubt in the minds of some stockholders. According to news reports, Hanley and his union hammered the Marriott family at every opportunity, implying that the proposal was only meant to line the family's pockets and increase their voting power.

In March, the shareholders approved the merger with Sodexho and eventual buyout of the food services division. Then, at the May 20, 1998, annual shareholder meeting, they were asked to approve the dual-class stock proposal. Bill received an overwhelming majority of the shareholder votes cast in person or by proxy, but unfortunately that amounted to only 47 percent of the outstanding shares—which fell just short of the 50-percent-plus-one-vote majority he needed for stock plan approval. There was little doubt that the combination of the large number of shareholders who didn't vote and the union's scare campaign getting out a negative vote had delivered the public defeat.

As reporters surrounded Bill to pummel him with questions about the defeat, he had reason to be upset and bitter. It was the first time shareholders had ever said no to a Marriott family proposal. Bill and his family had been prime movers in the company's enormous success, but the union had won by suggesting the family could no longer be trusted. With restraint, Bill said, "I'm disappointed but I'm not destroyed."[12]

The *Washington Post's* chief financial columnist, Jerry Knight, found Hanley's so-called "victory" to be brazenly hypocritical. He wrote: "The hotel and restaurant workers union's ability to muster moral suasion against what it portrayed as the Marriott family's efforts to enrich itself at the expense of investors is ironic considering (that) the union's longtime president (Hanley) was forced to resign last week by federal overseers, who alleged that he had ties to organized crime and enriched himself at the expense of union members."[13]

Hanley had reached a plea agreement with the Justice Department in order to avoid prosecution on racketeering charges. Several months later, the federal monitor's report was released. It concluded that Hanley had operated a virtual kleptocracy in which Hanley family members and friends lived lavish lifestyles at the expense of the lowest-paid union workers. Concluded the *Chicago Sun-Times:* "Headed by Hanley [the hotel workers union] has been run like a monarchy . . . an undemocratic union where funds were used as if they belonged to the organization's royal family."[14]

Bill put the defeat behind him, and in 1999 launched the "Spirit to Serve Our Communities Day." This was to be an annual event each third week of May in which employees across the world volunteered to work for local nonprofits. The company also pledged that on that day it would raise at least $4 million in donations for worthy local charities. The first event enlisted 145,000 employees in 58 countries who gave community service.

For many years, the idea of giving back had been very much at the forefront of Bill's mind. At both the national and local levels, the company was partnering with a wide variety of charities, including the Children's Miracle Network, Second Harvest food banks, and Habitat for Humanity. Most Marriott full-service hotel grand openings included a gala benefit for a worthy local cause.

Bill knew few people who exemplified the spirit of service and volunteerism better than his own mother. Allie worked hard for an array of nonprofits, including the Kennedy Center and the Arthritis Foundation. Bill honored her in 1992 by establishing an annual Alice S. Marriott Award for Community Service for the Marriott units that made the most outstanding contributions to their communities.

In the years following J.W.'s death, with the gentle Allie as his sole parent, Bill had been able to put his stormy relationship with his father in perspective, and he began to appreciate his father's uncompromising business philosophy. "My dad was never satisfied, which may have been his greatest strength," he told one management gathering. "My life experience tells me that success is never final, but the decisions we make along the way determine the end and final outcome."[15]

Meanwhile, the years were beginning to take their toll on Allie. "She has often said, 'Old age is hell,'" Bill acknowledged in a speech. "She has fallen many times and severely injured her lower back. She is in constant pain, yet whenever I have asked her how she feels, she always says, 'I'll feel better tomorrow.'"[16]

Allie had round-the-clock nursing care at her home, where she preferred to live her final years. On one of her few outings to corporate headquarters, to celebrate Bill's thirty-fifth anniversary with the company, she remarked: "Bill has been a wonderful son through the years and has added me to his long list of responsibilities. He supervises my health problems and finds me the best doctors and treatment. When he is traveling, he calls me every day from wherever he is and visits me several times a week when he is in town."[17]

For the most part, their visits were time to reminisce about younger days—like the day nineteen-year-old Allie met President Calvin Coolidge. She had just moved to Washington, D.C., with J.W., who was busy operating a tiny A&W root beer stand. "She had never been out of Salt Lake City before, and she was certain that when the root beer stand went broke, she'd return to Utah," Bill related. "So she took a few hours off each week to sightsee. In 1927, it was possible for anyone to visit the White House every day between noon and one p.m. to shake the president's hand. So she met silent Calvin Coolidge, who said 'Howdy do!'" And that was that.

Sometimes Bill joked with his mother about her parsimony in spite of substantial wealth. She had a drawer full of shopping coupons and bought glue by the gallon, pouring it into little bottles for thrift. Bill laughed with her about the recurring disagreement she had had with J.W. about her driving twenty miles across town to buy discounted prescriptions.

Allie and Bill often talked about the Hot Shoppes restaurants, including her 1987 visit to the last one Bill was about to open. "We went in, took a look around, and sampled some of the food," he recalled. "Mother was not impressed. She tasted the chili and said, 'That's not how I used to make it. They're using the wrong beans!' She called me the next day to make sure all her corrections were in place before the opening."[18]

By 1997, Allie was unable to travel to Salt Lake City to attend grandson David's wedding. Two years after that, she couldn't join Bill and Dick for the December 2 ceremony closing the last Hot Shoppe, in Marlow Heights, Maryland. The cafeteria-style restaurants were no longer sufficiently profitable, so when the lease expired in each of the last dozen, they were shuttered. Allie wanted to be present for this end of her era, but her own lease on life was close to expiration.

Alice S. Marriott died peacefully at the age of ninety-two on April 17, 2000. Longtime Marriott chauffeur and jack-of-all-trades Cornelius "Mack" McNeil had gotten a call from her earlier in the day.

"Mack, are you doing anything?" she asked him from her Georgetown University Hospital bed.

"Nothing much," he said.

"Well, why don't you come down here to the hospital? My mother is coming and I want you to meet her."

Allie's mother had been gone for almost forty years, but Mack was flooded with warm feelings about the reunion that Allie was anticipating with her mother. When Mack arrived, Dick was watching over his mother, so Allie asked Mack to wait in the hall to greet her mother, who would be coming in a few minutes. He stepped into the hall, and while he waited, Allie died, with Dick at her side.

At her funeral, Bill offered a tribute to his mother: "From my earliest memories she was my best friend, my teacher, and my advocate with a bigger-than-life father. When I was sick, she tenderly cared for me. When I was struggling with arithmetic in the second grade, she bought a small chalkboard and taught me how to add and subtract, and later to multiply and divide. As I worked on becoming an Eagle Scout, she encouraged me and drove me to all my appointments with my merit badge counselors. She always took me to church, as Dad was almost always going to another church meeting on Sunday. But mother and I never missed a Sunday. When I fell down, she picked me up, dusted me off, and encouraged me to keep going."

He recounted her invaluable partnership with his father in creating the Hot Shoppes chain of restaurants when she worked as the company's first CFO and executive chef. "She became very active in the community and in politics, but her family always came first. Her personal sacrifices for me and Dick and my family were enormous."

A few years earlier, Allie had written a note to her son about her funeral service. "My funeral doesn't need to be sad. It should be a celebration of a long life well lived. I know that my Redeemer lives."

Expanding on that theme, Bill said it was only fitting that she passed away at Easter time. "The first Easter, the resurrection of our Lord Jesus Christ, is the greatest miracle that has ever occurred. His resurrection was real, and it gave immortality to all mankind. Because He broke the bonds of death, so will we, and so will Mother. She will always be a strong presence in my life. I am honored and blessed to be her son, and I am grateful for the sure knowledge that she lives."[19]

CHAPTER 26

HEARTBREAK HOTEL AND HEROES

Five days after their mother's funeral, Bill and his brother, Dick, flew to Florida for the grand opening of the Tampa Waterside Marriott—the company's 2,000th hotel and a significant milestone.

Tampa had built a new convention center almost a decade earlier, but couldn't fill it because there wasn't a hotel big enough to house attendees for large conventions. Trammell Crow, one of America's largest developers, won the hotel bid and went looking for a partner. When Crow and Bill had met four decades earlier, Crow had been so impressed with the twenty-six-year-old vice president that he was ready to build Marriott's third hotel in Dallas, until the deal fell apart. Crow never forgot the astute young executive, and he enjoyed watching Bill's rise to become one of the world's premier hoteliers.

Now, decades later, the two men collaborated to build a twenty-seven-story, $110-million glass and steel tower on the Tampa waterfront. It opened April 27, 2000, fulfilling Bill's promise of "2,000 by 2000."[1]

It had taken nearly four decades for the Marriott corporation to reach 1,000 hotels in 1995, so Bill's announced goal of doubling that number in just five years had seemed overly ambitious. The fastest way to get there was to buy another hotel company. Marriott tried to buy the Inter-Continental chain in 1998 but was outbid.

Without another acquisition on the horizon, the only way the company could reach 2,000 by 2000 was by building, acquiring, or converting at least 300 hotels, one at a time, which was no easy feat. Two of the most difficult projects were in Philadelphia, which, together with the company-financed San Francisco Marriott, nearly broke the company due to unfortunate timing.

It had been a happy day at headquarters in 1989 when the Philadelphia Redevelopment Authority selected Marriott to build a $210-million hotel next to the city's new convention center, which was still in the design phase. "We were developing and selling over $1 billion per year of hotels and then taking them back on management contracts. We assumed we could do the same with Philadelphia," Bill recounted in a 1994 speech to Philadelphia businessmen. "The real estate market collapsed shortly after we had signed the deal. We were committed, but we didn't have a buyer nor did we have any financing. We took a deep breath and went ahead."[2] The Philadelphia hotel went up with Marriott cash and corporate borrowing. When it opened in 1995, it was the largest hotel construction project in the United States, and the last major convention hotel Marriott built.

Later that year, the company opened its only other Marriott-financed project, the Philadelphia Airport Marriott, which offered a new Marriott feature, The Room That Works. "Our guests said they needed more space and flexibility, better lighting, and a plug for their computer and a computer data port. They said they were tired of putting their work on top of the bed and then crawling around on the floor to find a plug for their computer," Bill said. The Marriott Room That Works featured a large, L-shaped workstation with a mobile desk, a console table, an upholstered ergonomic swivel chair, and an adjustable lamp. Two power outlets and a PC modem jack were mounted in the console top instead of along the floor. The Room That Works was such a success in attracting business that the company soon converted many of the guest rooms in full-service hotels to the concept, and its main features were copied by competitors.

While domestic hotels represented the majority of the 2,000 Marriotts, the company also built more foreign hotels than it had originally anticipated—in Puerto Rico, Egypt, Dubai, Kuala Lumpur, Bangkok, and Jakarta. It was a particularly exciting day when Marriott won the contract to manage the historic, five-star Plaza Hotel in Buenos Aires, Argentina, the first Marriott in South America.

Meanwhile, Marriott began adding a few important acquisitions in New York City, the most fateful of which was the Vista Hotel, nestled between the massive 110-story Twin Towers of the World Trade Center. When Hilton International opened the Vista in 1981, it was the first hotel built in lower Manhattan in more than a century. For a decade, the hotel had no competition in the financial district, until 1991, when Marriott opened the thirty-seven-story, 504-room Financial Center Marriott two blocks away on West Street.

Two years later, in February 1993, Islamic terrorists, attempting to bring down the Twin Towers, planted a bomb in the Vista International's parking garage. The explosion killed six people, injured 1,000 others, and caused major damage to the hotel. The power of the blast was felt at the nearby Financial Center Marriott.

Managers and associates of the Marriott rushed to help their Vista competitors, assigning space for a Vista command post and a place to hold press briefings. The Financial Center Marriott also provided complimentary housing for four days to 120 Port Authority officials and continuously delivered food to approximately 700 first responders and cleanup crews. The World Trade Center subsequently ran an ad in the *New York Times* proclaiming: "A million thanks, Marriott, for opening your doors to us." One of Marriott's associates told a journalist: "It's something you just do. You drop your competitiveness and reach out with your human side and say, 'What can we do to help you?'"[3]

At that point, the Port Authority owned the Vista. After the

The New York Marriott World Trade Center.

bombing, it was renovated and reopened in 1994. Host Marriott bought it for $141.5 million in 1995 and renamed it the New York Marriott World Trade Center. Bill was thrilled with the acquisition and had no qualms about another terrorist attack. For one thing, in spite of its international reach, the Marriott empire had so far escaped harm from global terrorism. Less than a year after the Vista purchase, Marriott *was* touched for the first time by terrorism when a homemade pipe bomb exploded in Atlanta's Centennial Park during the 1996 Olympics. Walking across the park at the time of the blast, thirty-six-year-old Marriott corporate food services manager Ron Smith was hit by shrapnel, losing a finger and the use of one foot. The incident alarmed Bill, but he made no connection to a possible threat at the WTC Marriott. Since that location had been bombed before, security in the hotel was extensive.

No one ever imagined that a threat would come from above.

Bill drove to his Bethesda, Maryland, office early on Tuesday, September 11, 2001. It was a brilliant, blue-sky morning on the East Coast. He was feeling rested after two weeks at Lake Winnipesaukee and was booked on a noon flight for New York City, where he would attend a World Trade & Tourism Council executive committee meeting.

A few minutes before nine a.m., Phyllis Hester interrupted a meeting in his office to tell him that a plane had just struck one of the World Trade Center's Twin Towers.

"I ran to the boardroom and turned on the big TV," he recalled. "The first images that came up showed billowing smoke and a gaping, fiery hole in one of the towers. My mind went straight to our guests and associates. Did the hotel team know what was going on? Were they already evacuating? Had anybody been hurt? The hotel's associates were well trained for emergencies, but this emergency was like nothing we'd ever seen before.

"We tried frantically to get through to the hotel staff by telephone from the boardroom, to no avail. As the minutes went by, more people came into the boardroom where, like millions of other viewers, we were transfixed by those surreal images. Then we saw the second plane hit the other tower. Total silence in the room. We were all devastated. We kept trying to get through to our people. We had no idea how bad things were for them, but knew it must be pretty terrible. More than a few of us in that boardroom could not hold back the tears."

Hijacked by terrorists and flying at 494 miles per hour, the American Airlines Flight 11 passenger jet had crashed into the north tower at 8:46 a.m. with a fiery explosion, sending debris crashing down to the streets. Part of the plane's landing gear crashed through the roof of the twenty-two-story Marriott below, landing in an office next to the pool and shaking the whole building. Front desk receptionist Amy Ting thought the grand piano on the mezzanine had dropped to the floor—"but then, out the windows, I saw pieces of building flying down onto the street like meteorites," she recalled.[4]

One hotel guest, Joyce Ng, later wrote to Bill describing that moment when she heard the explosion and looked out the window: "Fiery debris was raining outside my window. I saw a blizzard of glass, paper, debris, and chunks of metal avalanching to the ground into the plaza between the two towers. . . . I was shocked and horrified as I watched from my room as people ran for their lives, got hit by debris, and were killed. People were dying below me."

Ng ran down the stairs to the lobby and out the door, where a police officer was shouting, "Get out of this area and don't look up!" She did look up at the burning tower: "Then I saw the bodies coming out the windows and falling to the ground. People stopped and stared and could not peel their eyes away from the scene."

In the Marriott grand ballroom, 200 economists were having a breakfast meeting when the building shook and the chandeliers swayed. When noted economist Harvey Rosenblum had learned months before that the group was going to have breakfast in the expensive Windows on the World restaurant atop the north tower of the World Trade Center, he had protested. "I heard what the bill was going to be, and I raised a stink," recalled Rosenblum. "We moved it to the Marriott grand ballroom." Because of that, every one of the conferees in the Marriott ballroom lived. Everyone in the restaurant atop the north tower was killed.[5]

In the lobby, three Marriott associates gathered with walkie-talkies, as they had often practiced, to coordinate the evacuation—Rich Fetter, resident manager; Joe Keller, executive housekeeper; and Nancy Castillo, head of human resources for both the WTC Marriott and Financial Center Marriott. Several alarms were already sounding in the hotel, and the guest elevators automatically shut down. Unable to use the computers, Fetter found the last guest-list printout and gave it to Castillo for reference. He then dispatched associates to conduct a room-by-room check to make sure the guests were evacuating.

No one in the hotel could tell what had happened to the north tower because the gaping hole and fireball were not visible from any

Marriott vantage point. But most of the guests knew enough to get out, using the stairs. However, Leigh Gilmore, a forty-two-year-old woman from Chicago with multiple sclerosis who was dependent on her motorized wheelchair, could do nothing but huddle with her mother in her fifth-floor room. Then a second plane, American Airlines Flight 75, struck the south tower at 9:03 a.m. Minutes later, two Marriott maintenance men found the Gilmores and rushed them onto a freight elevator to get them to safety.

By this time, the Marriott had also become an evacuation portal for those fleeing the Twin Towers through the door that connected the hotel to the north tower. Companies of firemen and Marriott staff directed more than 1,000 frightened people through the lobby to an exit onto Liberty Street. Debris and bodies were still dropping from above, so a policeman stood at the exit door to hold up the line sporadically when falling objects were spotted. Because of that corridor of safety, the Marriott hotel saved many lives.

A year later, the *New York Times* heralded this effort: "It was only a hotel, a 22-story dwarf tucked under colossal buildings, but in its final 102 minutes, the Marriott Hotel at 3 World Trade Center served as the mouth of a tunnel, a runway in and out of the burning towers for perhaps a thousand people or more [because] a cadre of unsung Marriott workers, from managers to porters, stayed behind to make sure their guests got out."[6] One of those selfless heroes was audiovisual manager Abdu Malahi, who was last seen checking rooms for guests on the hotel's upper floors; he died in the courageous effort.

At 9:37 a.m., just a few miles from Marriott headquarters, American Airlines Flight 77 crashed into the Pentagon. CFO Arne Sorenson was driving to Marriott's Bethesda headquarters from a breakfast meeting in downtown Washington, D.C., when he spotted a cloud of smoke south of the city. As soon as he reached headquarters, he went to the boardroom, which had become a command center. "We were able to ascertain pretty quickly that our five hotels near the Pentagon—including one right across the street—had suffered no damage," Bill related. "In fact, our people threw open the hotel doors to take in evacuees from the damaged building. The lobby of our Residence Inn Arlington Pentagon City became an ad hoc triage center for Pentagon victims with injuries."

In his nineteenth-floor room at the WTC Marriott, guest Frank Razzano thought he was safe. The Washington, D.C., lawyer assumed firemen would put out the high-level conflagration, and he thought he had plenty of time to leave the hotel. He showered, shaved, and packed his belongings and legal papers. He was about to call for a bellman to pick up his luggage when the south tower, after burning for fifty-six minutes, collapsed at 9:59 a.m., registering 2.1 on the Richter scale.

The ten-second collapse occurred inside a veil of smoke, so it appeared that the building simply imploded, falling straight down, but that was not the case. The top thirty or forty floors broke off, pivoted, and fell eastward onto a neighboring office building. Other sections were propelled northwest toward Battery Park, while a few sections landed on the WTC Marriott, cleaving it in half.[7] As this curtain of concrete and debris fell past his window, Razzano hugged the wall next to the door, certain that these were the last few moments of his life. *Have I led a good life? Would my parents be proud of me?* he wondered.

Moments before, in the lobby, Marriott associates were talking with each other and the firemen, pleased that the evacuation seemed to be nearly complete. Joe Keller had managed to reach his wife, Rose, and reassure her that he was just fine, but she urged him to leave. She recalled: "He told me that he was evacuating the people, and I, selfishly, said, you get out. He said, 'I'll leave here when I can.'"

At the moment the tower fell onto the hotel, Keller was at the bellhop station talking to Rich Fetter, who was less than fifteen feet away. The immediate pressure from the impact lifted everyone into the air and carried them through the lobby. Fetter was caught by a fireman, who pulled him to a column and hugged him close. "I flew from the middle of the lobby to the corner," said Amy Ting. "I couldn't see. All I could hear were things crashing—it was like death had just passed you by." When the remaining firemen's flashlights flicked on, there was no sign of Keller or the other firemen behind a wall of debris. Reinforced beams installed in the hotel following the 1993 World Trade Center bombing had shielded a portion of the lobby from the crushing weight of the collapse. On-scene firefighter Patrick Carey said: "It was like the building was severed with scissors. If you were on one side of the line, you were okay. If you were on the other, you were lost." Keller was on the wrong side.

But he was still alive. Fetter managed to reach him on their walkie-talkies. "I'm in an air pocket. I'm on a ledge. There's a big hole and I can see down to the lowers levels of the hotel. Shouldn't be able to do that. There's two firemen in here with me and they seem to be hurt bad. I can't get to them." The firemen on the "safe" side of the lobby ordered the remaining trio of Marriott associates to evacuate immediately, and they began digging through the debris to rescue those on the other side.[8]

Meanwhile, the same reinforced I-beams had saved not only Razzano but also, in the southern stairwell, thirteen firemen led by Jeff Johnson of Engine Company 74. A single, narrow slice of the Marriott had survived. Razzano and the firemen found each other, and together they made an agonizingly slow thirty-minute descent down the stairs over and around blocking debris. They were at the second floor when the north tower collapsed at 10:28 a.m. after burning for 102 minutes. The rest of the Marriott hotel was crushed, as was everyone left inside, including Joe Keller. "There was only a few feet difference between making it or not," Nancy Castillo soberly reflected a decade later, crying without apology at the memory of her colleague.

Miraculously, the men in the southern stairwell, which was now crushed to about the third floor, were still alive. Recalled Razzano, "I heard what I can only describe as a freight train coming at me out of the sky, and then debris started to fall down on top of us." Fireman Johnson remembered thinking, "Please don't let me go like this. I'm too close." All fourteen subsequently made it out, the only people known to get out after the collapse of both towers.[9]

Bill set up a crisis center at headquarters that was staffed around the clock in the first days after the attack. Flaming debris from one of the towers started a raging fire in the building next to the Marriott Financial Center hotel, so firemen used the hotel for more than a day as a staging area to fight the fire. Windows were broken, and there was water damage throughout the hotel, requiring its closure.

The loss of life was, of course, far more impactful. When an accounting was later taken, it appeared that at least forty-one firefighters who had been trying to clear the WTC Marriott died when it was obliterated. Eleven of the 940 registered guests at the Marriott were unaccounted for and may have been among the numbers who died in the adjoining towers. Within hours of the collapse, Bill called the families of Joe Keller and Abdu Malahi. "I was deeply saddened by the loss of our men who, like their many colleagues that day, exhibited such bravery and dedication in the face of horrific tragedy," he later wrote. At the time, he told *Fortune* magazine: "This is the most difficult thing I've experienced in 45 years of business."[10]

Three days after the tragedy, Bill was invited to attend the "National Day of Prayer and Remembrance" at the National Cathedral in Washington, D.C. Clergymen from a variety of faiths—including the Imam of the Islamic Society of North America—participated. The main sermon was delivered by the Reverend Billy Graham, a longtime Marriott family friend, followed by remarks from President George W. Bush.

It was the same day Bill's son John made it home from London, where he had been conducting meetings as Marriott executive vice president of Sales and Marketing. Most commercial aircraft in the U.S. were grounded for a couple of days. John and his colleagues were able to catch a British Airways flight to Toronto, where they were picked up by a jet Bill dispatched to them.

On September 20, Bill was in New York to speak to his shell-shocked employees: "So many of you performed unbelievable acts of bravery in getting people to safety after the collapse of the towers—literally guiding people across steel girders that were all that was left of the lobby floor. Some of you remained at the hotel searching for coworkers and guests until firefighters forced you to leave when it was too dangerous to remain. I'll never forget all you've done here. You're all heroes in my eyes."

Many of them were moved by his remarks of deep gratitude and support. "He was incredibly compassionate," recalled Rich Fetter. "We felt very fortunate to be part of what was truly a caring, family company."

While there is never a "good time" for a catastrophic tragedy, this one could hardly have happened at a worse time for the travel and hospitality industry. During the Gulf War recession of 1990–91, the average REVPAR—revenue per available room—had fallen 5 percent. In the months *before* 9/11, an unexpected downturn had already caused a 10 percent REVPAR drop. "As soon as I saw the second plane hit, and I realized the weapon of choice for terrorists was a loaded airliner, I knew we were in trouble," Bill later said. "The images of those airplanes striking the two towers played like an endless loop in the imaginations of millions of travelers for months and years to come. Hotel reservations plummeted anywhere from 30 percent to 80 percent almost immediately. Air travel slowed to a trickle. When the stock market reopened for trading on September 18, our share price fell 20 percent by day's end. None of that reaction was surprising. Fear is a powerful force."

Marriott reservations dropped 94 percent as travelers canceled their trips. Bill told his management team to prepare for hotels at only 40 percent occupancy. But he was surprised when the reality wasn't quite that dire. And, "We found we could break even below 50 percent occupancy. We were never able to do this before. It's amazing how a crisis focuses the mind."

Bill wasted no time in rallying the industry to raise awareness in the government and among the public that staying home was not the answer to 9/11 or any other terrorist events. Two weeks after the terrible day, Bill led a group of travel company CEOs in a two-hour meeting with Secretary of Commerce Donald Evans. Since Congress was going to bail out the airline industry, Bill proposed that the government offer a significant tax credit for anyone traveling and staying in hotels for at least six months after the tragedy. He personally lobbied U.S. senators and testified before the Senate's subcommittee on tourism—all to no avail. There would be no help coming from that quarter.

Thus, at a time when he had to consider across-the-board layoffs, he was in a particularly rough spot when it came to his 1,100 employees from the two New York City hotels. Nevertheless, he and his associates pulled out all the stops to assist the traumatized group.

Bill announced that all workers from the affected hotels would be covered by the company's health insurance for a year. All of them would remain on the payroll until at least October 5. After that—because of the generosity of 1,500 Marriott associates donating more than $2 million of their vacation pay—all of them would be paid for a few months more. From his own family foundation, Bill wrote a $1-million grant to pay for survivor family expenses not covered by various federal and state emergency and relief organizations.

He knew it was critical to reopen the Financial Center Marriott as soon as possible so all those employees could get back to work, so he personally pushed the repair work along. As a result, when the hotel was reopened the following January 7, it was touted as the first hotel in lower Manhattan to reopen for business. New Mayor Michael Bloomberg, who had been in office only a few days, proudly cut the ribbon. He was again on hand three weeks later with Bill for the grand opening of the Ritz-Carlton Battery Park, a few blocks from Ground Zero.

These hotels, and another Ritz-Carlton that the company opened at Central Park in April, were bright spots in Bill's memory of the months following 9/11. There were others. Four days before Christmas, Bill was privileged to carry the Olympic torch on its way to Salt Lake City for the 2002 Olympic Winter Games in February. That event itself, managed by Bill's lifetime friend and Marriott board member Mitt Romney, was a symbol of hope, an American phoenix rising proudly out of the ashes of 9/11.

Five days after Christmas, a worker at Ground Zero found in the rubble the Marriott flag that had flown over the WTC Marriott. It was a bit burned, tattered, and torn. When Nancy Castillo delivered it to Bill at headquarters, he said he would donate it to the projected 9/11 museum. In the meantime, he directed that it be displayed in a glass case in the lobby at headquarters so every visitor would see it when coming through the main door. Intended to honor the heroism of all Marriott associates, the plaque beside it read:

> *Our Spirit to Serve*
> *From sacrifice . . . honor*
> *From adversity . . . resolve*
> *From grief . . . remembrance*

During his first four decades of hotel building, Bill rarely had to deal with on-the-job tragedies involving his employees. But beginning with the 9/11 tragedy, Marriott dealt with an increasing number of man-made and natural calamities:

• In August 2003, a suicide car-bomber linked to an Al Qaeda affiliated group targeted the JW Marriott Hotel in Jakarta, Indonesia. Two Marriott security guards died in their attempt to stop the terrorist. Another ten people were killed in the explosion, and about 150 were injured.[11]

• The day after Christmas, 2004, ten-year-old Tilly Smith was playing on the beach of the Marriott resort hotel on the island of Phuket, Thailand, when she noticed the sea disappear, revealing miles of new beach and fish flapping everywhere. Tilly was alarmed, and she shouted, "Mummy, we must get off the beach NOW!" Two weeks before, her geography teacher in Oxshott, England, had shown a film of a disappearing sea preceding large tsunami waves.

Tilly's family believed her warning and spread it quickly to others, including hotel resident manager Theera Kanjara. He ordered everyone off the beach and out of the pool area, evacuating them to higher floors of the Marriott. He was the last to leave in the face of the massive tsunami. While between 230,000 and 280,000 people in fourteen countries lost their lives from the 9.1–9.3 magnitude earthquake and subsequent tsunamis, not one guest or Marriott employee lost his or her life, all because of Theera's quick and decisive action.[12]

• When Hurricane Katrina lashed into New Orleans in August 2005, there were more than 400 guests and employees who had not yet evacuated from the downtown Marriott and Ritz-Carlton. With water four feet high around the hotels, the associates took care of guests for several days before the final evacuation could occur. There was no loss of life at the Marriott hotels, though it was months before they reopened—and when they did, Marriott gave the rooms to homeless employees and relief workers coming from across the country. Both Bill and Dick's family foundation and Marriott International donated millions of dollars to the relief effort. Many associates and Marriott customers redeemed their rewards points to send checks to the displaced for their housing and recovery.[13]

• In January 2007, a suicide bomber tried to enter the Marriott in Islamabad, Pakistan. A Marriott "loss prevention officer," Tariq Mehmood, successfully blocked the terrorist, who triggered his bomb in the entryway, killing only himself and Mehmood. Bill created a memorial wall at Marriott headquarters as a lasting tribute to employees who died while trying to help others escape harm. It began with five engraved names—the two who died at the Marriott World Trade Center, two more at the Jakarta Marriott, and Tariq Mehmood. At the time, Bill hoped he wouldn't have to add any more names.[14]

• A large dump truck packed with 1,300 pounds of explosives was stopped by a barrier and Marriott guards outside the same Islamabad Marriott hotel on the Saturday evening of September 20, 2008.

Realizing he could not go farther, the terrorist ignited the massive bomb, which could be heard from miles away and left a crater sixty feet wide and twenty-five feet deep. The explosion caused a natural gas leak in the hotel, which accelerated the initial fire into a conflagration. At least 54 people were killed and at least 266 were injured. Most of those who died were Marriott hotel employees.

"The entire security team on the ground at the entrance to the hotel was killed in the attack. These brave men were simply doing their jobs and gave their lives in an effort to protect the guests at their hotel, as well as their fellow associates. They will forever be remembered as heroes," Bill recorded. "While many of us will grieve over this incident for a long time, we must also realize that it is extremely important to move on. Our hotels serve as homes to travelers from many different cultures where all of our guests can do business and peacefully co-exist. We are truly a crossroads for communication. By traveling the world, we all learn that we have more in common than we have differences."[15]

• In 2009, bombs smuggled into both the Marriott and the Ritz-Carlton in Jakarta exploded, five minutes apart. Because the bombs were much smaller than the Islamabad explosive, the loss of life was much less—nine people. This was the second time the Jakarta Marriott had been targeted. Expressing condolences and pledges of aid to Jakarta associates and guests, Bill wrote:

"It is a sad truth in today's world that, if someone is willing to sacrifice his or her own life in an attack, there are no guarantees of safety. Nonetheless, we remain committed to do our best to implement tough and effective security procedures working with our associates, outside security experts and the authorities. And we remain committed to providing a place of hospitality, for public diplomacy, business and enjoyment for our guests, and providing opportunity for our wonderful associates who work in Jakarta and around the world."[16]

CHAPTER 27

MARRIOTT ON THE MOVE

As the twentieth century wound down, Bill became increasingly uneasy about the potential for his huge business empire to lose its edge. "I started my career in this business as a fry cook. I fell in love with this business because it moved so fast. When you've got six waitresses all hollering for their orders, you've got to move the food out," he told one audience of Marriott employees. "Today we're a big company and we are not very fast. We ponder too much, we overanalyze, we are simply too slow."

He told the gathering a story from his service on the Georgetown University board of trustees. At one board meeting he had spent time talking to a student who described the bureaucracy the student activities committee had slogged through to get permission to buy a live bulldog, the school mascot. "As I joined my fellow board members, we laughed about the eight months it took the bureaucracy to okay a dog. That reminds me a lot of our company. All I can say to you is to do it and do it now. Get on with it. Have a bias to action and accomplishment. Don't be afraid to make a mistake."[1]

At another meeting of Marriott managers, Bill continued the theme that was troubling him. "We are a big company. Some say our Marriott logo represents Pac Man—out there to gobble up anyone that

444

gets in our way. This may be true, but we cannot become complacent, and above all, we cannot become arrogant. So, at Marriott we must do everything we can to remain humble and teachable. Our competitors are aggressive and innovative. They copy everything we do. They move faster and are more creative in so many ways. We must be fast and fiercely competitive in all we do. Let's not forget where we've come from and how far we have to go. Success is never final."[2]

The road to success for Bill had been littered with challenges and mistakes to learn from. The business partner Bill regretted most in his long career was Hong Kong tycoon Dr. Henry Cheng. Bill had been happy enough about the $1-billion purchase in 1997 of Cheng's hotel management company, Renaissance Hotel Group (RHG), that he had invited Cheng to join the Marriott board, expanding the board to ten members to create a seat for him. "It was a big deal for him," recalled Bill Shaw. "He thought it was a big deal. After all, Bill Marriott was probably the best-known lodging person in the world, and now Henry was on his board." Cheng was welcomed by Marriott shareholders at the annual meeting in May, but when the applause died down, he didn't show up or call in for the next four board meetings.

Over the next couple of years, Cheng participated in fewer than half of the board's meetings, and the ones he did attend were by teleconference. Since Cheng was twelve hours ahead in Hong Kong, the morning board meetings in Maryland were late in the evening for him. At least once he could be heard snoring over the speakerphone in the boardroom. Bill tried to stroke Cheng's ego and interest by making him the board's "Asia expert," but Cheng did not share any expertise about the region that Bill didn't already possess. It was still a surprise when Cheng resigned three months after 9/11 with more than a year left in his term. As it turned out, Cheng was planning a major betrayal of his partners. It would be just one of several legal challenges Bill faced in the months following 9/11.

Cheng had split his empire much as Marriott had, into a real-estate arm, which owned the hotels, and RHG, which managed those hotels. For nearly $1 billion, Marriott had bought into RHG and the management rights. But in a brazen move to try to nullify the deal, four months after he resigned from the board, Cheng sued Marriott, charging Marriott with fraud and mismanagement. At the heart of the claim was the way Marriott used its own in-house procurement companies and other subcontractors. Cheng's suit tried to portray that as price fixing, but Marriott countered that it had all been spelled out in the original merger with RHG. Cheng even threatened to have the real-estate arm of his empire take its hotel-management contracts elsewhere. As Bill saw it, Cheng's hotels were suffering like everyone else in the downturn and Cheng was just trying to dun Marriott for its problems.

The suit was settled three years later when Marriott bought thirty-two of Cheng's hotels from him for $1.45 billion. That same day, the company turned around and sold thirteen of the hotels for $1 billion.[3] The other nineteen were sold over the next two years for a hefty profit, demonstrating that the best revenge is success.

In every legal challenge after 9/11, desperate hotel owners were trying to renegotiate Marriott management contracts because they were losing money in the lodging downturn. The biggest problem for the Marriott corporation was that the lawsuits such as Cheng's publicly besmirched the Marriott name with wild allegations. The company's only consolation was that Marriott wasn't the sole victim of this ploy. Sheraton, Hilton, Starwood, and Hyatt were all trying to fend off a flurry of similar lawsuits.

The most serious lawsuit against Marriott during that time had to do with the limited partnerships that had fueled the company's accelerated growth in the 1980s. Most of the investors who bought into collections of Marriott hotels were initially lured by the tremendous tax benefits the LPs offered. They were also impressed by optimistic Marriott projections of future profit, none of which took into account the possibility of a severe recession. In spite of those informal projections, Marriott had always been conservative in its final contractual promises. The company guaranteed a certain annual percentage of profit in the contract, and it made good on the guarantee to its own detriment during the 1990–91 recession.

Nevertheless, a host of disgruntled LP investors began filing lawsuits in the mid-1990s claiming fraud. Ultimately, the litigation was rolled into a single class action heard by a state court judge in San Antonio, Texas. One of the limited partners, Hall of Fame left-hander Whitey Ford, who played for the New York Yankees, became an effective spokesperson for the aggrieved limited partners.

Marriott lawyer Rick Hoffman said, "Whitey and more than a hundred other investors hadn't done so well and wanted Marriott to ante up. They claimed they were defrauded when it was really just a real estate dip." After a three-and-a-half-year legal battle, Marriott decided to settle the case out of court. The company bought back from the limited partners all the hotels involved, including 120 Courtyards, for more than $400 million. As it turned out, the limited partners were proven to be shortsighted. Within a few years, the economy rebounded, and Marriott sold the profitable Courtyards for a great deal more than it had paid in the settlement.

The Marriott spin-off that disappointed Bill the most was Host Marriott, the real-estate-owning company that Steve Bollenbach created in 1993 so Marriott International could concentrate on lodging management. The original intent of splitting the company in two was to form a mutually beneficial relationship, with one company owning hotels and the other managing them.

"Host Marriott should have been our growth vehicle," Bill reflected with some regret. "They had the money. They should have gone out and acquired more Marriott hotels." Having the same goal as Bill, Bollenbach had steered Host in the right direction during his two years as CEO. When he left to become Disney's CFO in 1995, Terence Golden, former General Services Administrator, got the job.

To Bill's dismay, Golden began moving Host away from its crucial ties to Marriott International. Publicly Golden said the right things about the alliance, but privately he began pulling the two companies apart. He did do one thing Bill appreciated. In 1999, Golden reorganized Host Marriott into a Real Estate Investment Trust (REIT). REITs pay out nearly all of their profits to shareholders in the form of dividends. That created a tax shelter that allowed Host to buy more hotels, none of which were Marriotts.

When Golden left Host in 2000, his number two, Chris Nassetta, was promoted to replace him. Again, Bill was disappointed when Nassetta widened the gulf between Host and Marriott International. Bill's son John saw this from the front lines, since he worked at Host for several of those years. "Terry and Chris clearly made it a separate company. They were not bashful about it. They were good people, but they did not have Marriott's interest at heart," John recalled. (Nassetta later left to be Hilton's CEO.)

The most serious unraveling between the two companies occurred in 2002 when, in that post–9/11 world, Host decided to hammer Marriott International with rounds of audits and demands for lower management fees. At the time, 110 of Host's 122 hotels were managed by Marriott International; Host was the largest single owner of Marriott-managed hotels. Though Host never took the fee dispute to court, the behind-the-scenes renegotiation was so unsettling that Bill resigned from the Host board.

Bill was disappointed with the way Host Marriott turned out, so in 2004 Marriott created a new REIT called DiamondRock Hospitality. The new company, which was organized to be everything Bill had wanted Host Marriott to be, rapidly began acquiring Marriott hotels— even from Host.

In 2005, the distance between Marriott and Host Marriott became very public and official. Nassetta cut a deal with Starwood Hotels and Resorts for Host to acquire thirty-eight luxury and upper-tier hotels for $4 billion. Since that would tip the percentage of Host's hotels to only 50 percent Marriott brands, Nassetta moved to change the name of the company from Host Marriott to Host Hotels and Resorts, which is its name today.

Other Marriott International changes in the early 2000s included selling its food-distribution and retirement-community businesses. When Bill's team took a close look at the company's sixty-year-old internal food distribution system in the early 1980s, they realized that "we were sitting on top of a potential new external business," he said. "What hadn't occurred to us before then was the potential of selling our distribution experience to others. We discovered our costs were lower than our competitors, so we had the confidence to move quickly to sign up outside clients for Marriott Distribution Services (MDS)."

With that plan in place, MDS opened a technologically advanced, 100,000-square-foot distribution center in Savage, Maryland, which quickly became one of the top two wholesale food distribution centers in the United States. A half dozen other new facilities sprouted up after that, turning MDS into a prodigious enterprise by the late 1990s, and more than half of its clients were not Marriott.

But at the turn of the century, MDS began losing money, so the company came up with a new idea: join with hotel competitors to create a new lodging procurement company whose combined purchasing clout would reduce all of the owners' costs. In fairly short order, four hotel chains—Hyatt, Accor, ClubCorp, and IHG—joined Marriott to found Avendra in 2001.

As the foremost hotel procurement company in the U.S. from its founding, Avendra took off like gangbusters and had an unmatched trajectory compared to other Marriott spin-offs. It took only a few years of dividends for Marriott to have its $13-million investment returned and to begin making sizable profits. Then, sixteen years after its creation, Avendra was sold to Aramark in 2017 for $1.35 billion. As a 55-percent owner-partner, Marriott's take was $650 million against its original $13-million investment.

Marriott had entered the retirement-community business in the 1980s because "it seemed like a natural extension of our lodging and dining experience," Bill said. "The housekeeping was similar to what we do in hotels: clean rooms, clean lobbies, mow the lawn, take care of the landscaping. And we had the food service down cold."

By 2003, Marriott Senior Living Services managed 126 properties in twenty-nine states with a resident capacity of 23,157. But SLS had become a serious drag on the bottom line because the business was fraught with problems. "You could run at 65 percent occupancy in hotels and make a profit, but you had to run 95 percent occupancy in these places to make money," Bill reflected. "The business was getting competitive, and liability insurance took almost all the profit out."

More important, the company was never comfortable with the medical side of the business. The majority of SLS residents needed health care—about 50 percent were assisted-living clients and 16 percent required skilled nursing care. "Caring for healthy people in a hotel setting is one thing; caring for frail or ill people in an assisted-living situation turned out to be much more difficult than we thought," Bill said. "We didn't have the expertise to do justice to all their special needs. If we couldn't do it all and do it well, then I decided it was better not to do it all."

In 2003, Marriott found a reputable buyer, Sunrise Assisted Living Inc. of McLean, Virginia, which paid $150 million for the Marriott holdings.

Throughout the previous seventy-six years of operation, Marriott had tried its hand at a panoply of businesses with varying degrees of success. These lines of business included family restaurants, airline catering, industrial food services, theme parks, cruise ships, airport concessions, toll-road restaurants, fast-food chains, home security, a travel agency, distribution services, and senior-living communities. All of them were either spun off or sold.

Thus, on April 1, 2003, for the first time in its history, Marriott was exclusively a hotel-management company.

Two years later, Bill and Donna commemorated their golden wedding anniversary. The post–9/11 recession had dissipated, and Marriott International was thriving, so Bill was in an ebullient mood to celebrate the anniversary with his family and friends in a special way—a chartered Mediterranean cruise aboard the legendary *Sea Cloud,* one of the last great tall ships and the largest private sailing yacht ever built.

From June 25 to July 2, 2005, the thirty-seven members of the Marriott family and a few friends sailed from Istanbul to ancient Troy, the Greek islands, and Ephesus, Turkey. Bill loved it all—the luxury ship, the water, the family, the friends. "It was a great way for him to decompress, to relax," said daughter-in-law Carrie. "No one could really reach him from the company unless they absolutely had to—which they didn't. So, in his jacket and long pants—I've never seen him in shorts—he sits there with his books and his best friends. They hang out and chat and watch the water as we sail along."

For the anniversary couple, the most memorable evening was the original skit that the grandchildren put on to celebrate the fifty-year marriage. The chorus crooned "Sweetheart of Sigma Chi" and "Sunrise, Sunset." The narration ended with, "So here we are sailing around on the *Sea Cloud* celebrating fifty years of marriage of two wonderful people who still love each other. They have both blessed the lives of countless others through their service and example in sickness and health, in good times and throughout tremendous challenges." Out came grandchildren representing Bill and Donna as the chorus belted out: "We're a couple of swells, we dine at the best hotels! . . . And we'll travel along, singing our song, side by side."[4]

In the immediate months following their return from the *Sea Cloud* voyage, Bill and John engaged in deep discussions destined to impact both the family and the company. When Bill had turned seventy, three years earlier, Wall Street and trade media pundits became more persistent in questioning who would be his successor as CEO. Bill Shaw was president, but wasn't interested in being CEO, as he expected to retire about the same time as Bill stepped down as CEO. The public speculation settled on two front-runners—CFO Arne Sorenson and John.

Sorenson was three years older than John and had been part of every major Marriott deal since he had joined the company. He was personable, a fine manager, and a favorite of Wall Street analysts. John was smart and an excellent hotel deal-maker, but he was more a gifted entrepreneur than a natural leader.

Bill had advanced John fairly quickly through the company ranks, putting him on the Marriott board in 2002 and promoting him a year later to be executive vice president of lodging. But Bill knew that John could only be elevated to the CEO post if the board and shareholders approved him as the best choice. "With his gold-plated name, his all-American good looks and a quarter-century in the family business, [John] would seem to be a perfect fit for his father's shoes. Not so fast, though, says his father," the *New York Times* wrote. "At 71, Bill Marriott keeps a vigorous pace, visiting 200 hotels a year. He said he has no plans to step down. 'I'm still having fun,' he said, and he emphasized that there was no shoo-in for leading the company in the future."

Two years later, *Wall Street Journal* reporter Christina Binkley zeroed in on the issue with a lengthy article headlined: "As Succession Looms, Marriott Ponders Keeping Job in Family." The Marriott family viewed it as a "hit" piece on John because it highlighted his occasional public awkwardness and inability to win over Wall Street analysts in comparison to the more suave and savvy Arne Sorenson.

Sorenson was quoted in the article highlighting the idea that Marriott International was a publicly owned company and not a

Marriott family sinecure—hence, the ultimate rationale for Bill's choice of successor would not necessarily be a blood tie. Sorenson told the reporter, "The [ongoing] role of the Marriott family has yet to be determined."[5] Bill was upset about the quote because it implied that Sorenson was pushing the family aside.

But after the article, it was time for father and son to talk in depth about the issue. It turned out that John had already decided that not only was he the wrong choice for CEO, but he didn't want the job. He had only left the possibility open because he thought it was what his father wanted. So, in October 2005, Bill made the announcement that John was resigning from Marriott International to serve as CEO of J.W.M. Family Enterprises, a private family partnership John had helped create in 1993. Family Enterprises had more than $600 million in assets, including ten Marriott-managed hotels.

It was obvious to everyone who knew him that, in the ensuing years, John was happier wheeling and dealing on his own for the family's private company, though, at the same time, he served as the vice chairman of the Marriott board. One of Bill's greatest sorrows came as his relationship with John disintegrated in the years that followed. Their personality differences became more apparent, and John pulled away from his previously close relationship with the family. At one point, John even sued his father over money issues. The suit was settled privately.

• • •

Of all the things Bill thought his job as CEO would include, becoming a blogger at age seventy-five was not on the list. He hired a new communications chief who was high on blogging as a way to connect Bill with his customers. But he has always been a technophobe. He takes handwritten notes on legal pads at business meetings. When visiting hotels across the world, he jots down his thoughts on note cards stored in his jacket pocket. He has found he can't do business without a cell phone, but he never owned a computer. In fact, he never learned to use a keyboard or typewriter. When he was assured that he could write his blog scripts in longhand or dictate them into a voice recorder, he was sold.

Bill's blog debuted on January 16, 2007: "A year ago, I didn't even know what a blog was [and] now I know this is where the action is if you want to talk to your customers directly and hear back from them." His signature closing became: "Thank you for helping me keep Marriott on the Move!"[6]

His first post got 151 comments; he read them all and responded to some of them. If customers wanted to gripe about a bad hotel room or poor service, they would go straight to Bill's blog and complain to the boss. His folksy weekly blogs, which averaged about 700 words, covered a wide variety of topics. He wrote about trips he took, what he learned from his employees, legislative issues, how his stint as a Latter-day Saint bishop helped him develop compassion, the importance of good tips for waitstaff, and his favorite place to relax with his golden retriever Murphy at Lake Winnipesaukee.

Bill's entry into the blogosphere was uniformly praised by business writers with headlines like: "An Old Dog Learns to Write a New Blog." The *Los Angeles Times* wrote that Bill's blog was consistently refreshing because "most CEO blogs read like they've been scrubbed of all life by publicists and lawyers." After five years of Bill's blogs, the *Washington Post* crowned him "Chairman of the Blog."[7]

When Bill flew to New York City for the announcement of a new partnership between Marriott and the children's TV channel Nickelodeon to create a chain of upscale resort hotels with water parks, he blogged about the ceremony. Standing next to SpongeBob SquarePants, Bill smiled as a bucket of Nickelodeon's trademark green slime was dumped over his head. "That's the highest honor you can get from Nickelodeon, so they tell me," he wrote. *Baltimore Sun* columnist Jay Hancock observed after the stunt: "Bill Marriott has perfected the art of being a CEO pitchman. Equal parts clown, maitre d'hotel and corporate royalty, he affects a ruffled dignity that draws attention without making shareholders think he's off his rocker."[8]

No veteran hotelier can forget the Great Bed Wars at the opening of the twenty-first century, when, at great expense, hotel chains "went to the mattresses" to outdo their rivals. From customer surveys, hoteliers learned that guests would pay more per night for a room with a better bed. Westin Hotels responded first with a "Heavenly Bed" campaign in 2000. Radisson advertised beds that allowed personalization with an air pump. Sheraton pushed its new Sealy Posturepedic Plush Top Sleeping System. Marriott upgraded many of its beds in 2002, but the new model didn't catch on. However, when the company launched a mattress makeover again three years later, backed by an award-winning advertising campaign, it was a booming success.

A January 2005 news conference unveiled the campaign. Executives and staff joined the "Pajama Party Rally" on the day of the announcement by showing up in sleeping attire. Bill and his sons posed for a photo in PJs and robes sitting on the end of one of the new beds, a stunt that drew widespread media coverage. To the assembled and amused journalists, Bill announced the company's "Clean for You" bedding campaign. Marriott would spend $190 million to replace 628,000 beds with better mattresses, softer sheets, and more pillows. Every king-sized bed in eight of Marriott's chains would be getting seven pillows instead of five, a pillow-top mattress cover, and a white duvet. No longer would guests find those scratchy, dark bedspreads that were not laundered more often than quarterly unless a housekeeper noticed distinctive spots. Not only the sheets but also the duvet cover would be washed after every checkout. Bill bragged on his blog that "this makes Marriott's new bedding the cleanest and freshest of any major hotel chain."[9]

Marriott opened its 3,000th hotel in Beijing in 2008, just a few months ahead of the Summer Olympics there. Among those 3,000

Bill and his sons roll out the new Marriott bedding.

properties was an increasing variety of brands. Three new chains had been spawned—SpringHill Suites, TownePlace Suites, and the "Autograph Collection."

The most interesting new brand was "Edition," a series of smaller, trendy hotels to be created by Ian Schrager, whom Arne Sorenson courted for a partnership with Marriott. Observed the *Washington Post:* "An almost perfect contrast with Marriott, a Mormon who does not drink, Schrager came up in the free-wheeling, New York disco days of the 1970s and 1980s, founding Studio 54 and Palladium." While some predicted disaster from this combination of opposites, others noted that Marriott might do for Schrager what Kohl's had done for Vera Wang and Target for Isaac Mizrahi. In fact, the partnership worked well, but the expansion of Edition was inevitably slowed down by the burst of the housing bubble, which began a recession in 2008.[10]

Two of the more important hotels constructed during this time were in Los Angeles and Washington, D.C. During the mid-2000s, in an effort to revitalize downtown Los Angeles, the city fathers and developer AEG forged ahead with the "L.A. Live" project: a $2.5-billion sports and entertainment complex next to the Staples Center and Los Angeles Convention Center. Marriott won the bid to be in the hotel tower. Opened in 2010, the JW Marriott hotel is on floors 3 to 21; a Ritz-Carlton hotel is on floors 22 to 26; and the final floors, 27 to 54, hold Residences at the Ritz-Carlton luxury condominiums.[11]

In the nation's capital, Marriott also won the contract to build a new hotel next to the Walter E. Washington Convention Center. Boasting 1,175 rooms, the $520-million Marriott Marquis is connected via underground concourse to the convention center. In its lobby is a fifty-six-foot-high sculpture, *The Birth of the American Flag*, by renowned Baltimore sculptor Rodney Carroll; it is the largest piece of artwork in any Marriott hotel. Bill felt more than a little nostalgic at the June 2014 opening of the hotel, which is located near the spot where a humble root beer stand had begun the Marriott empire. As the assembled dignitaries hoisted their mugs in a root beer toast, Bill announced that this was Marriott's 4,000th hotel.[12]

With the quantum leaps in Marriott's hotel acquisitions, nothing stands out as clearly as the lack of a hotel/casino. While Bill's major competitors were making a killing in Las Vegas, he could not bring himself to get into the gambling business. He had a chance in 1972 to sign a management contract in Las Vegas, but then even his board of directors warned it wouldn't be good for Marriott's image. In 1976, he passed on the opportunity to buy the Del Webb Company, including its Nevada casinos. In that case, the board again warned him away.

Bill had stockholders to please, so he was wary of falling back on his church's aversion to gambling as a reason to steer clear of a potentially lucrative line of business. Instead, he would frequently say the casino hotels were too expensive, or that Marriott had no expertise in running casinos. But in truth, in most cases, he could have found the money or hired the expertise. He just didn't want to.

In 2005, Bill had to decide one more time. Marriott was a major player in the convention business, and Las Vegas was a major convention town. There, hoteliers considered sleeping rooms to be an add-on to casinos. Marriott had smaller hotels in the gambling mecca, but none were "full service," because that would have meant a casino. Because of the nature of the full-service casino hotel, construction costs on the Las Vegas Strip in the early 2000s were running at $1 million a room.

Both the board and most of his top executives were pushing Bill to approve a 4,000-room hotel and casino as the last piece of their convention network. It would be built on a piece of land that Marriott already owned. During the board meetings, playing to Bill's well-known objections, executives assured the board that the operation could be a classic "Chinese Wall"—a thinly veiled division between the casino managed by hired experts in that field and the hotel benefiting from Marriott's considerable expertise. Bill approved millions of dollars in eighteen months of preplanning and design work, but that hit a snag when Architecture and Construction chief Brad Bryan became unrelenting in his gloomy forecasts of costs.

Bill told the company's developers and marketers that a buyer must be found in advance for the whole project. But the best they could do was find those willing to come up with, say, $2 billion. Bryan was adamant: it was not enough. The hotel was likely to cost $1 million a room, for a total of at least $4 billion. Las Vegas has a closed, unionized construction subcontracting market, and no one could be found to do it for less, he said. Bill believed him. The last thing he wanted was another San Francisco Marriott–like albatross of debt dragging the company down in what was shaping up to be another serious recession from the spreading subprime lending crisis. In spite of objections from most of his top men and some board members, Bill explained in mid-2008 that with no comprehensive buyer on hand, he was going to "put a hold on the project."

And then the bubble burst. Big time. Las Vegas was suddenly at the epicenter of the 2008 housing and building crash. "It was a bloodbath," Bryan said. The $3.1-billion Fontainebleau Hotel under construction in Las Vegas, of a similar size to the one envisioned by Marriott, filed for bankruptcy in mid-2009 when it was 70 percent built. Billionaire Carl Icahn later bought it at auction for $150 million. That would have been Marriott's fate also. Never again did Bill venture into gambling, and Marriott remained the only giant hotelier in the United States without casinos.

No matter how many hotels were added to the Marriott stable, and no matter how old he was, Bill was determined to go to most of the full-service hotel openings and continue his inspection visits of 100 to 200 hotels each year. He still carried paint remover to clean his pants if he brushed wet paint. And he eventually got over his surprise at the lengths to which some general managers would go to try to impress him. "One of them stationed a scout in the parking garage across the street with a pair of binoculars to watch my room in the predawn hours. When I turned the light on, he called the general manager and let him know that the boss was up and might be coming down soon."

The truth is that most of the general managers know there's almost nothing they can hide from Bill, as exemplified by a favorite story shared by Jim Quinn, general manager of the San Antonio Riverwalk Marriott: "I typically walk every inch of the property so I see everything before Mr. Marriott does when he comes," Quinn explained. "But in my haste [in 2011], I didn't go to the ballroom level. So when I walked into the ballroom ahead of Bill, I saw there was a piece of duct tape holding a worn spot of the carpet down."

Quinn covered the spot with his foot before Bill could see it, or so he thought. He pointed out every feature in the room, including the chandelier, without moving from the spot. When Quinn ran out of things to say, Bill asked, "How old is this carpet, Jim?"

"It's eight years old and it's due for a renovation, sir, but we keep getting it postponed by the owners," Jim responded.

"It looks pretty old—especially that spot that you're standing on right there," Bill said, smiling. When Jim sheepishly lifted up his foot, "my boss just starts cracking up and *his* boss is bowled over. They go, 'You fooled us! We had no idea!' It shows Mr. Marriott's attention to detail. He does not miss a beat."

Bill can be tough, but he can never be called a Scrooge because he consciously works to "pay it forward." He believes that those who have substantial means have an obligation to assist the less fortunate. He takes to heart a favorite Latter-day Saint hymn that begins: "Have I done any good in the world today? Have I helped anyone in need? Have I cheered up the sad and made someone feel glad? If not, I have failed indeed."[13] Both Bill and Donna have a deep-seated belief in giving back, a core value they have passed on to their children and grandchildren.

"The Marriott family's focus has always been, 'How do we use this [money] to help others?'" Bill Shaw said. Bill Marriott is not a soft touch, though a rare few have taken advantage of his largesse. His secretary Phyllis Hester has handled hundreds of letters from strangers petitioning him for money. One man asked Bill to buy him a nice RV so he could travel in style around the country.

Bill firmly believes in the admonition of Jesus in the Sermon on the Mount that those who follow Him should give their "alms in secret." He acknowledges that he pays a 10 percent tithing on his income to his church, but he otherwise does not detail his many charitable donations from his personal accounts, which one calculation suggests exceed more than $200 million given to worthy causes. A few stories have been shared by grateful recipients, like the following:

When a missionary at the Washington D.C. Temple was stricken with brain cancer, temple president Ed Scholz tried without success to arrange for transportation to her home in California. She had to travel on a stretcher, but no airline would accept her, even in two first-class seats. With no other alternative available, Scholz called Bill and explained the situation. "Is it at all possible that you could make an aircraft available to take her home to California?"

Bill replied: "You know that's going to be very expensive."

And then, Scholz recalled, "almost in the same breath Bill said, 'When do you need it?' The aircraft was made available to us."

Some philanthropy by the Marriotts is made public to encourage giving by others, particularly via challenge grants. Donna's extensive service on the boards of the American Heart Association and the Society for the Prevention of Blindness was undertaken in part to inspire others to assist in the research needed to combat these ailments. Bill has also served on the boards of the National Symphony Orchestra, the Goodwill Foundation, the Boy Scouts of America, and other nonprofit enterprises. At the personal request of First Lady Laura Bush in 2002, Bill spearheaded the creation of her Foundation for America's Libraries, including recruiting volunteers and raising $25 million for the foundation over a period of several years. After the devastating 2010 earthquake in Haiti, he and his company partnered with former President Bill Clinton and his foundation to help rebuild that country.

In general, there are three vehicles for Bill's charitable contributions: (1) personal donations; (2) Marriott corporation charitable programs, including educational and community efforts; and (3) the stewardship he and his brother have over the sizable foundation set up by their parents—and to which they have both added funds over the years. As a tax-exempt nonprofit, the J. Willard and Alice S. Marriott Foundation is obligated to publicly provide details of its charitable giving.

One review revealed that the single largest recipient has been the Marriott Foundation for People with Disabilities, which Bill's brother, Dick, started for the family in 1989. Its main program is Bridges from School to Work. "Simply put, it takes kids with disabilities and helps them find a job—but it's not so simple to execute," Bill explained.

461

Over three decades, Bridges has placed more than 20,000 young adults with disabilities in productive jobs in nine major cities.

The second-largest Marriott family foundation recipient is Brigham Young University, primarily through an endowment to the Marriott School of Management. Number three is the University of Utah, the alma mater for J.W., Allie, Bill, Dick, Donna, and John. Several hospitals are among the top twenty recipients, as are a variety of colleges with important hospitality programs, including Cornell, Purdue, and the Culinary Institute of America.

Coming in at number four is the Mayo Clinic. After Mayo's medical staff saved Debbie's life with open-heart surgery when she was only five, Bill and Donna began giving regularly to the clinic from their own funds and directing family foundation grants to the institution. The foundation gave Mayo $20 million for research on regeneration of damaged heart tissue.

Bill also served on Mayo's board of trustees for years, and he even accepted a daunting fund-raising task for the clinic. In 2005, Mayo asked Bill to lead a five-year campaign to raise $1.25 billion. He agreed, kick-starting it with $25 million from the family foundation. "Then I asked for a list of patients they had had with the most money," Bill recalled. "They were appalled, but they finally gave it to me. We started calling them, and they gave generously." When the campaign came to an end on the last day of 2009, Bill's leadership had brought in $1.35 billion in donations—$100 million more than the goal—from more than 286,000 benefactors in the middle of the economic crisis caused by the housing downturn.[14]

In all, the J. Willard and Alice S. Marriott Foundation has given nearly $500 million to more than 1,100 causes.

Not only did Bill give away money, he also donated much of his time as he continued to serve as a regional leader in various capacities for his church, maintaining a heavy travel schedule. His supervisor in one of those assignments, Cree-L Kofford, wrote Bill a letter: "In many people's minds, humility is most easily identified with 'the poor, the lame and the halt,' but seldom is the word used to describe a dynamic, successful leader. I think the thing that came most forcibly to my mind [during a meeting] was that you truly are a humble servant of our Heavenly Father."[15]

Part of the respect for Bill among the Church's leaders stems from the impact he has had on the Church's worldwide missionary work. He has placed hundreds of thousands of copies of the Book of Mormon in the company's hotel rooms alongside the Bible.

Beginning in 1977, he has hosted the annual "Festival of Lights" at the Washington D.C. Temple Visitors' Center, to which the public and prominent political leaders are invited. Typically, dozens of diplomats attend the event at Bill's invitation.

He often hosts other events for diplomats in Washington to mingle with officials of The Church of Jesus Christ of Latter-day Saints, with the aim of shoring up Church relations around the world.

In an interview, Elder Russell M. Nelson (who later became President of the Church) stressed that Bill helped pave the way for the Church's Christian missionary work in many countries because "the Marriott name carried so much weight with these people. They were doing cartwheels to get Marriott hotels in their countries, so when Bill hosted an activity, lending his good name and his great faith to the Lord's work, they came and they listened."

Whenever Bill opened a hotel in a foreign country where the Church had problems with missionary visas, he made sure Church leaders were on hand to meet the government's officials who attended his grand openings. Elder D. Todd Christofferson, an Apostle, never forgot what a difference it made for the Church's relations with the Mexican government when Bill introduced him to President Ernesto Zedillo at the opening of a Mexico City Marriott. "Bill was just so up front about the Church. He was not in the least reticent or embarrassed in any way about his membership and bringing it to the forefront."

Finally, at the age of seventy-nine, in June 2011, Bill was released from his last prominent Church leadership position—an office called Area Seventy. By that time, he had the longest tenure of anyone in the calling—fifteen years, or three times the normal service. Elder Kofford wrote him a note on the occasion: "It's a little like Mount Rushmore came tumbling down."

CHAPTER 28

THE WORK IS NEVER DONE

When Bill was sixty-four years old, Donna told an oral historian that she doubted he had it in him to retire. "He keeps saying, maybe when he turns sixty-five. But he's one year away from sixty-five and that is not going to happen. I just can't see Bill ever retiring because he doesn't really have any hobbies to go to." She knew her husband well.

In 2011, at the age of seventy-nine, Bill thought maybe it was time to step down as CEO of Marriott International. The leading candidate to succeed him was Arne Sorenson.

"It would make for a dramatic telling if I could say that I had a fireworks-and-marching-band epiphany while sitting on my dock in New Hampshire at sunset or while watching Arne deliver a flawless speech to a group of financiers. But, in all honesty, the choice of Arne was a gradual process, an evolution," Bill reflected in a 2012 revision of his *Spirit to Serve* book. "At some point I found myself listening to Arne's ideas with more than ordinary interest. He had a good grasp of the company's strengths and weaknesses, a feel for the future of the travel industry and a sense of direction that impressed me and others. He also seemed to 'get' our values and culture—key for anyone who might lead the company someday."[1]

Bill with Arne Sorenson.

Sorenson attributed his ascension to fortunate timing as much as anything else. "There's been a lot of great talent come through the company, including a few who tried to take over Bill's job at a time when he wasn't ready to give it up." Sorenson referenced the 2005 *Wall Street Journal* article as a turning point for Bill. In Bill's view, the *Journal* story had been "an unfair hatchet job on John." When Sorenson had been quoted in the article questioning the future role of the Marriott family in the company, Bill was upset with him. "Arne knew he made a mistake," Bill recalled. "He even apologized. It was a good thing in the end because he realized that the family was always going to have an influence and he needed to recognize that."

The *Journal* reporter had deliberately used Sorenson as an antagonist against John Marriott, the heir apparent. Despite the dustup, the article had prompted Bill to more seriously consider Sorenson as the potential CEO, especially after Bill and John mutually decided that John was a better fit to run JWM Family Enterprises, where some Marriott-managed hotels were parked.

With John's future decided, and no other family member ready yet for the CEO job, Bill's mind was free to look outside the family. Sorenson, who had been Marriott's CFO and its first nonfamily president, was the logical choice. At the time of the official announcement, Bill explained that he wasn't leaving the company. He would stay on as the executive chairman and chairman of the board, but he would give fifty-three-year-old Sorenson a fairly free hand in running the company. "Bill was determined not to be like his father, looking over Arne's shoulder every minute and questioning everything he does like his father had done with him," Donna explained.

Released from the day-to-day grind of company operations, Bill had more time to spend with his growing family of grandchildren. In the summer of 1993, Scott Harrison became the first grandchild to marry, and five years later he added the first great-grandchild to the family.

In 2013, Bill and Donna experienced the worst tragedy that can happen to parents—the loss of a child. At the age of fifty-four, Stephen finally lost his long struggle against the degenerative mitochondrial disease with which he was afflicted. A year before he died, Stephen submitted to an extensive interview about his life. He recounted favorite moments of his childhood; his love for his church, his wife, Julie, his children, and his five grandchildren; his satisfaction with his professional job performance as vice president of Corporate Culture; and his thoughts about the future. He was upbeat and full of hope.

> *Is your illness fatal?*
> "I don't know. The doctors don't know. Everybody has
>   to die sometime, though."
> *Have you ever been angry at God for suffering from this
>   illness?*
> "No."

Not once?

"No. It's just part of my trial here. I know that in the
next life I'll be fine."

When you die, how would you like to be remembered?

"That I was a good husband. That I was good and kind
to my wife, my children, and my grandchildren."

On May 30, the increasingly frail Stephen had a bad fall in his
home and was rushed to Suburban Hospital in Bethesda, Maryland.
After regaining consciousness, he was released to go home, only to suffer a grand mal seizure and return to the hospital. Further treatment
could not stop his rapid decline. On Thursday evening, June 20, Bill,
Ron, and Stephen's son-in-law Spencer Samuelian gave a final priesthood blessing to Stephen to comfort him and ease his pain. "The Spirit
was so strong. We held his hands, and he knew we were there," Debbie
recalled.

On Saturday, Bill wasn't able to visit until ten o'clock in the evening. "It was the night Stephen died. I held his hand for a half hour
or so, kissed him good night, and left. It was the last time I saw my
wonderful son alive." Stephen died peacefully at 3:08 a.m. on Sunday
morning, June 23, surrounded by his wife, three children, and two
sons-in-law. At home, Debbie woke up and looked at the clock. It was
3:08 a.m. "I said to myself, 'Stephen is dying.' Then I felt this really
peaceful feeling and I went back to sleep."

As president of the Washington D.C. Stake of The Church of Jesus
Christ of Latter-day Saints, Ron Harrison (Debbie's husband) conducted the funeral service. Debbie played the organ. Stephen's three
children gave eloquent and touching tributes to their father, followed
by Bill, who shared details of Stephen's early years and praised his character. "Donna and I have been deeply blessed to have raised such an
outstanding son. I bear my testimony that God lives, that Jesus is the
Christ, and there is indeed life eternal so that we look forward to the
day we will be gloriously reunited with Stephen."

Photo © Gale Frank-Adise

The last photo taken of the four Marriott siblings (left to right): David, Stephen, John, and Debbie.

Elder Jeffrey R. Holland, one of the Church's Twelve Apostles, was the concluding speaker. He talked about the privilege of knowing Stephen at BYU. The debilitating illness, Holland said, reminded him of the ancient Japanese practice of *kintsugi,* repairing cracks in precious porcelain objects with adhesive pure gold. "They enhanced the broken object, which thus became more beautiful and more valuable because of the damage it had experienced. None of us would have had Stephen face what he experienced from such an early age—its terrible, terrible effect. He was blessed and purified and made more beautiful because of the damage that was done to him and the challenges he faced. Through it all, I say and testify and know it to be true that this boy was absolutely pure gold."

For the present, he added, "It's wonderful to know that Stephen now sees better than any of us see. It is wonderful to know that he now hears better than any of us hear. . . . Stephen is not dead. I have it on the word of the Savior of the world, of Him who is the Resurrection and the Life that Stephen Marriott is not dead."

A few weeks later, when the family was attending church services at the lake, David's youngest son, four-year-old Henry, stood up on his chair, pointed toward the dais, and said to his mother, Carrie: "Look, Mom, there's Uncle Stephen." She thought he was referring to Ron, who was standing at the pulpit. "You mean Uncle Ron, right?" she responded.

"No, Mom, it's Uncle Stephen. Can't you see him?"

"No. Where is he?" she asked.

"He's sitting right next to Grandpa [Bill] up there on the stand."

Carrie gently asked, "What does he look like?"

"He looks like Jesus," the four-year-old said. "He looks really happy."

•　•　•

Marriott International continued to evolve. Just before he relinquished the CEO post, Bill and his team put together one last spin-off—Marriott Vacation Club International (MVCI), the time-share business founded in 1984. MVCI was the company's last capital-intensive business. The stock market was never going to properly value it, so it was spun off in 2011 as Marriott Vacations Worldwide Corporation. On its own, the spin-off's stock performed well, trading at $16 a share when it began and at $140 a share seven years later.

Sorenson's mandate from Bill had been to grow Marriott, and he pursued that idea with a kind of proselyting fervor. In 2010, Marriott partnered with the Spanish lodging group AC Hotels to help fuel the company's growth in Europe and Latin America. AC's ninety hotels in Spain, Italy, and Portugal were rebranded "AC Hotels by Marriott," and were managed by Marriott. In 2012, Marriott bought the Gaylord Hotel brand and the right to manage its four convention hotels in Nashville, Tennessee; Grapevine, Texas; Kissimmee, Florida; and Washington, D.C. The deal added 7,800 rooms to Marriott's 644,000, which consisted of seventeen brands around the world.

In 2013, Marriott partnered with Swedish furniture giant Ikea to launch a new budget hotel brand called Moxy. Targeted at young, price-conscious, well-traveled clientele, Marriott planned to build 150 franchised Moxy Hotels in the next decade throughout Europe. In 2014, Marriott bought Protea Hospitality Holdings of Cape Town, South Africa. The acquisition doubled Marriott's presence in Africa with 116 hotels in South Africa and six other sub-Saharan countries. Then, in January 2015, Marriott snapped up Delta Hotels and Resorts, with thirty-eight hotels across Canada.

Two months later, the *Washington Post* reported on Sorenson's dizzying pace. "Arne M. Sorenson is the first non-Marriott to head the hotel empire that bears the family's name. Three years into the job, it's become clear why Bill Marriott wanted Sorenson for the job: The company's stock is on a tear, and Marriott is adding tens of thousands of rooms worldwide annually, putting it on pace to pass one million rooms open or on the way this year."[2]

That didn't account for a massive acquisition only eight months later that wasn't on anyone's radar in early 2015.

Barry Sternlicht, founder of Starwood Hotels and Resorts, was a deal maker and an innovator. Starwood had acquired Westin Hotels & Resorts for $1.6 billion and soon bought Sheraton for $9.8 billion. Then Sternlicht invented the successful boutique W hotel brand. He seemed unstoppable, but he was not a good hotel operator and had trouble acquiring top talent.

In April 2015, the Starwood board announced that they were pursuing "strategic alternatives," which was the catchphrase for a sale. At first, Marriott wasn't interested. "The deal looked like it would be too expensive. Plus, they had a lot of real estate we didn't want, and the Sheraton segment looked like it needed a lot of work," Marriott's Rick Hoffman said. There were more than a dozen other interested parties by the time Sorenson persuaded Bill to jump in. It finally came down to Marriott and one other bidder—the Chinese Anbang Group.

What was most appealing about Starwood to Bill was Sorenson's "bigger is better" strategy, as well as the chance to take a significant competitor off the field. The November 15, 2015, announcement of a deal between Marriott and Starwood rocked the industry. Marriott was to pay $12.2 billion for Starwood, which would make Marriott the indisputable largest hotelier in the world—by a wide margin. Marriott's two dozen brands would be united with Starwood's brands. The combined company would leave Marriott with 5,500 properties and more than 1.1 million rooms around the world. The next-largest hotel company would be Hilton Worldwide with 4,500 properties and about 735,000 rooms.

Then, just days before the deal was to be finalized, Anbang's enigmatic chairman, Wu Xiaohui, outbid Marriott with a $13.2 billion all-cash offer. The politically well-connected Wu, who was married to the granddaughter of Chinese leader Deng Xiaoping, had been on a buying spree in the previous years. He had paid nearly $2 billion for the famous Waldorf Astoria in New York City and was in the process of buying Strategic Hotels & Resorts for $6.5 billion. News reports suggested that Anbang had more than $250 billion in assets. Bill could not hope to compete if Wu was all-in for Starwood.

"We thought for certain we would lose," Sorenson recalled. Then, inexplicably, Anbang bowed out. Well-informed reports in the *New York Times* subsequently deduced that Anbang had lost his political backing. The Chinese government was angered by his high-profile and seemingly hostile bidding war with the well-regarded Marriott company. Undoubtedly, he received orders to back off. Wu's fortunes rapidly went downhill. First, he was forced to resign from Anbang. And then, in 2018, two years after his contest with Marriott, he pled guilty to defrauding investors and was sentenced in a Chinese court to eighteen years in prison.[3]

At the celebration dinner in New York City following the closing of the landmark Marriott-Starwood merger, Sorenson offered a toast to the boss, Bill Marriott, now the undisputed heavyweight champion of the hotel world.

Bill declined taking any credit. "I didn't do anything."

"You did one really important thing," Sorenson responded. "You said 'Yes.'"

Sorenson was right. He was CEO, but if Bill had expressed any misgivings to the board, negotiations would have been dead in the water. "Mr. Marriott's fingerprints were all over that deal—from the people he let run it, to the ultimate decision to go ahead and do it," agreed Hoffman.

The most telling moment happened during the negotiations when Hoffman and Sorenson were still trying to persuade Bill to go after Starwood in earnest. Hoffman recalled, "At one point, Mr. Marriott paused and stopped talking altogether. We waited to hear what he was going to say next. . . . What Bill said echoed his old arguments with J.W. about risk vs. caution. 'I've become too complacent,' Bill said. 'I don't want to risk anything to change the good place we are in now. I can't sit back like that. Okay, let's go!'

"I understood what he was saying," Hoffman related. "Our stock was doing very well. Investors were happy with the company. We were executing on our strategy. We had these good, smaller acquisitions and we were growing like crazy. So we didn't have to take on Starwood with all the integration issues with our company. But Bill is the guy with the vision—even in his mid-eighties."

Bill Marriott lives by the motto he has always espoused: "Success is never final!" As soon as a person thinks it is, that person fails. It's the same with companies.

"Our corporate culture is restless, and we are never satisfied with current performance, but are always striving to do better," he told the San Francisco Century Club.[4] "When a company achieves a long period of sustained dominance, the human factors of pride, arrogance, and complacency seem to overtake many more noble qualities. We know the results of not changing are continual decline and eventual disappearance from the marketplace," he told another gathering.[5]

"Bill always tells me, 'Success is never final,' and that is in our corporate DNA," concluded Arne Sorenson. "He lives his life that way. He works harder than anyone else at the company, and I don't see that changing. No matter how well we are doing, he's always asking: 'What can we do better?' He applies that to himself. No matter how kind, how wonderful he is, he is sure he can be a better person if he works at it more. Bill Marriott won't ever stop working to improve until his heart stops."

AUTHOR'S NOTE

For me, there has not been a more reluctant subject of a biography than J. Willard (Bill) Marriott Jr. It took more than a year before he agreed with his daughter, Debbie, that a biography for his posterity would be a good thing. After six years of my working on this family history project, he finally allowed, albeit reluctantly, that the lessons of his life story might be beneficial to more than just his family.

There are many to whom I owe thanks for their help with this book. First and foremost is Bill himself. Over those years, he submitted—which is the right word—to more than fifty interviews, always responding candidly to questions. He reviewed every word of this manuscript and offered both important corrections and delightful additional stories. I am grateful also for the support of his wife, Donna; their marriage of sixty-three years and counting is a true model of love, respect, and loyalty. In addition to interviews with her, Donna's meticulously kept scrapbooks were a rich source of family memorabilia and news clippings not available elsewhere.

I am indebted to Bill's father, who was known in his adult life also as Bill or Bill Senior, which I abbreviated in this book to J.W. to more easily distinguish him from his son. I interviewed J.W. at length about his son on two occasions before he died in 1985. His handwritten journals stretching over four decades were a treasure trove for this biography, allowing him to speak posthumously in his own words throughout this book. Scrapbooks from his wife, Allie, were another helpful resource.

All of the Marriott family, including Dick and his family, were generous with their time, especially Debbie, who provided some of the most profound and memorable insights and stories in this book. Along the same line, Bill's close friends Ralph Hardy and Sterling Colton were longtime advocates of the importance of his biography and provided much-needed support and guidance. Also in this cadre were Bill's corporate assistants Phyllis Hester and Steve McNeil, who were both unstinting with their time and logistical support.

At Marriott International, CEO Arne Sorenson offered substantial insights and support. I was allowed unrestricted access to the minutes of meetings of the board of directors, which occurred through the kind assistance of corporate secretary Bancroft Gordon. General manager Marty Roth and staff at the Bethesda (MD) Marriott Suites made sure that my home-away-from-home for research purposes was as welcoming and friendly as possible.

Evidencing rare wisdom for a worldwide company, Marriott International has a corporate archives section, which is now helmed by Katie Dishman. It is part of the company's continued reiteration of its core values, including the spirit to serve, which have made Marriott so remarkably successful. This archive was an invaluable resource for my research, as was the J.W. and Allie manuscript collection contained under the auspices of the Special Collections section of the University of Utah's J. Willard Marriott Library. Not incidentally, most of this book was written in the friendly environs of the Ashburn, Virginia, public library, where the staff and associates (including Debbi Zisco and Becca Welt) were wonderfully helpful.

I interviewed more than 100 individuals for this biography, including many current and former Marriott employees. Prominent among them were Bill Shaw, Gary Wilson, Al Checchi, Brad Bryan, Jim Sullivan, and Rick Hoffman. Additionally, this work benefited substantially from oral history interviews conducted in 1995 and 1996 primarily by Kathi Ann Brown. In order to avoid overwhelming the reader with quotation citations, in most cases I do not specifically cite every quote from my own interviews or those from the oral history project in the Notes section.

This biography would never have occurred without the farsightedness of Jay Todd and Sheri Dew. It was Jay who, in 1982, assigned me to do a profile on Bill for the *Ensign,* an official magazine of The Church of Jesus Christ of Latter-day Saints. This began my association with the Marriott family; from that moment on, Bill became a personal hero and a North Star example of the right way to conduct oneself in life and in business.

A year after the *Ensign* assignment, Sheri Dew, then editor of *This People* magazine, asked me to write a cover story about Bill and his father. She later became Deseret Book's highly successful president and has moved "upstairs" to serve as executive vice president of Deseret Management Corporation. Due to her unfettered admiration of Bill, she was pivotal in finally convincing Bill to make his story available to the general public. She then facilitated this publication by Deseret Book's subsidiary, Shadow

Mountain. I am deeply grateful to Chris Schoebinger and the team at Shadow Mountain for their sensitive attention to this book, as well as the first-rate editing by chief editor Emily Watts.

I spent many years as a nationally syndicated columnist with Jack Anderson, exposing unethical or criminal activities of some of our nation's leaders. That work was important because I firmly believe that sunlight is the best disinfectant for keeping the country's leadership honest and true. But when I was done with that, it was time to turn my attention instead to promoting the good works of good people—their positive examples. Bill Marriott was always high on that list.

When I finally got the go-ahead to do his biography for his family, I was elated. As it turned out, I woefully underestimated the time it would take to do Bill justice. For six years, I toiled at the project; it became a mission. It certainly tested Bill's patience, but he hung in there and was always kind in his dealings with me in spite of his disappointment about the unexpectedly long, drawn-out process.

Writing is inherently a lonely business, and no one can continue day after day, year after year, without sufficient encouragement from close friends and family. Thus my greatest debt is to a quartet without whom I could never have completed this heartfelt mission. Daryl Gibson, my best friend since college, is an expert editor and writer in her own right. She has been involved in every aspect of this project, including mounting the first editing attack to slash the original 1,400-page manuscript to a more manageable size. My faithful friend and counselor Lynn Chapman read every word of the original manuscript and offered key suggestions. He buoyed my spirits throughout the project when he sensed I was flagging. The aforementioned Jay Todd, who has been like a second father to me, was a key cheerleader and editor of the manuscript as well.

And then there is Lynne, my wife of forty-four years. Throughout the long and challenging project, her faith in and support of me, as well as inspired editing suggestions, were of incalculable worth. Indeed, the best things in my life would not have been possible without her, including the adventure of this intense and inspiring project.

DALE VAN ATTA
Ashburn, VA
February 2019

NOTES

Please note: All quotations from Bill Marriott and others that are not referenced in these endnotes come from extensive interviews conducted by the author over the course of several months.

CHAPTER 1: PILGRIMS AND PIONEERS

1. From accounts of fellow *Pennell* passengers, in "Autobiography of Sarah B. Layton," *Women's Exponent* 19:18–19 (February 15 and March 1, 1901), 86–87; Diary of William L. Cutler, Ms. 1402, Church History Library, 124–53.
2. Elizabeth Stewart's autobiographical sketch as published by Hermoine Tracy Jex, *The Marriotts: Workers of Flock and Field* (Publishers Press, 1990), 497–98.
3. Ethel Marriott Tracy, in Jex, *Marriotts*, 497–98.
4. Bill Marriott, Remarks to Dayton (Ohio) East Stake Conference Adult Meeting, November 17, 2001.
5. Robert O'Brien, *Marriott: The J. Willard Marriott Story* (Deseret Book, 1977), 43–45.
6. O'Brien, *Marriott*, 58–59.
7. David Zuckerman, "J. Willard Marriott, a retrospective, 1900–1985," *Nation's Restaurant News*, October 7, 1985.
8. John G. Hubbell, "Everybody Likes to Work for Bill Marriott," *Reader's Digest*, January 1972.
9. Dale Van Atta, "The Marriotts: On David, Solomon, and Empire-Building," *This People*, October 1983; O'Brien, *Marriott*, 51–57.
10. Diary cited by Bill Marriott in Remarks, "Yerba Buena Hotel Opening," April 12, 1984.

CHAPTER 2: THE ROOT BEER STAND

1. "Drastic Action Is Taken by Officials," *Salt Lake Tribune*, October 10, 1918; *Ogden Standard*, October 16 and November 9, 1918.
2. J. Willard Marriott, in *Win If You Will: Thirteen Winners Show How* (Bookcraft, 1972), 246.
3. J. Willard Marriott Journal, December 22, 1919; hereafter "JWM Journal."
4. JWM Journal, February 25, 1920.
5. JWM Journal, January 12, February 3, and May 7, 1920.

6. JWM Journal, June 16, 1920; Pres. T.W. Tanner, *Liahona: the Elders' Journal,* 64, August 3, 1920.

7. JWM Journal, June 20, 1920.

8. JWM Journal, July 8, 1920.

9. JWM Journal, July 30, 1921.

10. Martin Buxbaum, "The Marriott Story," unpublished manuscript (1975), 29.

11. Robert O'Brien, *Marriott: The J. Willard Marriott Story* (Deseret Book, 1977), 97–98.

12. "Many Mourn for Bishop Sheets," *Deseret News,* January 10, 1919.

13. JWM Journal, January 28, 1972.

14. Rebecca Andersen, "The Baron Woolen Mills: A Utah Legend," *Utah Historical Quarterly* (Spring 2007), 116–23.

15. Martin Buxbaum, "The Story of Hot Shoppes," *Hot Sauce* (company newsletter), February 1955.

16. "Good Mormons Don't Go Broke," *Saturday Evening Post,* June 10, 1950.

17. Allie Marriott, Letter to J.W., Salt Lake City to D.C., March 14, 1929.

18. JWM Journal, March 7, 1984.

19. O'Brien, *Marriott,* 142–47.

CHAPTER 3: BILLY THE KID

1. See Dale Van Atta, "J. Willard Marriott, Jr.: 'A Time to Every Purpose,'" *Ensign,* October 1982; Martin Buxbaum, "The Marriott Story," unpublished manuscript (1975), 81–82.

2. Robert O'Brien, *Marriott: The J. Willard Marriott Story* (Deseret Book, 1977), 157–58.

3. Buxbaum, "Marriott Story," 85–86.

4. Woodrow Marriott interview, October 16, 2002.

5. Bill Marriott, in Hermoine Tracy Jex, *The Marriotts: Workers of Flock and Field* (Publishers Press, 1990), 831.

6. Woodrow Marriott interview, October 16, 2002.

7. Buxbaum, "Marriott Story," 72–73.

8. Related by Bill Marriott in Remarks, "Sales Leadership," Wardman Park, Washington, D.C., March 13, 2001.

9. *Hot Sauce* (company newsletter), August 26, 1938.

10. Quoted in Buxbaum, "Marriott Story," 88–89.

11. George H. Bushnell, *Fundamentals in the Development of Our Organization* (Madison Square Press, 1922); David Delbert Kruger, "Earl Corder Sams and the Rise of J.C. Penney," *Kansas History: A Journal of the Central Plains,* Autumn 2012, 164–85.

12. Woodrow Marriott interview, October 16, 2002.

13. O'Brien, *Marriott,* 185–89.

14. Russell S. Marriott, Jr., *Biography of Hyrum Willard Marriott (1863–1939)* (Family Heritage, 1979), 5–6.

15. James Zug, *The Long Conversation: 125 Years of Sidwell Friends School, 1883–2008* (Sidwell Friends School, 2008), 77.
16. Bill Marriott, in Jex, *The Marriotts*, 831.
17. Bill Marriott, "Productivity Speech," April 30, 1986.
18. Bill Marriott, "MINA Speech," Camelback Inn, Arizona, October 22, 2000.
19. Bill Marriott, Remarks to General Managers, Orlando, Florida, January 9, 1996.
20. J.W. Marriott, letter to family in D.C. from train, postmarked Chicago, October 7, 1941.

CHAPTER 4: THE WAR

1. Howard S. Bennion, Mervyn's younger brother, interviewed and corresponded with the *West Virginia's* survivors. He completed the most authoritative account of the last hours of the ship in 1943 in an unpublished manuscript, "One of the Lord's Noblemen: Mervyn Sharp Bennion, Captain, *U.S.S. West Virginia*, United States Navy"; see also Walter Lord, *Day of Infamy* (Henry Holt and Company, 1957), 70, 96–97.
2. Bill Marriott, in Hermoine Tracy Jex, *The Marriotts: Workers of Flock and Field* (Publishers Press, 1990), 830.
3. Martin Buxbaum, "The Marriott Story," unpublished manuscript (1975), 120–22.
4. Bill Marriott, in Jex, *The Marriotts,* 831.
5. Bill Marriott, in Jex, *The Marriotts,* 831.
6. Walter Shapiro, "The Empire Builder," *Washington Post,* September 19, 1982.
7. Bill Marriott, Remarks at Dinner upon Receipt of Boy Scouts of America's Citizen of the Year Award, February 4, 1986.
8. Elder Ezra Taft Benson, typed notecard ca. 1945, sent to Bill Marriott in a letter from then-President Benson, September 16, 1975.
9. Bill Marriott, Remarks at St. Albans Dinner, March 4, 2009.
10. Bill Werber, *Hunting Is for the Birds* (Naples Printing, 1981), 75–80.
11. Allie Marriott, interview with author, April 30, 1982.
12. Bill Marriott, Remarks at Outboard Marine Corp. Event, Key Biscayne, Florida, February 19, 1983.

CHAPTER 5: ANCHORS AWEIGH

1. "The Seniors 1950: John Willard Marriott, Jr.," *The Albanian,* 1950.
2. JWM Journal, January 1, 1950.
3. Bill Marriott, "Why I Believe," speech given December 26, 2000.
4. Sheri L. Dew, *Go Forward With Faith: The Biography of Gordon B. Hinckley* (Deseret Book, 1996), 143–51.
5. Ray Hart interview with author, May 31, 2012.
6. Bill Marriott interview with G. Wesley and Marian Johnson, November 7, 1995.

7. Martin Buxbaum, *The History of Fairfield* (booklet, 1968); Debbie Johnson *A Walking Historical Tour of Fairfield* (booklet, July 2010).

8. JWM Journal, September 16, 1952.

9. JWM Journal, December 31, 1952; Robert W. Barker, Chevy Chase Ward Bishop, Letter with Donation Receipts, January 15, 1954.

10. JWM Journal, March 28, 1953.

11. JWM Journal, June 17, 1953.

12. Bill Marriott, Founders Day Speech, University of Utah, March 10, 1983.

13. Brian T. West, "Marriott Foundation endows chair at U. in name of Royal Garff," *Deseret News,* September 29, 1988.

CHAPTER 6: HEAVENLY FLOWER

1. Louis (Lauritz) Garff, *Reminiscences,* unpublished manuscript, 58; C.C.A. Christensen, "By Handcart to Utah: The Account of C.C.A. Christensen," *Nebraska History,* Winter 1985, 337–44.

2. W. Dee Halverson, *The Life & Times of Royal L. Garff* (Aspen Digital Media, 2001), 1–7.

3. Royal Garff, Letters to Marba and children, August 6 and 17, 1944.

4. Royal Garff, Letters to daughter Donna Rae Garff, July 17, July 24, July 29, August 2, and August 5, 1947.

5. JWM Journal, December 19, December 20, and December 25, 1953.

6. Martin Buxbaum, "The Marriott Story," unpublished 1975 manuscript, 159.

7. Log Book of *U.S.S. Randolph* (CVA-15), commencing 1 January 1955 and ending 31 January 1955, U.S. National Archives.

8. Lieutenant Mickey Finn, Letter to Captain Alan Preil, January 26, 1955.

9. Reference to the *Washington Star*'s April 2 story was in "The Last Word," *Hot Sauce,* June 1955.

10. Bill Marriott, "Answering the Call: I Started as a Geedunk Officer," *Proceedings* (U.S. Naval Institute), November 2009.

11. Marriott, "Answering the Call."

CHAPTER 7: MOTOR HOTEL DIVISION CHIEF

1. JWM Journal, February 25, March 21, 22, and 26, 1955.

2. Bill Marriott, Remarks at Association Masters, Desert Ridge Resort, Phoenix, Arizona, June 19, 2003.

3. Bill Marriott, Remarks to Integrated Healthcare Symposium, Desert Springs Resort, Arizona, January 20, 1994.

4. Bill Marriott, Remarks at MINA Conference, San Francisco, California, November 16, 1998.

5. J.W. Marriott, Jr., and Kathi Ann Brown, *The Spirit to Serve: Marriott's Way* (HarperBusiness, 1997), 21–22.

6. JWM Journal, January 22, 1957.

7. Frank Hewlett, *Salt Lake Tribune,* October 6, 1957.

8. JWM Journal, March 28, 1959.

9. Bill Marriott, Remarks to Courtyard and Fairfield Inn General Managers, San Francisco, California, March 1, 1996.

10. JWM Journal, September 14, 1960.

11. JWM Journal, June 10, 1961; also, several J.W. interviews with his biographer, Robert O'Brien.

CHAPTER 8: THE SON RISES

1. JWM Journal, January 19 and March 8, 1960.

2. JWM Journal, October 19, 1960.

3. JWM Journal, March 25, 1960.

4. JWM Journal, May 21, May 27, July 3, and August 22, 1962.

5. Russell M. Nelson, interview with author, August 15, 2013.

6. JWM Journal, January 25 and February 25, 1963.

7. Jeffrey R. Holland, Remarks at BYU School of Management dinner, October 28, 1988.

8. Gwen Dobson, Women's Editor, "Luncheon With . . . J. Willard Marriott," *Washington Star,* March 13, 1970.

9. Robert O'Brien, *Marriott: The J. Willard Marriott Story* (Deseret Book, 1977), 267–69.

CHAPTER 9: NO TIME FOR SERGEANTS

1. Nancy Neill, "Bill Marriott Opens His Marquis," *Business Atlanta,* July 1985.

2. Richard M. Cohen, "The Spread of the Marriott Empire," *Washington Post,* December 23, 1974.

3. Ray Kroc with Robert Anderson, *Grinding It Out: The Making of McDonald's* (Henry Regnery Company, 1977), 58, 137–39, 163–64; John F. Love, *McDonald's: Behind the Arches* (Bantam, 1995), 217–22, 226–27, 293–95.

4. JWM Journal, January 8 and November 17, 1965.

5. George and Lenore Romney, Letters to J.W., December 4 and December 5, 1977, respectively; J.W., Letter to George Romney, December 13, 1977.

6. JWM Journal, December 7, 1967.

7. J.W., Letter to George Romney, October 3, 1967.

8. JWM Journal, July 17 and July 31, 1970.

CHAPTER 10: RISKY BUSINESS

1. Aaron D. Cushman, *A Passion for Winning: Fifty Years of Promoting Legendary People and Products* (Lighthouse Point Press, 2004), 161–66.

2. Bill Marriott, Remarks, "Goodwill Benefit," September 24, 1982.

3. Betty Beale, *Washington Evening Star,* quoted by *Hot Sauce,* "Lady Bird Johnson and Daughter Lynda Visit a Hot Shoppe," September 1966.

4. "White House Report on Beauty," *Washington Post,* April 28, 1967.

5. JWM Journal, June 13, 1968.

6. JWM Journal, July 24, 1966.

7. JWM Journal, September 17, 1968.
8. "The Marriott Story," *Forbes,* February 1, 1971.
9. JWM Journal, July 28, 1965.
10. Jack Anderson, "Nixon Puts an Eye on His Brother," *Washington Post,* February 16, 1972.
11. Bill Marriott, "Video Tribute to Jon Huntsman," University of Utah, September 17, 1997.
12. Jon Huntsman, interview with author, June 29, 2012; Matt Canham and Thomas Burr, *Mormon Rivals: The Romneys, the Huntsmans and the Pursuit of Power* (Salt Lake Tribune, 2015), 33.

CHAPTER 11: THE PERFECT STORM

1. William Rice, "Value: The World of Chefless Restaurants," *Washington Post,* January 23, 1977.
2. "The Marriott Pro-Team: The Sun Line Acquisition," February 1972.
3. "The Marriott Story," *Forbes,* February 1, 1971.
4. J.W., Letter to Elder Mark E. Petersen, October 18, 1971.
5. Allie entries in JWM Journal, January 1 and 13, 1972.
6. J.W., Speech, "Rededication to Excellence," Marriott Manager's Banquet, January 17, 1972.
7. John Getz, "Marriot [sic] Could Be on Road All Year if Projection Works Out," *Los Angeles Times,* December 30, 1971; J.W., Note to Bill, ca. December 30, 1971.
8. Dorothy McCardle, "GOP Party Not So Grand," *Washington Post,* August 21, 1972.
9. "Marriott's Hot Shop," *Newsweek,* May 22, 1972.
10. JWM Journal, November 20, 1972.
11. Ed Butterworth, "Spacious Marriott Center Dedicated," *BYU Alumni News,* February 1973; Jack Jarrard, "Rites Dedicate Center at BYU," [LDS] *Church News,* February 10, 1973.
12. JWM Journal, January 15, 17, and 18, 1974.

CHAPTER 12: BICENTENNIAL BISHOP

1. John Getz, "Marriot [sic] Could Be on Road All Year if Projection Works Out," *Los Angeles Times,* December 30, 1971.
2. Cary Koegle, "Groundbreaking in the skies; Marriott Corp. rises for occasion," Torrance (California) *Daily Breeze,* May 18, 1973.
3. Dick Turpin, "What It Takes to Open a New Hotel," *Los Angeles Times,* August 12, 1973.
4. "L.A.'s First Guest," *Marriott Crest,* July 1973.
5. William H. Jones, "New NBW Headquarters Set," *Washington Post,* October 26, 1974; William Taaffe, "Connecticut Avenue Hot Shoppes: Swing Era Landmark Closing," *Washington Star-News,* December 31, 1974.

6. Allie entries in JWM Journal, October 15 and 16, 1974.

7. John Carmody, "Bill Marriott Jr. looks ahead to $1 billion a year in Mighty Mo's, motels and mid-air mealtimes," *Potomac Magazine,* August 2, 1970.

8. Martin Buxbaum, "The Marriott Story," unpublished 1975 manuscript, 217–18.

9. Allie entry in JWM Journal, November 16, 1974.

10. JWM Journal, December 27, 1973.

11. Bill Marriott, Remarks at Chevy Chase Ward Conference, January 29, 1984, and Washington D.C. Stake Conference, April 23, 1988.

12. President Spencer W. Kimball, Letters to J.W., July 20 and August 17, 1976.

13. Canon Charles Martin, Headmaster, St. Albans, Letter to J.W., March 30, 1976.

14. Michael Creedman, "Interview: J. Willard Marriott, Jr.," Delta's *Sky Magazine,* August 1974.

15. Wade Franklin, "Great Marriott resort opens," *Chicago Sun-Times,* April 6, 1975; Aaron D. Cushman, *A Passion for Winning: Fifty Years of Promoting Legendary People and Products* (Lighthouse Point Press, 2004), 176.

16. JWM Journal, May 22, 1977.

17. President Jon Huntsman of the Washington D.C. Mission, interview with author, May 19, 1982.

18. Bill Marriott, interview with Kathi Ann Brown, October 17, 1996.

CHAPTER 13: HIGH ANXIETY AND MIRACLES

1. Jack Egan, "Marriott's 'Great America' Gamble," *Washington Post,* March 7, 1976.

2. Associated Press, "Marriott now operating roller coaster, too," Cleveland *Plain Dealer,* July 13, 1976.

3. William H. Jones, "Marriott at 50: Ready to Expand," *Washington Post,* February 27, 1977; "Marriott's Sales Top $1 Billion as Profits Rise 17%," *Washington Post,* September 8, 1977.

4. Jane Seaberry and Timothy S. Robinson, "Marriott Kidnaping Plot Foiled," *Washington Post,* August 3, 1977.

5. Jane Seaberry, "Court Hears Tape of Park Policeman, Undercover Agent in Marriott Case," *Washington Post,* October 28, 1977.

6. Eduardo Cue and Jane Seaberry, "Park Policeman Convicted in Marriott Kidnap Plot," *Washington Post,* November 4, 1977; Jane Seaberry, "Ex-Officer Given 15 Years in Marriott Kidnap Try," *Washington Post,* December 20, 1977.

7. "J.W. Marriott Elected to Board of Chamber of Commerce of the U.S.," *Chamber of Commerce News,* April 19, 1977; Alyssa Katz, *The Influence Machine: The U.S. Chamber of Commerce and the Corporate Culture of American Life* (Spiegel & Grau, 2015).

8. "Q&A: Marriott's Biggest Foes Are Inflation and Minimum Wage," *Los Angeles Examiner,* May 29, 1978.

9. Bill Marriott, Speech to the American Marketing Association, St. Louis, Missouri, "Pardon Me . . . Your Knee Is on My Chest," February 24, 1978.

10. Stephen Marriott Journal, April 2, 1979.

11. Rich Taylor, "John Marriott," *Corvette Quarterly,* April 1992; Gordon Pitts, "Marriotts succeed with front-line time," *Toronto Globe and Mail,* February 19, 2001.

12. Bill Marriott Journal, December 19, 1981.

13. Stephen Marriott Journal, January 7, 1983.

CHAPTER 14: HOTEL HOPPING

1. "Hotel opening lacks a big splash; Lifeguards act like pallbearers at a different kind of wake," *Seattle Times,* January 30, 1981.

2. "Mideast an Expansion Target," *Washington Post,* February 27, 1977.

3. "Abu Nowar opens Amman Marriott; Five-star hotel depicts confidence in Jordan," *Jordan Times,* January 27, 1982.

4. Phillip M. Kadis, "Marriott in Cairo," *Washington Star,* June 14, 1974; Lynn Langway, "Sibling Rivals in a Hotel Clan," *Newsweek,* September 3, 1979.

5. Bill Marriott, Remarks at Marketing Meeting, Mountain Shadows Resort, Phoenix, Arizona, April 25, 1983.

6. Minutes of Board Meeting, "Financial Reports," October 6, 1983.

7. J. Randy Taraborrelli, *The Hiltons: The True Story of an American Dynasty* (Grand Central Publishing, 2014), 349, 405.

8. John A. Jakle, Keith A. Sculle, and Jefferson S. Rogers, *The Motel in America* (Johns Hopkins University Press, 1996), 277–78.

9. Bill Marriott Journal, April 30, 1982.

10. Minutes of Executive Committee Meeting, September 9, 1976.

11. Marriott and Brown, *The Spirit to Serve,* 149–50.

12. JWM Journal, January 16, 1982; emphasis added.

13. JWM Journal, November 10, 1955.

14. JWM Journal, July 28, 1958.

15. JWM Journal, February 13, 1972.

16. Patricia Burstein, "Look, Pa, No Hands! Bill Marriott Jr. Wants to Take More Chances with His Dad's Empire," *People,* April 17, 1978.

CHAPTER 15: FULL SPEED AHEAD

1. Tom Curren, interview with Kathi Ann Brown, August 16, 1996.

2. Larry Peterson, "Western stars on hand to dedicate hotel," *The Register,* February 18, 1981; "Marriott Opening Praised," *Anaheim Bulletin,* February 18, 1981.

3. Allie entries in JWM Journal, October 20–23, 1981.

4. Associated Press, "Teen killed, eight hurt in roller coaster accident," *Lakeland Ledger,* March 31, 1980; Caroline E. Mayer, "Marriott Agrees to Pay $70,000 Fine to CPSC," *Washington Star,* January 27, 1981.

5. Mark Spencer, "Assault on the Mississippi," *Powerboat,* September 1982.

6. Shapiro, "The Empire Builder," *Powerboat,* September 19, 1982.

7. Mark Spencer, "A Joint Venture: Bill Marriott and Bob Nordskog take on The Northwest Passage," *Powerboat,* ca. 1983.

8. J. Willard Marriott, in Hermoine Tracy Jex, *The Marriotts: Workers of Flock and Field* (Publishers Press, 1990), 826.

9. JWM Journal, September 4, 1980.

10. JWM Journal, September 5, 1980.

11. JWM Journal, September 6, 1980.

12. JWM Journal, December 22, 1980.

13. Bill Marriott Journal, June 7, 1981.

CHAPTER 16: THE GUNSLINGERS

1. Ann Crittenden, "At Marriott, Volume Has Yielded to Profit," *New York Times,* August 6, 1978.

2. Dana Hedgpeth, "Marriott Faces the Future; Patriarch Mulls How to Preserve Values That Fueled His Company's Success," *Washington Post,* October 16, 2000.

3. Minutes of Board Meeting, "Hotel Limited Partnership Syndication," September 17, 1981.

4. Jane Carmichael, "Full speed ahead," *Forbes,* July 5, 1982.

5. "Marriott Filing," *New York Times,* January 19, 1982; "New Marriott Venture," *Washington Post,* January 19, 1982; "Marriott Plans Issue of Limited Interests in Hotel Partnership," *Wall Street Journal,* January 19, 1982.

6. Jerry Knight, "Marriott Expansion Set with Tax Shelter Sales," *Washington Post,* January 20, 1982.

7. Leslie Wayne, "Marriott Stakes Out New Territory," *New York Times,* September 22, 1985.

8. Jerry C. Davis, "Marquis: the top of Marriott's $3B empire," *New York Post,* October 23, 1984.

9. Carmichael, "Full speed ahead."

10. Bus Ryan interview by Kathi Ann Brown, September 3, 1996.

11. Joseph A. McCartin, *Collision Course: Ronald Reagan, the Air Traffic Controllers, and the Strike that Changed America* (Oxford University Press, 2011).

12. Carmichael, "Full speed ahead"; Sylvia Riggs, "Marriott makes lean years a season to grow," *Restaurants and Institutions,* August 15, 1982.

13. J.W. and Allie entries in JWM Journal, November 30, 1981.

14. Bill Marriott Journal, December 2, 1981.

15. J.W. Marriott, Jr., and Kathi Ann Brown, *The Spirit to Serve: Marriott's Way* (HarperBusiness, 1997), 143–49.

CHAPTER 17: THE CHAIRMAN'S GRAND EXIT

1. Lee Roderick, *Bridge Builder: Hugh Colton, from Country Lawyer to Combat Hero* (Probitas Press, 2010), 350–51.

2. Stephen Marriott Journal, September 29, 1985.
3. Nancy Peery Marriott, Funeral Program Transcript, August 17, 1985.
4. "J. Willard Marriott," Editorial, *Washington Post,* August 17, 1985.
5. President Ronald Reagan, White House, Letter to Allie, August 14, 1985; Lee Byrd, Associated Press, "Marriott Corp. Founder Dead at 84," August 14, 1985.
6. Jerry Ford, Letter to Allie, August 19, 1985.
7. Willard Mitt Romney, Bain Capital, Letter to Allie, August 26, 1986.
8. "Marriott family, firm, receive condolences," *Deseret News,* August 14, 1985.
9. Jack Anderson with Daryl Gibson, *Peace, War, and Politics: An Eyewitness Account* (Forge, 1999), 165.
10. George Romney, Letter to Bill Marriott, August 19, 1995.
11. Billy Graham, Letter to Bill Marriott, August 19, 1985.
12. Last entry in JWM Journal, by Allie, August 17, 1985.

CHAPTER 18: THE REFINER'S FIRE

1. Gary L. Wilson, Letter to Bill, Beverly Hills, California, September 11, 1985.
2. Associated Press, "J.W. Marriott Jr. Succeeds Father as Marriott Corp. Chairman," October 3, 1985.
3. "Artificial skin gives burn victim 2d lease on life," *New York Times,* December 29, 1981; Paul Vitello, "Dr. John F. Burke, 89; Created Synthetic Skin," *New York Times,* November 6, 2011.
4. "J.W. Marriott Jr. in Stable Condition After Explosion," *Washington Post,* August 26, 1985; William Matthews, "J.W. Marriott Jr. hurt in boat blast," *Washington Times,* August 26, 1985; Marilyn Montgomery, Ossipee Correspondent, "Marriott Hurt in Explosion," Laconia *Evening Citizen,* August 26, 1985.
5. Bill Marriott, "Remembering Dr. Burke, My Life-Saver," *Marriott on the Move* blog, February 13, 2012.
6. Stephen Marriott Journal, October 20, 1985.

CHAPTER 19: THE JEWEL BOX

1. Allie entry in JWM Journal, May 22, 1975.
2. JWM Journal, February 3, 1981.
3. Minutes of Board Meeting, "Reauthorization of NY Times Square Hotel," May 11, 1982; Bill Marriott Journal, June 15, 1982.
4. J.W. Marriott, handwritten memorandum, "Bill—re—Broadway," May 24, 1982.
5. Bill Marriott Journal, June 19, 1982.
6. J.W. Marriott, Jr., and Kathi Ann Brown, *The Spirit to Serve: Marriott's Way* (HarperBusiness, 1997), 73–75.
7. Damon Stetson, "Building Broadway's Marquis a Finely Tuned Performance," *New York Times,* January 12, 1984.
8. Stetson, "Building Broadway's Marquis."

9. Leslie Wayne, "Marriott Stakes Out New Territory," *New York Times,* September 22, 1985.

10. "The Forum: Here's To You, J.W.," *Lodging Hospitality,* March 1986.

11. Sharon Warren Walsh, "Marriott Profits Up 20% in 1st Quarter; Sales Rise 37%," *Washington Post,* April 15, 1987.

12. "[Darryl Hartley-Leonard] On His #1 Rival: Bill Marriott," *Chief Executive,* December 1988.

CHAPTER 20: THE FLAGSHIP AND FLEET EXPANSION

1. "Lessons of Leadership: The Marriott Man," *Nation's Business,* October 1979.

2. Richard Cohen, "Hard Work Produces 'Marriott Touch,'" *Washington Post,* December 22, 1974.

3. Bill Marriott, Remarks to Merchants and Manufacturers Association, 44th Annual Management Conference, Rancho Las Palmas, October 22, 1986.

4. Bill Marriott, Remarks, "Why I Believe," Oakton, Virginia, Stake Center Fireside, September 24, 1989.

5. Dieter Uchtdorf, interview with author, September 5, 2012.

6. Bill Marriott, Executive Chairman, Remarks at 2013 Award of Excellence Presentation to Mrs. Hester, May 14, 2013.

7. Debbie Marriott Harrison, Remarks at 2013 Award of Excellence Presentation to Mrs. Hester, May 14, 2013.

8. "Look, Pa, No Hands! Bill Marriott Jr. Wants to Take More Chances with His Dad's Empire," *People,* April 17, 1978.

9. Bill Marriott, "Phoenix Airport IV Presentation," December 9, 1987; "JW employees scale the Summit with finesse," *Marriott World,* January 1988; Christine Levite, "Reagan-Gorbachev Summit: Negotiating the Pressroom," *Meetings & Conventions,* February 1988.

10. "An Ordinary Guy," *Business Travel News,* March 2, 1987.

11. Larry Burger, "Marriott shuns Disney area 'rat race,'" *Miami News,* May 17, 1972.

CHAPTER 21: SEISMIC TREMORS

1. Charles Bernstein, "The human factor: Why Curtis rejected Marriott," *Nation's Restaurant News,* July 27, 1987.

2. Sharon Warren Walsh, "Marriott Restructures Its Divisions; Head of Hotel Unit," *Washington Post,* April 26, 1988.

3. J.W. Marriott, Jr., and Kathi Ann Brown, *The Spirit to Serve: Marriott's Way* (HarperBusiness, 1997), 59–60.

4. Barbara Basler, "Marriott Defies a Hong Kong Custom," *New York Times,* February 6, 1989.

5. Giselle Militante, "Marriott calls 1997 takeover a 'nonevent,'" *South China Morning Post,* February 28, 1989.

6. Carl Nolte, "New hotel got off to very shaky start; Loma Prieta Quake; The

1989 opening day rocked for downtown's Jukebox Marriott," *San Francisco Chronicle,* October 17, 2014.

7. Paul Farhi, "Economic Slowdown Hits Marriott Hard; Hotel Backlog Builds, Stock Price Falls," *Washington Post,* November 12, 1990.

8. Bill Marriott, Remarks on Richard E. Marriott's Twenty-Fifth Anniversary with Marriott Corporation, June 11, 1990.

9. Roddy Ray, "Marriott meets East Europe as posh Warsaw hotel opens," *Miami Herald,* October 31, 1989; Stuart Auerbach, "Marriott's Polish Pursuit: Hotel Chain Is First to Bring Western-Style Service to an Eastern Bloc Country," *Washington Post,* January 8, 1990.

10. Richard Kann, Commentary, "The Miracle on Chalubinskiego Street," *Hotels,* October 1990.

11. Bill Shaw, Transcript of Press Conference, December 18, 1989.

12. Nathaniel Sheppard Jr., "Thugs turn hotel into a prison of fear," *Chicago Tribune,* December 21, 1989.

13. "Quick! Hide in the Washing Machine," *New York Times,* January 21, 1990.

14. Candice Hughes, Associated Press, "Hotel Guests Cheer Arrival of U.S. Troops," December 21, 1989.

15. Stake President Bill Marriott, Remarks, "Obedience and Eternal Life," stake conference, April 22, 1990.

CHAPTER 22: "WHAT HAVE I DONE?"

1. Christopher Wood, *The Bubble Economy: The Japanese Economic Collapse* (Sidgwick & Jackson, 1992), 30–33.

2. Andrew Pollack, "Anxiety Under That Fabled Cypress," *New York Times,* September 8, 1990; Wood, *Bubble Economy,* 60–62.

3. Charles V. Bagli, "Ailing Asian Companies Unload Their Hotels," *New York Times,* January 24, 1999.

4. Bill Shaw interview by Kathi Ann Brown, July 2, 1996; Shaw interview by author, February 6, 2013.

5. Daniel Schorr, "Fearless forecasts," *Christian Science Monitor,* January 4, 1988.

6. Gus Carlson, "Hitting the green his playing years mostly over, Jack Nicklaus goes for a financial hole in one," *Miami Herald,* March 3, 1991.

7. Subrata N. Chakravarty, "Sails reefed," *Forbes,* November 30, 1987.

8. Bill Marriott, Remarks to Senior Management Meeting, May 10, 1990.

9. Bill Marriott, Remarks at Phillips Collection Meeting, May 7, 1990.

10. Bill Marriott, Remarks to Marketing Managers, Fort Lauderdale, Florida, April 9, 1990.

11. Karl Schoenberger, "Tokyo stocks were due for fall before crisis, analysts say," *Los Angeles Times,* August 27, 1990; Wood, *Bubble Economy,* 7–8.

12. Jonathan Dahl and Jim Carlton, "Rooms to Spare; Hotel Industry Suffers From Glut of Capacity and Faces Big Deficits," *Wall Street Journal,* November 21, 1990.

13. Stake President Bill Marriott, Stake Conference Remarks, "Developing Our Personal Reserves," October 27, 1990, and "Farewell Speech," October 28, 1990.

14. Paul Farhi, "Inns on the Outs," *Washington Post,* March 25, 1991.

15. J.W. Marriott, Jr., and Kathi Ann Brown, *The Spirit to Serve: Marriott's Way* (HarperBusiness, 1997), 32–34, 46–49.

CHAPTER 23: THE GREAT DIVIDE

1. Keith F. Girard, "What the Hell Happened to Marriott?: The Anatomy of Marriott's Debt Crisis," *Regardie's,* April 1991.

2. Bill Marriott, Business Roundtable Speech, February 6, 1991.

3. Skip Wollenberg, Associated Press, "Troubled Travel Industry Sponsors $6 Million Ad Program," March 20, 1991.

4. "Red Cross Steps Up Blood Collection," *Washington Post,* January 12, 1991; "Employees help reservists, families," *Marriott World,* April 1991.

5. Bill Marriott, Remarks at George Washington University, March 5, 1991.

6. Steve Bollenbach testimony, October 5, 1994, in Transcript of PPM America et al v. Marriott Corporation et al, 2516, 2523, 2525–28; hereafter PPM with specific page citations.

7. Barry Meier, "Stephen Bollenbach, Who Spared Donald Trump from Personal Bankruptcy, Dies at 74," *New York Times,* October 1, 2016.

8. The author was unable to interview Steve Bollenbach before he died in 2016. All otherwise unattributed Bollenbach quotes, such as this one, are from Steve Bollenbach interview with Kathi Ann Brown, August 7, 1996.

9. Matt Hart testimony, PPM, 2810.

10. Paul Farhi, "Marriott's Big Split; Restructuring Plan Sparks Lawsuits, Cries of Betrayal from Bondholders," *Washington Post,* July 19, 1993.

11. Allan Sloan, *Newsday* columnist, "Marriott's Fancy Financial Plan Leaves Bondholders in Lurch," *Washington Post,* October 20, 1992.

12. Farhi, "Marriott's Big Split."

13. Jean Christensen, "Two Easy Pieces," *Lodging,* September 1993.

14. Danielle Douglas, "Marriott makes way for a steady successor," *Washington Post,* December 19, 2011.

CHAPTER 24: PUTTIN' ON THE RITZ AND RENAISSANCE

1. David Remnick, "H. Ross Perot to GM: I'll Drive; GM to H. Ross Perot: 'Oh, Yeah?,'" *Washington Post,* April 19, 1987.

2. Kathleen Day, "GM's Move Symbolizes Wider Fight," *Washington Post,* October 27, 1992; Alison Leigh Cowan, "The High-Energy Board Room," *New York Times,* October 28, 1992.

3. Bill Marriott, Remarks to Integrated Healthcare Symposium, "The Culture of the Organization," Desert Springs, California, January 20, 1994.

4. Marriott, Remarks to Healthcare Symposium.

5. Bill Marriott, Remarks to Senior Management Meeting, November 14, 1991; "Marriott Easing Check-In," *New York Times*, August 18, 1992.

6. Susannah Vesey Rauscher, "ACOG's special ambassador: Albert Smith is on the short list of people who were the most influential in Atlanta's securing the Olympics," *Atlanta Journal and Constitution*, January 26, 1996.

7. Bill Marriott, Marriott Partnership Conference, Marco Beach, Florida, November 14, 1996.

8. William F. Powers, "The Host with the Most: Meet Stephen Bollenbach, The 'Good' Guy Who Helped Create the 'Bad' Marriott," *Washington Post*, June 13, 1994.

9. Jonathan Moore, Associated Press, "Marriott to Buy Stake in Ritz-Carlton Chain," March 6, 1995; Edwin McDowell, "Marriott to Acquire a Ritz-Carlton Stake," *New York Times*, March 7, 1995; Anthony Faiola, "Marriott Seeks to Expand into Luxury Hotels; Bethesda Firm to Buy Ritz-Carlton Stake with Eye Toward Acquisition," *Washington Post*, March 7, 1995.

10. Mike Wallace, Foreword, in Gordon B. Hinckley, *Standing for Something: Ten Neglected Virtues That Will Heal Our Hearts and Homes* (Times Books, 2000), vii–ix.

11. [Name removed for privacy], Letter to W. Don Ladd, vice president, Marriott International, April 26, 1997.

12. Gordon B. Hinckley, "This Thing Was Not Done in a Corner," *Ensign*, November 1996.

13. "Marriott International Strategy," *Plum Team Report*, November 22, 1994.

14. "British Brewer Buys U.K. Marriott Hotels," Associated Press, August 7, 1995.

15. Bill Marriott, Remarks at Opinion Leader Luncheon (UK), "Whitbread Brand Conversion," March 8, 1996.

16. Christina Binkley and Jon Bigness, "Marriott to Buy Renaissance Hotel Group; Agreement for $947 Million Pushes Out Doubletree from Purchase Accord," *Wall Street Journal*, February 19, 1997.

17. Kerry Diamond, "Power Move: Marriott Is Set to Go Global with Renaissance Buy," *Travel Agent*, February 24, 1997.

18. Judith Evans, "Marriott to Pay $1 Billion For Renaissance Hotels," *Washington Post*, February 19, 1997; Keith L. Alexander and Donna Rosato, "Marriott's $1B global reach; Deal catapults chain toward lofty target," *USA Today*, February 19, 1997.

CHAPTER 25: YOU'D BETTER BE RUNNING

1. John Marriott Journal at Masai Mara Game Reserve, June 25, 1998.

2. Pete Lyons, "Running of the Most Bulls: Miura's 35th reunion is largest-ever for Lamborghini's sex star of the '60s," *AutoWeek*, February 5, 2001.

3. Paul Blythe, "A Million-Dollar Mercedes Is a Big Deal," *Winchester Star* [Virginia], May 15, 1982, and, "So Fine: Introducing the World's Most Expensive Car," May 6, 1983.

4. Bill Marriott, Regional Representative, Youth Speech, "Letters from David," Suitland Maryland Stake Conference, June 12, 1994.

5. Michael S. Rosenwald, "Marriott's Youngest Son Makes His Mark; Fast Rise of Hotel Firm's Global Sales Chief Prompts Speculation About Succession," *Washington Post,* October 29, 2007.

6. Bill Marriott, Note to Carolyn Cullers, August 23, 1979.

7. Robert H. Bork, Jr., "The price of their toys," *Forbes,* October 28, 1985.

8. Blanche T. Sullivan, "From Hot Shoppes to Hotels & Hot Cars," *Low-country Monthly* [South Carolina], October 2007.

9. Bill Marriott, Remarks at Bill Shaw's Twenty-Fifth Anniversary Celebration, Ritz-Carlton, Tysons Corner, Virginia, October 21, 1999.

10. Liz Hamson, "Family values," *Property Week,* March 21, 2003.

11. "Mob Linked to Unions, Senate Panel Is Told," *New York Times,* April 28, 1983; Bill Keller, "Panel Links Mob and Hotel Union," *New York Times,* August 27, 1984; Peter Perl, "Senate Probe Finds 'Substantial' Mob Ties to Hotel Union," *Washington Post,* August 28, 1984.

12. Judith Evans, "Marriott's Two-Class Stock Plan Defeated; Lodging Company to Convert Shares," *Washington Post,* May 21, 1998.

13. Jerry Knight, "Marriott Faces Another Showdown with Angry Investors," *Washington Post,* May 25, 1998.

14. Cam Simpson, "High life of union's top brass revealed," *Chicago Sun-Times,* September 24, 1998; *Chicago Sun-Times,* Editorial, "A union run amok," September 25, 1998.

15. Bill Marriott, Remarks, Senior Management Meeting, January 22, 1999.

16. Bill Marriott, Remarks, National Association for Senior Living Industries Conference, December 10, 1991.

17. Allie Marriott, Speech on Bill's Thirty-Fifth Anniversary with Marriott, June 13, 1991.

18. "Marriott At 60: Hot Stuff; 9 Stools in '27, Now $6B in Sales," *Philadelphia Daily News,* May 20, 1987.

19. Bill Marriott, Remarks at Mother's Funeral, April 20, 2000.

CHAPTER 26: HEARTBREAK HOTEL AND HEROES

1. PR Newswire, "Grand Opening of the Tampa Marriott Waterside Marks 2,000th Hotel for Marriott International," April 26, 2000; Mark Albright, "Marriott showcases Tampa hotel," *St. Petersburg Times,* April 27, 2000.

2. Bill Marriott, Remarks, "1994 Market Facts Guide Breakfast," *Philadelphia Business Journal,* September 21, 1994.

3. "The World Trade Center Thanks a Good Neighbor," *Marriott World,* June 1993.

4. Ben Kaplan, "The Long Goodbye," *New York,* March 18, 2002; "Hotel Ground Zero," History Channel documentary, September 11, 2009.

5. Cheryl Hass, "Fed economist escaped being 9/11 statistic," *Dallas Morning News,* September 15, 2013.
6. Jim Dwyer and Ford Fessenden, "One Hotel's Fight to the Finish; At the Marriott, a Portal to Safety as the Towers Fell," *New York Times,* September 11, 2002.
7. Eric Lipton and James Glanz, "Slowed by Site's Fragility, the Heavy Lifting Has Only Begun," *New York Times,* October 13, 2001.
8. "The Heroes," *Newsweek,* September 27, 2001; Emily Gest, "Tragic Tales of Marriott's Last Minutes," *New York Daily News,* October 6, 2001.
9. David Segal, "At a Ground Zero Hotel, Room for Miracles," *Washington Post,* September 11, 2006.
10. Eryn Brown, "Heartbreak Hotel?," *Fortune,* November 26, 2001.
11. Keith Bradsher, "Indonesia bombing kills at least 10 in midday attack," *New York Times,* August 6, 2003; "Jitters in Jakarta," *Time,* August 18, 2003.
12. Duncan Larcombe, "Mummy, we must get off beach . . . Now," *The Sun* (London), January 1, 2005; "JW Marriott Phuket Associate Receives Chairman's Award," *Marriott World Express,* March 21, 2005.
13. Rebecca Mowbray, "Downtown N.O. hotels grow desperate to move guests; Coaches commandeered for other rescue efforts," New Orleans *Times-Picayune,* September 2, 2005; Michael S. Rosenwald, "Marriott Reports Solid Revenue; Company Seems to Have Weathered Hurricanes," *Washington Post,* October 7, 2005.
14. Salman Masood, "Deadly Suicide Bomber Attack at Hotel in Pakistan's Capital," *New York Times,* January 27, 2007; "Guard Blocks Bomber At Marriott," *Washington Post,* January 27, 2007.
15. Bill Marriott, "Marriott Remains Committed to Global Travel After Hotel Bombing," *Marriott on the Move,* September 23, 2008.
16. Bill Marriott, "Marriott Remains Committed to Hospitality in Jakarta and Around the World," *Marriott on the Move,* July 17, 2009.

CHAPTER 27: MARRIOTT ON THE MOVE

1. Bill Marriott, Remarks at Senior Management Meeting, May 24, 1999.
2. Bill Marriott, Remarks to Marriott Hotels, Resorts and Suites General Managers, New Orleans, Louisiana, March 3, 2000.
3. "Sunstone Hotel Investors, Walton Street Capital and Marriott International to Purchase 32 Hotels from CTF Holdings," *PR Newswire,* April 27, 2005; Ashby Jones, "Marriott buys hotels and goodwill," *Daily Deal/The Deal,* April 29, 2005.
4. Script, "Skit for Bill & Donna's 50th Anniversary," June 29, 2005.
5. Christina Binkley, "As Succession Looms, Marriott Ponders Keeping Job in Family," *Wall Street Journal,* May 19, 2005.
6. Bill Marriott, "Uncharted Territory," *Marriott on the Move,* January 16, 2007.
7. Michael S. Rosenwald, "An Old Dog Learns to Write a New Blog," *Washington*

Post, January 16, 2007; Molly Selvin and Michelle Quinn, "Internet: CEO postings can be hits or headaches," *Los Angeles Times,* July 13, 2007; Michael S. Rosenwald, "Bill Marriott: Chairman of the Blog," *Washington Post,* June 19, 2012.

8. Jay Hancock, "CEO's not afraid to play the fool," *Baltimore Sun,* June 6, 2007.

9. Christina Binkley, "Hotels 'Go to the Mattresses'; Marriott Is Latest to Make Huge Bet on Better Bedding; A Pledge to Wash the Covers," *Wall Street Journal,* January 25, 2005; Associated Press, "Marriott to replace 628,000 hotel beds," January 25, 2005; Jayne Clark, "Marriott's fresh look puts bedding concerns to rest," *USA Today,* January 28, 2005.

10. Peter Sanders, "Strange Bedfellows: Marriott, Schrager," *Wall Street Journal,* June 14, 2007; Alejandro Lazo, "Marriott, Boutique Hotel Pioneer Partner to Develop a New Brand," *Washington Post,* June 15, 2007; Ron Stodghill, "A Hotelier Is Breaking the Mold Once Again," *New York Times,* August 19, 2007.

11. Beth Barrett, "L.A. Live: $2.5 Billion transformation next door nearly halfway complete," Los Angeles *Daily News,* June 8, 2008; Elaine Glusac, "JW Marriott Opens In Downtown Los Angeles," *New York Times,* February 21, 2010.

12. "A Nod to the Past, A Vision for the Future—Marriott Celebrates the Grand Opening of Its 4,000th Hotel—The Marriott Marquis Washington, DC," *PR Newswire,* June 11, 2014.

13. "Have I Done Any Good?," *Hymns of The Church of Jesus Christ of Latter-day Saints* (1985), no. 223.

14. "Mayo Clinic Raises $1.35 Billion in First-Ever Comprehensive Philanthropy Campaign," *Business Wire,* January 26, 2010.

15. Elder Cree-L Kofford, Letter to Elder Bill Marriott, May 5, 1993.

CHAPTER 28: THE WORK IS NEVER DONE

1. J.W. Marriott, Jr., and Kathi Ann Brown, *Without Reservations* (Luxury Custom Publishing, 2012), 78, 80–81.

2. Jonathan O'Connell, "Sorenson puts imprint on Marriott hotel empire," *Washington Post,* March 8, 2015.

3. Ann M. Simmons, "China's vanishing bosses: Some have resurfaced, others not so lucky, as graft inquiries continue," *Los Angeles Times,* June 15, 2017; Alexandra Stevenson, "Chinese Tycoon Gets 18 Years in Prison for $10 Billion Fraud," *New York Times,* May 9, 2018.

4. Bill Marriott, San Francisco Century Club Speech, February 10, 1993.

5. Bill Marriott, Remarks to Healthcare Symposium, January 20, 1994.

INDEX

INDEX

INDEX

INDEX

INDEX